ENCOMIUM EMMAE REGINAE

The *Encomium Emmae Reginae* is a political tract in praise, as its title suggests, of Queen Emma, daughter of Duke Richard I of Normandy, wife of King Æthelred the Unready from 1002 to 1016, and wife of the Danish conqueror King Cnut from 1017 to 1035. It is a primary source of the utmost importance for our understanding of the Danish conquest of England in the early eleventh century, and for the political intrigue in the years which followed the death of King Cnut in 1035. It offers a remarkable account of a woman who was twice a queen, and of her determination to retain her power as queen-mother. This reprint, which contains the definitive text and translation of the *Encomium Emmae Reginae* first published in 1949, includes a supplementary introduction which reviews the career of Queen Emma and which defines as clearly as possible the historical context in which the *Encomium* was written.

SIMON KEYNES is Reader in Anglo-Saxon History at the University of Cambridge and a Fellow of Trinity College.

University of Edinburgh

Camden Classic Reprints is a select series of classic editions which are reissued on behalf of the Royal Historical Society by Cambridge University Press. The series serves to bring to light editions of private papers or diaries of particular historical significance which have been unavailable for some time. Each volume contains a new introduction by a recognised expert in the field which contains fresh insights informed by recent historical scholarship, and which places each text in an appropriate historical context.

The first titles in the series are:

1 *Kingsford's Stonor Letters and Papers 1290–1483* edited by CHRISTINE CARPENTER
2 *Thomas Wright's Political Songs of England* edited by PETER COSS
3 *Richard Symond's Diary of the Marches of the Royal Army* edited by C. E. LONG with a supplementary introduction by Ian Roy
4 *Encomium Emmae Reginae* edited by ALISTAIR CAMPBELL with a supplementary introduction by Simon Keynes

ENCOMIUM
EMMAE REGINAE

Edited by
ALISTAIR CAMPBELL

with a supplementary introduction by
SIMON KEYNES

CAMDEN CLASSIC REPRINTS 4

FOR THE ROYAL HISTORICAL SOCIETY
University College London, Gower Street, London WC1E 6BT

 CAMBRIDGE
UNIVERSITY PRESS

PUBLISHED BY THE PRESS SYNDICATE OF THE UNIVERSITY OF CAMBRIDGE
The Pitt Building, Trumpington Street, Cambridge CB2 1RP, United Kingdom

CAMBRIDGE UNIVERSITY PRESS
The Edinburgh Building, Cambridge, CB2 2RU, United Kingdom http://www.cup.cam.ac.uk
40 West 20th Street, New York, NY 10011–4211, USA   http://www.cup.org
10 Stamford Road, Oakleigh, Melbourne 3166, Australia

First published by the Royal Historical Society 1949, Camden Third Series volume 72
Reprinted with a supplementary introduction by Cambridge University Press 1998
© In the supplementary introduction The Royal Historical Society 1998

Typeset in MT old style 10/11 pt   [CE]

A catalogue record for this book is available from the British Library

Library of Congress cataloguing in publication data
Encomium Emmae Reginae, Richardi I ducis Normannorum filiae.
Encomium Emmae Reginae / edited by Alistair Campbell: with a supplementary
introduction by Simon Keynes.
p.   cm. – (Camden classic reprints: 4)
Originally published: London: Offices of the Royal Historical Society, 1949, in series: [Royal
Historical Society, London, Publications]. Camden third series: v. 72.
Includes bibliographical references and indexes.
ISBN 0 521 62307 3 (hardback). – ISBN 0 521 62655 2 (pbk.)
1. Emma, Queen, consort of Canute I, King of England, d. 1052.   2. Great Britain –
History – Edward, the Confessor, 1042–1066.   3. Great Britain – Politics and
government – 449–1066.   4. Great Britain – History – Ethelred II, 979–1016.
5. Power (Social sciences) – England – History.   6. Great Britain – History – Canute,
1017–1035.   7. Social history – Medieval, 500–1500.   8. Queens – Great Britain –
Biography.   9. Anglo-Saxons – Queens – Biography.   10. Eleventh century.
I. Campbell, A. (Alistair), 1907–   II. Keynes, Simon.
III. Series: Royal Historical Society Camden classic reprints: 4.
DA160.E53   1998
942.01'9'092–dc21
[B]   97–40934   CIP

ISBN 0 521 62307 3 hardback
ISBN 0 521 62655 2 paperback

Transferred to digital printing 2004

CONTENTS

CONTENTS

The preliminary pages of the 1998 reprint are paginated in square brackets

ILLUSTRATIONS

The illustrations are reproduced by permission of the British Library.

PREFACE TO THE 1998 REPRINT

Almost fifty years have elapsed since the publication of Professor Alistair Campbell's edition of the *Encomium Emmae Reginae*. It is difficult to see how the edition itself might be improved, and the main purpose of this reprint is simply to make a major source for English history in the first half of the eleventh century more readily accessible. The purpose of the supplementary introduction is to retrace the basic outline of Queen Emma's career, and in this process to define as clearly as possible the historical context in which the *Encomium* was written. Inevitably, the effect is to work over ground already covered by Professor Campbell, but enough has changed to make the exercise worthwhile. Primary texts which are central to the elucidation of the *Encomium* as a historical source have appeared in new editions; historians have become more sensitive to the importance of judging for what audience a work was written, and what purpose it was intended to serve; and advances in the understanding of one source have led to changes in the perception of another. The issues at stake in Norman and Scandinavian history of the late tenth and early eleventh centuries have been redefined; studies have been made of the reigns of Æthelred, Cnut, and Edward the Confessor; and the role of the queen has been brought in its own right to the centre of the stage. Numismatists have clarified the coinage in the 1030s, and have demonstrated its potential as a form of historical evidence. As we shall see, there is also a case for reopening some of the issues which Campbell discussed, ranging from the assumptions we might make about the authorship of the work (was it written in Flanders or in England?) to some of the finer details of its interpretation. Yet in no respect should the advance of scholarship be allowed to detract from the sheer pleasure of reading a text which transports us into the heart of eleventh-century politics, and which allows us to form our own impression of a woman who began her public career as the consort of one king, who retained her position after his death as the consort of another, and who played out her political role, with style, as the mother of their sons.

I am most grateful to Professor Michael Jones, Literary Director of the Royal Historical Society, for inviting me (in 1991) to provide a brief introduction for a reprint of Campbell's edition of the *Encomium Emmae*, and for his patience thereafter. I should also like to express my thanks to those who have given help or guidance on matters general and particular: Michelle Brown (British Library), Marjorie Chibnall, Julia Crick, Vicky Cuthill (Cambridge University Press), Richard Gameson, David Ganz, Liesbeth van Houts, David Howlett, Michel de Laburthe (Bibliothèque Méjanes, Aix-en-Provence), Andy Orchard, David Pelteret, Andrew Prescott (British Library), Nigel Ramsay,

PREFACE TO THE 1998 REPRINT

Pauline Stafford, Rod Thomson, Colin Tite, and Tessa Webber. My colleague Michael Lapidge kindly sacrificed his pristine copy of Campbell's edition for purposes of reproduction.

SIMON KEYNES

INTRODUCTION TO THE 1998 REPRINT
QUEEN EMMA AND THE
ENCOMIUM EMMAE REGINAE

The career of Queen Emma extended throughout the first half of the eleventh century, and involved a complex interplay of Norman, English, Danish, and Flemish political interests. She was born and brought up in the duchy of Normandy. She became the wife of King Æthelred the Unready in 1002, and remained so until his death on 23 April 1016. She was the wife of King Cnut from 1017 until his death on 12 November 1035. For thirty years a queen, accustomed to the trappings of royal power, Emma sought to preserve her position as queen-mother. In the closing weeks of 1035, Harold Harefoot (Cnut's son by Ælfgifu of Northampton) seized all of the best treasures which remained in Emma's keeping at Winchester, perhaps including the regalia. For her own part, Emma tried against the odds to secure a position for Harthacnut (her son by King Cnut), then preoccupied in Denmark; and when he failed to materialise, she switched her hopes to Edward and Alfred (her sons by King Æthelred), then in exile in Normandy. The plans came to nought, and in 1037, when Harold Harefoot was formally chosen as king over all England, Emma was driven in exile to Flanders. At first she tried to get Edward's help from Normandy, without success; whereupon she turned again to Harthacnut, in Denmark. After the death of Harold Harefoot on 17 March 1040, Emma was able to return, with Harthacnut, to a position of power in England; and mother and son were moved soon afterwards to invite Edward to join them. It was at this point that she commissioned the *Encomium Emmae Reginae*; but her moment of glory was short-lived. In November 1043, after the death of Harthacnut on 8 June 1042 and after the delayed coronation of Edward the Confessor at Easter in the following year, Emma was forcibly deprived of her treasures, for a second time; and although she soon recovered her position at court, she was left to pass the remainder of her life effectively in a state of retirement from the political scene. Queen Emma died on 7 March 1052, and was laid to rest in the Old Minster at Winchester, near the grave of her second husband, King Cnut, and also near that of King Harthacnut, their son.

Two eleventh-century artists have left us with striking visual images of Queen Emma. In 1031 she was depicted in association with King Cnut presenting a magnificent cross of gold and silver to the New Minster at Winchester (Ill. 1). About ten years later she was depicted with her two sons, and her Encomiast, but was herself the centre of attention (Ill. 2). These are the images which endure, and no doubt it is right that it should be so. Yet the story of Queen

Emma is bound to excite a modern imagination, not least because it satisfies our taste for scandal, intrigue, and dramatic reversals of fortune, and provides ample scope at the same time for the exercise of our historical judgement. When she began her career, in 1002, she was a pawn in a game of chess played by the political establishments in England and Normandy, with an eye towards Denmark; but she was from the outset a queen, so on reaching the eighth rank, as it were, in 1035, she became a player in her own right, and at once began to manipulate the pieces which remained on the board. The question is whether we should respect her political acumen and admire her capacity to survive in a world where so much depended on the entrenched power and status of men, especially the rulers of men; whether we should sympathise with her predicament at times of political upheaval (in 1016–17, in 1035–40, and again in 1042–3), for such times called for desperate measures if she was to have any chance of maintaining her position; or whether we should censure her for a certain inconstancy of feeling towards her children, which seems to have extended to a readiness to compromise their interests for the sake of securing her own; and so whether we should regard her discomfiture in 1043 as no more than her just desert. In the person of Queen Emma we are confronted with an image from the eleventh century which for once can come alive; and if it is not difficult to see through the conventions of the image-makers, we should not be surprised if we are soon disabused of any notion that Emma herself had ever been content to bask in the dignity of her exalted station.

The *Encomium Emmae Reginae* was written for the queen by an unidentified Flemish churchman – probably a monk from the abbey of Saint-Bertin, in Saint-Omer, Flanders – after the accession of Harthacnut in 1040, and after the return of Edward from Normandy to England in 1041, but before the death of Harthacnut in 1042. A glance at the synopsis of its contents (below, pp. [lii–liii]) reveals that the first two parts of the *Encomium* (Books I and II) comprise an account of the conquest of England by Swein Forkbeard and Cnut, serving to establish the political context in Anglo-Danish England which Emma had come to regard as her own. The third part of the work (Book III) is an account of the struggle for power in 1035–40, with much emphasis on the iniquity of Harold Harefoot, and culminating with a view of Queen Emma in her moment of glory at the beginning of the reign of Harthacnut (1040–2). Told in this way, it is a story which would have appealed most of all to Emma herself, and which might have helped to promote her interests in the early 1040s; but just as one cannot read the *Encomium* without understanding that it is highly politicised, so too can one see why it might have lost its appeal after Harthacnut's death. The work seems not to have been widely circulated in the middle ages, and made little or no impression on what became the mainstream of English historical tradition. It was only after its first appearance in print, in 1619, that the *Encomium* began to be used by historians concerned with the events and the aftermath of the Danish conquest of

England.[1] Few, however, made much attempt to explore and thereby to understand the author's methods and intentions. The *Encomium* was described by Sir Frank Stenton (in 1943) as 'in effect a panegyric of Cnut', and was dismissed by him as 'almost contemporary, but completely unreliable on points of fact'.[2] The proper appreciation of the *Encomium* was at last taken up, in the later 1940s, by Alistair Campbell (1907–74), who was at the time Lecturer in English Language at Balliol College, Oxford.[3] Quite apart from all the skills displayed in the establishment and translation of a difficult Latin text,[4] Campbell furnished his edition with an introduction, apparatus and commentary of a kind which afforded further display of his awesome range of learning. He made original and highly effective use of the evidence of Anglo-Saxon charters, the Anglo-Saxon Chronicle, and later Norman and Anglo-Norman sources; and he drew with command and touch on the evidence of skaldic verse, and on the substance of the later sagas in which the verse is embedded, in order to construct a detailed account of the Scandinavian supporters of Cnut.[5] The effect was to raise the profile of the *Encomium* itself among the store of primary sources for Anglo-Saxon history: its credentials were assessed at length,[6] and particular emphasis was placed upon its value 'for the illumination of character and motive', at the time of the Danish conquest of England in 1013–16 and during the political crisis precipitated by Cnut's death in 1035.[7] It remains true that the *Encomium* cannot be separated from the circumstances which obtained in 1041–2, or regarded as anything other than a tract for its times; but Campbell himself would have been the first to say that it is all the more interesting for being so tendentious.

---

[1] John Milton made some use of the *Encomium* in *The History of Britain, that Part Especially now Call'd England*, written in the 1640s and 1650s but first published in 1670; see J. Milton, *The History of Britain*, ed. G. Parry (Stamford, 1991), pp. 302, 312, and 318–21. The *Encomium* has played its part ever since in the formation and adjustment of historical tradition; its influence can also be traced on a number of historical novels, e.g. [Mary] Patry [and Dorothy F.] Williams, *I Am Canute* (London, 1938), Valerie Anand, *Gildenford* (London, 1978), and Ray Bryant, *Warriors of the Dragon Gold* (London, 1987).

[2] F. M. Stenton, *Anglo-Saxon England*, 3rd edn (Oxford, 1971), p. 697; see also *ibid.*, pp. 426–7.

[3] Campbell was Lecturer in English Language at Balliol College, 1946–53, University Lecturer in Medieval English, 1949–63, and Rawlinson and Bosworth Professor of Anglo-Saxon, and Fellow of Pembroke College, Oxford, 1963–74. An obituary of Professor Campbell was published in *The Times* (London), 11 February 1974. His books and papers are now housed in the library of the Pontifical Institute of Medieval Studies, in the University of Toronto; see A. B. Kingsmill, 'The Campbell Collection', *Old English Newsletter* 11.1 (1977), p. 6.

[4] Campbell's work on the *Encomium* has been described as 'a contribution of the first importance to eleventh-century Anglo-Latin literary studies' (M. Lapidge, 'Medieval Latin Philology in the British Isles', *La filologia medievale e umanistica Greca e Latina nel secolo XX* (Rome, 1993), pp. 153–88, at 166).

[5] *Encomium Emmae*, ed. Campbell, pp. 66–91.

[6] *Encomium Emmae*, ed. Campbell, pp. 1–lxix, esp. lxviii–lxix.

[7] *Encomium Emmae*, ed. Campbell, pp. xxii–xxiii; see also *EHD*, pp. 138–9, and no. 28.

QUEEN EMMA DURING THE REIGN OF KING ÆTHELRED

Emma was the daughter of Richard I, count of Rouen (942–96), by his second wife Gunnor, who was herself of Danish origin.[1] She was probably born in the mid or late 980s, at a time when the renewal of Viking raids in England had increased the tension between the political establishments in England and Normandy.[2] In November or December 990 Leo, bishop of Trevi, was despatched by Pope John XV to England, apparently to secure friendly relations between the English and the Normans; and on 1 March 991 the terms of a peace treaty were announced, in the form of a letter addressed by the pope 'to all the faithful'.[3] Relations between England and Normandy were brought under renewed and even greater strain by the activities of the Danish army which was at large in England in the 990s, and which in the summer of 1000 crossed over the channel to 'Richard [II]'s kingdom'.[4] If we can place some trust in a story told with evident relish by a Norman historian writing long after the supposed event, it may have been during this period, in the 990s, that King Æthelred launched a punitive but seemingly disastrous raid on the Cotentin peninsula.[5] Whatever the case, a fresh alliance seems to have been established between King Æthelred and Duke Richard II (996–1026), presumably in 1001 or 1002. In the words of an English chronicler, 'And then in the spring [of 1002] the Lady (*seo hlæfdige*), Richard [I]'s daughter, came to this land.'[6]

When Emma arrived in England, in the spring of 1002, she was probably between fifteen and twenty years old; King Æthelred was probably about thirty-five. Nothing is known in any detail of the part she played in the domestic affairs of the kingdom during the fourteen years which remained of Æthelred's reign, and we can only presume that in her capacity as 'the Lady',[7] she was accorded the

---

[1] Dudo, *GN* iv.125 (ed. Lair, p. 289); WJ, *GND* iv.18 (ed. van Houts, I.128–30). For the sons and daughters of Richard and Gunnor, see Searle, *Predatory Kinship*, pp. 132–40. For Emma's background, see also Stafford, *Queen Emma and Queen Edith*, pp. 209–18.

[2] For the general course of Viking raids during the reign of Æthelred the Unready, see Keynes, 'The Vikings in England, c. 790–1016', pp. 73–82.

[3] The letter of Pope John XV 'to all the faithful' was preserved in the late tenth-century 'Canterbury Letterbook' (BL Cotton Tiberius A. xv, fols. 144v–73r, at 172v–3r), and in WM, *GR* ii.166 (ed. Mynors, *et al.*, pp. 276–8). For a translation of the letter, see *EHD*, no. 230.

[4] It might be supposed that the 'Danish' armies active in England between 991 and 1005 came and went across the North Sea; but for the view that they represented a sustained and omnipresent threat, see Keynes, 'The Historical Context of the Battle of Maldon', pp. 88–95.

[5] WJ, *GND* v.4 (ed. van Houts, II.10–14). For Scandinavian place-names in the Cotentin, see Bates, *Normandy before 1066*, pp. 16–17, and map, p. 267. For further discussion of the raid, see *Encomium Emmae*, ed. Campbell, p. xlii; Campbell, 'England, France, Flanders and Germany', pp. 199–200; and Keynes, 'The Historical Context of the Battle of Maldon', pp. 94–5.

[6] ASC, MSS CDE, s.a. 1002.

[7] For the origin and usage of the style 'the Lady', see Stafford, *Queen Emma and Queen Edith*, pp. 56–64.

respect which befitted her station.[1] She immediately took or was given the name Ælfgifu (the name of Æthelred's first wife, and of his sainted grandmother), and at once began to attend meetings of the king and his councillors.[2] We get at least some impression of her standing at court from the position accorded to her in the witness-lists of the king's charters.[3] In the two earliest charters attested by Emma, one issued in the second half of 1002 and the other issued on 7 December 1004, she is placed after the king and the two archbishops but ahead of the athelings (the king's sons by his first wife) and the bishops;[4] in two charters of 1005 she is positioned after the king and the athelings but ahead of the archbishops and bishops;[5] and thereafter, in her further appearances between 1005 and 1012, she is accorded pride of place in immediate association with the king, ahead of the athelings, the archbishops, and the rest.[6] It should be emphasised, however, that the athelings, as a group, make a stronger impression than Queen Emma, often appearing in charters without her, as if they were more regularly in attendance at

---

[1] There seems to have been room, in a sense, for only one queen at a time in the royal household. The last attestation of King Æthelred's mother, Queen Ælfthryth, in a surviving charter is found in a charter dated 999 (S 896); she died on 17 November in that year, or in 1000 or in 1001 (Keynes, *Diplomas of King Æthelred*, p. 210 n. 203). Nothing is known of the fate of Æthelred's first wife, Ælfgifu; and it is as if it was Ælfthryth's death, rather than hers, that prompted the second marriage and the appearance of a new queen at court. Cf. Stafford, *Queen Emma and Queen Edith*, pp. 216-19.

[2] Campbell (*Encomium Emmae*, pp. xl-xli) made unnecessarily heavy weather of the date of the marriage and the date of Emma's 'change of name'. There is no reason to doubt the authenticity of the charter, dated 1002 and attested by 'Ælfgifu conlaterana regis', by which King Æthelred granted land at Little Haseley, Oxon., to his thegn Godwine (S 902, preserved at Abingdon). It is the case, however, that while the queen was known officially as Ælfgifu, she continued to be known privately and popularly as Imme (Emma): see *Encomium Emmae*, ed. Campbell, pp. xli and 55-8, and below, pp. [lxxiv] n. 5 and [lxxviii] n. 5; cf. Stafford, *Queen Emma and Queen Edith*, pp. 8 n. 9, 11-12, and 61 n. 30.

[3] The evidence of the witness-lists is best interpreted in a way that allows a set of attestations in the name of a particular person to be differentiated from and judged in relation to sets of attestations of other persons; that at the same time allows the evidence of one charter to be judged in relation to the evidence of other charters preserved in the same or in different archives; and that makes it possible to discern any changes in a person's position, or to discern a pattern of appearances in relation to non-appearances. For an attempt to display the evidence in tabular form, see Keynes, *An Atlas of Attestations in Anglo-Saxon Charters*.

[4] S 902 and 909. She was accorded the same position in S 923, dated 1011.

[5] S 910 and 911.

[6] S 943, 916, 915, 918, and 926; the exception is S 923 (above, n. 4). Campbell (*Encomium Emmae*, pp. xli and 64-5) took the view that Emma's status in 1002-16 was marginally 'lower' than Ælfthryth's had been in the 980s and 990s. In so far as we can judge this matter merely from the analysis of witness-lists, the position is in fact rather more interesting. Ælfthryth was generally 'prominent' in the period 978-84 (when she was evidently a significant power at court), wholly absent in the period 984-93 (when she seems to have been out of favour), and present again but not generally so prominent in the period 993-9. Emma's status in Æthelred's reign was much the same as Ælfthryth's status in the early 980s; and it was certainly far higher than that of Æthelred's first wife, Ælfgifu, who does not attest any of the king's charters and who appears in this respect to have been eclipsed by her mother-in-law. See also Stafford, *Queen Emma and Queen Edith*, p. 221.

meetings of the councillors than the queen herself. It is striking, moreover, that Emma's two sons by Æthelred were not accorded special treatment, in the sense that they take their place after their elder half-brothers:[1] Edward (born 1002 x 1005) makes his first appearances in charters dated 1005, and Alfred (perhaps born a few years later) appears for the first time in 1013.[2] Æthelred and Emma also had a daughter, Godgifu; it is not clear whether she was born before or after Alfred.[3]

A few months after his marriage to Emma, King Æthelred 'ordered to be slain all the Danish men who were in England . . . because the king had been informed that they would treacherously deprive him, and then all his councillors, of life, and possess this kingdom afterwards'.[4] It is conceivable that the king's marriage had strengthened his position in a way that some found threatening, and that gave the king himself the confidence to take action against his enemies; or perhaps the event proceeded from a combination of these and other factors. The so-called 'Massacre of St Brice's Day', on 13 November 1002, was directed (arguably) not at the 'Danes' settled in eastern and northern England, but at those members of the Danish army who had remained in the country after the payment of tribute (gafol) at the beginning of the year, and also, it seems, at those identifiable as 'Danes' (whether merchants, mercenaries, or recent settlers), wherever they might be found.[5] The possibility exists, therefore, that there might have been a connection of some kind between the events of November 1002 and the first recorded event in 1003: 'In this year Exeter was stormed on account of the French *ceorl* Hugh, whom the Lady had appointed as her reeve, and the Danish army then destroyed the borough completely and seized much booty there.'[6] In other words, it would

---

[1] Stories subsequently developed to the effect that Edward was marked for kingship from an early age: see Edward's supposed charter for St Peter's, Ghent, issued in 1016 (Keynes, 'The Æthelings in Normandy', pp. 177–81); the *Inventio et miracula sancti Vulfranni*, ch. 18 (ed. Laporte, pp. 29–30), from Saint-Wandrille in Normandy (a house in contact and competition with St Peter's, Ghent, over the relics of St Wulfram), cited and discussed by van Houts, 'Historiography and Hagiography', esp. pp. 247–8 and 251; and *VÆdR* i.1 (ed. Barlow, p. 12). These stories are of the kind which would develop after a king's accession, as a sign of his distinction; and they would bear comparison in this respect with the stories of Alfred's 'coronation' at Rome in 853. They are to be distinguished from the evidence that Edward was sometimes accorded status as 'king' during his exile in Normandy (Keynes, 'The Æthelings in Normandy', pp. 186–93).

[2] For Edward and Alfred, see Barlow, *Edward the Confessor*, pp. 29–30, and Stafford, *Queen Emma and Queen Edith*, pp. 222–3.

[3] For Godgifu, see *Encomium Emmae*, ed. Campbell, pp. xliii, xlv n. 3, and xlix–l, and Barlow, *Edward the Confessor*, p. 30. It was later alleged that King Æthelred was unfaithful to his wife; see WM, *GR* ii.165.12–13 (ed. Mynors, *et al.*, p. 276).

[4] ASC, MSS CDE, s.a. 1002, and *EHD*, no. 127. For a later, Norman, view of the event, see WJ, *GND* v.6 (ed. van Houts, II.14–16); see also WM, *GR* ii.165.12 (ed. Mynors, *et al.*, p. 276), JW, *Chron.* s.a. 1002 (ed. Darlington and McGurk, II.452), and HH, *HA* vi.2 (ed. Greenway, p. 340).

[5] Keynes, *Diplomas of King Æthelred*, pp. 203–5; *idem*, 'The Vikings in England', pp. 77–8.

[6] ASC, MSS CDE, s.a. 1003. Emma is said to have put Hugh in charge of Devon: see JW, *Chron.* s.a. 1003 (ed. Darlington and McGurk, II.454).

appear that Queen Emma had appointed one of her own Norman associates to look after her particular interests in Exeter, and that it was in consequence of his actions that the Danes ransacked the city in 1003. It may be (as supposed by Anglo-Norman historians writing in the first half of the twelfth century) that Hugh had betrayed the English and encouraged the Danes;[1] but Exeter does seem to have had a 'Scandinavian' element in its population in the late tenth century,[2] and it is conceivable, therefore, that Queen Emma's reeve had in fact done something to antagonise the Danish occupants of the borough, precipitating the ferocious attack. If Æthelred's marriage was symbolic of a renewed and sustained alliance with Normandy, the alliance may have been invoked in 1009, when the king is said (albeit on uncertain authority) to have sent messengers to Duke Richard 'to seek his advice and assistance'.[3] It is not known whether any help was forthcoming; but if it was, it was seemingly to no avail, for from August 1009 until April 1012 the English suffered under the worst and most crippling invasion they had ever had to endure. It was apparently in the aftermath of the ravaging of southern England by 'Thorkell's Army' that the king granted Queen Emma a property in the centre of Winchester, on the north side of the High Street and not far from the precincts of the New Minster.[4] The charter recording this grant, dated 1012, is anomalous in form and content, yet if allowances are made for a transaction involving the king and his queen, there is no decisive objection to its authenticity.[5] Emma is known, of course, to have held land elsewhere, in different parts of the kingdom;[6] but it is a pleasant thought that in the closing years of

---

[1] JW, *Chron.* s.a. 1003 (ed. Darlington and McGurk, II.454); HH, *HA* vi.2 (ed. Greenway, pp. 340-2).

[2] For the Scandinavian element at Exeter, see Smart, 'Moneyers of the Late Anglo-Saxon Coinage 973-1016', pp. 263 and 271, and 'Moneyers of the Late Anglo-Saxon Coinage: The Danish Dynasty', p. 305. See also Insley, 'Some Scandinavian Personal Names from South-West England', and 'Some Scandinavian Personal Names from South-West England from Post-Conquest Records'.

[3] HH, *HA* vi.5 (ed. Greenway, p. 344).

[4] The property had once been called 'Ælfric's *godebegeaton*' ('Ælfric's bargain'), presumably after a former owner, and was later known as the manor of Goodbegot. For the name, and the location of the property in Winchester, see *Winchester in the Early Middle Ages*, ed. Biddle, pp. 37-8, 158-9, 340-2 (with map), and 553; see also Stafford, *Queen Emma and Queen Edith*, p. 252 (map).

[5] The charter (S 925: KCD 720), preserved at the Old Minster, Winchester, was entered among some later twelfth-century additions in the 'Codex Wintoniensis' (BL Add. 15350, fol. 11r); for its form and content, see '*Liber Vitae*' *of the New Minster*, ed. Keynes, p. 34 n. 173. The property was bequeathed by Queen Emma to the Old Minster, Winchester, and was confirmed to the Old Minster by King Edward the Confessor (S 1153: *Writs*, ed. Harmer, no. 111).

[6] According to S 1148 (*Writs*, ed. Harmer, no. 104), she had held estates at Islip, where Edward was born, and at Marston, Oxon., and had given them to Edward on the day of his birth. The poet Gaimar, writing in the late 1130s, remarks that King Æthelred gave Emma *en duaire* (as her dowry) Winchester (Hants.), Rockingham (Northants.), and Rutland, 'which Ælfthryth [mother of King Æthelred] had owned before'; see *L'Estoire des Engleis by Geffrei Gaimar*, ed. A. Bell, Anglo-Norman Texts 14-16 (Oxford, 1960), p. 131, lines 4130-5. Campbell (*Encomium Emmae*, p. xliv) may well be right to imply that Gaimar had no authoritative basis for his remark. For Emma's landed interests, see also below, p. [xxvi] n. 5.

Æthelred's reign she passed much of her time pacing up and down the High Street at Winchester.

When Swein, king of Denmark, invaded England in the summer of 1013, the English were still recovering from the effects of the activities of Thorkell's army in the previous years. Thorkell himself was now the leader of a mercenary force in the employment of the English king, and for a while stood firm with King Æthelred at London; but by the end of the year the king had been forced to accept the reality of what for him was an untenable situation. The surviving athelings by Æthelred's first wife (Æthelstan, Edmund, and Eadwig) appear to have remained at large in England, but the king himself, the queen, and the younger children were obliged to take refuge elsewhere. In the words of a contemporary English chronicler:

Then King Æthelred was for a time with the fleet which lay in the Thames, and the Lady (*seo hlæfdige*) went across the sea to her brother Richard, and with her Abbot Ælfsige of Peterborough, and the king sent Bishop Ælfhun across the sea with the athelings Edward and Alfred, that he should take care of them. And the king then went from the fleet to the Isle of Wight at Christmas and spent that festival there; and after the festival went across the sea to Richard and was there with him until the happy event of Swein's death.[1]

William of Jumièges, writing in the 1060s, put a slightly different construction on the events:

King Æthelred, who at that time was at Winchester and who found himself completely deserted by the English, dug up his treasure from the earth and went with his wife and sons, Edward and Alfred, to Duke Richard in Normandy, where he was suitably welcomed by Richard with a great display of splendour and for the whole length of his visit remained with him at Rouen.[2]

King Æthelred, Queen Emma, and their children were in Normandy for little more than three or four months. King Swein died on 3 February 1014. After some negotiations with the English people, the king and the athelings returned to England in the spring, presumably accompanied by Emma,[3] with every prospect of greater things to come. The death of the atheling Æthelstan, the king's eldest son by his first wife, on 25 June 1014, must therefore have had quite an unsettling effect on the newly re-established regime, undoing the expectations of some,

---

[1] ASC, MSS CDE, s.a. 1013. For Ælfsige, abbot of Peterborough (1006–42), in Normandy, see *The Chronicle of Hugh Candidus*, ed. W. T. Mellows (Oxford, 1949), pp. 48–9. For Bishop Ælfhun, see *Charters*, ed. Robertson, pp. 384–5.

[2] WJ, *GND* v.7 (ed. van Houts, II.18).

[3] William of Jumièges (*GND* v.8 (ed. van Houts, II.20)) states that Æthelred and Emma returned to England, leaving Edward and Alfred in Normandy. That the athelings came back is clear from charters of 1014–15 (Keynes, 'The Æthelings in Normandy', p. 176 n. 20); that Emma came back is implied by the evidence that she was in London in 1016 (below, p. [xxi] n. 4).

creating new opportunities for others, and generally causing loyalties to unravel.[1] Cnut, son of King Swein, brought the Danes back to England in August 1015, in the midst of a political crisis which had exposed all the weaknesses of the king's government.[2] The king himself was again in London; and it was in London that he died, on St George's Day (23 April) 1016, having held his kingdom 'with great toil and difficulties as long as his life lasted'.[3] There is reason to believe that Emma was with the king, at London, in 1016,[4] but it is uncertain exactly what became of her, and of her children, during the brief reign of Edmund Ironside, initially as (notional) king of all the English and latterly, after his defeat at the battle of Ashingdon and the consequent division of the kingdom, as king of Wessex. Edmund died on 30 November 1016, and Cnut succeeded to the whole kingdom. Queen Emma would appear to have remained in England;[5] but Edward and Alfred were driven into exile. Edward was in Flanders in December 1016,[6] though it is not clear whether he was accompanied at this stage by his younger brother Alfred;

---

[1] The date of the atheling Æthelstan's death is established by a reading of his will (S 1503) in conjunction with the fact that his obit on 25 June was recorded both at Christ Church, Canterbury (BL Arundel 68, fol. 32r), and at the Old Minster, Winchester (BL Add. 29436, fol. 73r); see EHD, no. 129, Keynes, Diplomas of King Æthelred, p. 267, and Keynes, 'Cnut's Earls', p. 71 n. 156. Æthelstan was buried at the Old Minster. The impact of his death on the political situation in 1014, and on the advancement into prominence of his younger brother Edmund (Ironside), affords much scope for fruitful speculation. Cf. N. J. Higham, The Death of Anglo-Saxon England (Stroud, 1997), pp. 44–7 and 56–9.

[2] Keynes, 'A Tale of Two Kings', pp. 214–16; Stafford, Queen Emma and Queen Edith, pp. 223–4.

[3] ASC, MSS CDE, s.a. 1016.

[4] TM, Chron. vii.40–1 (ed. Trillmich, pp. 396–8; EHD, no. 27); see also Keynes, 'The Æthelings in Normandy', pp. 176–7. WJ, GND v.9 (ed. van Houts, II.20); see also van Houts, 'The Political Relations between Normandy and England', p. 81. The Norse poem Liðsmannaflokkr, vv.8–10, can also be taken to imply that Emma was in London during Cnut's siege in 1016: see Poole, 'Skaldic Verse and Anglo-Saxon History', pp. 290–2; Poole, Viking Poems, pp. 89–90; and Medieval Scandinavia, ed. Pulsiano, p. 391. For what it may be worth, the story told in Knytlinga Saga, ch. 9 (Pálsson and Edwards, p. 31), depends on the belief that Emma was captured by the Danes before she could escape to Normandy; see also the so-called 'Supplement to Jómsvíkinga saga', in Encomium Emmae, ed. Campbell, pp. 90 and 93.

[5] See further below, p. [xxiii–xxiv]. William of Malmesbury (GP v.263 (ed. Hamilton, pp. 419–20)) tells a colourful story to the effect that Emma returned to Normandy after Æthelred's death, passed the time at Rouen, and returned to England thereafter bearing relics of St Ouen, giving the body to Canterbury and keeping the head for herself. For ramifications of this story, see Heslop, 'The Production of de luxe Manuscripts', pp. 183–4. It is the case that Emma would have had many opportunities for obtaining relics from her friends in Rouen (cf. OV, HE iii (ed. Chibnall, II.42), for her gift, possibly during Æthelred's reign, of an illuminated Psalter to her brother Robert, archbishop of Rouen); and it is not clear whether William had any basis, apart from his own imagination, for supposing that she obtained the relics during an alleged return to Rouen in 1016–17.

[6] Edward visited St Peter's abbey, Ghent, in December 1016, and promised that in the event of his becoming king he would restore certain lands to the monks: see Keynes, 'The Æthelings in Normandy', pp. 177–81.

sooner or later, however, both Edward and Alfred seem to have found their way safely to Normandy.[1]

QUEEN EMMA DURING THE REIGN OF KING CNUT

The most familiar aspect of the political career of Queen Emma is the fact that within eighteen months of the death of her first husband, King Æthelred the Unready, she married his Danish conqueror, King Cnut. It is far from certain in what circumstances the second marriage took place, and precisely what political significance should be attached to it. A contemporary English chronicler represented the matter in seemingly unambiguous terms: 'And then before 1 August [1017] the king ordered the widow of King Æthelred, Richard [I]'s daughter, to be fetched as his wife (*het se cyng feccean him . . . him to wife*).'[2] Ralf Glaber, a monk of Saint-Bénigne at Dijon (Burgundy), writing in the 1030s, presumed the marriage to be symbolic of a treaty between Cnut and Duke Richard, whereby Richard was assured of military aid whenever it was required.[3] The author of the *Encomium Emmae*, writing for Emma herself about twenty-five years after the event, gives a striking picture of Cnut as the suitor and Emma as the ultimate prize:

Everything having been thus duly settled, the king lacked nothing except a most noble wife; such a one he ordered to be sought everywhere for him, in order to obtain her hand lawfully, when she was found, and to make her the partner of his rule, when she was won. Therefore journeys were undertaken through realms and cities and a royal bride was sought; but it was with difficulty that a worthy one was ultimately found, after being sought far and wide. This imperial bride was, in fact, found within the bounds of Gaul, and to be precise in the Norman area, a lady of the greatest nobility and wealth, but yet the most distinguished of the women of her time for delightful beauty and wisdom, inasmuch as she was a famous queen.[4]

It should be noted, however, that the marriage is presented not as the occasion of an alliance between the political orders in England and Normandy, but as a symbol of lasting reconciliation between the English and the Danes.[5] A monk of Saint-Wandrille, in Normandy, writing apparently in the 1050s, presumed that

---

[1] See further below, pp. [xxviii–xxix]. Cambridge, University Library, MS Ee.3.59 (Westminster, s.xiii med.), contains an attractive series of drawings depicting events in the life of Edward the Confessor, including Swein's oppressive rule and the flight of Emma and her sons to Normandy: see M. R. James, *La Estoire de Seint Aedward le Rei* (Oxford, 1920), and N. J. Morgan, *Early Gothic Manuscripts 1250–85*, Survey of Manuscripts Illuminated in the British Isles 4.2 (London, 1987), no. 123.

[2] ASC MSS CDE, s.a. 1017.   [3] RG, *Hist.* ii.3 (ed. France, pp. 54–6).

[4] *EER* ii.16 (ed. Campbell, p. 32). See further below, pp. [lx–lxi].

[5] *EER* Arg. and ii.16 (ed. Campbell, pp. 6 and 32); and see further below, p. [lx]. Campbell (*Encomium Emmae*, p. xxi) points out, not unreasonably, that the English might not have regarded Emma with special affection, and prefers to regard the marriage as a move towards a reconciliation between Cnut and Normandy (*Encomium Emmae*, pp. xxi and xlv–xlvi).

Cnut had married Emma with her brother's approval.[1] William of Jumièges, writing in the 1060s, creates a rather different impression of the event: 'He [King Cnut] took Queen Emma from the city [London] and married her a few days later according to the Christian custom. In return for her he handed over her weight in gold and silver to the army.'[2] Adam of Bremen, writing in the 1070s, knew from the *Liber Vitae* of his church that Cnut, Emma, and Harthacnut had entered into confraternity with the church of Bremen, and put the marriage in the context of others.[3] The Anglo-Norman historians, writing in the first half of the twelfth century, would have been able to draw their own conclusions from what they read in the Anglo-Saxon Chronicle, but might otherwise not have had any privileged information. John of Worcester and Henry of Huntingdon report the event without comment;[4] but William of Malmesbury has no hesitation in presuming Cnut's purpose to have been in part to conciliate the English and in part to establish good relations with Duke Richard II, not least in order to discourage the duke from intervening in England on behalf of the exiled athelings.[5] The point at issue is whether we should assume that Queen Emma had returned to Normandy after King Æthelred's death in 1016, and was then formally given in marriage by her brother Duke Richard II to King Cnut;[6] or whether Emma had remained in England after Æthelred's death, and was still there in 1017 when Cnut decided to marry her in the furtherance of his own political ends. If Emma was 'fetched' from Normandy, there would be every reason to suppose that the marriage reflected Cnut's earnest desire quickly to establish an alliance with Duke Richard, for all the reasons first suggested by William of Malmesbury.[7] If, on the other hand, Cnut had ordered that Emma be

---

[1] *Inventio*, ch. 18 (ed. Laporte, p. 30); van Houts, 'Historiography and Hagiography', p. 251.

[2] WJ, *GND* v.9 (ed. van Houts, II.20). For pertinent comment on the custom of 'marriage by seizure', see van Houts, 'The Political Relations between Normandy and England', pp. 87–8 and 94 n. 16, and *William of Jumièges*, ed. van Houts, II.21 n. 4.

[3] AB, *GHEP* ii.52, Schol. 37 (ed. Trillmich, p. 290; transl. Tschan, p. 91), and 54 (ed. Trillmich, p. 292; transl. Tschan, p. 92).

[4] JW, *Chron.* s.a. 1017 (ed. Darlington and McGurk, II.504), and HH, *HA* vi.15 (ed. Greenway, p. 362). For a later and more spirited account of the events of the early eleventh century, focussing on Æthelred, Earl Godwine, and Cnut, see WMp, *DNC*, Dist. v.3–5 (ed. James, pp. 410–36).

[5] WM, *GR* ii.180.11 (ed. Mynors, *et al.*, p. 318) and esp. ii.181.3 (ed. Mynors, *et al.*, p. 322). See also WM, *GP* v.263 (ed. Hamilton, p. 419).

[6] Campbell (*Encomium Emmae*, pp. xliv–xlv; see also p. xlviii, with n. 5) had no doubt that Emma returned to Normandy in 1016 and was there when 'fetched' by Cnut in 1017; see also above, p. [xxi] n. 5.

[7] The prevailing view of the marriage is as a continuation of the 'Norman alliance': e.g. Stenton, *Anglo-Saxon England*, pp. 397 and 399; *Encomium Emmae*, ed. Campbell, pp. xlv–xlvi; Barlow, *Edward the Confessor*, pp. 37–8; [M. W.] Campbell, 'Queen Emma and Ælfgifu of Northampton', pp. 66–7; John, 'The *Encomium Emmae Reginae*', pp. 79–80; John, 'The Return of the Vikings', p. 207; Stafford, *Unification and Conquest*, p. 72; Lawson, *Cnut*, pp. 86–7; and John, *Reassessing Anglo-Saxon England*, pp. 156–7. It has also been suggested that Cnut wished to marry Emma because she was a Norman, and because the Normans were renowned as conquerors; see Searle, 'Emma the Conqueror', esp. pp. 287–8.

'fetched' from safe-keeping of some kind in England, the marriage would look rather less like the renewal of an alliance with Normandy, and much more like a move on Cnut's part intended to secure Emma's support, perhaps involving her abandonment of her children by Æthelred (and his abandonment of his children by Ælfgifu of Northampton), on the understanding that the succession would belong to the child of them both, in straightforward defiance of what might be regarded as Norman political interests (symbolised by the presence of the athelings in Normandy).[1] Our understanding of the political drift in the 1020s and 1030s turns out to depend squarely, therefore, on our view of the Encomiast's credibility in the matter of Cnut's marriage to Emma; and it is precisely in this matter that the Encomiast is at his most notoriously tendentious.[2] The athelings themselves remained in Normandy for the duration of Cnut's reign, under the care of their uncles Duke Richard II (996–1026) and Robert, archbishop of Rouen (989–1037), and would have soon come to know their cousins Duke Richard III (1026–7) and Duke Robert (1027–35), not to mention Duke Robert's son, William. It is no surprise, under the prevailing circumstances, that the athelings were treated with honour and accorded the respect which befitted their station, with consequences that are very well known.[3]

King Cnut and Queen Emma appear to have drawn strength from each other in a way that seems not to have been true of Æthelred and Emma; and if the Danish conqueror and his Norman queen were astute enough to cultivate the double act, one senses, perhaps, that their subjects were quick to appreciate the performance.[4] The evidence of the queen's attestations in royal charters suggests that she maintained a more regular attendance at meetings of the king and his councillors than had been the case during Æthelred's reign, and that she was consistently accorded 'high' status: it is true that initially, in charters of 1018–19, she was placed after the king and archbishops,[5] representing a slight 'demotion' from the position normally accorded to her in Æthelred's charters;[6] but she was

---

[1] The year's delay before remarriage may have been occasioned by considerations of English law (as suggested by van Houts, 'The Political Relations between England and Normandy', p. 88, citing *V Æthelred* 21.1. and *II Cnut* 73). It should also be borne in mind that the Normans had already declared their interests by giving shelter to the athelings, and that in this respect Duke Richard II had already turned against the Danes (a point stressed and developed by Bates, *Normandy before 1066*, pp. 67–8). For further discussion of the marriage, see Keynes, 'The Æthelings in Normandy', pp. 181–5, and Stafford, *Queen Emma and Queen Edith*, pp. 225–31. For the rather intriguing suggestion that an early eleventh-century Norman poem, *Semiramis*, can be interpreted as a satire, composed in 1017, ridiculing Emma's relationship with King Cnut, see van Houts, 'A Note on *Jezebel* and *Semiramis*', pp. 20–3, and Stafford, *Queen Emma and Queen Edith*, pp. 12 and 34.

[2] See further below, pp. [lx–lxi].   [3] See further below, pp. [xxviii–xxix].

[4] Cnut's skalds were not so quick on the uptake: see Frank, 'Cnut in the Verse of his Skalds', p. 112.

[5] S 951, 953, 950 (reproduced in *The Golden Age of Anglo-Saxon Art*, ed. Backhouse, *et al.*, no. 169, and in Stafford, *Queen Emma and Queen Edith*, p. 194, Fig. 8), 956, 955.

[6] Cf. above, p. [xvii]; see also *Encomium Emmae*, ed. Campbell, pp. xlvi–xlvii and 65.

accorded pride of place, after the king and ahead of the archbishops, in 1022–3,[1] and although she reverted to a place after the archbishops in the late 1020s,[2] she resumed her accustomed position, after the king and ahead of the archbishops, in 1032–5.[3] The stature which Queen Emma enjoyed in Cnut's reign is suggested by other forms of evidence which reflect what seems to have been the general perception of a king who acted in association with his queen. In 1020 Archbishop Wulfstan directed a writ 'to his lord King Cnut and to the Lady Ælfgifu' ('Ælfgyfe þa hlæfdian'), informing them that Æthelnoth had been consecrated archbishop of Canterbury.[4] In another document, King Cnut 'and the Lady Ælfgifu' ('Ælfgifu seo hlædige') granted permission to their priest Eadsige to dispose of certain estates when he became a monk.[5] At lower levels of the social hierarchy, Mantat the Anchorite announced his will in the form of a document addressed to King Cnut and Queen Emma ('Emma hlæfdie');[6] and Leofflæd, daughter of Ealdorman Byrhtnoth, appears to have done much the same.[7] Emma is said to have been in Cnut's company when he visited Ely abbey.[8] The symbolic importance attached to the queen's presence in royal ceremonial is suggested more particularly by a contemporary chronicler's account of the translation of the mortal remains of Archbishop Ælfheah from London to Canterbury in 1023. On Saturday 8 June, the body of St Ælfheah (martyred by Thorkell's army, at Greenwich, on 19 April 1012) was ceremonially removed from its resting-place at St Paul's, transported across the Thames to Southwark, and taken thence to Rochester; on Monday 10 June, Queen Emma joined the gathering, 'with her royal child Harthacnut', and on the next day the assembled company conveyed the archbishop in state to Canterbury; and a few days later,

---

[1] S 958, 980, 984, 977, 960.   [2] S 962, 983, 963, 971.

[3] S 964, 970 ('Ego Cnut rex Anglorum cum regina mea Ælfgyfu'), 968, 967, 972 (cf. S 970), 973, 975, 976. The evidence of Emma's attestations is presented in tabular form in Keynes, *Atlas of Attestations*; see also Stafford, *Queen Emma and Queen Edith*, pp. 231–2. The fact that the changing pattern can be detected at all suggests that it should be meaningful. It might be related in some way to changes in personnel which affected her position in relation to others; and while it is interesting that she should start with a 'demotion' and yet soon recover the position which she had enjoyed before, it is difficult to guess what might account for her temporary demotion in the late 1020s. Emma was prominent among the witnesses to a spurious document which concerns Cnut's grant of Folkestone to Christ Church, Canterbury: see S 981 (*Charters*, ed. Robertson, no. 85). Her style in this document is 'Ælfgyua Imma seo hlæfdige'; cf. S 1228, from St Albans, cited below, p. [lxxiv] n. 5.

[4] S 1386 (*Writs*, ed. Harmer, no. 27). A copy of the writ was entered in the 'MacDurnan Gospels' (London, Lambeth Palace, MS 1370, fol. 69v), a book which had been given to the see of Canterbury by King Æthelstan, and which was used in the eleventh century for the safe-keeping of documents concerning the archbishops themselves.

[5] S 1465 (*Charters*, ed. Robertson, no. 86). Eadsige became archbishop of Canterbury in 1038.

[6] S 1523 (*Wills*, ed. Whitelock, no. 23).   [7] S 1520 (*LE* ii.88 (ed. Blake, pp. 157–8)).

[8] *LE* ii.85 (ed. Blake, p. 153).

on Saturday 15 June, the body was formally laid to rest in the cathedral, on the north side of the altar.[1] Cnut and Emma were also associated with each other in acts of conspicuous patronage conducted on a scale reminiscent of King Æthelstan as a donor of books, and probably to much the same purpose.[2] Both were named, for example, in the inscription on a shrine which they presented to Abingdon abbey, during the abbacy of Abbot Æthelwine (1018–30).[3] The ultimate and most abiding expression of the partnership between the king and his queen is, however, the familiar image which serves as a frontispiece in the 'Liber Vitae' of the New Minster, Winchester, produced at the beginning of the abbacy of Abbot Ælfwine, in 1031 (Ill. 1).[4] It is in certain respects a development of the equally familiar image of King Edgar which serves as a frontispiece in the 'Foundation Charter' of the New Minster; yet while the image in the charter focusses attention on the importance of the king's role in the monastic reform movement, the image in the 'Liber Vitae' acknowledges the importance of the queen as well as the king in the Anglo-Danish regime.

On her own terms, Queen Emma comes across as one who had interests in different parts of the kingdom, but who was nonetheless identified most closely with the ecclesiastical establishments at Winchester.[5] Her association with or patronage of Stigand, the royal priest given charge of the minster at Ashingdon (Essex) in 1020, was perhaps one aspect of links which she soon developed in East Anglia.[6] She is known to have acquired rights of jurisdiction in the eight and a half hundreds of Thingoe (Suffolk), giving her strong interests in and around the newly

---

[1] ASC MS D, s.a. 1023 (ed. Cubbin, p. 64). See also Rumble, 'Translatio Sancti Ælfegi Cantuariensis archiepiscopi et martyris', p. 312.

[2] Encomium Emmae, ed. Campbell, pp. xlvii–xlviii; see also Heslop, 'The Production of de luxe Manuscripts', esp. pp. 156–62 and 182–8.

[3] The object is lost, but the inscription was recorded in the twelfth-century chronicle-cartulary of the abbey; see Heslop, 'The Production of de luxe Manuscripts', pp. 156 (for Ælfgyth read Ælfgifu) and 182–3.

[4] For the 'Liber Vitae' of the New Minster (BL Stowe 944), see 'Liber Vitae' of the New Minster, ed. Keynes, pp. 37–9 (date and circumstances of its production), 66–8 (Abbot Ælfwine, possibly the artist responsible for the image of Cnut and Emma), and 79–80 (prefatory image). For reproductions of the image in colour, see The Vikings in England and in their Danish Homeland, ed. Roesdahl, et al., p. 153, and 'Liber Vitae' of the New Minster, ed. Keynes, plate V. For discussion of its significance, see (e.g.) Gerchow, 'Prayers for King Cnut', pp. 222–30; Frank, 'Cnut in the Verse of his Skalds', p. 117; Stafford, 'Emma: The Powers of the Queen', pp. 3–4; Stafford, Queen Emma and Queen Edith, pp. 178–9; and Halpin, 'Anglo-Saxon Women and Pilgrimage', pp. 112 and 119.

[5] For Emma's landed interests, see Encomium Emmae, ed. Campbell, p. xlviii; Meyer, 'The Queen's "Demesne" in Later Anglo-Saxon England', pp. 83–4, and Stafford, Queen Emma and Queen Edith, pp. 123–42.

[6] For Emma and Stigand, see Smith, 'Archbishop Stigand', esp. pp. 199–200.

Ill. 1   The cross of gold and silver placed on the altar of the New Minster, Winchester, by King Cnut and Queen Ælfgifu (Emma). *Liber Vitae* of the New Minster (1031), prefatory image. BL Stowe 944, fol. 6r.

[xxvii]

refounded abbey of Bury St Edmunds.[1] Elsewhere, she is said to have governed, in some sense, the monastery at Evesham (Worcestershire);[2] and when a substantial estate at Newington, in Oxfordshire, was forfeited by a thegn called Ælfric to King Cnut, Emma was able to acquire the property and then to arrange for it to be given to the community of Christ Church, Canterbury.[3] Any or all of this might pale into insignificance if only more were known for certain of Emma's landed interests and personal attachments; and in our ignorance of her political activities in Cnut's reign, beyond the presumption that she maintained a presence beside the king, we can but imagine that she passed much of the time in her house at Winchester, and kept good company there with her Anglo-Scandinavian friends.[4] The two recorded children of the marriage, Harthacnut and Gunnhild, were probably born in the period 1018–20. Harthacnut was no more than five or six years old when put on public display in June 1023; and the fact that he does not attest any of the surviving charters of the king is consistent with the tradition that he was despatched to Denmark, at about that time, for his upbringing.[5]

While Cnut and Emma presided over their affairs in England, and (in Cnut's case) further afield, the athelings Edward and Alfred remained in exile in Normandy. It is not known whether they were given a permanent home in the ducal monastery at Fécamp on the coast; but whatever the case, there is every reason to believe that they were well looked after.[6] It was apparently in 1033 that Duke Robert sent envoys to King Cnut asking that the athelings be allowed to return to England; but Cnut would have nothing to do with the suggestion, whereupon Duke Robert assembled an invasion force at Fécamp. A storm drove

---

[1] It is not known when Emma acquired these interests (*Writs*, ed. Harmer, pp. 145–8); but the fact that she lost them temporarily in 1043–4 (below, p. [lxxiii]) indicates that she had possessed them earlier, presumably in the 1020s and 1030s, if not before. According to a Bury interpolation in a manuscript of the Worcester Chronicle, Emma was involved with Cnut, Bishop Ælfwine, and Earl Thorkell in the refoundation of Bury St Edmunds; see *Chronicle of John of Worcester*, ed. Darlington and McGurk, p. 643, but cf. Keynes, 'Cnut's Earls', p. 56 n. 65.

[2] S 1423 (*Charters*, ed. Robertson, no. 81, with comment on p. 405); see also Lawson, *Cnut*, p. 155.

[3] A record of this transaction was subsequently entered in a gospel-book at Canterbury (BL Cotton Claudius A. iii, fol. 6r). It is registered as S 1229 (*Charters*, ed. Robertson, no. 96); the archbishop of Canterbury held an estate of fifteen hides at Newington in 1066 and 1086 (GBD 155r (*DB Oxon*. 2.1)). See further below, p. [lxxvii].

[4] For references to 'Scandinavian' elements at Winchester in the eleventh century, see Yorke, *Wessex in the Early Middle Ages*, pp. 143–4, and '*Liber Vitae*' of the New Minster, ed. Keynes, p. 40 n. 227.

[5] ASC MS C, s.a. 1023; Keynes, 'Cnut's Earls', pp. 56–7 and 63.

[6] WJ, *GND* vi.9 (ed. van Houts, p. 76); WP, *GG* i.14 (ed. Davis and Chibnall, pp. 18–20). On the treatment of the athelings in Normandy, see van Houts, 'The Political Relations between England and Normandy', pp. 89–93, and Keynes, 'The Æthelings in Normandy', p. 185. According to the *Inventio et miracula sancti Vulfranni*, written at Saint-Wandrille in the 1050s, Duke Richard II raised his nephews as if they were his sons: see *Inventio*, ch. 18 (ed. Laporte, p. 30), and van Houts, 'Historiography and Hagiography', p. 251.

the fleet westwards, round the peninsula to Jersey; and when it became clear that they could make no further progress, Duke Robert decided to abandon his projected invasion of England, and returned to the mainland at Mont-Saint-Michel.[1] It is said that Cnut subsequently sent envoys to Duke Robert offering to return 'half the kingdom of England' to the sons of King Æthelred, because he was seriously ill;[2] but it seems that the negotiations, if ever set in motion, came to nothing. Cnut and his retinue of housecarls appear by this stage to have developed a special liking for Dorset,[3] and it was at Shaftesbury that the king died, on 12 November 1035. His body was brought back to Winchester, and he was laid to rest there in the Old Minster.

QUEEN EMMA IN 1035–42

The death of King Cnut created a highly charged political situation. Secular authority in England appears to have polarised in the early 1030s into two factions, personified by Earl Godwine (representing the new aristocracy of the Anglo-Danish regime), on the one hand, and Earl Leofric (representing entrenched political interests north of the river Thames), on the other.[4] There were two surviving sons of Cnut, neither of whom was without political ambition and both of whom had politically active mothers. Unfortunately Harthacnut, who would appear to have been regarded by his supporters as the designated heir to Cnut's throne,[5] was still in Denmark; and while Harold Harefoot, son of Cnut by Ælfgifu of Northampton, had the distinct advantage of being in England, there were doubts about his paternity which those opposed to him would scarcely fail to bring forward against him.[6] The English athelings, sons of King Æthelred the Unready, remained in Normandy, but it seems that no one was prepared to stand up for either of them. One contemporary chronicler reported that Harold sent to Emma at Winchester, 'and had all the best treasures taken from her, which she could not

---

[1] For all these events, see WJ, *GND* vi.9–10 (ed. van Houts, II.76–8), and WM, *GR* ii.180.11 (ed. Mynors, *et al.*, pp. 318–20). The story has been regarded by modern historians with all due circumspection (e.g. Stenton, *Anglo-Saxon England*, p. 409; Bates, *Normandy before 1066*, p. 68); but it gains support from the analysis of Norman charters (Keynes, 'The Æthelings in Normandy', pp. 186–94; Lawson, *Cnut*, pp. 110–11). See also Stafford, *Queen Emma and Queen Edith*, pp. 234–5.
[2] WJ, *GND* vi.11 (ed. van Houts, II.78–80).
[3] S. Keynes, 'The Lost Cartulary of Abbotsbury', *Anglo-Saxon England* 18 (1989), pp. 207–43 at 230–1. One of Cnut's Scandinavian associates was called Orc, founder of Abbotsbury abbey in Dorset; Orc's wife was called Tola, who is said to have come from Rouen (*ibid.*, p. 236).
[4] See Keynes, 'Cnut's Earls', pp. 53 (Table 4.1), 70–4 (Godwine), 77–8 (Leofric) and 78–87 (discussion).
[5] *EER* Arg. (ed. Campbell, p. 6) and ii.16 (ed. Campbell, p. 32).
[6] ASC MSS CD and EF, s.a. 1035; *EER* iii.1 (ed. Campbell, pp. 40–2); *VÆdR* i.3 (ed. Barlow, p. 32); JW, *Chron.* s.a. 1035 (ed. Darlington and McGurk, II.520); WM, *GR* ii.188.1 (ed. Mynors, *et al.*, p. 334).

keep back, which King Cnut had possessed; yet she continued to stay there as long as she was allowed'.[1] Another, scarcely less hostile to Harold but more inclined to take Earl Godwine's side, explained the course of events in different terms:

> And immediately after his [Cnut's] death there was an assembly of all the councillors at Oxford. And Earl Leofric and almost all the thegns north of the Thames and the shipmen in London chose Harold to the regency of all England, for himself and for his brother Harthacnut, who was then in Denmark. And Earl Godwine and all the chief men in Wessex opposed it as long as they could, but they could not contrive anything against it. And it was then determined that Ælfgifu, Harthacnut's mother, should stay in Winchester with the housecarls of her son the king, and they should keep all Wessex in his possession; and Earl Godwine was their most loyal man.[2]

The outcome of the deliberations at Oxford was apparently a form of shared rule, with King Harold Harefoot and Earl Leofric firmly established north of the Thames, and with Queen Ælfgifu (for the absentee Harthacnut) and Earl Godwine established south of the Thames.[3] Yet if this was the situation which obtained in 1035–6, the balance of political power soon began to change. The underlying factor was doubtless Earl Godwine's decision to transfer his allegiance from Harthacnut's party to Harold Harefoot, itself prompted by Emma's decision to switch her own attention from Harthacnut to Edward.[4] It would appear that Emma had soon realised that her initial position, waiting at Winchester for Harthacnut to return to England, was hopeless, and that her only chance of maintaining herself in power as queen-mother was to place her faith in her sons by Æthelred the Unready, in exile in Normandy. Yet while she might have had much to gain from the return of the athelings, Earl Godwine would have had everything to loose; for he was the archetypal 'new noble', who had risen to power in the entourage of King Cnut, and who would have reason to fear the restoration of the native dynasty. It is not entirely clear whether it was Emma who summoned the athelings to England in 1036, or whether they decided to return of their own accord; but whatever the

---

[1] ASC MSS CD, s.a. 1035; see also *The Abingdon Chronicle*, ed. Conner, p. lv.

[2] ASC MSS EF, s.a. 1035.

[3] References to 'the Lady' in documents which might have been issued within the period 1035 x 1037 could be to an otherwise unknown wife of Harold Harefoot, or to Ælfgifu of Northampton, or to Queen Emma. The will of Ælfric, bishop of Elmham, of the period 1035 x 1040, includes a bequest to 'my lady' ('mire hlefdigen'); see S 1489 (*Wills*, ed. Whitelock, no. 26). The will of Leofgifu, of the period 1035 x 1044, similarly includes bequests to her lady ('mine lauedi'); see S 1521 (*Wills*, ed. Whitelock, no. 29). Both wills have strong connections with Bury St Edmunds; and the most likely 'Lady' in question would have been Emma herself, suggesting that she may have retained her status for the while, among friends. Cf. Stafford, *Queen Emma and Queen Edith*, p. 244.

[4] *Encomium Emmae*, ed. Campbell, pp. lxvi–lxvii; Barlow, *Edward the Confessor*, pp. 43–4; *'Liber Vitae' of the New Minster*, ed. Keynes, p. 39. Stenton, *Anglo-Saxon England*, pp. 420–1, is curiously opaque in his account of these events, regarding Godwine as one of those 'who seem to have felt that Alfred's presence would delay the settlement of the kingdom'.

case, it seems that Edward chose the most direct route to his mother at Winchester, that Alfred came from a different direction, and that both would have been hoping to take advantage of the prevailing uncertainties of the political climate and thereby to gather much needed support. The contemporary English sources say nothing of Edward's expedition, not (one suspects) without good reason; so it is the Norman sources alone which tell of his arrival at Southampton with a force of forty ships, and of his hasty return to Normandy, albeit 'richly laden with booty'.[1] The bitter truth about the atheling Alfred's expedition could not be so easily concealed. He went first from Normandy to Flanders, and crossed thence from Wissant (near Calais) to Dover.[2] As a chronicler put it:

[1036] In this year the innocent atheling Alfred, the son of King Æthelred, came into this country, wishing to go to his mother who was in Winchester, but Earl Godwine would not allow him, nor did the other men who had great power, because feeling was veering much towards Harold, although this was not right.[3]

The different sources put their different spins on the story; but in essence it seems that Alfred and his companions were at first entertained and then betrayed by Earl Godwine, at Guildford, in Surrey, and, once delivered by him into the hands of the forces of Harold Harefoot, were variously massacred, mutilated, or enslaved.[4] Alfred himself was taken in captivity to Ely abbey in the fens, where he was blinded on board ship, and then handed over to the monks: 'And he dwelt there as long as he lived. Then he was buried as well befitted him, very honourably, as he deserved, in the south chapel at the west end, full close to the steeple. His soul is with Christ.'[5] Alfred's obit was commemorated at Ely on 5 February, so it

---

[1] WJ, *GND* vii.5 (ed. van Houts, II.104–6); WP, *GG* i.2 (ed. Davis and Chibnall, pp. 2–4); cf. JW, *Chron.* s.a. 1036 (ed. Darlington and McGurk, II.522 and 524). Edward's expedition is not mentioned by Stenton in his account of this period (*Anglo-Saxon England*, p. 421). For further discussion, see *Encomium Emmae*, ed. Campbell, p. lxvii; Barlow, *Edward the Confessor*, pp. 44–6; Keynes, 'The Æthelings in Normandy', pp. 195–6; Stafford, *Queen Emma and Queen Edith*, p. 239.

[2] *EER* iii.4 (ed. Campbell, p. 42), 'taking only a few men of Boulogne'; WJ, *GND* vii.6 (ed. van Houts, II.106), 'with a considerable military force'.

[3] ASC MSS CD, s.a. 1036 (ed. Conner, pp. 12–13; ed. Cubbin, p. 65). MS E (pro-Godwine) is deafeningly silent on the matter.

[4] ASC MSS CD, s.a. 1036 (ed. Conner, pp. 13–14; ed. Cubbin, pp. 65–6); *EER* iii.4–6 (ed. Campbell, pp. 42–6); *VÆdR* i.3 (ed. Barlow, pp. 32–4); WJ, *GND* vii.6 (ed. van Houts, II.106); WP, *GG* i.2–3 (ed. Davis and Chibnall, pp. 2–4); and JW, *Chron.* s.a. 1036 (ed. Darlington and McGurk, II.522–4). See also WM, *GR* ii.188.5 (ed. Mynors, *et al.*, p. 336), and HH, *HA* vi.20 (ed. Greenway, pp. 370–2). For an attempt to clear Earl Godwine of complicity in Alfred's death, see E. A. Freeman, *A History of the Norman Conquest of England*, 6 vols. (Oxford, 1867–79), I (2nd edn) 484–97 and 755–64; for a response, see *Two of the Saxon Chronicles Parallel*, ed. C. Plummer, 2 vols. (Oxford, 1892–9), II.211–15, and *Encomium Emmae*, ed. Campbell, pp. lxiv–lxvii. For further discussion from different points of view, see Barlow, *Edward the Confessor*, pp. 44–6; Stafford, *Queen Emma and Queen Edith*, pp. 239–40; Walker, *Harold: The Last Anglo-Saxon King*, pp. 14–16; and Higham, *Death of Anglo-Saxon England*, pp. 111–12.

[5] ASC MSS CD, s.a. 1036.

would appear that the events of his return, capture and blinding had taken place in the closing months of 1036, and that he died on 5 February 1037.[1]

It is not difficult to see what the chronicler might have meant by his remark that in 1036 'feeling was veering much towards Harold, although this was not right'. The vital insight is provided by a remarkable letter written in July or August 1036 by Immo, then a priest at the court of the Emperor Conrad II, to Azeko, bishop of Worms.[2] Conrad's son Henry (the future Emperor Henry III) had married Gunnhild, daughter of Cnut and Emma, in June 1036;[3] and Immo was bursting to tell his friend about the messengers who had just come from England to see Gunnhild at the German court:

Porro autem nec illud vos latere volo, quod legati Anglorum nostrae iuniori domnae, nuper infirmae, nunc autem, Deo gratias! valenti, missi sunt; qui vero dixerunt sibi haec: 'infelix ergo', inquiunt, 'et iniusta noverca vestra, Arduichenut, germano vestro, regnum fraude subripere cupiens, universis primatibus nostris convivia maxima celebravit, et nunc eos prece, nunc pretio corrumpere satagens, iuramentis sibi suoque nato subiugare temptavit; qui vero non solum ei in aliquo huiusmodi non consenserunt, verum etiam nuntios prefato germano vestro, quatenus ad eos cito redeat, unanimes transmiserunt.' Sed illi quidem talia.

Yet nor do I wish it to escape your notice that envoys of the English were sent to our younger lady (recently unwell, but now, thanks be to God, much better). This is what they told her. 'Your wretched and wicked step-mother, wishing to deprive your brother Harthacnut of the kingdom by fraud, organised a great party for all our leading men, and, eager to corrupt them at times with entreaty and at times with money, tried to subordinate them with oaths to herself and to her son; yet not only did the men not give their consent to her in any such way, but of one accord they despatched messengers to your aforesaid brother, so that he might soon return to them.' But to her, indeed, (they said) such things.

Immo's letter testifies most effectively to the methods employed by Ælfgifu of Northampton in her determination to suborn her political opponents, and thereby to deprive Harthacnut of his share of the kingdom. Her campaign finds further and even more striking reflection in the numismatic evidence. Initially (probably

---

[1] Alfred's obit was recorded in an Ely calendar (Cambridge, Trinity College, MS O. 2. 1, fol. K2v); see Gerchow, *Die Gedenküberlieferung der Angelsachsen*, p. 344. The local Ely tradition is disappointingly derivative: see *LE* ii.90 (ed. Blake, pp. 158–60); Barlow, *Edward the Confessor*, p. 46 n. 7. On the alleged commemoration of Alfred in the calendar in the Crowland Psalter (Oxford, Bodleian Library, MS Douce 296), see Keynes, 'The Crowland Psalter', pp. 361–2.

[2] For the text (and context) of this letter, see H. Bresslau, *Jahrbücher des Deutschen Reichs unter Konrad II*, 2 vols. (Leipzig, 1879–84), II.532–3, and W. H. Stevenson, 'An Alleged Son of King Harold Harefoot', *English Historical Review* 28 (1913), pp. 112–17, at 115–16. It could be said that the letter deserved rather more attention, in relation to the *Encomium Emmae*, than Campbell saw fit to give it in his edition; cf. *Encomium Emmae*, ed. Campbell, p. lxiv n. 2.

[3] For Gunnhild's marriage, see *VÆdR* i.1 (ed. Barlow, p. 16); WJ, *GND* v.9 (ed. van Houts, II.20); WM, *GR* ii.188.7 (ed. Mynors, *et al.*, p. 338); and HH, *HA* vi.17 (ed. Greenway, p. 366). See also *Encomium Emmae*, ed. Campbell, p. xlix (for Beatrix, daughter of Henry and Gunnhild, who became abbess of Quedlinburg); and Keynes, 'Giso, Bishop of Wells', p. 206 n. 12.

in 1035–6), coins of the same basic type (*Jewel Cross*) were being minted in the name of each king at mints respectively north (Harold) and south (Harthacnut) of the river Thames, with mints *on* the Thames (including London) operating more even-handedly for both parties, and with a handful of the mints north of the Thames operating for Harthacnut as well as for Harold; but, interestingly, the balance soon began to change (probably in 1036–7), for while the mints which had previously operated for Harthacnut stopped doing so, more of the mints lying south of the Thames began to operate for Harold, until (during the course of 1037) the coinage in Harthacnut's name was effectively replaced by a ubiquitous coinage in Harold's name (the late varieties of *Jewel Cross*).[1] It is apparent, in other words, that there was a shift of loyalty in 1036–7 which was to Harold's advantage and Harthacnut's disadvantage, and which when it had run its course left Harthacnut stranded without any significant support.

The interpretation of the events of 1036 turns largely upon our understanding of one issue in particular: under what circumstances and so with what expectations did the athelings Edward and Alfred return to England? We are scarcely in a better position today to understand the events than were many observers in the eleventh century, and there is much scope, therefore, for the creative exercise of historical judgement. At the heart of the matter lies the Encomiast's extraordinary story of how Harold Harefoot forged a letter purporting to be from Queen Emma to Edward and Alfred, in which she urged one or other of them to come to her in England, and by which means Harold hoped to entice them into a fatal trap.[2] In effect, we have to make a choice between four options. First, whether to accept the Encomiast at his word, and to suppose that Harold Harefoot forged a document purporting to be a letter from Emma to her sons, in order to lure the athelings back. Secondly, whether to suppose that Queen Emma's letter was in fact genuine, and that the Encomiast was obliged to maintain that it was a forgery in order to transfer the blame for its immediate consequences (notably the death of Alfred) from Emma to Harold Harefoot.[3] Thirdly, whether to suppose that the athelings returned to England on their own initiative, and that the Encomiast fabricated the story in the spirit of the underhand methods known to have been employed by Emma's opponents in 1036–7 and in the hope of ensuring that Harold, not Emma, would be blamed for enticing them back. Or fourthly, whether to suppose that Emma in some way encouraged the athelings to return to England, at a time when she had begun to

---

[1] For details and further references, see Talvio, 'Harold I and Harthacnut's *Jewel Cross* Type Reconsidered', and Talvio, *Anglo-Saxon Coins: Harold I and Harthacnut*, pp. 1–3.

[2] *EER* iii.3 (ed. Campbell, pp. 40–2).

[3] See John, 'The *Encomium Emmae Reginae*', pp. 85–6, and John, *Reassessing Anglo-Saxon England*, pp. 164 and 166. The view that the letter is genuine is also adopted by Stafford, *Queen Emma and Queen Edith*, pp. 241–2 and 245.

despair of Harthacnut, and that the Encomiast fabricated the story of the forged
letter as yet another way of casting a slur upon Harold, by making it appear that
Harold had been responsible for initiating a sequence of events which had such a
disastrous outcome, and as the most direct way, at the same time, of insisting
that Emma herself had not been party to Alfred's coming.[1] If the letter was
forged by Harold, and the Encomiast's story is true, it would provide the perfect
illustration of the campaign described in Immo's letter (but there attributed to
Ælfgifu of Northampton), and striking evidence at the same time of the use of
forged documents for political purposes. If the letter was written by Emma, and
the Encomiast's story is quite brazenly untrue, it would be scarcely less
remarkable as a surviving example of a written communication from the queen to
her sons, cast (more or less) in the appropriate diplomatic form, and would
constitute telling evidence of Emma's actual part in these events. It is arguable,
however, that the object was to implicate Harold at the start of a sequence of
events leading to the death of Alfred; and it is the way the letter, so phrased,
serves the particular purposes of the Encomiast, as opposed to the nefarious
purposes of Harold or the political purposes of Emma, that recommends the
presumption that the whole story is a glorious fabrication.[2] It is entirely likely
that it was Emma who encouraged Edward and Alfred to return to England; but
in the retrospect of the early 1040s, Harold was to be blamed not only for
Alfred's death, but also for enticing him back to England in the first place. What
Edward would have made of the story is another matter, and perhaps the least of
the Encomiast's concerns.

In 1037 'Harold was chosen as king everywhere, and Harthacnut was deserted
because he was too long in Denmark; and then his mother, Queen Ælfgifu
[Emma] was driven out without any mercy to face the raging winter.'[3] It is a
matter of central importance to our understanding of Emma's career that she did
not return to the bosom of her family in Normandy, but chose instead to seek
refuge in Flanders.[4] 'And then she went across the sea to Bruges, and Earl
Baldwin received her well there and maintained her there as long as she had
need.'[5] The contacts maintained between England and Flanders from the late

---

[1] *Encomium Emmae*, ed. Campbell, pp. xxiii n. 6, lxiv, lxvii, and lxix; Barlow, *Edward the Confessor*,
p. 44; Keynes, 'The Æthelings in Normandy', p. 196 n. 113.

[2] For further discussion, see below, p. [lxiii].   [3] ASC MSS CD, s.a. 1037.

[4] Campbell (*Encomium Emmae*, p. xlviii) suggested that Emma did not go to Normandy because the
duchy 'was in the disorders of a minority rule'. Emma's nephew, Duke Robert I, had died in 1035, and
had been succeeded by his son, William I (1035–87); her brother Robert, archbishop of Rouen, died in
1037; but doubtless she would have had other friends and supporters. It is more to the point, however,
that Emma would not have wished to commit herself, as it were, to the atheling Edward, and that she
might have preferred to keep her options open. See Keynes, 'The Æthelings in Normandy', p. 196;
Stafford, *Queen Emma and Queen Edith*, p. 246.

[5] ASC MSS CD, s.a. 1037.

ninth century onwards are well attested,[1] and are extended, in a sense, by the contacts which developed in the eleventh century between England and Lotharingia.[2] For various reasons the rulers of Flanders would seem to have been instinctively sympathetic to the political interests in England which might be characterised as Anglo-Danish.[3] Baldwin IV, count of Flanders (988–1035), would appear to have been on friendly terms with King Cnut; and Cnut is well known to have passed through Flanders when on his way to Rome, in 1027 or perhaps on a later occasion.[4] Baldwin V, count of Flanders (1035–67), might be expected to have inherited the same political proclivities; and although matters became progressively more complicated, it is not difficult to understand why (for example) King Edward should have sided with the emperor Henry III against him in 1049, or why Baldwin should have given refuge to Earl Swein (son of Earl Godwine) in 1049–50, or why Earl Harold might have been made welcome in Flanders in November 1056, when he attested a charter of Baldwin V drawn up at Saint-Omer in favour of St Peter's, Ghent.[5] Emma herself settled at Bruges, on the north-east coast of Flanders, evidently with Count Baldwin's blessing, and would have been well positioned there to keep in touch with her friends and supporters elsewhere.[6] Moreover, she would have established contact, sooner or later, with the community of the ancient monastery founded by St Omer on the island of Sithiu, on the river Aa, known after its first abbot as the monastery of Saint-Bertin, and then under the rule of Abbot Roderic (1021–42).[7] Emma might

---

[1] The classic and indispensable account of this subject, covering the ninth, tenth and eleventh centuries, is P. Grierson, 'The Relations between England and Flanders before the Norman Conquest', *Transactions of the Royal Historical Society* 4th ser. 23 (1941), pp. 71–112, repr. in *Essays in Medieval History*, ed. R. W. Southern (London, 1968), pp. 61–92. See also McGurk and Rosenthal, 'The Anglo-Saxon Gospelbooks', pp. 251–6; and *Two Old English Apocrypha*, ed. Cross, pp. 16–21.

[2] For England and Lotharingia in the eleventh century, see Keynes, 'Giso, Bishop of Wells', pp. 205–13.

[3] For a survey of the history of Flanders, see Nicholas, *Medieval Flanders*, esp. pp. 45–9 (Baldwin IV) and 49–56 (Baldwin V). See also John, 'The *Encomium Emmae Reginae*', pp. 86–7.

[4] *EER* ii.20–1 (ed. Campbell, p. 36); see also below, pp. [lxi–lxii].

[5] P. Grierson, 'A Visit of Earl Harold to Flanders in 1056', *English Historical Review* 51 (1936), pp. 90–7, at 91–2. The charter (which survives in its original single-sheet form) is registered in *Diplomata Belgica*, ed. Gysseling and Koch, I.203 (no. 100), and is printed in A. van Lokeren, *Chartes et documents de l'abbaye de Saint Pierre au Mont Blandin a Gand*, 2 vols. (Ghent, 1868), I.95–6 (no. 133). It was written by a monk called Folcard; see further below, p. [xxxvii] n. 1.

[6] For Bruges in the eleventh century, see Nicholas, *Medieval Flanders*, pp. 34–6; see also Grierson, 'Relations between England and Flanders', pp. 96–7.

[7] For the history of Saint-Bertin, in general, see H. de Laplane, *Les abbés de Saint-Bertin*, 2 vols. (Saint-Omer, 1854–5), and D. Haigneré, *Les chartes de Saint-Bertin d'après le Grand Cartulaire de Dom Charles-Joseph Dewitte* I [AD 648–1240], Société des Antiquaires de la Morinie (Saint-Omer, 1886). For Abbot Roderic, see B. Guérard, *Cartulaire de l'abbaye de Saint-Bertin*, Collection des Cartulaires de France 3 (Paris, 1841), esp. pp. 171–9; see also F. Morand, *Appendice au Cartulaire de l'abbaye de Saint-Bertin* (Paris, 1867).

also have come into contact with the canons who served the church of Sainte-Marie, on an adjacent hill. The two religious houses were separate but connected;[1] and the place had developed by the eleventh century into the town of Saint-Omer (now France, Département du Pas-de-Calais).[2] Monks from Saint-Bertin had moved to England on more than one occasion in the past, in the way represented most conspicuously by Grimbald of Saint-Bertin (who came to the court of King Alfred the Great in the 880s),[3] and by the group of monks from Saint-Bertin who found refuge at Bath in the 940s.[4] Emma could rely at Saint-Omer, as at Bruges, on the good standing which she enjoyed as Cnut's widow; so she would have found herself among friends, and in contact with a renowned centre of learning.[5] Perhaps we may permit ourselves the speculation that she needed and therefore secured the services of a priest, for her own household at Bruges; and that whoever entered her service at this time might later have returned with her to England. It was through an association with Herman, bishop of Ramsbury, who had been a monk at Saint-Bertin in 1055–8, under Abbot Bovo (1042–65), that Goscelin of Saint-Bertin came to England, in the late 1050s or early 1060s,[6] and began to pursue his career as a professional hagiographer.[7] Folcard of Saint-Bertin came to England at about the same time; and it has been suggested that Folcard might be the otherwise unidentified

---

[1] *Encomium Emmae*, ed. Campbell, pp. xix–xx.

[2] For Saint-Omer, see Nicholas, *Medieval Flanders*, pp. 36–7, and Derville, *et al.*, *Histoire de Saint-Omer*, esp. pp. 23–7.

[3] For Grimbald's career at Saint-Bertin in the second half of the ninth century, see P. Grierson, 'Grimbald of St. Bertin's', *English Historical Review* 55 (1940), pp. 529–61, at 542–5; see also J. Bately, 'Grimbald of St Bertin's', *Medium Ævum* 35 (1966), pp. 1–10. For the charters composed or attested by Grimbald, between 867 and 885, see *Diplomata Belgica*, ed. Gysseling and Koch, nos. 38, 40, 42, and 46.

[4] Folcwin, *Gesta Abbatum S. Bertini Sithiensium*, ch. 107 (*EHD*, no. 26), in 'Gesta Abbatum S. Bertini Sithiensium', ed. O. Holder-Egger, MGH, Script. 13 (Hanover, 1881), pp. 600–73, at 628–9; see also S. Keynes, 'King Athelstan's Books', *Learning and Literature in Anglo-Saxon England: Studies Presented to Peter Clemoes*, ed. M. Lapidge and H. Gneuss (Cambridge, 1985), pp. 143–201 at 161.

[5] *Encomium Emmae*, ed. Campbell, p. xx, *Life of King Edward*, ed. Barlow, p. xlvii. For surviving manuscripts from the monastery of Saint-Bertin and from the chapter of Saint-Omer, see H. Michelant, 'Manuscrits de la bibliothèque de Saint-Omer', *Catalogue général des manuscrits des Bibliothèques Publiques des Départements* III (Paris, 1861), pp. 1–386, and H. Michelant, 'Manuscrits de la bibliothèque de Boulogne-sur-mer', *Catalogue général des manuscrits des Bibliothèques Publiques des Départements* IV (Paris, 1872), pp. 565–699. For an impression of activity at Saint-Bertin in the late tenth and early eleventh centuries, see A. Wilmart, 'Les livres de l'abbé Odbert', *Bulletin historique de la Société des Antiquaires de la Morinie* 14 (1922–9), pp. 169–88, and Oursel, *et al.*, *Nord roman*, pp. 267–97.

[6] For Herman, see *Life of King Edward*, ed. Barlow, pp. xlvii–xlix. It should be noted that Herman may not have been in a position to take charge of the diocese of Sherborne until the early 1060s (Keynes, 'Giso, Bishop of Wells', pp. 208–9).

[7] For Goscelin, see *Life of King Edward*, ed. Barlow, pp. xlvi–lii and 133–5.

Flemish monk who was commissioned by Queen Edith to write the *Vita Ædwardi Regis*.[1]

If we may believe the Encomiast, Emma lost little time, once safely established at Bruges, in asking her son Edward to visit her in Flanders; whereupon he came to his mother, insisted that he was in no position to help her, recommended that she seek help from Harthacnut instead, and then returned to Normandy.[2] So she despatched messengers to Harthacnut, told him of her great sorrow (a reference to the blinding and death of Alfred), and urged him to come; if we may believe the Encomiast, again, Harthacnut burned with a desire to avenge his (half-) brother's injuries, and to obey his mother.[3] By this time, Harthacnut had been absent from England for about fifteen years, and, for all we know, had not seen his mother at all during that period, let alone either of his half-brothers. It is difficult to imagine that Harthacnut would have been moved in particular by a wish to avenge Alfred, and one suspects that it was resentment of Harold's seizure of power that provided him with a more powerful incentive; whatever the case, he sailed from Denmark to Bruges in 1039, and was there reunited with Emma. Harold Harefoot died in Oxford on 17 March 1040.[4] The councillors 'sent to Bruges for Harthacnut, thinking that they were acting wisely';[5] so in June 1040 Emma and Harthacnut were able to return to England, to take up the position which had been denied them for nearly five years. Emma was, of course, accorded a prominent place after the king among the witnesses to Harthacnut's charters,[6] and she is also found with the king (styled 'Ælfgeofu his modor') as a witness to a Worcester lease issued in 1042;[7] a writ issued in the names of Harthacnut and Queen Ælfgifu, granting land at Hemingford, Hunts., to Ramsey abbey, affords further evidence of the truth that she was now back at the centre of the stage.[8] It is evident, however, that Harthacnut's regime was deeply unpopular. To judge from the Anglo-Saxon Chronicle, the unpopularity would appear to have been a function of the excessive levels of taxation imposed on the

---

[1] For Folcard, see *Life of King Edward*, ed. Barlow, pp. lii–lix. Perhaps it should be noted in this connection that the charter of Count Baldwin V issued in November 1056 (above, p. [xxxv] n. 5), in the presence of Earl Harold, was drawn up at Saint-Omer by 'Folkardus monachorum ultimus', conceivably none other than the monk of Saint-Bertin.

[2] *EER* iii.8 (ed. Campbell, p. 48). Campbell (*Encomium Emmae*, pp. lxvii–lxviii) suggested that the story of Edward's visit to Flanders may be apocryphal; cf. Barlow, *Edward the Confessor*, p. 47.

[3] *EER* iii.8 (ed. Campbell, p. 48).

[4] ASC, MSS EF, s.a. 1039 for 1040. For Harold's last illness, see S 1467 (*Charters*, ed. Robertson, no. 91).

[5] ASC, MSS CD, s.a. 1040.

[6] S 995, 982, 993, 994. Stafford, *Queen Emma and Queen Edith*, p. 247.

[7] S 1394 (*Charters*, ed. Robertson, no. 94).

[8] S 997 (*Writs*, ed. Harmer, no. 57). The grant was confirmed in the 1040s by Edward the Confessor (S 1106 (*ibid.*, no. 58)).

people in 1040 and 1041; but other factors may well have contributed to the general hostility now felt towards the Anglo-Danish regime. Ælfric Puttoc, who had been prior of the Old Minster, Winchester, before becoming archbishop of York (1023–51), and certain other persons unnamed, are said on what should be good authority to have accused Earl Godwine and Lyfing, bishop of Worcester (1038–46), of complicity in the blinding of the atheling Alfred.[1] It seems that Lyfing was briefly deprived of his see (1040–1), and it may be no coincidence that the men of Worcestershire appear to have resisted the king's tax-gatherers at just this time;[2] it is said of Earl Godwine that he gave Harthacnut a fully equipped ship, and swore 'that it had not been by his advice or at his wish that his brother was blinded, but that his lord King Harold had ordered him to do what he did'.[3] It was conceivably in this connection that Harthacnut and Emma invited the atheling Edward to return from Normandy to England, in 1041, and one can understand why they might have been keen to associate him with themselves in the appearance of joint rule.[4] In other words, it seems likely that in 1040–1 there was much debate about the circumstances in which the atheling Alfred had been murdered, that Earl Godwine contrived to exculpate himself by asserting under oath that he had only been acting under King Harold's orders, and that Emma and Harthacnut took the initiative in asking Alfred's elder brother Edward to return to England, presumably for what was perceived to be their own good. The question, perhaps, is whether Queen Emma's own activities had been called into question during the course of the debate about Alfred; and whether it might have been in circumstances of this kind that she decided to commission a Flemish priest in her service to put together an account of some of the more recent events in her life.

---

[1] JW, *Chron.* s.a. 1040 (ed. Darlington and McGurk, II.530–2); for another version of the same story, see WM, *GR* ii.188.6 (ed. Mynors, *et al.*, pp. 336–8). It is by no means improbable that Lyfing was a staunch supporter of Harold Harefoot. He had been abbot of Tavistock, and was appointed bishop of Crediton in 1026 or 1027. When Brihtheah, bishop of Worcester, died, on 20 December 1038, Lyfing was soon afterwards given Worcester as well, for he is found before the end of the year issuing a lease of Worcester property with the express permission of King Harold and Earl Leofric (S 1392). Most significantly, Lyfing, described as 'bishop of Devonshire', was at Harold's side at Oxford in 1040, when the king was dying (S 1467).

[2] ASC, MSS CD, s.a. 1041; JW, *Chron.* s.a. 1041 (ed. Darlington and McGurk, II.532).

[3] JW, *Chron.* s.a. 1040 (ed. Darlington and McGurk, II.530–2); see also below, p. [lxv] n. 2. The charge against Godwine was revived by Robert of Jumièges, archbishop of Canterbury, in 1051; see *VÆdR* i.3 (ed. Barlow, pp. 32–4), and *Life of King Edward*, ed. Barlow, p. 32 n. 71.

[4] ASC, MSS CD, s.a. 1041; *EER* iii.13–14 (ed. Campbell, p. 52). S 993, a charter by which King Harthacnut granted land at Farnborough, Berks., to Abingdon abbey, was issued *in regali uilla* at Sutton, in 1042, and is attested by the king, his mother Ælfgifu, and his brother Edward, among others (including a number of royal priests). For further discussion, see Barlow, *Edward the Confessor*, pp. 48–50; and, for the 'trinity' of power, Stafford, *Queen Emma and Queen Edith*, pp. 247–8.

INTRODUCTION TO THE 1998 REPRINT

THE *ENCOMIUM EMMAE REGINAE*

The author and date of the *Encomium Emmae Reginae*

The author of the *Encomium Emmae* states unequivocally that he had been present at Saint-Omer when King Cnut had passed through the town on his way to Rome, most probably in 1027.[1] He describes himself in the same context as the 'servant' (*uernula*) of St Omer and St Bertin,[2] with the implication that he was or had formerly been either a canon of Saint-Omer or a monk of Saint-Bertin. It is otherwise apparent that the author had been commissioned to write the *Encomium* by Queen Emma herself,[3] and that he discharged this task during the reign of Harthacnut (1040-2), after the return of Edward to England in 1041.[4] Professor Campbell warned against the assumption that the author was necessarily a monk of Saint-Bertin, if only to leave open the possibility that he was a canon of Saint-Omer;[5] yet it must be admitted that the frontispiece in the surviving mid-eleventh-century manuscript (Ill. 2) appears to depict the author with a tonsure, so the likelihood must be that he was a monk.[6] Campbell noted that Bovo, who became abbot of Saint-Bertin in 1042 or 1043, claimed to have written a historical work, and he wondered, therefore, whether Bovo himself might be the author of the *Encomium*.[7] Whatever the case, the impression we derive from Campbell's introduction is that the *Encomium* was written in Flanders in 1041-2, probably by a monk of the monastery of Saint-Bertin, and that a copy of the work was then brought from Flanders to England for presentation to Queen Emma. The question arises, however, whether the *Encomium* is likely to have been written by a person in Saint-Omer who had been commissioned (and briefed) by Queen Emma when she was still in Flanders, and who might not have had ready access to information about the Danish conquest of England in 1013-16, or about the politics of 1035-40; or whether the nature of the work is more readily compatible with the supposition that it was written by a person who had entered into the service of Queen Emma while she was based at Bruges in 1037-40, and who had then returned with her to England in 1040.[8] As Campbell showed, the author was

---

[1] *EER* ii.20 (ed. Campbell, p. 36). For Cnut's visit to Rome, see below, pp. [lxi–lxii].
[2] *EER* ii.21 (ed. Campbell, p. 36).   [3] *EER* Prol. (ed. Campbell, p. 2).
[4] *EER* Arg. (ed. Campbell, pp. 6-8) and iii.13-14 (ed. Campbell, p. 52).
[5] *Encomium Emmae*, ed. Campbell, p. xix n. 3.
[6] Cf. *Encomium Emmae*, ed. Campbell, p. vi, for Francis Wormald's view that it is not possible to decide 'whether the artist [of the frontispiece] intended to depict the Encomiast as a monk or as a secular cleric, though the former appears the more likely'.
[7] *Encomium Emmae*, ed. Campbell, pp. xx–xxi; Gransden, *Historical Writing*, p. 56.
[8] There are no obvious or decisive clues as to the author's location. The Encomiast claims to have seen many of those men who were captured with the atheling Alfred in 1036 (*EER* iii.5 (ed. Campbell, p. 44)), perhaps because they had been able to get back to Boulogne. The ending is conceivably

certainly well trained in the classics (notably Sallust, Virgil, Lucan, and Caesar; perhaps also Lucretius, Ovid, Horace, and Juvenal),[1] though there is rather less to recommend Campbell's supposition that the author was also familiar with Dudo of Saint-Quentin's *Gesta Normannorum*.[2] Points of this nature may, however, reflect no more than the Encomiast's training in Flanders; and since he would appear to have been familiar with Asser's *Vita Ælfredi regis Angul-Saxonum*,[3] and since he seems to have been in a position to draw information (and disinformation) from those who frequented the Anglo-Scandinavian court,[4] it is conceivable that when he wrote the *Encomium* he was in fact resident in England. On this hypothesis we might imagine that the Encomiast was a Flemish monk who, like Grimbald before him and like Goscelin soon after him, had left the monastery of Saint-Bertin in order to pursue a more high-profile career across the channel. It would remain

---

suggestive: 'Here there is loyalty among sharers of rule, here the bond of motherly and brotherly love is of strength indestructible' (*EER* iii.14 (ed. Campbell, p. 52)).

[1] *Encomium Emmae*, ed. Campbell, pp. xxiii–xl. For the Encomiast's knowledge of Lucretius (*ibid.*, p. xxxii), see *Texts and Transmission: A Survey of the Latin Classics*, ed. L. D. Reynolds (Oxford, 1983), pp. 219–20.

[2] *Encomium Emmae*, ed. Campbell, pp. xxii and xxxiv–xxxv; cf. L. Musset's review of Campbell, in *Annales de Normandie* 2 (1952), p. 87. For Dudo, see G. C. Huisman, 'Notes on the Manuscript Tradition of Dudo of St Quentin's *Gesta Normannorum*', *Anglo-Norman Studies* 6 (1984), pp. 122–35, and E. A. Hanawalt, 'Dudo of Saint-Quentin: The Heroic Past Imagined', *Haskins Society Journal* 6 (1995), pp. 111–18; an English translation, by Eric Christiansen, is forthcoming.

[3] *Encomium Emmae*, ed. Campbell, pp. xxxv–xxxvi, with reference to the glosses for Ashingdon (*EER* ii.8) and Sheppey (*EER* ii.9), apparently reflecting familiarity with equivalent glosses in Asser, ch. 37 and ch. 3. For further discussion of the former gloss, see Townend, '*Assandun* and *Assatun*'. Campbell (*Encomium Emmae*, p. xxxvii) also made a connection between the author's reference to the magic raven banner (*EER* ii.9; cf. *Encomium Emmae*, ed. Campbell, pp. 96–7) and a similar passage in the so-called 'Annals of St Neots' (*Annals of St Neots with Vita Prima Sancti Neoti*, ed. Dumville and Lapidge, p. 78), suggesting on this basis that the Encomiast and the compiler of the annals drew on a lost version of the *Vita Ælfredi regis* which contained its own account of the magic banner. The hypothesis was dismissed, not unreasonably, by Dumville and Lapidge (*Annals of St Neots with Vita Prima Sancti Neoti*, pp. xxxvi n. 28, and lxiii n. 124). The possibility thus arises that the twelfth-century compiler of the 'Annals of St Neots' was acquainted, directly or indirectly, with the account of the raven banner in the *Encomium Emmae*; and one would imagine that the passage was then simply interpolated, in the late sixteenth century, from the 'Annals of St Neots' into certain transcripts of Asser (to form ch. 54b in Stevenson's edition). The notion (propounded by Smyth, *Alfred the Great*, pp. 162–3 and 169) that the author of the *Encomium Emmae* drew the glosses, and the information on the raven banner, from a lost 'East Anglian' chronicle which itself lies behind the 'Annals of St Neots' is fraught with complications which cannot be pursued here; much depends on one's understanding of the composition of the 'Annals of St Neots', and, in particular, on the likely date when certain Norman or Frankish sources would have been available in eastern England (see *Annals of St Neots with Vita Prima Sancti Neoti*, ed. Dumville and Lapidge, esp. pp. xliii–xlvii, lii–lviii and lxv, and cf. Hart, 'The East Anglian Chronicle', pp. 251–4, 258–61 and 274).

[4] For evidence that the author derived information from English witnesses, see *Encomium Emmae*, ed. Campbell, pp. xxxvi–xxxvii.

[xl]

uncertain whether he passed the rest of his days in the service of Queen Emma, perhaps based at Winchester, or whether he later returned to Saint-Omer.

Manuscripts and transcripts

The sole surviving medieval manuscript of the *Encomium Emmae* (BL Add. 33241) was written towards the middle or perhaps during the third quarter of the eleventh century. Campbell was able to show from textual evidence that an early copy of the author's autograph had introduced certain scribal errors, and that the surviving manuscript, and another eleventh-century manuscript now lost, were derived independently from the same early copy.[1] The surviving manuscript contains a prefatory image in which the seated or enthroned Queen Emma is depicted receiving the book from the kneeling author, while two bearded young men, presumably her sons Harthacnut and Edward (one of whom has a hand on the open book), look admiringly towards her from behind the architectural frame (Ill. 2).[2] The question immediately arises whether it follows that this particular manuscript was produced for presentation to the queen, and may thus once have belonged to Emma herself, or whether a frontispiece of this nature would have been regarded as necessarily integral to any early copy of the work. The manuscript was written by two collaborating scribes.[3] The first scribe, who was clearly a master of his craft, was responsible (so it seems) for drawing the frontispiece (1v), for writing the Prologue (2r–5r, beginning with the decorated initial S on 2r (Ill. 3)), and for writing the greater part of the main text (8r–41r, line 9 (from *EER* i.1 to *EER* ii.10, line 18), beginning with the decorated initial R on 8r (Ill. 4), and with a smaller initial M at the beginning of Book II on 19v); the parchment was prepared for 15 lines, which with wide margins gave space for about fifty words per page. The second scribe wrote the Argument (5r–7v, beginning with a crude initial F, probably supplied by another hand), and seems to have taken over again half-way down the first leaf of the sixth quire (41r, line 9), continuing thereafter to the end of the whole work (67r), leaving a blank space for the initial M on 54r (at the beginning of Book III); interestingly, once he had completed the sixth quire (on a

---

[1] *Encomium Emmae*, ed. Campbell, p. xii n. 3.

[2] BL Add. 33241, fol. 1v. For an excellent reproduction in colour, see *The Vikings in England and in their Danish Homeland*, ed. Roesdahl, *et al.*, p. 156. For further discussion of the portrait, see Neuman de Vegvar, 'A Paean for a Queen'; Stafford, 'Emma: The Powers of the Queen', pp. 4–6; and Stafford, *Queen Emma and Queen Edith*, pp. 38–9. For the wider iconographic context, see Gameson, 'The Gospels of Margaret of Scotland', esp. pp. 159–60.

[3] *Encomium Emmae*, ed. Campbell, p. xi. The collation is as follows: I⁸ (fols. 1–8), II⁸ (fols. 9–16), III⁸ (fols. 17–24), IV⁸ (fols. 25–32), V⁸ (fols. 33–40), VI⁸ wants 8 (fols. 41–7), VII⁸ (fols. 48–55), VIII⁸ (fols. 56–63), IX⁴ (fols. 64–7). Fol. 1r was left blank, and now carries later medieval library marks; fol. 1v bears the prefatory image; the text of the *Encomium* occupies fols. 2r–67r; fol. 67v was left blank. The manuscript was rebound in 1978, and each quire was mounted on a separate guard.

Ill. 2   Queen Emma receiving the *Encomium Emmae Reginae* from its author; her sons
Harthacnut and Edward behold the scene. *Encomium Emmae Reginae*, prefatory image.
BL Add. 33241, fol. IV.

[xlii]

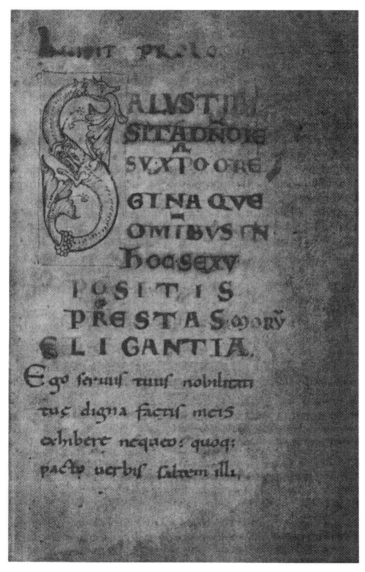

Ill. 3   The Encomiast's address to Queen Emma. *Encomium Emmae Reginae*, Prologue.
BL Add. 33241, fol. 2r

leaf now missing between fols. 47 and 48), still with 15 lines per page, he seems to have decided to use a more economical format, so that the last three quires were prepared for 18 lines, which with narrower margins gave space for eighty or ninety words per page (as shown, for example, on fol. 56r (Ill. 5)). A curious feature of the manuscript is the thorough and wholly effective erasure of one-and-a-half lines at the beginning of Book III (54r, lines 6–7), by someone who appears to have taken exception to the Encomiast's remarks on Cnut's burial at Winchester; for rather more text has been erased than simply a reference to Winchester itself, and it is not clear what else might have been said.[1]

It is generally presumed, on grounds of content, script, and decoration, that the manuscript was written on the continent.[2] If so, the most natural place of origin would be Saint-Omer, in Flanders,[3] but the view has also been expressed that the manuscript was written in Normandy.[4] The matter may yet be settled by the identification of one or other, or both, of the scribes in another manuscript context, whether Flemish, Norman, or English. One has to admit, however, that in the conditions which obtained in the central decades of the eleventh century, it might be difficult to tell whether a manuscript was produced in a continental scriptorium under 'English' influence, or by 'continental' scribes active in England; and since monks were as transportable as manuscripts were portable, it is as hazardous to assume that a scribe could not move from one place to another as it is to draw inferences about a book's origin from information about its later provenance.[5] If it proves to be the case that the manuscript was written in Normandy, it would be interesting to have such evidence of 'Norman' interest in Emma before the Norman Conquest; and one might then ask how the *Encomium*

---

[1] *EER* iii.1 (ed. Campbell, p. 38, and textual note *b*); Campbell's presumption that the erasure was made *after* the late medieval marginal annotation (which refers to Cnut's burial at Winchester) may not be safe. Another eleventh-century manuscript of the *Encomium* appears to have had simply 'Wyntonie' at this point, and if only to judge from the transcript there was no evidence of erasure (Paris, Bibliothèque nationale, Fonds Lat. 6235, fols. 7v–14v, at 12v). For intimations of controversy, cf. Crook, 'The Movement of King Cnut's Bones', pp. 169–73.

[2] BL Add. 33241 is not included in E. Temple, *Anglo-Saxon Manuscripts 900–1066* (London, 1976), presumably because it was regarded as not English; cf. D. J. A. Matthew, 'The English Cultivation of Norman History', *England and Normandy in the Middle Ages*, ed. D. Bates and A. Curry (London, 1994), pp. 1–18, at 3 n. 5.

[3] *Encomium Emmae*, ed. Campbell, p. xii. For manuscripts from Saint-Bertin and Saint-Omer, see above, p. [xxxvi] n. 5.

[4] *The Golden Age of Anglo-Saxon Art*, ed. Backhouse, *et al.*, p. 144 (no. 148); Brown, *Anglo-Saxon Manuscripts*, p. 18; *St Augustine's Abbey Canterbury*, ed. Gem, p. 84; all with reproduction of fols. 1v–2r. For Norman manuscripts of this period, see J. J. G. Alexander, *Norman Illumination at Mont St Michel 966–1100* (Oxford, 1970); F. Avril, *Manuscrits Normandes XI–XIIème siècles* (Rouen, 1975); and A. Lawrence, 'Anglo-Norman Book Production', *England and Normandy in the Middle Ages*, ed. D. Bates and A. Curry (London, 1994), pp. 79–93.

[5] On movements between England and Flanders in the eleventh century, see Crick, in *Two Old English Apocrypha*, ed. Cross, pp. 16–21.

was transmitted from Flanders, or England, to Normandy, and whether the work was known in 'Norman' political circles.[1] It might be better, on the other hand, to leave the matter open, pending further palaeographical, art-historical, and literary study, and in the meantime to bear in mind the possibility that the *Encomium*, and the extant manuscript of the *Encomium*, might have been written in England. The manuscript, wherever it originated, is known to have been in the library of St Augustine's, Canterbury, in the later middle ages.[2] It is conceivable that it was given to the abbey by Queen Emma herself, along with her other gifts;[3] but this would depend, of course, on the assumption that the manuscript was the very copy which had been made for presentation to the queen, and it is arguable that the rough and unfinished aspects of the second scribe's work, in particular, should tell against such an assumption. The manuscript may have remained at Canterbury for some while after the dissolution of St Augustine's abbey in 1538,[4] but what became of it in the seventeenth and eighteenth centuries is a mystery. It belonged in 1819 to the 10th duke of Hamilton, and was acquired by the British Museum in 1887.[5]

A transcript of the *Encomium Emmae*, probably derived from the extant 'Canterbury' manuscript, was made in the third quarter of the sixteenth century by the antiquary Thomas Talbot; unfortunately, the transcript has not survived, and all that is known of its origin, date, and textual affiliations has to be worked out from other transcripts, and a printed edition, which can be seen to have been derived directly or indirectly from it.[6] Talbot was a member of the 'College of Antiquaries', formed towards the end of the reign of Elizabeth I,[7] and contributed

---

[1] For whatever the information may be worth, there is no sign of a copy of the *Encomium* in the list of over 300 books at Saint-Bertin in the early twelfth century; see G. Becker, *Catalogi Bibliothecarum Antiqui* (Bonn, 1885), pp. 181–4. Nor is there any clear indication that the *Encomium* was known to 'Norman' authors (William of Jumièges, William of Poitiers, Orderic Vitalis), and it does not appear in any of the booklists in G. Nortier, *Les bibliothèques médiévales des abbayes bénédictines de Normandie*, rev. edn (Paris, 1971).

[2] It is registered in the catalogue as 'Gesta Cnutonis Regis cum A, 20 fo. *meis*': see M. R. James, *The Ancient Libraries of Canterbury and Dover* (Cambridge, 1903), p. 294 (no. 907), and *Encomium Emmae*, ed. Campbell, p. xii n. 4; see also N. R. Ker, *Medieval Libraries of Great Britain: A List of Surviving Books*, 2nd edn (London, 1964), p. 40.

[3] For Emma's gifts to St Augustine's, see below, p. [lxxvii].

[4] For the fate of the library in the mid-sixteenth century, see James, *Ancient Libraries*, pp. lxxxi–lxxxii, and *St Augustine's Abbey Canterbury*, ed. Gem, pp. 148–9.

[5] *Encomium Emmae*, ed. Campbell, pp. xii–xiii.

[6] *Encomium Emmae*, ed. Campbell, pp. xiii–xv.

[7] The standard account of this most interesting association of learned men remains L. van Norden, 'The Elizabethan College of Antiquaries', unpublished Ph.D. thesis, Univ. of California at Los Angeles (1946), of which there is a copy in the library of the Society of Antiquaries of London. See also L. van Norden, 'Sir Henry Spelman on the Chronology of the Elizabethan College of Antiquaries', *Huntingdon Library Quarterly* 13 (1949–50), pp. 131–60; J. Evans, *A History of the Society of Antiquaries* (Oxford, 1956), pp. 8–13; and C. E. Wright, 'The Elizabethan Society of Antiquaries and the Formation of the

short papers to its proceedings in the early 1590s.[1] It is not clear under what circumstances he had encountered the *Encomium Emmae*, or why he took a special interest in it;[2] but it seems that he made the transcript in 1566, at which time the manuscript may still have been at Canterbury, and that it was he who gave the work its familiar title.[3] The particular importance of the Talbot transcript derives from the fact that some time after it was made, probably in the late sixteenth or early seventeenth century, a leaf was lost or removed from the 'Canterbury' manuscript, between fols. 47 and 48. It so happens that the missing leaf contained a passage of particular historical importance; and we are thus dependent on Talbot for our knowledge of the passage in question.[4]

The Talbot transcript seems to have passed from Talbot into the hands of his fellow antiquary and collector, Sir Robert Cotton (1571–1631),[5] and while in the Cottonian library it was copied at least twice. In 1618 the celebrated French antiquary Nicolas-Claude Fabri de Peiresc (1580–1637) sought help from William

---

Cottonian Library', *The English Library before 1700*, ed. F. Wormald and C. E. Wright (London, 1958), pp. 176–212. There is a brief notice of Talbot in the *Dictionary of National Biography*; see also M. McKisack, *Medieval History in the Tudor Age* (Oxford, 1971), p. 78.

[1] 'Of the Time, when England was first divided into Shires, and the Reason of such Division', printed in [J. Ayloffe], *A Collection of Curious Discourses Written by Eminent Antiquaries*, 2 vols. (London, 1771), I.27–8 (no. 9), from Talbot's autograph in BL Cotton Faustina E. v, fol. 25r, and a tract on sterling money, printed [Ayloffe], *A Collection of Curious Discourses*, II.379–80 (no. 59), from his autograph in BL Cotton Faustina E. v, fol. 71r.

[2] Further study of Talbot's collections may yield clues; suffice it to say that nothing germane to the purpose emerges from BL Cotton Vespasian D. xvii (on which see A. G. Watson, *The Manuscripts of Henry Savile of Banke* (London, 1969), pp. 78–82) or BL Harley 2223.

[3] A volume of extracts from miscellaneous writers, compiled by the Kentish antiquary William Lambarde, with dated entries ranging between 1568 and 1578, contains a single page of notes headed 'Ex Encomio Emmæ Reginæ, incerti autoris, quod scriptum est ea vivente . . .' (BL Cotton Vespasian A. v, fol. 43r), without any further indication of source. One might suppose that Lambarde had seen the manuscript itself, c. 1570. It is the case, however, that Lambarde's heading is strikingly similar to the title given in Duchesne's edition of 1619 (below, p. [xlvii] n. 5), and the common denominator is most likely to have been a heading in Talbot's transcript. Lambarde's excerpts include part of the passage on the magic banner (*EER* ii.9), and the opening words of the Prologue.

[4] *EER* ii.16 (ed. Campbell, p. 32, lines 6–16). Campbell (p. xiv n. 5) remarks that the passage on the lost leaf 'contained the supposed allegation of Queen Emma's virginity at the time of her marriage to Knútr', and suggested, therefore, that 'this was perhaps too much for the patience of some reader, who accordingly destroyed the leaf'. This is a pleasant idea, but perhaps a bit far-fetched. It may be more to the point to observe that the missing folio was the last leaf of the sixth quire (above, p. [xli] n. 3), and that the ink on 48r is different from the ink on 47v, as if the missing folio was a place where a scribal stint changed. Perhaps the missing leaf was a singleton which ultimately became detached from the rest of the manuscript. The text of this passage in the Talbot transcript is supported by the text in Paris, Bibliothèque nationale, Fonds Lat. 6235, fol. 11rv, derived from the 'Edwardian recension' of the *Encomium*, on which see further below.

[5] For Cotton, see C. G. C. Tite, *The Manuscript Library of Sir Robert Cotton*, Panizzi Lectures 1993 (London, 1994), and the papers assembled in *Sir Robert Cotton as Collector*, ed. C. J. Wright (London, 1997).

INTRODUCTION TO THE 1998 REPRINT

Camden (1551–1623), in connection with the projected publication of a collection of texts bearing on the history of Normandy.[1] On 10 February Peiresc wrote to Camden asking for any texts about the Normans, for inclusion in his collection.[2] Camden responded by sending Peiresc a copy of the text of the *Encomium*, evidently made for the purpose from the (Talbot) transcript in the Cottonian library.[3] Peiresc wrote again to Camden on 5 March, acknowledging receipt of the text:

J'ay receu l'Encomium de vostre Reyne Emma, que nous ferons imprimer en son rang et ordre dans le recueil des Historiens de Normandie. C'est bien la verité qu'il appartient plus à l'Angleterre qu'à la Normandie; mais il ne sera pas tant mal seant entre ceux de Normandie, puisqu'elle estoit Normande; et que son alliance fut la premiere planche aux conquestes de Guillaume son neveu. Il se trouve si peu d'escrivains de ce siecle la, que je n'en sçaurois point negliger.[4]

Peiresc forwarded the copy of the *Encomium* to his collaborator, André Duchesne (1584–1640); and the text was duly printed in the following year.[5] There is no reason to believe that Duchesne would have felt obliged to return the copy of the

---

[1] For an early life of Peiresc, first published in Latin in 1641, see P. Gassendi, *The Mirrour of True Nobility and Gentility, being the Life of the Renowned Nicolaus Claudius Fabricius Lord of Peiresk*, trans. W. Rand (London, 1657); for a modern translation, see R. Lassalle with A. Bresson, *Peiresc 1580–1637: vie de l'illustre Nicolas-Claude Fabri de Peiresc . . . par Pierre Gassendi* (Paris, 1992). For modern accounts of Peiresc, see C. T. H. Wright, *Nicholas Fabri de Peiresc* (London, 1926), and G. Cahen-Salvador, *Un grand humaniste: Peiresc 1580–1637* (Paris, 1951); see also L. van Norden, 'Peiresc and the English Scholars', *Huntingdon Library Quarterly* 12 (1948–9), pp. 369–89. Letters from Peiresc to Camden, written in 1617–22 and preserved in BL Cotton Julius C. v, are printed in P. Tamizey de Larroque, *Lettres de Peiresc*, 7 vols. (Paris, 1888–98), VII: *Lettres de Peiresc à Divers 1602–1637* (Paris, 1898), pp. 759–826; see also R. Lebègue with A. Bresson, *Peiresc: lettres à Divers | Supplément au tome VII de l'édition Tamizey de Larroque et errata* (Paris, 1985), p. 191, and below, n. 3. Material gathered by Peiresc from the Cottonian library is in Carpentras, Bibliothèque Inguimbertine, MS 1772 (*Catalogue général des manuscrits des bibliothèques publiques de France, Départements, XXXV: Carpentras II* (Paris, 1899), pp. 191–8).

[2] Letter from Peiresc to Camden, 10 Feb. 1618, printed in *Lettres de Peiresc*, VII.770–2, from BL Cotton Julius C. v, fol. 233.

[3] Copies of eight letters from Camden to Peiresc are preserved in Aix-en-Provence, Bibliothèque Méjanes, MS 203 (*Catalogue général des manuscrits des bibliothèques publiques de France, Départements, XVI: Aix* (Paris, 1894), pp. 124–5). Seven of these letters were written in 1617, and the eighth was written on 23 Dec. 1618. Further work on the scattered correspondence of Peiresc, Camden, Cotton, and Duchesne may yet throw further light on the dealings between them in Feb.–Apr. 1618.

[4] Letter from Peiresc to Camden, 5 Mar. 1618, printed in *Lettres de Peiresc*, VII.773–6, from BL Cotton Julius C. v, fols. 237–8 (at 237r). See also van Norden, 'Peiresc and the English Scholars', p. 384, and van Houts, 'Camden, Cotton and the Chronicles of the Norman Conquest of England', pp. 156–7.

[5] A. Duchesne, *Historiae Normannorum Scriptores Antiqui* (Paris, 1619), pp. 161–78 (acknowledging that the source was a copy of the text transmitted from the Cottonian library via Camden and Peiresc). The title is: 'Emmæ Anglorum Reginæ, Richardi I. Ducis Normannorum Filiæ, Encomium. Incerto Authore, sed coæterno.' The title may have been suggested by a heading in Talbot's transcript; see above, p. [xlvi] n. 3, and cf. *Encomium Emmae*, ed. Campbell, p. xviii.

transcript to Peiresc, or indeed to Camden or Cotton, and, sadly, it is now lost;[1] so it is on the evidence of Duchesne's printed text that the copy is seen to have been derived from the Talbot transcript. A transcript of a manuscript of William of Poitiers' *Gesta Guillelmi* was sent (from the Cottonian library) by Camden to Peiresc (for Duchesne's collection), at just the same time, and it was in response to Peiresc's request that Camden subsequently sent him the manuscript as well; in this case, neither the transcript nor the manuscript seems ever to have been returned.[2] A second transcript of the *Encomium* was made by the Welsh antiquary Robert Vaughan of Hengwrt (1592–1667), in about 1624, and was evidently derived from a copy of the text closely related to and probably identical with the transcript presumed then to be in the Cottonian library.[3] Vaughan's transcript ends, most usefully, 'Transcriptum et excerptum a vetustissi[mo] exemplari manuscripto per Thom. Talbot anno Domini 1566'; and it is on this basis that the transcript in the Cottonian library is known to have been made by Talbot, in 1566. The Talbot transcript may have remained in the Cottonian library for the duration of the seventeenth century. It was not, however, included in Thomas Smith's catalogue of the library,[4] suggesting that by 1696 it had been lost, or lent and not returned; but if it was omitted from the catalogue because it was perceived to be

---

[1] Instead, it would appear that Peiresc or Duchesne sent complimentary copies of the book to England. In a letter to Cotton, Camden writes: 'Good Sir, Mr Bill sent to me 2 Copies Rerum Normannicarum, but without Titles, Prefaces, or Lettre. I doubt not but they were sent by Mr Peiresc, or by Chesne, to you and me, and therefore I have sent you one of them' (BL Cotton Julius C. iii, fol. 6or, undated). See also K. Sharpe, *Sir Robert Cotton 1586–1631: History and Politics in Early Modern England* (Oxford, 1979), pp. 58 and 103.

[2] In February 1618 Camden had sent Peiresc a transcript of another Cottonian manuscript containing a text which he thought might be of interest; in the letter of 5 March, Peiresc identified the text in question as William of Poitiers, and asked for the loan of the manuscript itself for editorial purposes (*Lettres de Peiresc* VII.774–5); Camden sent it on 2 April, and on 29 April Peiresc thanked him for it, and reported on progress (*Lettres de Peiresc* VII.777–81, from BL Cotton Julius C. v, fols. 254–5). It seems unlikely that the original manuscript was ever returned (whatever Peiresc's best intentions may have been, as reported in his letter to Sir Robert Cotton, 4 July 16[19], in BL Cotton Julius C. iii, fol. 291v); if it was returned, it was overlooked when the library was catalogued by Thomas Smith in 1696, and must be presumed to have been destroyed in the fire of 1731. There remains some hope that another 'lost' manuscript of William of Poitiers, mentioned by Peiresc as being in the collection of Pierre Pithou, may yet be discovered (*The Gesta Guillelmi of William of Poitiers*, ed. Davis and Chibnall, pp. xv and xliii–xlv). The 'Fragmentum vitae Willelmi I', separately registered in an early catalogue of the Cottonian library (BL Harley 6018, fol. 58r, no. 102, as noted by van Houts, 'Camden, Cotton and the Chronicles of the Norman Conquest of England', p. 161 n. 33) appears to be distinct from what is now BL Cotton Vespasian A. xix, fols. 104–21 (cf. *Orderic*, ed. Chibnall, IV, p. xiv), and remains unidentified.

[3] Aberystwyth, National Library of Wales, MS Peniarth 281(Hengwrt 158), pp. 1–21, discussed in *Encomium Emmae*, ed. Campbell, pp. xiii–xiv.

[4] T. Smith, *Catalogue of the Manuscripts in the Cottonian Library 1696*, ed. C. G. C. Tite (Cambridge, 1984).

merely a transcript,[1] one would then have to assume that it was a casualty of the fire which ravaged the library in 1731, since it does not survive to the present day.[2]

There is evidence for the existence of another eleventh-century manuscript of the *Encomium*, derived from the same early copy of the author's autograph as the 'Canterbury' manuscript yet representing what in certain respects was a significantly different recension of the text.[3] In this manuscript, the account of Emma's sorrow after the death of the atheling Alfred, and of her flight to Flanders, was reduced (for whatever reason) from a long paragraph to a single sentence,[4] as was the account of Harthacnut's joyous reunion with his mother.[5] The ending of the text was also rewritten, to take account of Harthacnut's death and to transfer the emphasis to Edward, perhaps in his capacity as the reigning king:[6]

His itaque fratribus concorditer regnantibus mors media intercidit et regem Hardechnutonem uitalibus auris abstulit. Regem mater et frater maximo cum luctu honorifice sepeliunt. Mortuo Ardechnutone in regnum successit Edwardus, heres scilicet legitimus, uir uirium eminentia conspicuus, uirtute animi consiliique atque etiam ingenii uiuacitate preditus et, ut omnia breuiter concludam, omnium expetendorum summa insignitus.	While the two brothers were thus reigning in concord, death came between them and carried off Harthacnut to heaven. The mother and the brother buried the king honourably, with great sorrow. After Harthacnut's death, Edward, who was the legitimate heir, succeeded to the kingdom: a man conspicuous for the eminence of his strength, endowed with vigour of mind and purpose, and also with tenacity of character, and – if I may draw briefly to a close – possessed with the best of all the desirable qualities.

---

[1] There are other instances where early modern transcripts were omitted from the 1696 catalogue, presumably because they were not deemed to be worthy of inclusion in their own right. The transcript of Asser's *Vita Ælfredi regis Angul-Saxonum*, in BL Cotton Otho A. xii*, is a case in point.

[2] Further consideration should perhaps be given to the late eighteenth-century transcript of Book I of the *Encomium Emmae* (*EER* i.1–5), made by John Haddon Hindley (1765–1827) and now BL Add. 6920, fols. 105–14. Campbell (*Encomium Emmae*, pp. xiv–xv) dismissed the text as 'worthless', and suggested that it may have been derived from Duchesne's printed edition, or from a transcript intermediate between Talbot's transcript and Duchesne's edition. The fact remains that Hindley appears to have copied the text from a manuscript which also contained a version of the *Historia Brittonum* (fols. 26–82) and other 'Arthurian' items. The heading on fol. 105 is: 'In hoc Nennii Codice inter Civitates &c., i.e. Librum de Civitatibus et Librum de mirabilibus Britonum, folium ("13 Sueinus Rex" notatum) occurrit, eodem charactere rotundiori ut prioribus, et forsan eodem Amanuensi operatum; omnia sicut inventa transcripsi.'

[3] *Encomium Emmae*, ed. Campbell, pp. xv–xvii.

[4] *EER* iii.7 (ed. Campbell, p. 46, textual note *d*). Campbell (*Encomium Emmae*, pp. xvi and xl) considered it likely that the abbreviated version of this chapter was the work of an eleventh-century redactor.

[5] *EER* iii.10 (ed. Campbell, p. 50, textual note *a*). In this case, the possibility exists that the act of abbreviation was the work of a later transcriber.

[6] *EER* iii.14 (ed. Campbell, p. 52, textual note *b*), and *Encomium Emmae*, ed. Campbell, pp. xv–xvii and xl. See also Barlow, *Edward the Confessor*, pp. 128–9, and Lifshitz, 'The *Encomium Emmae Reginae*', p. 49.

INTRODUCTION TO THE 1998 REPRINT

Campbell was prepared to entertain the thought that the Encomiast 'revised his work in a copy retained in Flanders, while the copy sent to England remained unrevised';[1] but it seems just as likely that the changes were introduced in a copy made in England, perhaps by the Encomiast himself, to respect the different sensitivities which prevailed after the accession of Edward the Confessor. Unfortunately, the manuscript which contained what might be termed the 'Edwardian recension' of the *Encomium Emmae* is now lost. We are dependent for our knowledge of its text on a transcript, written on vellum, in a late English Hybrida / Bastard Secretary script (*c.* 1500).[2] The scribe began by copying some passages descriptive of Britain, under the heading 'Excerpta ex Gilda',[3] and he continued, under the heading 'Ex eodem Gilda in historia de Sueyno et Knuctone quam in gratiam scripsit ad reginam Emmam', with extended excerpts from the *Encomium Emmae*.[4] It would appear to follow that the scribe was under the impression that Gildas wrote the *Encomium*, or, and perhaps more usefully, that the two works happened to occur together in the same manuscript.[5] The transcript, which does not otherwise afford an indication of any distinctive features of its immediate exemplar, belonged in the later sixteenth century to William Cecil, 1st Baron Burghley (1520–98), of Burghley House, near Stamford in Lincolnshire.[6] One could not wish, of course, for a more interesting provenance; and it remains to be seen whether any light may be thrown on this version of the *Encomium* by a study of the manuscript in relation to other manuscripts in Lord Burghley's collection.[7]

---

[1] *Encomium Emmae*, ed. Campbell, pp. xvi and xl; see also Stafford, *Queen Emma and Queen Edith*, p. 39 n. 29.

[2] Paris, Bibliothèque nationale, MS Fonds Lat. 6235, fols. 7–14. My knowledge of this manuscript is based on a photocopy of fols. 1–14.

[3] The extracts are from Gildas, *De Excidio Britanniae*, chs. 3–11 (cf. *Gildas: The Ruin of Britain and Other Works*, ed. M. Winterbottom (Chichester, 1978), pp. 89–92).

[4] The Prologue and the Argument are not represented, except by the heading; but the excerpts otherwise cover *EER*, Books I–III.

[5] The question arises whether it may be significant that the eighteenth-century transcript of part of the *Encomium* in BL Add. 6920 keeps similar company (above, p. [xlix] n. 2).

[6] The contents of Burghley's library are known from the sale-catalogue produced when it was dispersed, as part of the library of Lord Aylesbury, in November 1687; see *Bibliotheca Illustris* (London, 1687), esp. pp. 80–92 (Manuscripts). The *Encomium* formed part of a composite collection of historical texts (Manuscripti Latini, no. 98), and is covered in the description of the contents of this collection by the heading 'Gildæ Abbatis flores Historiarum'. Among Burghley's other Latin manuscripts, we find 'Wilhelmus Gemmeticensis de Normannorum Ducum gestis' (no. 17), 'Vita gloriosi Regis Edwardi Confessoris' (no. 75), and 'Asserii Menevensis Chronicon' (no. 92).

[7] Burghley is known to have acquired some of his manuscripts from the library of Robert Glover (1544–88), Somerset Herald; see P. M. Selwyn, '"Such speciall Bookes of Mr Somersettes as were sould to Mr Secretary": the Fate of Robert Glover's Collections', *Books and Collectors 1200–1700: Essays Presented to Andrew Watson*, ed. J. P. Carley and C. G. C. Tite (London, 1997), pp. 389–401, and cf. the list of Glover's 'old books', as opposed to his heraldic books, in BL Lansdowne 58, fols. 105–6. He also had at least one by William Lambarde (below, p. [li] n. 2); for Burghley and Lambarde, see R. M. Warnicke,

INTRODUCTION TO THE 1998 REPRINT

The Cecil library was dispersed at auction in 1687,[1] and the manuscript containing excerpts from the *Encomium* passed overseas.[2]

It is possible that there was another medieval manuscript of the *Encomium*, in the library of Glastonbury abbey. A short list of books seen at Glastonbury by John Bale, in the mid-sixteenth century, ends with one described as 'De Canuto Anglorum et Dacorum rege'; and it has been suggested that this might be a reference to a copy of the *Encomium*.[3]

The structure of the *Encomium Emmae Reginae*

The *Encomium Emmae Reginae* was divided by its author into a Prologue, an Argument, and three books; and within each book some further subdivisions of the text were clearly intended. In the earliest surviving manuscript (BL Add. 33241) provision was made for decorated initials at the beginning of the Prologue (fol. 2r), at the beginning of the Argument (fol. 5r), and at the beginning of each book (fols. 8r (Bk I), 19v (Bk II), and 54r (Bk III)). Internal divisions of the text presumably indicated in the immediate exemplar, perhaps originating in the author's draft, are marked by blank lines, or parts of lines, on fols. 11r (beginning of *EER* i.2), 15r (beginning of *EER* i.4), 26r (in *EER* ii.3, line 8/9), 30r (beginning of *EER* ii.6), 33v (in *EER* ii.7, line 9), 42v (beginning of *EER* ii.12), 47r (beginning of *EER* ii.16), 54r (beginning of *EER* iii.1), and 61r (beginning of *EER* iii.7). Other divisions intended by the author may be indicated by initial letters which bear a lower grade of decoration, or by space left for initials and not always filled in; but of course it is difficult to judge what might have been done in this respect on the whim of the

---

William Lambarde: Elizabethan Antiquary 1536–1601 (Chichester, 1973), pp. 79–80 and 87–92 and 124. Burghley's other associates included Matthew Parker and Laurence Nowell.

[1] *Bibliotheca Illustris* (London, 1687). For this sale, see Selwyn, 'Fate of Robert Glover's Collections', p. 397, and D. Huws, 'Sir Thomas Mostyn and the Mostyn Manuscripts', *Books and Collectors 1200–1700*, ed. Carley and Tite, pp. 451–72, at 457 (and 472 n. 46).

[2] According to annotated copies of the sale-catalogue (BL, Dept. of Ptd Books, 821.i.8 (1); Cambridge, St John's College, Dd.9.10, art. 13), the manuscript was bought by 'Mr Frasier' for £6.15.0d. It passed into the Colbertine library (MS 5337), thence into the royal library and so ultimately into the French national collection (Paris, Bibliothèque nationale, MS Fonds Lat. 6235, fols. 7–14). For the Colbertine library (founded by Jean Baptiste Colbert (1619–83)), see L. Delisle, *Le Cabinet des Manuscrits de la Bibliothèque Impériale / Bibliothèque National*, 3 vols. (Paris, 1868–81), I.439–86. The 'Asser' manuscript (above, p. [l] n. 6), which was in fact a transcript of the Annals of St Neots made by Lambarde in 1567, was also bought at the sale by 'Mr Frasier', passed into the Colbertine library, and is now Paris, Bibliothèque nationale, MS Fonds Lat. 6236; see *The Annals of St Neots*, ed. Dumville and Lapidge, p. xxv.

[3] *English Benedictine Libraries: The Shorter Catalogues*, ed. R. Sharpe, J. P. Carley, R. M. Thomson and A. G. Watson, Corpus of British Medieval Library Catalogues 4 (London, 1996), pp. 238–45, at 245 (no. 69). The *Encomium* had been described as the 'Gesta Cnutonis regis' by a late medieval hand on the first page of the surviving eleventh-century manuscript (BL Add. 33241, fol. 1r).

scribe. The main scribe of Add. 33241 supplied a suitably grand display for the opening of the Prologue (fol. 2r, with lines in capitals alternating in red, green, and blue), a fine initial for the beginning of Book I, and a rather less imposing initial for the beginning of Book II; he also provided a rubricated heading for the account of the removal of Swein's body to Denmark (*EER* ii.3, on fol. 25r). The second scribe made a point of displaying the text of the forged letter to the athelings (*EER* iii.3, on fol. 56rv); he also supplied low-grade decoration for initial letters on fols. 42v (beginning of *EER* ii.12), 46r (beginning of *EER* ii.15), 57r (beginning of *EER* iii.4), and 59v (beginning of *EER* iii.6). Several of the chapter-divisions familiar from the printed text thus have at least some basis in the surviving manuscript. A number of them were, however, introduced by the first modern editor of the *Encomium*, G. H. Pertz, in 1866. Pertz's divisions were modified by M. Cl. Gertz (1920); but Campbell chose to follow Pertz.[1]

The simplest way to comprehend the structure of the *Encomium* as a whole is to reduce its contents to tabular form, using the modern chapter-divisions:

---

[1] *Encomium Emmae*, ed. Campbell, pp. xvii–xviii and 3. Campbell expressed particular approval of Gertz's arrangement at the beginning of *EER* i.2 (ed. Campbell, pp. xviii n. 6, and 10 n. 1); but the blank line in the manuscript on fol. 11r supports Pertz against Gertz.

It is apparent from this table that although the *Encomium* was once designated the *Gesta Cnutonis Regis*, it is something rather more complex than an account of the deeds of King Cnut. It is equally apparent that while its more familiar title is wholly consistent with the spirit of the author's prefatory remarks, the work was not obviously devised solely in praise of Queen Emma. One of the attractions of the *Encomium* is, of course, that it will be found to respond to exposition and analysis at many different levels; yet if we may presume on the one hand that the author was not simply determined to prostitute his literary powers in the hope of personal reward, we may suspect on the other hand that he had not been persuaded to take up his pen simply in order to provide posterity with a considered account of Emma's life. So what is the work about?

Ill. 4   On the happiness and good fortune of Swein Forkbeard, king of the Danes.
Encomium Emmae Reginae, Book I, ch. 1. BL Add. 33241, fol. 8r

INTRODUCTION TO THE 1998 REPRINT

The story told in the *Encomium Emmae Reginae*

We cannot use the *Encomium* as a source of historical information until we have formed some judgement of the Encomiast's purpose, and we cannot judge his purpose until we have some sense of the manner he displays in his treatment of particular persons and historical events. The Encomiast's account of the Scandinavian conquest of England in 1013–16 (*EER* i.1–ii.11), and its immediate aftermath in 1016–17 (*EER* ii.12–15), is of interest in part because it is independent of and therefore complements the annals in the Anglo-Saxon Chronicle (written probably by a Londoner, *c.* 1020),[1] and in part because it represents what is effectively a 'Danish' as opposed to an 'English' point of view. Although written at the behest of a queen who had lived through the period on the receiving end of sustained military aggression, the account of these events was directed towards an audience in the early 1040s which was clearly expected to enjoy being reminded of a victorious campaign fought twenty-five years before – and which would certainly not have worried too much about the details. Swein Forkbeard appears from the outset in a positive light.[2] For all the difficulties which he had once had with his father (Harold Bluetooth), he was a good, popular, and successful ruler of Denmark (*EER* i.1–5). Indeed, it was in the favourable conditions created by King Swein's rule that Thorkell had embarked on his ravaging of England (1009–12); yet Thorkell had defected to the English with forty ships, and the general wish among the Danes was that Swein should attack England in order to punish him. The Encomiast waxes lyrical on the splendour of the Danish forces organised for war, in a way which has more to do with literary hyperbole than with historical reality;[3] and he stresses how King Swein took his elder son (Cnut) with him to England, leaving his younger son (Harold) in charge of the kingdom of Denmark. The fleet was truly magnificent, and the invasion a triumphant success. After a brief and glorious reign King Swein fell ill, appointed his son Cnut as his successor,

---

[1] For the date and authorship of the account of these events in the Anglo-Saxon Chronicle, see Keynes, 'The Declining Reputation of King Æthelred the Unready', pp. 229–36. It is now possible to compare the chronicler's account of Æthelred's reign with modern critical editions of the three main twelfth-century chronicles which to a greater or lesser extent are dependent upon it: JW, *Chron.* (ed. Darlington and McGurk); WM, *GR* (ed. Mynors, *et al.*); and HH, *HA* (ed. Greenway). See also Hart, 'The Early Section of the *Worcester Chronicle*', p. 300.

[2] For a reassessment of King Swein, accounting for the 'negative' portrayal of the king in most of the available sources and urging that the Encomiast's view should be taken more seriously, see Sawyer, 'Swein Forkbeard and the Historians'.

[3] *EER* i.3 (ed. Campbell, pp. 10–12). For more recent accounts of Danish military organisation in the eleventh century, see Lund, 'The Armies of Swein Forkbeard and Cnut', esp. pp. 112–18; Lund, 'Danish Military Organisation', esp. pp. 110–11 and 117–21; and Lund, *Lið, Leding og Landeværn*, pp. 110–25; see also Campbell, 'The Late Anglo-Saxon State', p. 46. For the arrangements which surfaced in the Anglo-Danish kingdom, see Hooper, 'Military Developments in the Reign of Cnut'.

and died (February 1014). Cnut returned to Denmark, with sixty ships, in order to consult King Harold. He proposed that they should divide the kingdom of Denmark, conquer the kingdom of England, and then each take one or the other; and when Harold refused, Cnut was content to leave the matter for God to resolve. The two brothers made further preparations, and also fetched their mother from the land of the Slavs.[1] An unnamed English woman (*quaedam matronarum Anglicarum*) took it upon herself to bring the mortal remains of King Swein from England back to Denmark, for burial in the monastery which Swein had built (at Roskilde) – an event evidently regarded as akin to the translation of a saint.[2] Cnut invaded England on his own account (in 1015), with a force of 200 ships (*EER* ii.4–5); again, the fleet was magnificent, and the English were determined to resist. The Encomiast's account of the military campaign in 1015–16 is of great interest, but leaves much to be desired. Thorkell disembarked at Sandwich (in Kent), and engaged the English in battle at Sherston (in Wiltshire);[3] his success prompted Eirik, 'leader and prince of the province called Norway', to subdue some other part of the country;[4] and Cnut laid siege to the city of London. It is at this point that the Encomiast remarks upon the death of 'the prince (*princeps*) who was in command of the city within', an oblique or deliberately obscure reference to the death of King Æthelred the Unready; and when 'the son of the deceased prince' (Edmund Ironside) secretly left the city, Cnut entered London 'and sat on the throne of the kingdom'.[5] It should be noted, perhaps, that the Encomiast had an imperfect grasp of chronology. He creates the impression that all this took place in the summer months (of 1015), before Cnut retired from London to Sheppey for the winter (of 1015–16); but of course it is well established that King Æthelred died on 23 April 1016, 'before the ships arrived', and that the siege of London began soon after the ships reached Greenwich on or about 7 May. The Encomiast puts Edmund Ironside back in London for the winter (of 1015–16), and goes on to describe how the warfare came to its glorious climax at the battle of Ashingdon,

---

[1] *EER* ii.2 (ed. Campbell, p. 18); see also TM, *Chron.* vii.39 (ed. Trillmich, p. 396; *EHD*, no. 27, p. 348). For the Slavic connection, see Keynes, 'Cnut's Earls', pp. 64–5.

[2] *EER* i.5 and ii.3 (ed. Campbell, pp. 14 and 18). A similar story involving an unnamed English-woman ('quaedam matrona . . . etsi indigena') was told in TM, *Chron.* vii.37 (ed. Trillmich, p. 394; *EHD*, no. 27, p. 348). For further comment, see *Encomium Emmae*, ed. Campbell, p. lvii, and esp. Demidoff, 'The Death of Sven Forkbeard', pp. 32–5.

[3] *EER* ii.6 (ed. Campbell, pp. 20–2). Far from being a preliminary skirmish fought soon after the arrival of the Danish fleet in 1015, at which Thorkell displayed his loyalty to Cnut, the battle of Sherston was fought between the Danes and King Edmund Ironside, after midsummer in 1016 (ASC).

[4] *EER* ii.7 (ed. Campbell, p. 22). It is not clear what the Encomiast may have had in mind at this point, as little is known of Eirik's contribution, beyond the fact that Cnut appointed him earl of the Northumbrians quite early in 1016 (ASC). For his presence at the siege of London, see *Encomium Emmae*, ed. Campbell, pp. 70–1.

[5] *EER* ii.7 (ed. Campbell, p. 22). The Encomiast was evidently aware that London was effectively the capital of the kingdom in the first half of the eleventh century.

apparently in the following spring (*EER* ii.8–11); in fact the battle of Ashingdon took place on 18 October 1016. The rest, it seems, was history: the partition of the kingdom between Cnut (in the north) and Edmund (in the south), proposed by Earl Eadric; the death of Edmund Ironside (30 November 1016), and his honourable burial; Cnut's assumption of rule over the whole kingdom; and the execution (in 1017) of those who had wavered between the two warring sides, including Earl Eadric.[1]

The Encomiast's account of these events is obviously garbled, one-sided, and incomplete, to an extent which requires that it be treated with all due circumspection. It is also clear that he injected certain extraneous elements into the story, and we should expect that he applied a spin to the whole which was calculated to serve his own literary purposes. Apart from Swein and Cnut, the account revolves around four men in particular: Thorkell the Tall, Eirik (son of Hákon), Edmund Ironside, and Eadric Streona. The Encomiast appears to have been especially concerned to explain the role of Earl Thorkell at every stage in the proceedings. He could probably presume on his audience's general awareness of Thorkell's ravaging of England in 1009–12, which had had such a devastating effect on Æthelred's kingdom,[2] and it seems to have been enough to explain that Thorkell had gone to England in order 'to avenge his brother, who was killed there'. The Encomiast made a virtue of Thorkell's subsequent realignment with the English, as a factor which prompted Swein's invasion, and explained that although Thorkell remained in England after Swein's death (in 1014), he was ready nonetheless to assist the Danish cause when Cnut returned. The story continues in much the same vein: Cnut's presumption (when conferring with his brother Harold in 1014) that Thorkell would be against them; Thorkell's return to Denmark (in the spring or early summer of 1015), to affirm his support for Cnut, and his role in urging Cnut to invade England; Thorkell's brave demonstration of loyalty to the Danish cause, displayed at the battle of Sherston, which inspired the others and won its due reward; and his inspiring remarks when the magic raven banner fluttered immediately before the decisive battle of Ashingdon (in 1016). Thorkell is not mentioned by the Encomiast thereafter, though it is known from other sources that he held a very prominent position in England in the opening years of Cnut's reign, that he was outlawed in 1021, that he was reconciled to the king in Denmark in 1022–3, and that subsequently he held Denmark on Cnut's behalf, with custody of the king's son (Harthacnut).[3] It seems clear that in his account of the Scandinavian

---

[1] *EER* ii.12–15 (ed. Campbell, pp. 28–32).

[2] ASC, MSS CDE, s.a. 1009–12. For the involvement of Olaf Haraldsson, see *Encomium Emmae*, ed. Campbell, pp. 76–82, and Fell, 'Víkingarvísur'. See also Keynes, *Diplomas of King Æthelred*, pp. 216–21, and Keynes, 'The Vikings in England', pp. 75 and 79–81.

[3] For further discussion of the twists and turns in Thorkell's career, see *Encomium Emmae*, ed. Campbell, pp. 73–6; [M. W.] Campbell, 'Queen Emma and Ælfgifu of Northampton', pp. 70–1;

conquest of England the Encomiast was concerned, above all, to portray Thorkell as one whose actions in 1009–12 could be explained and excused, and whose loyalty to the Danish cause in 1014–16 was not in doubt.[1] The historical truth may well have been different; but while Campbell was inclined to suppose that Thorkell had been loyal to the English, from his first employment as a mercenary in 1012 until soon after the death of Edmund Ironside in November 1016,[2] it seems rather more likely that Thorkell, having been in King Æthelred's service in 1012–13 and perhaps again after the king's restoration in 1014, transferred his allegiance to the Danish cause in 1015, or during the course of Cnut's invasion in 1015–16, and was duly rewarded for his support.[3] Yet why was the Encomiast apparently so concerned to portray Thorkell as one whose loyalty to the Danes was not in doubt? Campbell observed in this connection that the Encomiast was writing at a time (in the early 1040s) when a certain Earl Harold, presumed with good reason to be Thorkell's son, 'was alive and married to a near relative of the king';[4] and it is true that Earl Harold, and his wife Gunnhild (Harthacnut's cousin), would appear to have been significant figures at Harthacnut's court.[5] We should also bear in mind that if Thorkell played an important part on the Danish side in the events of 1015–16, and if (in particular) the forty ships manned by 'Danish' soldiers which Eadric is said to have seduced from King Æthelred towards the end of 1015 in fact represented the surviving bulk of Thorkell's mercenary army,[6] it would follow that many of Thorkell's men might well have ended the war in the service of the earl of Mercia, and might even have been among those who settled in the west midlands and whose loyalty in the 1030s was thus to Earl Leofric and Harold Harefoot.[7] Nor should we forget that Thorkell himself seems to have played an important part in

---

Williams, 'Danes and English in the Western Midlands', pp. 10–11; Poole, *Viking Poems*, pp. 100–7; and Keynes, 'Cnut's Earls', pp. 54–7.

[1] That is to say, the impression made of Thorkell for the audience in mind is positive, not negative; cf. John, 'The *Encomium Emmae Reginae*', pp. 65–73, 81–2, and 93, and John, *Reassessing Anglo-Saxon England*, pp. 153–4.

[2] *Encomium Emmae*, ed. Campbell, pp. liv–lv, 74–5 and 84 n. 8.

[3] John, 'The *Encomium Emmae Reginae*', p. 73; Keynes, 'Cnut's Earls', p. 55, with n. 62.

[4] *Encomium Emmae*, ed. Campbell, pp. 84–5 (esp. p. 84 n. 8).

[5] Harold may be the son of Thorkell who was brought up by Cnut in England (ASC, MS C, s.a. 1023), in which case it is appropriate that he should have married Cnut's niece (? in the early 1030s) and that he became an earl in his own right. Earl Harold is seen at court in 1042 (S 1396), but left England for Denmark after the king's death (Keynes, 'Cnut's Earls', p. 66). His wife Gunnhild, daughter of King Cnut's sister and widow of Earl Hákon (son of Eirik), seems to have remained in England; but she was banished in 1044, with her sons Hemming and Thorkell, and went via Bruges to Denmark. See ASC, MS D, s.a. 1044 (ed. Cubbin, p. 67), and JW, *Chron.* s.a. 1029 and 1044 (ed. Darlington and McGurk, pp. 510 and 540). Gunnhild's mother was possibly the Santslave, sister of Cnut, who was commemorated at the New Minster, Winchester; see *'Liber Vitae' of the New Minster*, ed. Keynes, p. 95.

[6] ASC, MSS CDE, s.a. 1015; JW, *Chron.* s.a. 1015 (ed. Darlington and McGurk, p. 480).

[7] For the Scandinavian settlements in the west midlands, see Williams, 'Danes and English in the Western Midlands', and Keynes, 'Cnut's Earls', p. 80.

Danish politics in the 1020s, that he was entrusted by Cnut with the upbringing of Harthacnut, and that Harthacnut's men might have respected Thorkell's memory. The *Encomium Emmae* was written for presentation to Queen Emma and (by reasonable extension) for consumption at Harthacnut's court; so it may be that Thorkell was given due prominence in the story for the benefit of an audience which would have included not only Earl Harold, son of Thorkell, but also some of Thorkell's friends and followers, as well as Harthacnut himself, and, one imagines, a number of the king's friends and followers whom Harthacnut had brought with him to England from Denmark.

There are not necessarily any special considerations lurking behind the Encomiast's treatment of the three other men who feature prominently in his account of the Scandinavian conquest of England. Eirik, son of Hákon, had succeeded Thorkell in 1021 as Cnut's principal earl, and was seemingly dislodged from that position by Earl Godwine in 1023;[1] Hákon, son of Eirik, who was prominent in the 1020s among the Scandinavians who had settled in the west midlands, died at sea in 1030, and his widow Gunnhild, daughter of Cnut's sister, seems then to have married Earl Harold, son of Earl Thorkell. It is not clear, however, whether this helps in any way to explain the attention which the Encomiast gives to Eirik, as one who was inspired by Thorkell's example to ravage an unspecified part of the country, who seems to have been present at the siege of London, and who was instrumental in the execution of Eadric Streona.[2] It is also appropriate that an account of the Scandinavian conquest of England should give all due attention to Edmund Ironside.[3] It may be, of course, that the Encomiast could not afford to give any offence to Edward, son of Æthelred and Emma, and that he chose for this reason not to exult explicitly in Æthelred's defeat, and to portray Edmund (not untruthfully) as a noble and worthy opponent who was grievously let down by one of his own men. An interesting aspect of this part of the *Encomium*, from an historian's point of view, is the Encomiast's perception that Eadric Streona played a central role in the fall of the English.[4] This was clearly the opinion of the contemporary English chronicler, and became a tradition which improved much in the retelling;[5] but it is useful to have what amounts to the judgement of an early

---

[1] Keynes, 'Cnut's Earls', pp. 57–8 and 84. For Eirik, see also *Encomium Emmae*, ed. Campbell, pp. 66–71.

[2] *EER* ii.7 and 15 (ed. Campbell, pp. 22 and 30–2); see also *Encomium Emmae*, ed. Campbell, pp. 70–1.

[3] *EER* ii.7–14 (ed. Campbell, pp. 22–30).

[4] For Eadric's treachery to Edmund Ironside at the battle of Ashingdon (1016), see *EER* ii.8–9 (ed. Campbell, pp. 24–6); for his advice to Edmund and his councillors, urging a division of the kingdom, see *EER* ii.12 (ed. Campbell, p. 28); and for his execution, see *EER* ii.15 (ed. Campbell, pp. 30–2).

[5] See, e.g., JW, *Chron.* s.a. 1006–17, *passim* (ed. Darlington and McGurk, pp. 456–504); WM, *GR* ii.165.9, 179.4, 180.1, 180.4–7 and 9, and 181.1–2 (ed. Mynors, *et al.*, pp. 274, 310, 312, 314–18, 320);

and independent source (perhaps representing Emma's own opinion). The Encomiast was otherwise concerned to draw the appropriate lesson from the manner of Eadric's death, 'so that soldiers (*milites*) may learn from this example to be faithful, not faithless, to their kings'. The point was not to explain why the English lost, but to remind the Anglo-Danish audience (perhaps including Earl Godwine himself) of the fate in store for those who deserted their rightful lord in order to take up service with another.

The Encomiast's treatment of the reign of King Cnut, from his marriage to Queen Emma in the spring of 1017 until his death on 12 November 1035 (*EER* ii.16–24), is of value as a connected account to set beside whatever can be derived from the evidence of charters, law-codes, letters, and coins, supplemented by the bare record of events in the Anglo-Saxon Chronicle; and of course its special interest is that Emma does not lie very far behind the Encomiast's presentation of events. Our attention is focussed initially on the circumstances of Cnut's marriage to Emma in 1017, and on the arrangements made for Emma's children.[1] The Encomiast's passing reference to Emma as 'a famous queen' before her marriage to Cnut, and his fond supposition that the marriage would help to effect a reconciliation between the English and the Danes,[2] suggest that he had not been instructed by Emma to deny, in effect, that she had been in England before what was thus tacitly admitted to be her second marriage. The Encomiast's explicit statement that Cnut's agents had found Emma in Normandy arises from the fact that it was desirable for his purposes to gloss over the first stage of Emma's career, and in this way to avoid unnecessary complications; yet it has given rise in turn to the supposition which prevails among modern historians, that the marriage was a renewal of the Anglo-Norman alliance. It must be stressed, therefore, that the Encomiast gives no hint of the formation of any such alliance. Indeed, he presents the marriage negotiations as a political arrangement made between Cnut and Emma, not between Cnut and Duke Richard II; and although his point was that the marriage created conditions in which two armies rejoiced, joined forces, and subdued peoples,[3] the two armies in question were not the Danes and the Normans but the Danes and the English. The truth was, perhaps, that Emma had been fetched from some form of captivity in England, and that she wished, not unreasonably, to create a rather different impression.[4] Moreover, the arrangement described by the Encomiast – that Cnut swore 'that he would never set up the son of any wife other than herself to rule after him', obviously directed at Harold Harefoot (Cnut's son by

---

and HH, *HA* vi.4, 5, 10, 13, 14 (ed. Greenway, pp. 344, 346, 354, 356–8, 360–2). See also WMp, *DNC*, Dist. v.4 (ed. James, p. 428).

[1] *EER* ii.16–18 (ed. Campbell, pp. 32–4).
[2] *EER* Arg. and ii.16 (ed. Campbell, pp. 6 and 32).   [3] *EER* ii.17 (ed. Campbell, p. 34).
[4] Above, pp. [xxii–xxiv]. Cf. Lawson, *Cnut*, pp. 86–7, and Stafford, *Queen Emma and Queen Edith*, p. 228.

Ælfgifu of Northampton) – represents only one side of the bargain. The athelings Edward and Alfred were out of the king's reach, in Normandy; and with Emma on his side Cnut could at least ensure that she would not make trouble for himself on their behalf. In blatant extension of the process of obfuscation, the Encomiast remarks further that Cnut and Emma sent 'other noble sons [*alios uero liberales filios*] to Normandy to be brought up', keeping their son Harthacnut with them, 'in as much as he was to be the heir of the kingdom';[1] and while he does state that Harthacnut was later sent to Denmark, there is no suggestion that this was part of a reciprocal arrangement with Earl Thorkell.[2]

The Encomiast writes enthusiastically of Cnut's distinction as 'emperor of five kingdoms' (Denmark, England, Wales, Scotland, and Norway), and expounds his naturally favourable view of the king's enforcement of law and of his support for the church. It is in this context that the Encomiast claims to have seen Cnut at Saint-Omer, en route for Rome, and gives a moving account of the king's various acts of devotion.[3] The question arises when this visit or pilgrimage took place. There can be no doubt that Cnut was in Rome at Easter 1027, for the coronation of the Emperor Conrad,[4] and that it was on this occasion that he despatched the second of his remarkable letters to the English people;[5] moreover, the town of Saint-Omer was certainly on a natural route from England to Rome.[6] It is apparent from the letter, however, that in 1027 Cnut travelled to and returned from Rome via Denmark (which might render it unlikely that he would have passed through Saint-Omer), and besides, the Encomiast implies that the visit occurred not long before the king's death. There is no objection in principle to the supposition that Cnut travelled to Rome on more than one occasion, and that it was thus on an occasion in the early 1030s that he passed through Saint-Omer; moreover, a contemporary chronicler seems to have believed that Cnut went to Rome in 1031,[7] and there is evidence of what would appear to be another visit, in

---

[1] *EER* ii.18 (ed. Campbell, p. 34). Campbell's translation, to the effect that Cnut and Emma 'sent in fact their other legitimate sons to Normandy to be brought up', represents no more than the Encomiast may have intended, but is perhaps too loaded. See also *EER* iii.1 (ed. Campbell, p. 38).

[2] *EER* ii.19 (ed. Campbell, p. 34); cf. ASC, MS C, s.a. 1023. See also Keynes, 'Cnut's Earls', pp. 56–7, and above, p. [lviii] n. 5.

[3] *EER* ii.20–2 (ed. Campbell, pp. 36–8).

[4] Wipo, *Gesta Chuonradi II Imperatoris*, ch. 16 (*Quellen*, ed. Trillmich, p. 570; transl. T. E. Mommsen and K. F. Morrison, *Imperial Lives and Letters of the Eleventh Century* (New York, 1962), p. 79). For Cnut and Conrad, see Keynes, 'Giso, Bishop of Wells', pp. 205–6.

[5] For the letter of 1027, see JW, *Chron.* s.a. 1031 (ed. Darlington and McGurk, II.512–18), and WM, *GR* ii.183 (ed. Mynors *et al.*, pp. 324–30); see also *EHD*, no. 53, and *Councils & Synods*, ed. Whitelock, *et al.*, I.506–13.

[6] On routes to Rome, see Grierson, 'Grimbald of St. Bertin's', p. 541, and Grierson, 'Relations between England and Flanders', pp. 74–81.

[7] ASC, MSS DE, s.a. 1031; JW, *Chron.* s.a. 1031 (ed. Darlington and McGurk, II.512).

1035, or more probably in 1030.[1] It must be admitted, however, that it is all too easy to see how memories of the events of 1027 might stray from one context in order to dignify another;[2] and in the absence of more compelling evidence for a later visit it would perhaps be as well to suppose that Cnut went to Rome on only the one occasion, and made a point of visiting Saint-Omer on the outward or on the return journey.[3] It is most unfortunate that the Encomiast did not see fit to say any more about Cnut's rule, and that he did not enlarge on the personal qualities of the king. His account of Cnut's death and burial is, however, written with an intensity of feeling which seems entirely genuine. If we may risk some psycho-history, it would seem that Emma was fully conscious of what she owed to the king who had rescued her from political oblivion in 1017: her relationship with Cnut eclipsed whatever had passed between her and King Æthelred, and cast a lengthening shadow over her relations with her sons.

The Encomiast's account of the events of 1035–6 (*EER* iii.1–6) is perhaps the most highly charged part of his work, and is of the greatest value in as much as it provides an unashamedly prejudiced (and therefore all the more interesting) view of a period full of incident, subterfuge, treachery, and murder. One can but sympathise with Emma in the immediate aftermath of Cnut's death: her sons by King Æthelred had been abandoned in 1016; her son by King Cnut had been despatched to Denmark in the mid-1020s; Cnut himself had now died, leaving her politically exposed in a kingdom dominated by factions personified on the one hand by Earl Godwine and on the other hand by Earl Leofric; and it would not be easy to maintain the political interests of her absent son (Harthacnut) against the supporters of the late king's elder son (Harold Harefoot). The Encomiast implies that in 1035 a thought was spared for Edward and Alfred in the dispute which now broke surface between the supporters of Harthacnut (absent in Denmark) and Harold Harefoot;[4] but we have to bear in mind, as always, that he was writing in the early 1040s, under the circumstances which had come to obtain by that time, and it is perhaps unlikely that the sons of Æthelred would

---

[1] Goscelin, *Translatio S. Mildrethe*, cc. 10 and 17 (Rollason, 'Goscelin of Canterbury's Account', pp. 167–8 and 175–6). For 1030, as opposed to 1035, as the date intended, see Sharpe, 'The Date of St. Mildrith's Translation'.

[2] The reference to the expedition in 1031, in ASC, MSS DE, is probably a garbled reference to the expedition of 1027 (*Councils & Synods*, ed. Whitelock, *et al.*, p. 507), and the same may be true of Goscelin's stories (Barlow, 'Two Notes', pp. 50–1). The chronicler's reference became attached to a notice of Cnut's expedition to Scotland, which probably took place in 1031; see Hudson, 'Cnut and the Scottish Kings'. Glaber's account of an intervention by Cnut in Scotland (RG, *Hist.* ii.3 (ed. France, pp. 54–6)) clearly relates to an earlier and separate occasion; see Lawson, *Cnut*, pp. 104–5.

[3] Campbell (*Encomium Emmae*, pp. lxii–lxiii) opted for two visits; see also John, 'The *Encomium Emmae Reginae*', pp. 76–7, n. 2, Lawson, *Cnut*, pp. 102–4, and John, *Reassessing Anglo-Saxon England*, pp. 154–6.

[4] *EER* iii.1 (ed. Campbell, pp. 38–40).

have been uppermost in the minds of those with political power. It is no surprise that the Encomiast should subscribe to the seemingly common view that Harold Harefoot was of lowly birth, and had been intruded surreptitiously into the bed of Cnut's concubine, Ælfgifu of Northampton;[1] and we may imagine that he took some pleasure in relating how Æthelnoth, archbishop of Canterbury, refused to consecrate and crown Harold as king, and how badly the king conducted himself thereafter.[2] Yet the matter which seems to be at the heart of the *Encomium* is the sequence of events which led to the capture and blinding of the atheling Alfred, in 1036.[3] According to the Encomiast, it was Harold Harefoot who conceived the plan to lure the athelings from Normandy to England, by forging a letter from Queen Emma to Edward and Alfred, in which she apprised them of Harold's activities, assured them that they had support among the chief men, and urged one or other of them to come back soon in order to receive her advice. The athelings replied that one of them would come; and in the event it was Alfred, the younger of the two, who went from Normandy to Flanders and crossed over thence to England. Of course it is well known that both Edward and Alfred came over to England in 1036, that Edward returned to Normandy, and that Alfred was captured, blinded, and left at Ely to die.[4] Yet can we believe that either Harold (if the letter was indeed forged by him) or Emma (if it is genuine) would have written to the athelings in terms which would be so conveniently compatible with the outcome of events? The prospective successor was quite obviously Edward, but the letter is cast in terms so loose that Edward is left aside and Alfred is able to make the fateful response; and just as it would have been in the Encomiast's interests to say nothing about Edward's abortive expedition, so too would he have wished to create the impression that it was not Emma who had invited Alfred to come to England but Harold who had so deviously enticed him to his death. It is difficult, therefore, to believe that the Encomiast's story is anything other than an elaborate fiction, devised five years after the event; and, accordingly, we may doubt that Emma's letter, which if 'genuine' would be a document of intrinsic diplomatic interest, is anything other than the product of yet another flight of the Encomiast's fancy.[5] The Encomiast goes on to describe how Earl Godwine took Alfred under his protection, and became his man (*miles*); but he is very careful to make it plain that it was Harold's men, not Godwine and his men, who were responsible for capturing

---

[1] ASC, MSS CDE, s.a. 1035; *EER* iii.1 (ed. Campbell, pp. 38–40); JW, *Chron.* s.a. 1035 (ed. Darlington and McGurk, p. 520).
[2] *EER* iii.1 (ed. Campbell, p. 40). Campbell (*Encomium Emmae*, pp. lxiii–lxiv) rejected the whole story; but it is not unlikely that Æthelnoth stalled until 1037, and then gave in (cf. John, *Reassessing Anglo-Saxon England*, p. 165).
[3] *EER* iii.2–6 (ed. Campbell, pp. 40–6).
[4] Above, pp. [xxx–xxxii].   [5] Above, pp. [xxxiii–xxxiv].

Ill. 5   The forged letter from Emma to her sons Edward and Alfred. *Encomium Emmae Reginae*, Book III, chs. 2–3. BL Add. 33241, fol. 56r

Alfred and his 'few men of Boulogne', and for inflicting evil upon them.[1] Again, there can be little doubt that Godwine was in fact deeply involved in and perhaps even directly responsible for Alfred's capture, blinding, and death; but the Encomiast was writing at a time when Godwine was at the height of his power, and it might well have been necessary for him to tread carefully in this particular respect.[2] The English chronicler who wrote of Alfred's capture and death was clearly moved deeply by the event ('No more horrible deed was done in this land since the Danes came and peace was made here'), and one can sense from his account that there were the makings here of the cult of a martyred innocent. The Encomiast, while professing concern to spare Emma's maternal feelings, raises the event to a 'martyrdom', lingering on the horror of the crime and reporting on the occurrence of miracles at Alfred's tomb.[3] In effect, therefore, a plan for which Emma must have been blamed when it went so disastrously wrong was turned quite effectively to her own advantage, and exploited for all that it was worth.

The denouement of the Encomiast's tale, from Queen Emma's 'decision' to go into exile (in 1037) to her triumphant return (in 1040), is another brilliantly contrived set piece (*EER* iii.7–14). The focus of attention is at last the queen herself, grieving for her murdered son, and wondering what remained of her life and position. The Encomiast seems to have been aware that Emma was open to criticism for having managed to avoid death in 1036, when her son had not been so fortunate, which is about as close as he comes to an overt display of pleading the case for her defence against those who would be her detractors. He then justifies her decision to seek refuge overseas (in this respect making a virtue of necessity), and describes how she was presently established by Baldwin, count of Flanders, in a house at Bruges. She made an approach to Edward, who declined to help (on the grounds that 'the English nobles had sworn no oath to him'), urging her to turn instead to Harthacnut; and with some intervention from divine providence Harthacnut joined her in Flanders, in order to put right what was wrong. It so happened that Harold Harefoot died; whereupon Harthacnut and Emma returned to England, to the great sorrow of those who had come to know her in Flanders and of course to the joy of the English. After a reference to the return of Edward, at Harthacnut's invitation, the *Encomium* ends with a verbal flourish: Emma and

---

[1] *EER* iii.4–5 (ed. Campbell, pp. 42–4). The Encomiast's account of the evils inflicted on Alfred's men seems to echo ASC, MSS CD, s.a. 1036.

[2] *Encomium Emmae*, ed. Campbell, pp. lxv and lxix n. 1; Barlow, *Edward the Confessor*, p. 46. The fact that the Encomiast took the trouble to note that Godwine had sworn an oath to Alfred, his lord, may be a thinly veiled response to Godwine's own assertion, in 1040–1, that he was acting under Harold's orders (above, p. [xxxviii]); see also John, 'The *Encomium Emmae Reginae*', pp. 87–8, and John, *Reassessing Anglo-Saxon England*, pp. 164–5.

[3] *EER* iii.6 (ed. Campbell, pp. 44–6).

her two sons are happily established as sharers of royal power, harking back to the image placed at the beginning of the book.

A reading of the *Encomium Emmae Reginae*

It would be easy to dismiss the *Encomium* as a thoroughly unreliable and tendentious piece of work, which it is, though to do so would be to deny oneself a useful account of the Scandinavian conquest of England in 1013–16, a contemporary impression of Cnut's rule, and an inside view of English politics in the immediate aftermath of Cnut's death. We may be sure, however, that it was not the Encomiast's intention to provide posterity with anything of the sort. We might reasonably expect the historical value of the *Encomium* to reside in the details which it provides of the vicissitudes of Emma's career from her marriage to Cnut in 1017 to her triumphant return to England in 1040; yet while the *Encomium* was written when Queen Emma was at the height of her power, it cannot be said that the Encomiast was concerned to divulge much about his subject on a personal level – whether her good works as queen, or the intensity of her devotion to God, or the quality of her shining example. Campbell himself took the view that the *Encomium* deserves the greatest attention 'for the illumination of character and motive';[1] but it is in this respect, more so than in any other, that the work needs to be treated with all due circumspection. In fact the special value of Campbell's own exposition of the *Encomium* lies in his command of the literary traditions generated in the different parts of the Scandinavian world; for he knew full well that the complexities and inter-relationships of the traditions represented on the one hand by Danish historiography of the twelfth century, and on the other hand by the Norwegian synoptic histories of the same period, need to be fully understood before any use can be made of the 'Scandinavian' material bearing on English history in the eleventh century, and that the same applies – with compound interest – to the verses and stories contained in the later Icelandic productions ranging from the various sagas of St Olaf to *Heimskringla*, *Knytlinga saga*, *Jómsvíkinga saga*, and the rest.[2] Campbell brought this vast and varied literature into an instructive relationship with the *Encomium*; but while much of the literature is more readily accessible than it was before, and while there are respects in which Campbell's judgements might be affected by the natural advance of scholarship in the past fifty years,[3] it is arguable that the line of enquiry expects

---

[1] *Encomium Emmae*, ed. Campbell, pp. xxii–xxiii and 1–lxix.

[2] Keynes, 'Cnut's Earls', pp. 47–8, and references.

[3] Campbell made use of what he called the 'Supplement to Jómsvíkinga saga', which follows the recension of that saga contained in 'Flateyjarbók'. For an account of the main recensions of *Jómsvíkinga saga*, see Blake, *The Saga of the Jomsvikings*, pp. xv–xxi; *Jómsvíkinga Saga*, ed. Halldórsson, pp. 7–12; and the pertinent entry in *Medieval Scandinavia*, ed. Pulsiano, pp. 343–4 (with bibliography). For

too much of the material, and that to pursue it much further would be to obscure the better possibilities. We might choose to fasten, for example, on the value of the *Encomium* as a source for queenship and family politics in the eleventh century; for while we can detect some of the tensions which lie beneath the surface of recorded events in the ninth and tenth centuries, it is largely by virtue of the *Encomium* that the tensions in Emma's case are fully exposed.[1] Our approach towards the *Encomium* should, however, be guided in the first instance not so much by a determination (against the odds) to separate the hard information from the rhetorical or polemical embellishment, and then to reduce the available sources to some kind of harmony, as by a wish to understand why Queen Emma should have commissioned a work of this nature in the early 1040s, and how the Encomiast set about the task in hand.

It is axiomatic in the study of a work like the *Encomium Emmae* that the circumstances of its composition – authorship, date, purpose, and intended audience – must be fully understood before any use can be made of it as a source of historical information. In his introduction to the present edition, published in 1949, Professor Campbell took the view that what Emma commissioned in 1041–2 was 'a laudatory work on the history of the Danish dynasty in England', that it was written 'purely for the personal glorification of Emma and her relatives', and that 'it is not in any sense a piece of political propaganda defending the Danish occupation of England';[2] in short, the Encomiast intended his book 'to be entirely devoted directly or indirectly to Emma's praise'.[3] R. W. Southern approached the *Encomium* in a way which has the distinct advantage of keeping faith with the author's declared intention to heap praise upon the queen, reading it (most effectively) as 'the story of a woman behind the scenes who saved a kingdom from ruin', and judging it to be 'not only a work of great literary skill, but even of some nobility and historical insight'.[4] Other commentators have been similarly inclined to take the *Encomium* at face value, as a work which for all its distinctive features was primarily a work written in praise of the queen.[5] The irresistible temptation, however, has long been to identify a contemporary political purpose behind the Encomiast's tale. In 1964 Sten Körner argued that the Encomiast did have a

---

further discussion of the 'Supplement to Jómsvíkinga saga', see Campbell, 'Knút's Saga'. For *Knytlinga saga*, see *Medieval Scandinavia*, ed. Pulsiano, pp. 359–60 (with bibliography).

[1] For much perceptive discussion of these matters, see Stafford, *Queens, Concubines and Dowagers*; Stafford, 'The Portrayal of Royal Women in England'; Stafford, 'Emma: The Powers of the Queen'; and Stafford, *Queen Emma and Queen Edith, passim.*

[2] *Encomium Emmae*, ed. Campbell, p. xxi.

[3] *Encomium Emmae*, ed. Campbell, p. xlvi; cf. *EER*, Arg. (ed. Campbell, p. 8).

[4] Southern, 'Aspects of the European Tradition of Historical Writing', pp. 186–7. Further appreciation of the Encomiast's literary skill is likely to emerge from studies which David Howlett and Andy Orchard have in hand; see also John, 'The *Encomium Emmae Reginae*', p. 89 n. 2.

[5] Gransden, *Historical Writing*, pp. 56–60; Lawson, *Cnut*, pp. 54–6.

political agenda, and, in effect, that he was writing in support of Harthacnut's interests against those of Edward.[1] In 1970 Christopher Brooke described the *Encomium* as 'a contemporary defence of Queen Emma',[2] with the implication that it was written in response to contemporary criticism; and in the same year Frank Barlow suggested that the *Encomium* 'was intended, among other things, to discredit Edward's claim to the throne', by showing that Harthacnut's claim was the stronger.[3] It has also been argued, variously, that the *Encomium* was written in support of Harthacnut and Edward, against Swein Estrithsson;[4] that the author's purpose in praising Emma was to warn the English that 'they would despise Queen Emma at their peril', and at the same time to convey the message that she, and only she, was 'the bearer of legitimacy';[5] that the emphasis was on Emma's role as the maker of peace between peoples, because she was a Norman and the Normans were conquerors;[6] and that the work was commissioned by Emma while in exile in Flanders in the late 1030s, as part of her campaign against Harold Harefoot, that its purpose was to assert the legitimacy of Harthacnut's cause and to gain the support of Count Baldwin V, and that by the time it was completed in the early 1040s Edward could be represented as heir-apparent.[7] More generally, and most recently, it has been suggested that the *Encomium* was written in order 'to justify and bolster a family trinity of power in which mother and two sons rule together'.[8]

The *Encomium* is transparently 'political', yet evidently its author's intentions were not so straightforward that it is easy for a modern reader to judge what particular political cause it was intended to serve. It might be helpful, in such circumstances, to return to first principles. It is clear that the *Encomium* was written by a monk (or former monk) of Saint-Bertin, in Saint-Omer, Flanders, some time after Edward's return to England in early 1041 and before Harthacnut's death in June 1042. It is also clear (from the Prologue) that the Encomiast had been commissioned to produce the work by Queen Emma herself, and we have his own word (in the Argument) that 'the course of this book is devoted entirely to the

---

[1] Körner, *The Battle of Hastings, England, and Europe 1035–1066*, pp. 47–74, esp. 69–70. Körner's particular interpretation of the *Encomium* was soon challenged by Lindqvist, 'Encomium Emmae'.

[2] Brooke, 'Historical Writing in England', pp. 236–7.

[3] Barlow, *Edward the Confessor*, pp. 47 and 49; *Life of King Edward*, ed. Barlow, p. xxiii.

[4] [M. W.] Campbell, 'The *Encomium Emmae Reginae*', esp. p. 38.

[5] John, 'The *Encomium Emmae Reginae*', pp. 94 and 91. In John's reading of the *Encomium*, the portrait of Thorkell would recall 'the horrors of the world of illegitimate kings' and Emma would be seen as one who 'ushered in a new era of peace and stability' (*ibid.*, pp. 81–2, 93–4). See also John, *Reassessing Anglo-Saxon England*, pp. 151–3.

[6] Searle, 'Emma the Conqueror', esp. pp. 286–7 and 288.

[7] Lifshitz, 'The *Encomium Emmae Reginae*', pp. 46–7; see also Fletcher, *Who's Who*, p. 197.

[8] Stafford, 'The Portrayal of Royal Women in England', pp. 162 and 163–5; see also Stafford, *Queen Emma and Queen Edith*, pp. 28–40.

praise of Queen Emma'. It is unlikely, however, that Emma intended the Encomiast to pander to her own sense of vanity and self-esteem, and more probable that she intended the work, in praising her, to serve a particular political or polemical purpose. It would be interesting to know whether the work was written in Flanders or in England, and whether its intended audience was (for example) Count Baldwin V, or the queen and her immediate entourage, or members of the Anglo-Danish royal court; and while the natural assumption is that it was written in Flanders for consumption by Emma in England, we should not rule out the possibility that it was written in England by a Flemish monk who had entered into Queen Emma's service, for consumption at the Anglo-Danish court. The key to our understanding of the *Encomium* may be, quite simply, that it was written during the reign of Harthacnut, at a time (1041–2) when Harthacnut's rule was becoming increasingly unpopular, when a cult of the martyred innocent was developing around the atheling Alfred, and when Alfred's brother Edward had just returned to England, at Emma's request, in order to take his place as co-ruler beside his mother and his half-brother.[1] The Encomiast was writing at a time of considerable turmoil in England, in response to a commission from a person who had just recovered her place at court and her power in the kingdom after three years in political exile. We cannot expect him to display objectivity and balance, and we should not be surprised if he takes a particular line on a particular aspect of Emma's career; indeed, we might even admire the way he picked his way through past events, and maintained his composure to the end. It was hardly germane to the Encomiast's purpose that he should say anything about Emma's background in Normandy, or about her marriage to King Æthelred in 1002, or her role as queen from 1002 to 1016;[2] he was, after all, writing for those who had ousted the native dynasty by force of arms, and it was more convenient for his purposes to take the line that Emma was in Normandy when Cnut sought to marry her in 1017, and that her sons Edward and Alfred were sent to Normandy by Emma and Cnut.[3] The account of the Scandinavian conquest of England appears to contribute nothing to the praise of Queen Emma herself, except by indirect association; but the Encomiast's intention may have been to remind his audience, or readers, that the origins of the Anglo-Danish regime lay in a concerted effort which had led to a splendid victory over an enemy divided against itself, and in this way to generate a sense of collective pride in the achievement of the Danes. It may be that the message was directed towards a particular faction at court in the early 1040s, comprising many of those who had previously supported Harold

---

[1] Above, pp. [xxxvii–xxxviii].

[2] For discussion of the Encomiast's treatment of Emma's marriage to Æthelred, see *Encomium Emmae*, ed. Campbell, p. xlvi.

[3] Above, pp. [lx–lxi]. See also *Encomium Emmae*, ed. Campbell, pp. xliv–xlvi, and Keynes, 'The Æthelings in Normandy', p. 184.

Harefoot, with the aim of impressing upon them a view of the past calculated to serve the interests of the present; and it could be that the emphasis on the role of Earl Thorkell, and on the splendour of the Danish fleet, reflects the Encomiast's (and Emma's) concern to acknowledge the special part which Thorkell and others had played in these momentous events. The account of Cnut's rule would serve in its own way to evoke the glorious past, and to remind the audience that their loyalty belonged to the regime which he had established in England. Yet it is in Book III that we reach what is arguably the heart of the matter. The Encomiast's view of the events of 1035–40 is certainly one-sided, and all the more interesting for precisely that reason. The reader is told that it was Harold Harefoot, not Emma, who lured the athelings back to England; no mention is made of Edward's expedition in 1036, and attention is focussed instead on his younger brother Alfred; Earl Godwine might have been expected to help, but anyway it was Harold's men who perpetrated the crime and who were thus responsible for Alfred's death; Alfred was an innocent martyr, and Emma was utterly devastated by his loss; she was obliged for good reason to leave the country, though she did so with a heavy heart; she sought help first from Edward, who for good reason could not oblige, and then from Harthacnut, who burned with desire to avenge the murder of his brother Alfred; and there was great sadness when Emma left Flanders, where she was so much loved. It may be that the Encomiast took outrageous liberties with what we perceive or presume to have been the historical truth, and in certain respects his testimony must be set aside as worthless; but for all its imperfections as a historical record, it is important to judge the *Encomium* on its own terms. The death of Harold Harefoot in 1040 created new political opportunities, but at the same time it set in motion waves of recrimination about the capture and blinding of the atheling Alfred in 1036; so, when Emma and Harthacnut returned to England, Emma would have needed not only to secure the loyalty of those who until recently had been the supporters of her enemy Harold Harefoot, including Earl Godwine and Earl Leofric, and to gain acceptance for Harthacnut (and his followers from Denmark), but also to clear herself of the charge that she had encouraged the athelings to return to England and might thus be considered responsible for initiating the sequence of events which led to Alfred's death. Her answer was to commission a work which might help to restore political faith in the Anglo-Danish regime established in the first instance by King Cnut, and which would represent her case, and her view of events, to those in positions of power and influence. There would have been few persons in her service on whom Emma could rely, and she gave the commission to one who had learnt his literary trade as a monk of Saint-Bertin, and who had come to know the queen while she was in exile at Bruges.

The *Encomium* must be judged as the product of circumstances which proved to be short-lived, but which determined the shape and the substance of a work which is now put to a completely different use. So, while the modern reader who expects the *Encomium* to provide a portrait of a great and distinguished queen at the height of her power will be disappointed, and might well despair of an author who could suppress, misrepresent, and garble what we know or think to have been the truth, a reader more sympathetic to the author's purpose will be rewarded with an extraordinary view of English politics in the early 1040s and will properly appreciate all the dissimulation and artful dissembling. Yet the purpose of the *Encomium Emmae* was not to establish Harthacnut's claims against Harold Harefoot, or against the atheling Edward, or indeed to establish the legitimacy of one party as opposed to another; for it was not merely the succession which mattered in 1041–2, but the very survival of a political order. The *Encomium* was intended for consumption by men and women who were already beholden to the Anglo-Danish cause: they did not need to be told that the Scandinavian conquest of England was justified, and they did not need to be reminded of Emma's place in the political regime which they supplanted; rather, they needed to be reminded of the circumstances in which Danish rule had been established in England, and they needed to be told that Emma stood for the furtherance of Cnut's political intentions. In the process Harold Harefoot was vilified; and as the cult of the martyred innocent gathered momentum, it was impressed upon the reader that responsibility for leading Alfred to his death could in no way be laid at Emma's door. In short, when we seek to judge the *Encomium* as a historical source, there is little to be gained from censuring the author for his 'suppression' of Emma's marriage to Æthelred, or for the various misconceptions which pervade his account of the Scandinavian conquest of England, or for seeming to represent Edward and Alfred as sons of Emma and Cnut. We should marvel, instead, at the wondrous audacity which lies behind the Encomiast's exposition of events which took place in the 1030s, for example in the invention of the forged letter from Emma to her children, or in his treatment of Earl Godwine's part in the story of Alfred's capture and death, and we should relish the thought that Emma should have commissioned a work of this nature in order to secure her political objectives. The *Encomium* represents the triumph of literary artifice over historical truth; and while truth is still there, it is a truth which lies hidden in the artifice.

QUEEN EMMA DURING THE REIGN OF EDWARD THE CONFESSOR

The frontispiece of the *Encomium Emmae* (Ill. 2) depicts Queen Emma in the panoply of royal power, with her sons Harthacnut and Edward relegated to a decidedly subordinate position. It was not, however, a situation destined to last; for Harthacnut died unexpectedly on 8 June 1042, whereupon the people received Edward as king, 'as was his natural right'.[1] The chronicler's statement may in fact

---

[1] ASC, MSS CD, s.a. 1042.

conceal a period of political manoeuvring, precipitated by Harthacnut's death; and there is reason to believe that Swein Estrithsson (son of Cnut's sister Astrith) took an interest in the succession at about this time.[1] It may be significant in this connection that several months elapsed before Edward was consecrated king, at Winchester, on Easter Sunday (3 April) 1043. In November of that year, nearly eighteen months after his accession, the king rode with his earls from Gloucester to Winchester:

And they came unexpectedly upon the Lady, and deprived her of all the treasures which she owned, and which were beyond counting, because she had formerly been very hard to the king, her son, in that she did less for him than he wished both before he became king and afterwards as well. And they allowed her to stay there afterwards.[2]

The implication seems to be that Edward had cause to resent his mother's actions not only in the twenty-five years before his accession, while he was in exile in Normandy, but also in the eighteen months or so which had passed since his accession in June 1042; and one imagines, therefore, that Emma was not wholly confident, in 1042–3, that she would continue to prosper politically during Edward's reign.[3] It has long been recognised that a passage in Goscelin's account of the miracles which took place some time after the Translation of St Mildrith from Minster-in-Thanet to St Augustine's, Canterbury, on 18 May 1030, sheds welcome light on the alleged circumstances of Queen Emma's 'disgrace' in November 1043:[4]

Sic, Dei prouidentia ordinante omnia prout uult, suscepit Anglia indigenam regem Eaduuardum, Æthelredo rege et Emma progenitum. Quo Salomonica pace regnante, ipsa eius genitrix accusabatur regem Northuuegorum, Magnum nomine, ad inuadendum Anglicum imperium concitasse suosque thesauros infinitos secum illi dedidisse. Hinc proditrix regni, hostis patrie, insidiatrix filii iudicatur, uniuersaque substantia eius regi proscribitur.

And so, in accordance with the dispensation of God who governs all things, England received as king the native-born Edward, offspring of King Æthelred and Emma. While he was reigning in peace, like Solomon, his own mother was accused of having incited the king of the Norwegians, who was called Magnus, to invade England, and of having given countless of her treasures to him, as well as her support. Wherefore this traitor to the kingdom, enemy of the country, betrayer of her son, was judged, and all of her property was forfeited to the king.

---

[1] AB, *GHEP* ii.77–8 (ed. Trillmich, p. 318; transl. Tschan, p. 108).

[2] ASC, MS D, s.a. 1043 (ed. Cubbin, p. 67); JW, *Chron.* s.a. 1043 (ed. Darlington and McGurk, II.534).

[3] For a rather different view of Emma's relations with Edward, see [M. W.] Campbell, 'Emma, reine d'Angleterre'. Campbell challenges Freeman's notion that there was deep-rooted ill-feeling between mother and son (*Norman Conquest*, II (2nd edn), 59–62), on the grounds that there is no good evidence of such ill-feeling before Harthacnut's death in 1042; and he suggests instead that in acting against Edward in 1042–3 Emma was motivated by her determination to curb the growing influence of Earl Godwine.

[4] Goscelin, *Translatio S. Mildrethe*, c. 18 (Rollason, 'Goscelin of Canterbury's Account', pp. 176–7; *Anglo-Saxon Chronicle*, ed. Whitelock, *et al.*, p. 107 n. 8).

The interesting point for the modern historian is that Emma should here be said to have made an approach to Magnus of Norway, at a time when Magnus was extending his rule into Denmark and would have had good cause to entertain a design or an aspiration in the general direction of England;[1] but of course the point for Goscelin was that St Mildrith intervened on behalf of Queen Emma, and that through her intervention Emma was restored to her rightful position.[2] A direct consequence of Emma's fall from grace in November 1043 was the discomfiture of her friend Stigand, who had been appointed bishop of the East Angles in the previous year. He was deprived of his bishopric, 'and all that he owned was placed in the king's control because he was closest in his mother's counsel, and because it was suspected that she did as he advised'.[3] The reality of Emma's fall is demonstrated most effectively by a writ of King Edward, addressed to Bishop Grimketel in his capacity as bishop of the East Angles, and issued, therefore, during the brief period after Stigand's removal from office in 1043 and before his restoration in the following year.[4] The king declares that the land at Mildenhall, Suffolk, and the sokes of the eight and a half hundreds pertaining to Thingoe, are to belong to Bury St Edmunds 'as fully and as completely as my mother possessed it', as if he were making new arrangements occasioned by the turn of events. Sooner or later, however, Emma recovered at least part of her rights in Suffolk;[5] and the fact that Stigand recovered his bishopric in 1044 is itself a sign that Emma was restored to favour, with or without St Mildrith's help.

It would appear, therefore, that Emma's fall from grace in 1043 was short-lived, and that she was soon restored to an honourable position in the kingdom, even if she no longer played much part in public affairs. In the one charter of 1042 she is positioned after the archbishop of Canterbury and before the bishops (in other words notionally 'lower' than her position in the latter part of Cnut's reign);[6] and in a charter of 1043 (perhaps issued before her fall in November) she is positioned immediately after the king.[7] She appears again in two 'Winchester' charters issued in 1044 (before the death of Ælfweard, bishop of London, on 25 July), positioned immediately after the king.[8] Emma does not seem to have attested the king's

---

[1] Stenton, *Anglo-Saxon England*, pp. 426–7; *Encomium Emmae*, ed. Campbell, pp. xxii and xlix n. 4; *Life of Edward*, ed. Barlow, p. 17 n. 37; Barlow, *Edward the Confessor*, pp. 76–7; Stafford, *Queen Emma and Queen Edith*, pp. 249 and 251; Walker, *Harold: The Last Anglo-Saxon King*, pp. 17–18.

[2] Goscelin, *Translatio S. Mildrethe*, c. 18 (Rollason, 'Goscelin of Canterbury's Account', pp. 177–8); Barlow, 'Two Notes', pp. 51–5.

[3] ASC, MS C, s.a. 1043; Smith, 'Archbishop Stigand', pp. 200–1.

[4] S 1069 (*Writs*, ed. Harmer, no. 9); see also Barlow, *Edward the Confessor*, p. 77. S 1070 (*Writs*, ed. Harmer, no. 10) is spurious. For Stigand's restoration, see ASC, MS E, s.a. 1044.

[5] See below, p. [lxxv]. [6] S 998, from Sherborne (ex Horton abbey); styled *regina humillima*.

[7] S 999, from Abingdon; styled *regis mater*.

[8] S 1001 and 1006, from the Old Minster, Winchester; styled *regis mater*. S 1006 is a grant of land at Pitminster, Somerset, to the Old Minster; and it would appear from later Winchester tradition that

charters after 1044,[1] and it is probably significant that her 'disappearance' coincides, in effect, with the king's marriage to Edith, daughter of Earl Godwine, in 1045.[2] In the less formalised protocol of the vernacular charters, we also find Emma initially in close association with her son the king. A document recording a certain Thurstan's bequest of land in Essex to Christ Church, Canterbury, was drawn up at a meeting attended by the king, 'the Lady Ælfgifu' ('Ælfgifu seo hlæfdige'), and many others;[3] since the others include 'Stigand the priest', the meeting took place before Stigand's appointment as bishop in 1043, and so before Emma's discomfiture later in the same year. A document recording how Ælfwine, bishop of Winchester, leased an estate in Oxfordshire to a certain Osgod was drawn up at a meeting attended by the king, 'the Lady Ælfgifu' ('Ælfgyfu seo hlefdige'), and many others;[4] in this case the others include Ælfweard, bishop of London, so the meeting took place some time before the bishop's death on 25 July 1044. The record of a grant of land by Æthelwine the Black to St Albans abbey was drawn up at a meeting attended by the king, 'Ælfgifu Emma his mother' ('Ælfgyfe Imma his modor'), and others;[5] since the others include Eadnoth, bishop of Dorcester, the meeting took place some time before Eadnoth's death on 18/19 September 1049. The last two of these documents could have been drawn up before, or after, Emma's fall from grace in November 1043, and do not necessarily show, therefore, that she was restored in 1044 to an honourable position. It is interesting, however, that a document recording an agreement between a certain Æthelric (Bigga) and Eadsige, archbishop of Canterbury, was drawn up at a

---

King Edward was in this instance confirming a grant which Queen Emma had made for the soul of King Harthacnut (below, p. [lxxviii] n. 3).

[1] Emma does not attest three other 'south-western' charters issued in 1044 (S 1003–5). Emma is included in the witness-lists of three other charters which are not authentic in their transmitted form: S 1000 (Coventry), dated '1043', attested by 'Ælfgyfa mater regis' and 'Eadgith regina'; S 1002 (St Peter's, Ghent), dated '1044', attested by 'Ælfgyfu mater regis'; and S 1011 (Westminster), dated 1 Aug. 1045, attested by 'Ælfgyfu Imma mater regis' and 'Eadgytha collaterana regis'. There is a genuine basis to the witness-lists in all three of these charters, but in view of the connections between them it would be hazardous to place much confidence in S 1000 and S 1011 as instances of the joint appearance of Emma and Edith.

[2] Cf. above, p. [xvii] n. 1. For various (very familiar) reasons Edith's own position at court in the later 1040s was far from secure, though it improved again in the later 1050s; she is 'the Lady Edith' in the 1060s (e.g. S 1426 (*Charters*, ed. Robertson, no. 117)).

[3] S 1530 (*Wills*, ed. Whitelock, no. 30). The *terminus post quem* is 1042 (Edward's accession). The witnesses include Ælfric, son of Wihtgar, who (at this stage or later) looked after Emma's interests in Suffolk; see below, p. [lxxv] n. 7.

[4] S 1391 (*Charters*, ed. Robertson, no. 98). The *terminus post quem* is 1042 (Edward's accession), not 1043 (cf. *Charters*, ed. Robertson, p. 433).

[5] S 1228. The *terminus post quem* is 1042 (Edward's accession). For the vernacular text of this charter, see S. Keynes, 'A Lost Cartulary of St Albans Abbey', *Anglo-Saxon England* 22 (1993), pp. 253–79 at 267–8. The witnesses include Ælfric, son of Wihtgar, who was a kinsman of Æthelwine the Black and who looked after Emma's interests in Suffolk; see below, p. [lxxv] n. 7.

meeting held apparently at Canterbury and attended by the king, 'the Lady
Ælfgifu' ('Ælfgyfu seo hlæfdige'), and many others;[1] since the others include
Wulfric, abbot of St Augustine's, and Ælfwine, bishop of Winchester, the meeting
must have taken place after Wulfric was consecrated abbot, on 25 December
1045,[2] and before Bishop Ælfwine's death, on 29 August 1047.[3] Emma may have
been down in the later 1040s, but perhaps she was not yet out.

It is generally presumed, in the absence of evidence but not without good
reason, that Emma was based at Winchester in the 1040s and that she remained
there up to the time of her death in 1052.[4] What little evidence there is bears on
activities of a nature largely resistant to interpretation as part of a historical
narrative. The most striking aspect of Emma's activities is the variety and
multiplicity of the interests which she maintained in religious houses across
southern England; for while there is little direct documentation, and no surviving
copy of a will, we still cannot fail to get the impression that she was a woman who
left her mark wherever she went. At what may have been a relatively early stage in
her public career, she is known to have given an illuminated Psalter to her brother
Robert, archbishop of Rouen (980–1037);[5] latterly, it seems that she provided
funds for or in some other way contributed to the building of the church of Saint-
Hilaire at Poitiers, dedicated in 1049.[6] It is not clear how effectively or for how
long she was able to maintain her connections with houses in eastern England. Her
special interest in Bury St Edmunds had probably originated in the early 1020s,
and found expression in the personal contacts which she established with the local
aristocracy of that area. As we have seen, she lost some of her rights in Suffolk in
1043–4; and although King Edward seems soon afterwards to have restored to his
mother the sokes of the eight and a half hundreds pertaining to Thingoe, it is
interesting that they are said to have been administered on Emma's behalf by
Ælfric, son of Wihtgar, who was a prominent landowner in Suffolk and Essex, and
founder of a house of secular canons at Clare (Suffolk).[7] In a writ issued soon after

---

[1] S 1471 (Charters, ed. Robertson, no. 101).
[2] ASC, MS E, s.a. 1045.   [3] ASC, MSS CDE, s.a. 1047.
[4] For Emma at Winchester, see Encomium Emmae, ed. Campbell, pp. xlviii–xlix; 'Liber Vitae' of the
New Minster, ed. Keynes, pp. 39–41; and Stafford, Queen Emma and Queen Edith, p. 253; see also above,
p. [xix] n. 4.
[5] See above, p. [xxi] n. 5; see also Alexander, Norman Illumination at Mont St Michel, pp. 112, 133,
150, 190 and 237–8.
[6] 'Istud monasterium magna ex parte construxerat regina Anglorum, per manus Gauterii Coorlandi'
(La Chronique de Saint-Maixent, ed. Verdon, p. 126). See also Beech, 'England and Aquitaine', pp. 87–8
and 92–3, and The Gesta Guillelmi of William of Poitiers, ed. Davis and Chibnall, pp. xvii–xviii.
[7] S 1078 (Writs, ed. Harmer, no. 18) shows that control of the sokes passed from Emma (and Ælfric,
son of Wihtgar) to the king himself, and that the king transferred it to the abbey of Bury St Edmunds
in the 1050s; S 1084 (ibid., no. 24) shows that the king confirmed the privilege to Abbot Baldwin, soon
after his appointment in 1065. For Ælfric, son of Wihtgar, see Wills, ed. Whitelock, p. 188; Charters, ed.

the fall of Earl Godwine in 1051 (and before Emma's death in March 1052), King Edward declared that his mother should be allowed to have an estate at Kirby, Norfolk, as fully as her retainer Leofstan had held it;[1] soon afterwards she bequeathed the estate to Bury St Edmunds, but it was illegally occupied by a certain Semer, and the king had to issue another writ confirming it to the abbey.[2] For whatever reason, the king also had occasion in the 1040s to issue a writ declaring that Ramsey abbey was to have the land at Hemingford, Hunts., which had been given to the monks by Harthacnut and Emma.[3] Yet it is part of the interest of Emma's activities as an exponent of the art of conspicuous patronage that she did it with far more than grants of land and privileges. Much could be accomplished with books, with well-chosen and well-aimed relics, and with other forms of treasure.[4] At Ely abbey Emma was remembered in particular as donor of a stunning array of precious textiles:[5]

Insignem quoque purpuram, aurifriso undique cinctam, fecit et per partes auro et gemmis pretiosis mirifico opere velud tabulatis adornavit illicque optulit, ut nulla alia in Anglorum regione talis operis et pretii inveniatur. Opus quippe illius materiam precellere videtur atque ceteris sanctis nostris pannum sericum unicuique, licet minoris pretii, auro et gemmis intextum, optulit, que penes nos hactenus reponuntur. Fecit etiam indumenta altaris, magnam pallam viridi coloris insignem cum laminis aureis, ut in faciem altaris per diem sollempnem celsius appareret, et desuper bissus sanguineo fulgore in longitudinem altaris ad cornua eius attingens usque ad terram cum aurifriso, latitudinem habens pedis, spectaculum decoris magni pretii administrat.

She also made and gave to this place a marvellous *purpura* encircled everywhere with gold edging, and adorned it in places with gold and precious gems of marvellous workmanship, as if it were panelled, such that no other is to be found in the land of the English of such workmanship and costliness. Her work seems indeed to transcend the subject; and for each of our other saints she gave a silk covering, although of lesser value, covered with gold and gems, which are preserved with us to this day. She also made altar cloths – a large and glorious hanging of green colour with bands of gold, so that at the front of the altar it might appear more wonderful on festival days, and on the top, along the length of the altar, a covering blood-red in splendour with gold edging, a foot wide, reaching right to the ground at its corners, presents a beautiful spectacle of great costliness.

Robertson, p. 425; *Writs*, ed. Harmer, p. 550; and Clarke, *English Nobility*, pp. 43–4, 50, 52–3 and 357–63 (Wihtgar, son of Ælfric). The Leofgifu who drew up her will in 1035 x 1044 (S 1521: *Wills*, ed. Whitelock, no. 29), and who may have considered herself close to Emma (cf. above, p. [xxx] n. 3), gave land in Suffolk to her kinsman Ælfric, son of Wihtgar; see also above, p. [lxxiv] n. 3. Ælfric, son of Wihtgar, appears to have been succeeded as Emma's agent by a certain Ordgar; see *RRAN* 41 and 292, and *Charters*, ed. Robertson, p. 426.

[1] S 1076 (*Writs*, ed. Harmer, no. 16).

[2] S 1077 (*Writs*, ed. Harmer, no. 17). For 'Semer', cf. S 1608.

[3] S 1106 (*Writs*, ed. Harmer, no. 58).

[4] For Emma as patron of various religious houses, see Heslop, 'The Production of *de luxe* Manuscripts', pp. 182–8, and Halpin, 'Anglo-Saxon Women and Pilgrimage', pp. 108–9.

[5] *LE* ii.79 (ed. Blake, p. 149); S. Keynes and A. Kennedy, *Anglo-Saxon Ely: Records of Ely Abbey and its Benefactors* (forthcoming).

Most of these items can be recognised in the inventory of the abbey's treasures compiled for Bishop Nigel (1133–69), in 1134. For example, the first item was clearly the pall, of *purpura*,[1] 'surrounded by a gold fringe and splendidly decorated with gems, which Queen Emma gave to St Æthelthryth', most notable for its later history;[2] and the first of the two altar cloths was perhaps the frontal 'well worked in gold and silver, which the worthy Queen Emma had made in honour of St Æthelthryth – but the Christ in Majesty lacks its throne'.[3] Moving from eastern England into Kent, it comes as no surprise that Emma extended her patronage to the two principal houses in Canterbury. Her gifts to Christ Church included land at Newington and Britwell (Prior), Oxon.,[4] and 'two dorsals from a pall, and two copes with golden tassels, and a chalice with a paten in which there were thirteen marks of pure gold'.[5] Her gifts to St Augustine's included costly palls for all the saints of that house.[6] Elsewhere, Emma's attention was focussed naturally enough on the religious houses at Winchester, within sight of her own dwelling on the High Street. She bequeathed to the Old Minster an estate of ten hides at Hayling

---

[1] For *purpura*, apparently shot-silk taffeta (and by extension something made of this material), see R. Dodwell, *Anglo-Saxon Art: A New Perspective* (Manchester, 1982), pp. 145–50.

[2] It was evidently this pall, said to have been given by Queen Emma as a covering for St Æthelthryth's tomb, which Bishop Nigel sold to the bishop of Lincoln in 1144/5 (when in need of cash), which the bishop of Lincoln (Alexander) offered to Pope Eugenius III in 1145 (when in need of a favour), which the pope (to his credit) refused to accept, which the bishop (to his shame) tried to strip of its gold, and which was duly recovered by the monks of Ely, only to be sold again to the bishop of Lincoln when Nigel needed more cash to pay to the king. See *LE* iii.122 (ed. Blake, pp. 372–3).

[3] *LE* iii.50 (ed. Blake, pp. 288–94, at 292 and 294); cf. Dodwell, *Anglo-Saxon Art*, p. 141. An analysis of the inventory will appear in Keynes and Kennedy, *Anglo-Saxon Ely*.

[4] The estate at Newington had been acquired by Emma from King Cnut, and was given by him to Christ Church (S 1229 (*Charters*, ed. Robertson, no. 96), cited above, p. [xxviii]); the estate at Britwell (Prior) was perhaps Emma's own gift to the community, made on a later occasion (S 1638, on which see below).

[5] 'et Imma regina que dedit ecclesie Christi Niwentun et Brutewelle, et duo dorsalia de pallio, et duas cappas cum tassellis aureis, et calicem cum patena in quibus fuerunt tredecim marce de puro auro' (BL Royal 7. E. VI, fol. 14v (8 March)). The record of this gift probably derives from an obituary maintained at Christ Church, Canterbury, in the eleventh century, represented by the surviving fragments of a late eleventh-century obituary (e.g. in BL Cotton Nero C. ix, fols. 19–21) which cover August–December. The information was copied, apparently from the lost obituary, into the 'Old Martrology' of the Christ Church community (BL Royal 7. E. VI), and made its way thence into later manifestations of the commemorative liturgy at Christ Church (BL Cotton Galba E. iii, fol. 32r; BL Cotton Nero C. ix, fol. 7r; BL Arundel 68, fol. 19rv); see '*Liber Vitae*' of the New Minster, ed. Keynes, p. 60 n. 91, and cf. Fleming, 'Christ Church Canterbury's Anglo-Norman Cartulary', p. 92 n. 49. A record of the same grant (registered as S 1638) was included in the (lost) Anglo-Norman cartulary of Christ Church, probably based in this instance on the information in the obituary, and (for no good reason) dated '997'; see Fleming, 'Christ Church Canterbury's Anglo-Norman Cartulary', pp. 92 and 137 (P 56).

[6] Heslop, 'The Production of de luxe Manuscripts', p. 184; *Charters of St Augustine's, Canterbury*, ed. Kelly, p. xx.

Island, Hants., assigning five hides to the monks and five hides to Wulfweard White (with reversion to the Old Minster); though after Emma's death Wulfweard managed to extend his life-interest over the whole estate.[1] She is also said to have given the Old Minster an estate at Wargrave, in Berkshire.[2] More generally, she was remembered at the Old Minster as the donor of 'many ornaments in gold and silver, in gems and precious textiles', along with land at Westwood (Wilts.) and Pitminster (Somerset); also, as the donor of nine estates, one for each of the hot ploughshares she walked over when proving her innocence of allegations of impropriety with Ælfwine, bishop of Winchester (1032–47); and as the former owner of the great cross decorated with images of Mary and John, which Bishop Stigand gave to the church.[3] She was remembered at the New Minster as the donor of land at Piddletrenthide (Dorset), and, perhaps more particularly, as the donor of an elaborate reliquary of Byzantine workmanship, containing the head of St Valentine.[4] Some of the gifts to the Winchester houses were made specifically for the soul of King Harthacnut; and one can imagine that as the years passed at Winchester, Emma looked back to Harthacnut's reign as the culmination of her own political career.

Queen Emma died on 7 March 1052, and was buried alongside her second husband in the Old Minster at Winchester.[5] She was, in a sense, the organising

---

[1] S 1476 (*Charters*, ed. Robertson, no. 114), drawn up in the period 1053 x 1057, probably soon after Earl Harold's succession to his father's earldom in April 1053. Campbell (*Encomium Emmae*, p. xlviii) is in this instance unnecessarily sceptical. By 1066 the estate seems to have been held by Wulfweard from Queen Edith, *in alodium*, and by 1086 it belonged to St Peter's abbey, Jumièges (GDB 43v (*DB Hants.* 10.1)). In 1086 the monks of the Old Minster claimed, not untruthfully, that Queen Emma had given half of the estate to the monks and half to Wulfweard, with reversion to the Old Minster, but it seems that they forgot to mention the modification of the terms of her bequest, represented by S 1476. The story later arose that Hayling was one of a number of estates given by Emma to the Old Minster after she had cleared herself, by ordeal, of the charge that she had had an affair with Ælfwine, bishop of Winchester (1032–47); see further below, n. 3.

[2] S 1062 (*Charters*, ed. Robertson, no. 118), though not authentic in this form.

[3] Richard of Devizes, 'Annals of Winchester' (Cambridge, Corpus Christi College, MS 339), printed in *Annales Monastici* II, ed. H. R. Luard, Rolls Series (London, 1865), pp. 18 and 20–5. For the authorship and date of the 'Annals of Winchester', see Gransden, *Historical Writing*, p. 252. For the gift of Pitminster, see above, p. [lxxiii] n. 8. For the tale of the ploughshares, see Freeman, *Norman Conquest*, II (2nd edn). 569–71; see also Crook, 'The Movement of King Cnut's Bones', pp. 181–2, and Stafford, *Queen Emma and Queen Edith*, p. 250.

[4] See *'Liber Vitae' of the New Minster*, ed. Keynes, pp. 40–1 and 105–6.

[5] ASC, MS C, s.a. 1051 ('14' March), and MS D, s.a. 1052 ('6' March). For the day of her death, see Keynes, 'The Crowland Psalter', p. 369 n. 33. On the fate of Emma's bones at Winchester, see Crook, 'The Movement of King Cnut's Bones', pp. 171, 181, 183, 188–9 and 190. It was perhaps Ælfwine, abbot of the New Minster (1031–57), who ensured that she was duly commemorated in the calendar in his prayerbook (7 March: 'Imma obiit regina'); her obit was also commemorated at the New Minster in the calendar in the Vitellius Psalter (7 March: 'Emma regina'). For 'Ælfwine's Prayerbook' (BL Cotton Titus D. xxvi–xxvii), see *Ælfwine's Prayerbook*, ed. Günzel, and *'Liber Vitae' of the New Minster*, ed.

principle of English politics in the first half of the eleventh century: everything that turned touched her, and she turned everything she touched. Godfrey of Cambrai, prior of Winchester (1082–1107), celebrated her virtues in one of his epigrams on the great and the good of his age;[1] and Henry of Huntingdon acclaimed her as 'Emma, jewel of the Normans (*Emma Normannorum gemma*)',[2] describing her more prosaically as 'the wife of kings and the mother of kings (*uxor regum et mater regum*)'.[3] Her career had spanned a period of exactly fifty years; and if she was not in her dotage the power she had once been in her prime, she had enjoyed far more of her time in the cultivated garden of English politics than she ever endured in the wilderness. Through her the English were brought into political relationship with a nascent power across the channel; through her a Danish conqueror sought in one way or another to secure his own rule; through her the English were drawn after Cnut's death into a period of high political drama; and through her Edward the Confessor found his way back from Normandy to England, albeit with a grudge and a debt. The interest of Emma's story lies in the way she developed her political strength in her role as a queen, and then sought to extend and to take advantage of that strength in her role as a mother; and just as we may try to form an impression of her relationship with each of her husbands, so too may we try to judge her feelings towards her sons Edward, Alfred, and Harthacnut. The historian can then make up for his impertinence by giving due consideration to the weightier matters which are properly his business. In the first half of the twelfth century Emma's marriage to King Æthelred the Unready was already regarded as the fateful beginning of a sequence of events that led inexorably to the Norman Conquest.[4] Of course it was not the case that the marriage had given Duke William any formal right of succession to the English throne, through his great-aunt. Rather, the marriage gave rise to circumstances which took Emma's sons Edward and Alfred to Normandy in 1016; which led the young Alfred to his death, twenty years later, in a manner which shocked all parties to the core; and which gave Edward cause to be grateful for Norman

---

Keynes, pp. 68–9 and 111–23; for the 'Vitellius Psalter' (BL Cotton Vitellius E. xviii), see Pulsiano, *Psalters 1: Descriptions*, pp. 50–6, and '*Liber Vitae*' *of the New Minster*, ed. Keynes, pp. 67–8 and 114–15. Emma ('Ymma regina') was commemorated at Ely as one who had entered into confraternity with the abbey through her benefactions (Cambridge, Trinity College, MS O. 2. 1, fol. K3v (7 March); Gerchow, *Die Gedenküberlieferung der Angelsachsen*, p. 345). For her commemoration at Christ Church, Canterbury, see above, p. [lxxvii] n. 5.

[1] *The Anglo-Latin Satirical Poets and Epigrammatists of the Twelfth Century*, ed. T. Wright, 2 vols., Rolls ser. (London, 1872) i.xvi–xvii, and ii.148; see also *Encomium Emmae*, ed. Campbell, p. xlvii n. 3, and Stafford, *Queen Emma and Queen Edith*, pp. 26–7 and 253.

[2] HH, *HA* vi.2 (ed. Greenway, p. 340).   [3] HH, *HA* vi.22 (ed. Greenway, p. 376).

[4] William of Malmesbury, *Vita S. Dunstani*, ch. 34 (*Memorials of Saint Dunstan*, ed. W. Stubbs (London, 1874), p. 322); HH, *HA* vi.1 (ed. Greenway, p. 338, with the editor's note); OV, *HE* xi.38 (ed. Chibnall, vi.168). For a modern restatement of the same view, see Freeman, *Norman Conquest*, i.301–2.

recognition and support. In 1041, after twenty-five years in exile, Edward returned to his homeland; after a while he began to advance the interests of his Norman friends and associates, and, in a heady moment of political freedom in 1051, he entered into an understanding with Duke William which appears to have had something to do with the succession.[1] It so happened that whatever transpired in that year was overtaken in England by the restoration of Earl Godwine and his family, in 1052; but the view of events was different from Normandy, and Edward's promise to Duke William was one which the Normans would have been neither minded nor likely to forget.

---

[1] 'Then forthwith Count William came from overseas with a great force of Frenchmen, and the king received him and as many of his companions as suited him, and let him go again' (ASC, MS D, s.a. 1051 (ed. Cubbin, p. 71); cf. Keynes, 'The Æthelings in Normandy', p. 200 n. 128). It is a pleasant thought that William may have come in order to see his great-aunt Emma, in what would prove to be the closing months of her life; see Barlow, *Edward the Confessor*, pp. 116–17, and Stafford, *Queen Emma and Queen Edith*, pp. 253–4. It is, however, the thrust of the unfolding course of events which commends the view that he came in order to be apprised of his political prospects.

ABBREVIATIONS AND BIBLIOGRAPHY

Primary sources are cited by means of the abbreviations listed below; full references are given in the bibliography. Other items cited in the introduction are either given in full on the first occasion and in an abbreviated form on a subsequent occasion, or given in an abbreviated form throughout and in full in the bibliography. The bibliography serves in its own right as a list of publications which have appeared since 1950 and which bear in one way or another on the *Encomium Emmae* and its historical context.

ABBREVIATIONS

AB, *GHEP*	Adam of Bremen, *Gesta Hammaburgensis ecclesiae pontificum* (ed. Trillmich, transl. Tschan)
ASC	Anglo-Saxon Chronicle, MSS A–G (transl. Whitelock)
BL	London, British Library
DB	*Domesday Book* (ed. Morris)
Dudo, *GN*	Dudo of Saint-Quentin, *Gesta Normannorum* (ed. Lair)
EER	*Encomium Emmae reginae* (ed. Campbell)
EHD	*English Historical Documents* (ed. Whitelock)
GDB/LDB	Great Domesday Book / Little Domesday Book
HH, *HA*	Henry of Huntingdon, *Historia Anglorum* (ed. Greenway)
Inventio	*Inventio et miracula sancti Vulfranni* (ed. Laporte)
JW, *Chron.*	John of Worcester, *Chronicon* (ed. Darlington and McGurk)
LE	*Liber Eliensis* (ed. Blake)
OV, *HE*	Orderic Vitalis, *Historia ecclesiastica* (ed. Chibnall)
RG, *Hist.*	Rodulfus Glaber, *Historiarum libri quinque* (ed. France)
RRAN	*Regesta Regum Anglo-Normannorum*, I (ed. Davis), with number of charter
S	P. H. Sawyer, *Anglo-Saxon Charters: An Annotated List and Bibliography* (London, 1968), with number of charter
TM, *Chron.*	Thietmar of Merseburg, *Chronicon* (ed. Trillmich)
VÆdR	*Vita Ædwardi regis* (ed. Barlow)
WJ, *GND*	William of Jumièges, *Gesta Normannorum Ducum* (ed. van Houts)
WM, *GP*	William of Malmesbury, *Gesta Pontificum* (ed. Hamilton)
WM, *GR*	William of Malmesbury, *Gesta Regum* (ed. Mynors, *et al.*)
WMp, *DNC*	Walter Map, *De nugis curialium* (ed. James)
WP, *GG*	William of Poitiers, *Gesta Guillelmi ducis Normannorum et regis Anglorum* (ed. Davis and Chibnall)

BIBLIOGRAPHY

Backhouse, J., *et al.*, eds., *The Golden Age of Anglo-Saxon Art 966–1066* (London, 1984)

Barlow, F., 'Two Notes: Cnut's Second Pilgrimage and Queen Emma's Disgrace in 1043',

English Historical Review 73 (1958), pp. 649–56, repr. in (and cited from) his *The Norman Conquest and Beyond* (London, 1983), pp. 49–56

Edward the Confessor (London, 1970), new edn, with bibliographical addenda (New Haven and London, 1997)

Barlow, F., ed., *The Life of King Edward who Rests at Westminster, Attributed to a Monk of Saint-Bertin*, 2nd edn (Oxford, 1992)

Bates, D., *Normandy before 1066* (London, 1982)

Beech, G., 'England and Aquitaine in the Century before the Norman Conquest', *Anglo-Saxon England* 19 (1990), pp. 81–101

Biddle, M., ed., *Winchester in the Early Middle Ages: An Edition and Discussion of the Winton Domesday*, Winchester Studies 1 (Oxford, 1976)

Blake, E. O., ed., *Liber Eliensis*, Camden 3rd ser. 92 (London, 1962)

Blake, N. F., *The Saga of the Jomsvikings* (London, 1962)

Brooke, C. N. L., 'Historical Writing in England between 850 and 1150', *La Storiografia altomedievale*, 2 vols., Settimane di studio del Centro italiano di studi sull'alto medioevo 17 (Spoleto, 1970), pp. 223–47 and 259–60

Brown, M. P., *Anglo-Saxon Manuscripts* (London, 1991)

Campbell, A., 'Knúts Saga', *Saga-Book of the Viking Society for Northern Research* 13 (1946–53), pp. 238–48

Campbell, J., 'England, France, Flanders and Germany in the Reign of Ethelred II: Some Comparisons and Connections', *Ethelred the Unready*, ed. D. Hill (Oxford, 1978), pp. 255–70, repr. in (and cited from) J. Campbell, *Essays in Anglo-Saxon History* (London, 1986), pp. 191–207

'The Late Anglo-Saxon State: A Maximum View', *Proceedings of the British Academy* 87 (1994), pp. 39–65

Campbell, M. W., 'Queen Emma and Ælfgifu of Northampton: Canute the Great's Women', *Mediaeval Scandinavia* 4 (1971), pp. 66–79

'Emma, reine d'Angleterre: mère dénaturée ou femme vindicative?', *Annales de Normandie* 23 (1973), pp. 99–114

'The *Encomium Emmae Reginae*: Personal Panegyric or Political Propaganda?', *Annuale Mediaevale* 19 (1979), pp. 27–45

Chibnall, M., ed., *The Ecclesiastical History of Orderic Vitalis*, 6 vols. (Oxford, 1968–80)

Clarke, P. A., *The English Nobility under Edward the Confessor* (Oxford, 1994)

Conner, P. W., ed., *The Abingdon Chronicle, A.D. 956–1066 (MS. C, with reference to BDE)*, The Anglo-Saxon Chronicle: A Collaborative Edition 10 (Cambridge, 1996)

Crook, J., '"A Worthy Antiquity": The Movement of King Cnut's Bones in Winchester Cathedral', *The Reign of Cnut, King of England, Denmark and Norway*, ed. A. R. Rumble (London, 1994), pp. 165–92

Cross, J. E., ed., *Two Old English Apocrypha and their Manuscript Source: 'The Gospel of Nichodemus' and 'The Avenging of the Saviour'*, Cambridge Studies in Anglo-Saxon England 19 (Cambridge, 1996)

Cubbin, G. P., ed., *MS. D*, The Anglo-Saxon Chronicle: A Collaborative Edition 6 (Cambridge, 1996)

Darlington, R. R., and P. McGurk, ed., *The Chronicle of John of Worcester*, II: *The Annals from 450 to 1066* (Oxford, 1995)

INTRODUCTION TO THE 1998 REPRINT

Davis, H. W. C., ed., *Regesta Regum Anglo-Normannorum 1066–1154*, I: *Regesta Willelmi Conquestoris et Willelmi Rufi 1066–1100* (Oxford, 1913)

Davis†, R. H. C., and M. Chibnall, eds., *The Gesta Guillelmi of William of Poitiers* (Oxford, 1998)

Demidoff, L., 'The Death of Sven Forkbeard – in Reality and Later Tradition', *Medieval Scandinavia* 11 (1978–9), pp. 30–47

Derville, A., *et al.*, *Histoire de Saint-Omer* (Lille, 1981)

Dumville, D., and M. Lapidge, eds., *The Annals of St Neots with Vita Prima Sancti Neoti*, The Anglo-Saxon Chronicle: A Collaborative Edition 17 (Cambridge, 1985)

Fell, C., 'Víkingarvísur', *Speculum Norroenum: Norse Studies in Memory of Gabriel Turville-Petre*, ed. U. Dronke, *et al.* (Odense, 1981), pp. 106–22

Fleming, R., 'Christ Church Canterbury's Anglo-Norman Cartulary', *Anglo-Norman Political Culture and the Twelfth-Century Renaissance: Proceedings of the Borchard Conference on Anglo-Norman History, 1995*, ed. C. W. Hollister (Woodbridge, 1997), pp. 83–155

Fletcher, R., *Who's Who in Roman Britain and Anglo-Saxon England* (London, 1989)

France, J., ed., *Rodulfi Glabri Historiarum Libri Quinque / Rodulfus Glaber: 'The Five Books of the Histories'* (Oxford, 1989)

Frank, R., 'Cnut in the Verse of his Skalds', *The Reign of Cnut, King of England, Denmark and Norway*, ed. A. R. Rumble (London, 1994), pp. 106–24

Gameson, R., 'The Gospels of Margaret of Scotland and the Literacy of an Eleventh-Century Queen', *Women and the Book: Assessing the Visual Evidence*, ed. J. Taylor and L. Smith (London, 1997), pp. 149–71

Gameson, R., ed., *The Study of the Bayeux Tapestry* (Woodbridge, 1997)

Gem, R., ed., *English Heritage Book of St Augustine's Abbey Canterbury* (London, 1997)

Gerchow, J., *Die Gedenküberlieferung der Angelsachsen, mit einem Katalog der libri vitae und Necrologien*, Arbeiten zur Frühmittelalterforschung 20 (Berlin, 1988)

'Prayers for King Cnut: The Liturgical Commemoration of a Conqueror', *England in the Eleventh Century: Proceedings of the 1990 Harlaxton Symposium*, ed. C. Hicks (Stamford, 1992), pp. 219–38

Gransden, A., *Historical Writing in England*, I: *c. 550–1307* (London, 1974)

Greenway, D., ed., *Henry, Archdeacon of Huntingdon: 'Historia Anglorum' / The History of the English People* (Oxford, 1996)

Günzel, B., ed., *Ælfwine's Prayerbook (London, British Library, Cotton Titus D. xxvi + xxvii)*, Henry Bradshaw Society 108 (London, 1993)

Gysseling, M., and A. C. F. Koch, eds., *Diplomata Belgica ante Annum Millesimum Centesimum Scripta*, 2 pts, Bouwstoffen en Studiën voor de Geschiedenis en de Lexicografie van het Nederlands 1 (Brussels, 1950)

Halldórsson, Ó., ed., *Jómsvíkinga Saga* (Reykjavík, 1969)

Halpin, P. A., 'Anglo-Saxon Women and Pilgrimage', *Anglo-Norman Studies* 19 (1997), pp. 97–122

Hamilton, N. E. S. A., ed., *Willelmi Malmesbiriensis Monachi De Gestis Pontificum Anglorum Libri Quinque*, Rolls Series (London, 1870)

Harmer, F. E., *Anglo-Saxon Writs* (Manchester, 1952)

Hart, C., 'The East Anglian Chronicle', *Journal of Medieval History* 7 (1981), pp. 249–82

'The Early Section of the *Worcester Chronicle*', *Journal of Medieval History* 9 (1983), pp. 251–315

Heslop, T. A., 'The Production of *de luxe* Manuscripts and the Patronage of King Cnut and Queen Emma', *Anglo-Saxon England* 19 (1990), pp. 151–95

Hooper, N., 'Military Developments in the Reign of Cnut', *The Reign of Cnut, King of England, Denmark and Norway*, ed. A. R. Rumble (London, 1994), pp. 89–100

van Houts, E. M. C., 'The Political Relations between Normandy and England before 1066 according to the "Gesta Normannorum ducum"', *Les mutations socio-culturelles au tournant des xie–xiie siècles*, Actes du IVe Colloque international Anselmien, ed. R. Foreville and C. Viola (Paris, 1984), pp. 85–97

'Historiography and Hagiography at Saint-Wandrille: The "Inventio et Miracula Sancti Vulfranni"', *Anglo-Norman Studies* 12 (1990), pp. 233–51

'A Note on *Jezebel* and *Semiramis*, Two Latin Norman Poems from the Early Eleventh Century', *Journal of Medieval Latin* 2 (1992), pp. 18–24

'Camden, Cotton and the Chronicles of the Norman Conquest of England', *British Library Journal* 18.2 (1992), pp. 148–62, repr. in *Sir Robert Cotton as Collector*, ed. C. J. Wright (London, 1997), pp. 238–52

van Houts, E. M. C., ed., *The Gesta Normannorum Ducum of William of Jumièges, Orderic Vitalis, and Robert of Torigni*, 2 vols. (Oxford, 1992–5)

Hudson, B. T., 'Cnut and the Scottish Kings', *English Historical Review* 107 (1992), pp. 350–60

Insley, J., 'Some Scandinavian Personal Names from South-West England', *Namn och Bygd* 70 (1982), pp. 77–93

'Some Scandinavian Personal Names from South-West England from Post-Conquest Records', *Studia Anthroponymica Scandinavica* 3 (1985), pp. 23–58

James, M. R., ed., *Walter Map: De Nugis Curialium / Courtiers' Trifles*, revised by C. N. L. Brooke and R. A. B. Mynors (Oxford, 1983)

John, E., 'The *Encomium Emmae Reginae*: A Riddle and a Solution', *Bulletin of the John Rylands Library* 63 (1980), pp. 58–94

'The Return of the Vikings' and 'The End of Anglo-Saxon England', *The Anglo-Saxons*, ed. J. Campbell (Oxford, 1982), pp. 192–213 and 214–39

Reassessing Anglo-Saxon England (Manchester, 1996)

Kelly, S. E., ed., *Charters of St Augustine's Abbey, Canterbury, and Minster-in-Thanet*, Anglo-Saxon Charters 4 (Oxford, 1995)

Keynes, S., 'The Declining Reputation of King Æthelred the Unready', *Ethelred the Unready: Papers from the Millenary Conference*, ed. D. Hill, British Archaeological Reports, British Series 59 (Oxford, 1978), pp. 227–53

The Diplomas of King Æthelred 'the Unready' 978–1016: A Study in their Use as Historical Evidence (Cambridge, 1980)

'The Crowland Psalter and the Sons of King Edmund Ironside', *Bodleian Library Record* 11.6 (1985), pp. 359–70

'A Tale of Two Kings: Alfred the Great and Æthelred the Unready', *Transactions of the Royal Historical Society* 5th ser. 36 (1986), pp. 195–217

'The Historical Context of the Battle of Maldon', *The Battle of Maldon AD 991*, ed. D. Scragg (Oxford, 1991), pp. 81–113

'The Æthelings in Normandy', *Anglo-Norman Studies* 13 (1991), pp. 173–205

'Cnut's Earls', *The Reign of Cnut, King of England, Denmark and Norway*, ed. A. R. Rumble (London, 1994), pp. 43–88

INTRODUCTION TO THE 1998 REPRINT

'Giso, Bishop of Wells (1061–88)', *Anglo-Norman Studies* 19 (1997), pp. 203–71

'The Vikings in England c. 790–1016', *The Oxford Illustrated History of the Vikings*, ed. P. Sawyer (Oxford, 1997), pp. 48–82

An Atlas of Attestations in Anglo-Saxon Charters, c. 680–1066, University of Cambridge, Department of Anglo-Saxon, Norse, and Celtic (1993), publication forthcoming

Keynes, S., ed., *The 'Liber Vitae' of the New Minster and Hyde Abbey, Winchester*, Early English Manuscripts in Facsimile 26 (Copenhagen, 1996)

Körner, S., *The Battle of Hastings, England and Europe 1035–1066*, Bibliotheca Historica Lundensis 14 (Lund, 1964)

Lair, J., ed., *De moribus et actis primorum Normanniae ducum auctore Dudone Sancti Quintini decano*, Mémoires de la Société des Antiquaires de Normandie 23 (Paris, 1865)

Laporte, J., ed., *Inventio et miracula sancti Vulfranni*, Mélanges publiés par la Société de l'Histoire de Normandie, 14th ser. (Rouen, 1938)

Lawrence, A., 'Anglo-Norman Book Production', *England and Normandy in the Middle Ages*, ed. D. Bates and A. Curry (London, 1994), pp. 79–93

Lawson, M. K., *Cnut: The Danes in England in the Early Eleventh Century* (London, 1993)

Lifshitz, F., 'The *Encomium Emmae Reginae*: A "Political Pamphlet" of the Eleventh Century?', *Haskins Society Journal* 1 (1989), pp. 39–50

Lindqvist, O., 'Encomium Emmae', *Scandia* 33 (1967), pp. 175–81 (with English summary)

Lund, N., 'The Armies of Swein Forkbeard and Cnut: *leding* or *lið*?', *Anglo-Saxon England* 15 (1986), pp. 105–18

'Danish Military Organisation', *The Battle of Maldon: Fiction and Fact*, ed. J. Cooper (London, 1993), pp. 109–26

'Cnut's Danish Kingdom', *The Reign of Cnut, King of England, Denmark and Norway*, ed. A. R. Rumble (London, 1994), pp. 27–42

Lið, Leding og Landeværn: Her og samfund i Danmark i ældre middelalder (Roskilde, 1996) (with English summary, pp. 291–301)

McGurk, P., and J. Rosenthal, 'The Anglo-Saxon Gospelbooks of Judith, Countess of Flanders: Their Text, Make-Up and Function', *Anglo-Saxon England* 24 (1995), pp. 251–308

Meyer, M. A., 'The Queen's "Demesne" in Later Anglo-Saxon England', *The Culture of Christendom: Essays in Medieval History in Commemoration of Denis L. T. Bethell*, ed. M. A. Meyer (London, 1993), pp. 75–113

Morris, J., ed., *Domesday Book*, 35 vols. (Chichester, 1975–86) (cited by county abbreviation)

Musset, L., (review of *Encomium Emmae*, ed. Campbell), *Annales de Normandie* 2 (1952), pp. 86–8

Mynors†, R. A. B., R. M. Thomson, and M. Winterbottom, eds., *William of Malmesbury: Gesta Regum Anglorum | The History of the English Kings*, I: *Text & Translation* (Oxford, 1998)

Neuman de Vegvar, C., 'A Paean for a Queen: The Frontispiece to the "Encomium Emmae Reginae"', *Old English Newsletter* 26.1 (1992), pp. 56–8

Nicholas, D., *Medieval Flanders* (London, 1992)

Oursel, H., C. Deremble, and J. Thiébant, *Nord roman: Flandre, Artois, Picardie, Laonnois*, La nuit des temps 82 (Pierre-qui-Vire, 1994)

Pálsson, H., and P. Edwards, *Knytlinga Saga: The History of the Kings of Denmark* (Odense, 1986)

Poole, R. G., 'Skaldic Verse and Anglo-Saxon History: Some Aspects of the Period 1009–1016', *Speculum* 62.2 (1987), pp. 265–98

Viking Poems on War and Peace: A Study in Skaldic Narrative, Toronto Medieval Texts and Translations 8 (Toronto, 1991)

Pulsiano, P., *Anglo-Saxon Manuscripts in Microfiche Facsimile 2: Psalters 1: Descriptions*, Medieval and Renaissance Texts and Studies 137 (Binghamton, NY, 1994)

Pulsiano, P., ed., *Medieval Scandinavia: An Encyclopedia* (New York, 1993)

Robertson, A. J., ed., *Anglo-Saxon Charters*, 2nd edn (Cambridge, 1956)

Roesdahl, E., *et al.*, eds., *The Vikings in England and in their Danish Homeland* (London, 1981)

Rollason, D. W., 'Goscelin of Canterbury's Account of the Translation and Miracles of St. Mildrith *(BHL 5961/4)*: An Edition with Notes', *Mediaeval Studies* 48 (1986), pp. 139–210

Rumble, A. R., ed., 'Textual Appendix: *Translatio Sancti Ælfegi Cantuariensis archiepiscopi et martyris (BHL 2519)*: Osbern's Account of the Translation of St Ælfheah's Relics from London to Canterbury, 8–11 June 1023', *The Reign of Cnut, King of England, Denmark and Norway*, ed. A. R. Rumble (London, 1994), pp. 283–315

Sawyer, P., 'Swein Forkbeard and the Historians', *Church and Chronicle in the Middle Ages*, ed. I. Wood and G. A. Loud (London, 1991), pp. 27–40

Searle, E., *Predatory Kinship and the Creation of Norman Power, 840–1066* (Berkeley, CA, 1988)

'Emma the Conqueror', *Studies in Medieval History Presented to R. Allen Brown*, ed. C. Harper-Bill, *et al.* (Woodbridge, 1989), pp. 281–8

Sharpe, R., 'The Date of St. Mildreth's Translation from Minster-in-Thanet to Canterbury', *Mediaeval Studies* 53 (1991), pp. 349–54

Smart, V. J., 'Moneyers of the Late Anglo-Saxon Coinage 973–1016', *Commentationes de nummis saeculorum IX–XI in Suecia repertis*, II (Stockholm, 1968), pp. 193–276

'Moneyers of the Late Anglo-Saxon Coinage: The Danish Dynasty', *Anglo-Saxon England* 16 (1987), pp. 233–308

Smith, M. F., 'Archbishop Stigand and the Eye of the Needle', *Anglo-Norman Studies* 16 (1994), pp. 199–219

Smyth, A., *Alfred the Great* (Oxford, 1995)

Southern, R. W., 'Aspects of the European Tradition of Historical Writing 1: The Classical Tradition from Einhard to Geoffrey of Monmouth', *Transactions of the Royal Historical Society* 5th ser. 20 (1970), pp. 173–96

Stafford, P., *Queens, Concubines and Dowagers: The King's Wife in the Early Middle Ages* (London, 1983)

Unification and Conquest: A Political and Social History of England in the Tenth and Eleventh Centuries (London, 1989)

'The Portrayal of Royal Women in England, Mid-Tenth to Mid-Twelfth Centuries', *Medieval Queenship*, ed. J. C. Parsons (New York, 1993; Stroud, 1994), pp. 143–67

'Emma: The Powers of the Queen in the Eleventh Century', *Queens and Queenship in Medieval Europe: Proceedings of a Conference Held at King's College London April 1995*, ed. A. Duggan (Woodbridge, 1997), pp. 3–26

Queen Emma and Queen Edith: Queenship and Women's Power in Eleventh-Century England (Oxford, 1997)

Talvio, T., 'Harold I and Harthacnut's *Jewel Cross* Type Reconsidered', *Anglo-Saxon Monetary History: Essays in Memory of Michael Dolley*, ed. M. A. S. Blackburn (Leicester, 1986), pp. 273–90

Royal Coin Cabinet, Stockholm, IV: Anglo-Saxon Coins: Harold I and Harthacnut, 1035–1042, Sylloge of Coins of the British Isles 40 (Oxford, 1991)

Thomson, R. M., ed., *William of Malmesbury: Gesta Regum Anglorum / The History of the English Kings, II: Commentary* (Oxford, forthcoming)

Townend, M., '*Assandun* and *Assantun*: The Value of Skaldic Evidence for English Place-Name Studies', *Journal of the English Place-Name Society* 27 (1995), pp. 21–9

Trillmich, W., ed., *Thietmar von Merseburg: Chronik*, Ausgewählte Quellen zur deutschen Geschichte des Mittelalters 9 (Darmstadt, 1957)

Quellen des 9. und 11. Jahrhunderts zur Geschichte der Hamburgischen Kirche und des Reiches, Ausgewählte Quellen zur deutschen Geschichte des Mittelalters 11 (Darmstadt, 1961)

Tschan, F. J., *Adam of Bremen: History of the Archbishops of Hamburg-Bremen* (New York, 1959)

Verdon, J., ed., *La Chronique de Saint-Maixent 751–1140*, Les Classiques de l'histoire de France au moyen âge (Paris, 1979)

Walker, I. W., *Harold: The Last Anglo-Saxon King* (Stroud, 1997)

Whitelock, D., ed., *Anglo-Saxon Wills* (Cambridge, 1930)

English Historical Documents c. 500–1042, 2nd edn (London, 1979)

Whitelock, D., with D. C. Douglas and S. I. Tucker, eds., *The Anglo-Saxon Chronicle: A Revised Translation* (London, 1961)

Whitelock, D., M. Brett, and C. N. L. Brooke, eds., *Councils & Synods with Other Documents Relating to the English Church, I: A.D. 871–1204, Part I: 871–1066* (Oxford, 1981)

Williams, A., '"Cockles amongst the Wheat": Danes and English in the Western Midlands in the First Half of the Eleventh Century', *Midland History* 11 (1986), pp. 1–22

Yorke, B., *Wessex in the Early Middle Ages*, Studies in the Early History of Britain (London, 1995)

PREFACE

A new edition of the *Encomium Emmae Reginae* calls for no excuse, for it has not been separately edited before, its language has not been previously studied, and the only earlier historical commentary upon it is that contained in the obsolete annotations of Langebek (1773). This is a remarkable state of affairs, for the importance of the text is shown by the number of allusions to it which occur in the pages of all writers on the English and Scandinavian history of the eleventh century.

The Text and Textual Notes of the present edition have been prepared from the manuscripts and from photostatic reproductions of them. They will be found more accurate even than those in the edition of Gertz, which suffer slightly because the editor had not MS. L or a reproduction of it before him but worked from a collation previously made in London. At the request of the Royal Historical Society I have added a translation : this should be used only in conjunction with the Linguistic Notes, where alternative renderings of many passages will be found.

In the historical sections of the Introduction and in the Appendices, I have attempted to give an orderly presentment of everything that can be learned from the sources, English, Welsh, Scandinavian and continental, concerning Queen Emma and her Encomiast, and about the Scandinavian supporters of Knútr, whose deeds bulk so large in the *Encomium*. The historical content of the *Encomium* is carefully considered, every statement being severely tested, and a general estimate of its historical value, based upon this detailed examination, is offered. The place of the work in eleventh-century historiography is also indicated.

In § C of the Introduction, and in the Linguistic Notes and Glossary, I have attempted to make an adequate study of the Encomiast's language, to show its relationship to the Latin in general use in its period, and to estimate the degree to which it is ornamented with elements from classical writers. The Encomiast's spelling of proper names is discussed in the light of Old English and Old Norse phonology, and of what little is known of the ancient language of Flanders.

I have not considered an edition of a single text a suitable place for a detailed bibliography concerning either the history of the Danish conquest of England or the latinity of the Encomiast's period. I wish, however, to direct the attention of those who use Scandinavian sources for the history of the eleventh century to Bjarni Aðalbjarnarson's excellent work *Om de norske kongers sagaer* (Oslo, 1937) and to the enduring value of Sigurður Nordal's *Om Olaf den helliges saga* (Copenhagen, 1914).

Place-names are used in current modern forms. Old English personal names are spelt as in contemporary documents, while for Scandinavian ones normalised Old Norse spelling is used, but in both cases *th* is substituted for þ and ð. No attempt is made to give the names of persons, who happen to be mentioned in Latin documents only, in vernacular form.

I am particularly grateful to Mr. G. Turville-Petre for much advice on Scandinavian matters, and for the valuable Additional Notes in Appendix V, which are due entirely to him. Mr. Francis Wormald has been kind enough to examine a reproduc-

v

tion of the illumination on fo. IV of L, and informs me that he does not consider that it is possible to decide whether the artist intended to depict the Encomiast as a monk or as a secular cleric, though the former appears the more likely (cf. p. xix, n. 3). I wish also to express my thanks to the Royal Historical Society for accepting for publication an edition with considerably more commentary than they normally allow.

ABBREVIATIONS AND METHODS OF REFERENCE

Names of classical and early medieval writers and works and of books of the Vulgate are generally given in the abbreviated forms used in the *Latin Dictionary* of Lewis and Short, though slightly fuller forms are occasionally employed.

If no edition is specified, medieval historians and biographers are quoted by the divisions of the text in the *Monumenta Germaniae Historica*.

The Old Norse Sagas are quoted by the chapter divisions of the standard editions, except *Fagrskinna*, which is quoted by the pages of Finnur Jónsson's edition (Copenhagen, 1902–3).

The following abbreviations are freely used :

B.	Birch, W. de G., *Cartularium Saxonicum*.
Baxter. . . .	Baxter, J. H., and Johnson, C., *Medieval Latin Word-list* (Oxford, 1934).
Earle	Earle, J., *A Hand-Book to the Land-Charters, and other Saxonic Documents*.
Gertz	Gertz, M. Cl., *Scriptores minores historiæ Danicæ medii ævi* (Copenhagen, 1917–20).
Gertz, Trans.. .	Gertz, M. Cl., *Kong Knuts liv og gerninger eller aereskrift for dronning Emma oversat af* (Copenhagen, 1896).
K.	Kemble, J. M., *Codex diplomaticus aevi Saxonici*.
M.G.H.S. . . .	*Monumenta Germaniae Historica ; Scriptores*.
N.C.	Freeman, E. A., *The History of the Norman Conquest of England* (Vols. I and II are quoted by the pagination of the third edition).
N.E.D. . . .	*New English Dictionary*.
Patrologia . .	Migne, J. P., *Patrologia Latina*.
R.	Robertson, A. J., *Anglo-Saxon Charters*.
Skjaldedigtning .	Jónsson, Finnur, *Den Norsk-Islandske Skjaldedigtning*.
Stenton . . .	Stenton, F. M., *Anglo-Saxon England*.
Stolz-Schmalz .	Leumann, M., and Hofmann, J. B., *Lateinische Grammatik* (Munich, 1928 ; = Stolz-Schmalz, fifth edition).
Storm	Storm, G., *Monumenta Historica Norvegiæ*.
Thes.	*Thesaurus Linguae Latinae*.
Thorpe . . .	Thorpe, B., *Diplomatarium Anglicum ævi Saxonici*.
W.	Whitelock, D., *Anglo-Saxon Wills*.

INTRODUCTION

A. *Manuscripts and Editions*

The following are the existing manuscripts of the *Encomium Emmae Reginae* [1]; the prefixed capitals are the sigla by which reference is made to them in the present work:

L. British Museum, Additional 33241.
V. National Library of Wales, Hengwrt 158 (= Peniarth 281).
B. British Museum, Additional 6920.
P. Bibliothèque Nationale, Fonds Lat. 6235.

L is a manuscript of the mid-eleventh century, consisting of 67 vellum leaves (17·5 × 11 cm.). On fo. 1r a late medieval hand has written *Gesta Cnutonis Ri*, and, on the same line, a press-mark of the library of St. Augustine's, Canterbury. [2] Below this, the same hand has written ' Lib. sci. aug. Cant '. On fo. 1v there is an illumination, tinted in blue, green and red. It depicts a queen, crowned and enthroned, receiving a book from a kneeling ecclesiastic ; two men are standing beside her. These figures undoubtedly represent Queen Emma, her two sons, Hörthaknútr and Eadweard, and the author of the *Encomium*. The text of the *Encomium* occupies fos. 2r–67r. It will appear below that a leaf has been lost in modern times between fos. 47 and 48. [3] The initial *S* at the beginning of the text is elaborately ornamented : it extends down before the first six lines, which are written in large letters, and contain only the opening fourteen words, ' Salus . . . sexu '. Ornamented initials are used to begin all three books, and occasionally to begin paragraphs. Although the writing is similar throughout the manuscript, a slight change in its character occurs on fo. 41r, with the words *Qui licet deuictus* (II, 10, 23), and, from this point onwards, -*q*. instead of -*q*: is the prevailing contraction for final -*que*. A change of hand must therefore be presumed at this point. From fo. 48r onward the average number of lines on a page is 18 ; since it is only 15 in the preceding part of the manuscript, the British Museum *Catalogue of Additions* [4] assumes that the hand changes on fo. 48r (while not recognising the change on fo. 41r). In this, however, it is probably mistaken. The lower half of fo. 5r containing the beginning of the Argument (' Fortasse . . . facturum. Quod ') is probably in the hand of the scribe of fos. 41–67. The rest of the Argument (fos. 5v–7v) is either in the hand of the scribe of fos. 41–67 or in that of a third scribe : it is not in the prevailing hand of fos. 2–41. In the text only familiar contractions are used. The names of Knútr and Emma are nearly always, and those of other royal persons are frequently, written in uncial letters. In spelling, punctuation, and word-division the manuscript follows the usual practices of. its period. Both scribes frequently correct slight errors made by themselves or inadvertently copied from their exemplar. The word *Geldefordia*, III, 4, 18, seems to be due to a corrector practically contemporary with the original scribes.

Two annotators have been active on L : one is of the late medieval period, the other

---

[1] On this title, see below, p. xviii.
[3] See below, p. xiv.
[4] Vol. for 1882–7, p. 281.

[2] X. *Gra*. III Cn. A.

clearly of the sixteenth century.[1] They make corrections and worthless comments,[2] alter the punctuation and word-division to conform with the habits of their own period, and draw hands in the margins to indicate points of interest. They are also responsible for a marginal drawing of Knútr against the opening words of II, 15, and another of two eyes against the episode of the blinding of Ælfred in III, 6. One of them proposes various emendations, to three of which it will be necessary to make frequent reference below. They are *uiuebat* for *muniebat*, I, 1, 18 ; *remitti* for *remissi*, I, 1, 19 ; insertion of *affectus* after *precordiis*, I, 1, 22. I refer to the work of these two annotators as L'. It is occasionally not possible to decide if a slight correction is due to L' or to the original scribe.

L is clearly not the author's autograph, but a copy made by two scribes, either from that autograph or a very early copy of it.[3] In view of its careful execution and the illustration, it is probable that it is either the copy sent to Queen Emma or a close reproduction of that copy. The illumination of the manuscript appears to belong to a continental centre subject to English influence ; since St. Omer was just such a centre, it is extremely likely that L was written there for presentation to the Queen.

The inscription on fo. 1r mentioned above shows that L was at St. Augustine's, Canterbury, in the later Middle Ages, and it is entered in the fifteenth-century catalogue of the library of that foundation.[4] In 1566 it was copied by Thomas Talbot under circumstances now unknown.[5] In 1819 it was in the library of the tenth Duke of Hamilton, and was described as follows in the *Repertorium Bibliographicum* published at London in that year by William Clarke (pp. 259–60) :

Cnutionis Magni Gesta.—A MS. of great antiquity : it is dedicated to Queen Emma, the widow of Canute, and is supposed to have been written about the year 1030 : prefixed is a drawing of the author presenting his book to the Queen.

This notice attracted the attention of Pertz to the manuscript and led to his visit to Scotland to study it in 1862.[6] Hardy's attention was first drawn to the manuscript by the publication of Pertz's edition. Its existence had escaped him when first dealing with the *Encomium* in his *Descriptive Catalogue* (i. 627 ff.), so he devoted a supplementary entry to it, giving a translation of the Latin preface to Pertz's edition and opposing Pertz's opinion that the *editio princeps* was derived from it (*op. cit.*, iii. 1 ff.). L was also noticed briefly in the *First Report of the Royal Commission on Historical Manuscripts* (p. 114). The manuscript was acquired at the sale of the Hamiltonian library in 1882 by the Royal Library, Berlin.[7] It was bought by the British Museum in 1887, together with other

---

[1] Gertz states that the hand of one of these annotators belongs to the seventeenth or eighteenth century, but this is not possible, as the annotator in question is responsible for the three emendations to be mentioned below, and hence his activity antedates the making of Talbot's copy in 1566 (see below, p. xiii).

[2] Generally these are merely indications of the content of the adjacent part of the text.

[3] It will appear below (p. xvi) that there was probably a copy intermediate between the author's autograph and L, from which L and P are independently derived, and which introduced some errors common to L and P.

[4] See M. R. James, *The Ancient Libraries of Canterbury and Dover*, p. 294. The medieval catalogue gives the title and press-mark in agreement with L, fo. 1r (see above, p. xi, n. 2), and quotes the first word of fo. 2, so it is certain that the book referred to is L.

[5] See below, p. xiii.

[6] See below, p. xvii.

[7] M. Manitius, *Geschichte der lat. Lit. des Mittelalters*, ii. 331, fails to realise the identity of the Berlin and London manuscripts, and also alleges incorrectly that MSS. Cott. Claud. D ii and Harley 746 contain the *Encomium*. (These two manuscripts do actually contain brief texts about Knútr ; see Hardy, *Descriptive Catalogue*, i. 626.)

Hamiltonian manuscripts.[1] The manuscript was briefly described in the *Catalogue of Additions to the Manuscripts in the British Museum in the Years 1882–7* (p. 281).

V is a paper manuscript containing copies of texts, mostly of an historical nature, made by Robert Vaughan (1592–1667), the collector of the Hengwrt MSS. The first item in it (pp. 1–21) is the *Encomium*. This begins without title, and the last words are followed by the note ' Transcriptū et excerptū a vetustissi (*sic*) exemplari manuscripto per Thom. Talbot, an° Dni 1566 '. This note is followed by four trifling verses about Queen Emma said to be ' Ex Chronicis Th. Rudburni '. Vaughan's text of the *Encomium* agrees closely with that of L and even reproduces the three emendations of L' mentioned above,[2] giving the first two in the margin marked *al*, but accepting the third into the text without comment. This use of the late notes written on L would be alone practically sufficient proof that the ultimate source of V is L, and the matter is placed beyond doubt by the fact that, where L has an erasure, V usually leaves a gap.[3] Now, since the note at the end of the *Encomium* in V states that the text was copied by Thomas Talbot [4] from an ancient manuscript, and since we have seen that V is derived from L,[5] it follows that the ancient manuscript copied by Talbot was L, and that V is derived from Talbot's copy, with or without intervening links. V generally follows the practices of its own period in spelling, punctuation and word-division.

V has always been among the Hengwrt MSS., which Vaughan himself collected. The compiler of the Hengwrt catalogue of 1658 [6] dealt with V in some detail, and described the first item as ' the History of Cnute and Swayne, by the Archbishop of Canterbury '. I can offer no explanation for this assumption of archiepiscopal authorship for the *Encomium* : it is repeated in the catalogues of both W. W. E. Wynne [7] and Aneurin Owen,[8] but Gwenogvryn Evans [9] modifies it to the equally absurd ' History of Cnute and Swayne by Thom. Talbot 1556 '. Hardy drew attention to the V text of the *Encomium* in his *Descriptive Catalogue* (i. 627) but, nevertheless, Pertz and Gertz do not refer to it in their editions, and seem not to have been aware of its existence.

Before considering MSS. B and P it will be convenient to discuss the *editio princeps*, which appeared in 1619, when A. Duchesne included the *Encomium* in his collection *Historiae Normannorum Scriptores Antiqui* (pp. 161–78), published at Paris. Duchesne states in his preface that manuscripts of the *Encomium* and William of Poitiers were transmitted to him by William Camden through Nicolaus Fabricius de Petrisco, and that both manuscripts were from the library of Robert Cotton. He says that the manuscript of William of Poitiers was very old, but concerning that of the *Encomium* he offers no

---

[1] On the paper fly-leaf bound in with the manuscript there is a note of its present number, and it is stated that it was purchased 2 April 1887 from Dr. Lippmann (who, no doubt, represented the German authorities).

[2] P. xii.

[3] See Textual Notes to III, 1, 2 ; III, 4, 15. It may also be observed that V frequently reproduces marks of punctuation added to L by L'.

[4] On this active antiquary, see *D.N.B.*, xix. 337.

[5] From L, not merely from an early copy of L, for V gives the emendations of L', and it follows that Talbot's copy, the source of V, was made from an exemplar, which had the notes of L'. Talbot copied, therefore, from a manuscript which was ancient, but had the sixteenth-century notes of L', and this could only be L itself. Comparison of the annotations on L with Talbot's autograph shows that he was not himself responsible for them.

[6] Printed in the *Cambrian Register*, iii. 278 ff.

[7] *Archæologia Cambrensis*, 1869, p. 363.

[8] *Transactions of the Cymmrodorion*, ii. 4 (1843), p. 409.

[9] *Report on Manuscripts in the Welsh Language*, i. 1099.

information. Pertz apparently assumed that the manuscript sent to Duchesne was L, and though Hardy suspected that this was not the case, Gertz formed the same opinion as Pertz.[1] Duchesne's text is obviously derived ultimately from L, for it accepts the three marginal emendations of L' already referred to. It also, like V, frequently reproduces marks of punctuation added to L by L'. But both V and Duchesne add at the end the four verses attributed to Rudbourne, and they have many common errors.[2] It is therefore evident that they are derived from L through an intermediate common source. Since Talbot copied directly from L, and since V is derived from Talbot's copy, it follows that Duchesne is also derived directly or indirectly from Talbot's copy. Gwenogvryn Evans dates V about 1624,[3] and, since his authority in such a matter is very great, it appears likely that Vaughan copied a manuscript other than that sent to France, for Duchesne seems never to have returned the manuscripts sent to him : at least the ancient manuscript of William of Poitiers has not been heard of since. The innumerable errors in Duchesne's text, which are not found in V, suggest that what Camden sent to France was a very bad transcript derived directly or indirectly from that of Talbot, and that Vaughan used either Talbot's copy or a good transcript derived from it. It is, at least, certain that the texts of Vaughan and Duchesne are derived from Talbot's transcript of L, and, accordingly, I use T to denote the agreement of V and C (= Duchesne's printed text).[4]

A comparison of T and L shows that a leaf has been lost in L between the present fos. 47 and 48. The passage lost in L occurs in II, 16, and it is present in P as well as in C and V.[5] P is, as usual,[6] full of errors in this passage, and the text of C and V must be adopted, though P is of value in confirming certain readings. The chief value of V is that it confirms the text of C in this passage, for, as has already been pointed out, C is in general a much worse text than V. C and V agree exactly in this passage apart from details of spelling, and, when P diverges from them, its readings are manifestly inferior.

B is a paper manuscript containing transcripts in the hand of the Rev. John Haddon Hindley (1765–1827),[7] including on fos. 105–14 the first book of the *Encomium*. Hindley claims to have copied from a manuscript, but this can only have been a transcript derived ultimately from Talbot's. B has both the independent errors of C, and those which are common to V and C[8]; like C, it accepts the three emendations of L' into the text ;

---

[1] Pertz's words are, that he found the Hamiltonian manuscript to be the identical codex ' cuius apographum Chesnius typis expressit '. These words do not imply that Duchesne used a copy of L, though Gertz so interprets them with disapproval (*Scriptores Minores*, ii. 384). Cf. Hardy, *Descriptive Catalogue*, iii. 5.

[2] Examples of such common errors of V and C are : *puerili* for *pueruli*, I, 1, 8 ; *baculis* for *batulis*, II, 5, 6 ; *habet* for *habes*, II, 19, 15.

[3] *Loc. cit.*

[4] It is impossible that C is derived from V or V from C. C has innumerable independent errors in places where V agrees with L. On the other hand, V has some errors which are not in C, and sometimes writes in the first place errors which are also in C, but afterwards corrects them (e.g., in II, 1, 10, C has *vitam* for *in tam*, V *uitam* altered to *in tam*). I have not considered it worth the space to exemplify the independent errors of C and V.

[5] The loss of a leaf after fo. 47 in L is certain, as fo. 47v ends in the middle of a word (*regio|ne*). The lost leaf contained the supposed allegation of Queen Emma's virginity at the time of her marriage to Knútr, and this was perhaps too much for the patience of some reader, who accordingly destroyed the leaf.

[6] See below, p. xvi.

[7] On this scholar, see *D.N.B.*, ix. 895.

[8] I again spare space by not exemplifying the errors of B, for which I refer to Gertz's apparatus.

like C, it has a marginal note *contingere* against *contingi*, I, 1, 2. It is therefore evident, either that B is derived from C, or that B and C are derived independently from a copy which formed a link between Talbot's transcript and C. Hindley heads his text of the first book of the *Encomium* with the words 'Narratio de Sweyno Rege'. He makes a number of independent errors in copying, and his text can be dismissed as worthless. B was presented to the British Museum together with a number of other volumes of Hindley's collections (Additional MSS. 6913–7057) by Mrs. M. B. Williamson in 1829. Attention was drawn to its text of the *Encomium* by Gertz, who, however, believed it to be an early seventeenth-century manuscript, and to have been used by Duchesne.[1]

It appears, from what has now been said, that V, C, and B, although their inter-relations may not be entirely clear, are all derived ultimately from a transcript of L made in 1566 by Thomas Talbot. Accordingly, B is useless to an editor of the *Encomium*, and V and C are of use to him only in the passage now missing in L. Almost the only other interest of these descendants of Talbot's transcript is that they show that the three emendations of L', which they all know, were already written on L in 1566.[2]

P is a manuscript on vellum, probably of the sixteenth century.[3] A note on fo. 1 shows that the manuscript was at one time in the possession of William Cecil, Lord Burghley (1520–98) : its previous history is unknown. It is well known to contain a copy of William of Malmesbury's *Gesta Pontificum*. The portion which concerns the present inquiry (fos. 7–14) is in a hand not found elsewhere in the manuscript, and was evidently originally in no way connected with the material with which it is now bound up. On fo. 7r and the upper half of fo. 7v there are a number of sentences from Gildas, headed 'Excerpta ex Gilda', and these are followed on fos. 7v–14 by a text of the *Encomium* headed 'Ex eodem Gilda in Historia de Sueyno et Knuctone, quam in gratiam scripsit ad reginam Emmam'.[4] The Prologue and Argument are not given, and the first book is severely abridged, but the second and third books are given fairly fully, although several passages are omitted and others are shortened.[5] These passages are all of a rhetorical nature, and it is evident that the scribe of P was interested in the *Encomium* only as an historical document. Hardy[6] appears to suggest that the passages missing in P are less authentic than the rest of the *Encomium* : this is most unlikely for P professes only to be 'excerpta'. It may be noted that the reading of P's text of the *Encomium* shows that the scribe knew the Prologue, if not the Argument, for otherwise he would not have known that the work was written 'in gratiam ad reginam Emmam'. P differs from L in the conclusion of the final chapter : the description of the unanimity of Emma and her sons ('Hic fides . . . Amen') is replaced by a brief account of the death of Hörthaknútr and

---

[1] *Scriptores Minores*, ii. 382, 384.
[2] L' proposes a good many other emendations : some of these (e.g., *ignari* for *incogniti*, II, 10, 26) T evidently did not accept, as they are not found in V and C ; others are found in V and C, but are mere corrections of an obvious nature, and prove nothing concerning the relationships of the manuscripts.
[3] Practically all writers who refer to the MS. P date it in the fifteenth century. An exception is Stubbs (William of Malmesbury, *Gesta Pontificum*, Rolls Series, p. xxii), who places the manuscript in the sixteenth century, and this appears to be correct at least of the leaves containing the *Encomium*.
[4] Occasional similarities of phrase and vocabulary probably explain why the scribe of P thought that the *Historia Gildae* and the *Encomium* were by the same writer.
[5] See Textual Notes on I, 1, 14 ; I, 2, 1 ; I, 5, 1 ; II, 4, 5 ; III, 6, 19 ; III, 7, 1 ; III, 9, 5 ; III, 10, 2 ; III, 11, 2.
[6] *Descriptive Catalogue*, i. 628.

the accession of Eadweard, followed by an eloquent testimony to the merits of the latter.[1] This ending has clearly been substituted for that preserved in L after the death of Hörthaknútr. The text of P is abnormally bad : it is full of errors, accidental omissions (varying in length from one to about a dozen words) and foolish alterations.[2]

It is very difficult to determine the relationship of L and P. The question which most concerns an editor is whether P is derived from L or whether it is descended from the author's autograph through a chain in which L is not a link. If the latter were the case, P would be of some value, for it has a number of unusual forms in common with L, and could be regarded as confirming these, or, at least, proving that they were already present in the *Encomium* at an older stage than L in its transmission. If, on the other hand, it were decided that P was derived from L, it would be of no value except in the passage now lost in L,[3] and in its own version of the final sentences. It may be noted that L and P have a number of common errors [4] ; this might suggest either that P is derived from L, or that L and P are independently derived from a manuscript in which these errors were already present. But in a few cases P has errors which L had at first, but which the scribes have themselves corrected.[5] This suggests that L and P are independently derived from a manuscript which had these errors, and that the scribes of L corrected them after inadvertently copying them, while they were retained in another copy made from the same exemplar and from which P is ultimately derived. P is so full of independent errors that certainly cannot be reached in this matter, but I have considered it likely that P is independent of L, and that it preserves an occasional glimpse of an older stage than L in the transmission of the *Encomium*, by showing that certain doubtful forms found in both L and P go back to a manuscript older than L.[6] Furthermore, P seems to give an occasional hint as to how L is to be corrected.[7] In III, 1, 2, it preserves a place-name erased in L. It offers, however, practically no readings which are better than those of L.[8]

The date of the revised version of the ending found in P is uncertain. This passage, with its rhetorical style and Virgilian reminiscence,[9] is certainly not the work of the scribe of P, whose Latin, as exhibited in his summaries of parts of the text, is singularly bald. It probably dates back to the reign of Eadweard the Confessor, for the spiritual merits of that monarch would be more strongly emphasised by a late eulogiser. Its author has caught the style of the *Encomium* admirably. It is, of course, not impossible that the Encomiast himself revised his work in a copy retained in Flanders, while the copy sent to England remained unrevised. It will appear below (p. xl) that III, 7, was probably revised at the same time as the ending.

The existence of a text of the *Encomium* in P is pointed out neither in the catalogue

---

[1] See Textual Note on III, 14, for P's version of the ending.

[2] I refer the reader to the editions of Pertz and Gertz for the errors of P : both these editors give an excellent selection of them, and it would be mere waste of space to do this again.

[3] In this passage P has a definite value, even if it be regarded as derived from L, for, while its text is very inferior to that of T, it confirms the anomalous form *iusiurando* and the readings *temporum* and *illi* (cf. Linguistic Note on II, 16, 7).

[4] See Textual Notes on II, 2, 1 ; II, 7, 13 ; II, 10, 22 ; II, 13, 10 ; III, 1, 19 ; III, 5, 12 ; cf. III, 13, 4.

[5] See Textual Notes on II, 18, 2 ; II, 20, 1.

[6] See Textual Notes on II, 3, 6 ; II, 7, 11 ; II, 8, 9 ; II, 9, 7 ; II, 9, 14 ; II, 21, 8 ; III, 1, 24 ; III, 3, 8 ; III, 5, 3 ; III, 5, 16 ; III, 6, 16 ; III, 9, 16 ; cf. also below, p. xxxvi, on forms in which L and P have inorganic *h*.

[7] See Textual Notes on II, 11, 4 ; II, 13, 18 ; III, 6, 11 (*postquam*) ; III, 9, 2 ; III, 10, 11.

[8] For possible exceptions, see Textual Notes on II, 2, 12 ; II, 16, 21.

[9] *Vitalibus auris* ; cf. *Aen.* i. 387–8.

of the French royal manuscripts nor in the catalogue of the Burghley sale, although many of its other contents are recorded in those works,[1] but was first brought to the attention of scholars in Hardy's *Descriptive Catalogue* (i. 627–9), where most of P's summary of Book I and its peculiar ending are printed.   In their editions of the *Encomium*, Pertz and Gertz follow P in the passage missing in L.   Since these editors have also given a good illustrative selection of P's errors in their footnotes, I have thought it necessary to include in my Textual Notes only its major variants and such readings as are of interest for the reasons outlined above.

Duchesne's text of the *Encomium* is reprinted in the following collections of texts. (1) Jacobus Langebek, *Scriptores rerum Danicarum medii aevi*, ii (1773), pp. 472–502. The editor adds copious historical notes.   (2) Francis Maseres, *Historiæ Anglicanæ circà tempús conquestús Angliæ a Gulielmo Notho, Normannorum duce, Selecta Monumenta* (London, 1807), pp. 3–36.   The editor gives a marginal summary in Latin and a few notes in English.   The first part of this work, containing the *Encomium* and William of Poitiers, was set long before 1807, and some copies of this part were printed and issued privately without the editor's name in 1783.   (3) Migne's *Patrologia*, cxli (1853), cols. 1373–98. The editor notes a few of the verbal parallels with classical authors and quotes by way of introduction a passage from the *Histoire Littéraire de la France*, vii (1746), pp. 573–4, in which the Encomiast's good latinity and poetical style are commented upon.   (4) Short extracts from Duchesne's text of the *Encomium* are printed in the *Recueil des historiens des Gaules et de la France*, xi (1767), pp. 5–8, with a few introductory remarks of an obvious nature.

Modern work on the *Encomium* began in September 1862, when G. H. Pertz, having observed the notice of L in Clarke's *Repertorium*, went to Scotland and copied the manuscript.   He also knew of the existence of P (probably from Hardy's *Descriptive Catalogue*) and he published an edition of the *Encomium*, in which the text follows L and copious variants are given from P.   Pertz removed most of the errors of Duchesne, but he introduced a few new ones,[2] and the variants which he gives from P are not always accurate. Pertz's edition was published in *Monumenta Germaniae Historica, Scriptores*, xix (1866), pp. 508–25, and also separately at Hanover in 1865 in the series of texts from the *Monumenta* re-issued *in usum scholarum*.   Both issues of Pertz's edition are entitled ' Cnutonis Regis Gesta sive Encomium Emmae Reginae auctore monacho Sancti Bertini ' : it has a brief introduction, describing L, P, and C.

An extremely careful edition of the *Encomium* was published by M. Cl. Gertz in vol. ii (pp. 376–426) of his *Scriptores minores historiæ Danicæ medii ævi* (2 vols., Copenhagen, 1917–20).   He worked on L in London in June 1906, and on P in Copenhagen, whither it was sent for his use, in January 1914.   In London he also presumably discovered and collated B.   His edition follows L, and all the variants of P, C, and B which are of any interest are given in the apparatus.   The existence of V seems to have escaped him (as it had previously escaped Pertz).   In his introduction, Gertz gives excellent descriptions of L, P, and B, though, as has already been observed, he dates B incorrectly.   Gertz's

---

[1] See *Catalogus codicum manuscriptorum bibliothecæ regiæ*, iv (1744), p. 218 ; *Bibliotheca Illustris* (London, 1687), p. 85, no. 98.

[2] Since the errors of Pertz are carefully pointed out by Gertz in his apparatus, I have not thought it necessary to record them again, but it is desirable that attention should be drawn to the fact that Pertz wrongly alleges an agreement of P and C against L in a number of places.   The readings concerned are *posthabitis*, II, 9, 4, *iniquo* III, 2, 4, *reuehitur*, III, 8, 6, where Pertz incorrectly states that L has *postpositis*, *maligno*, *reuertitur*.   Pertz states that P and C have *omnis*, II, 1, 3, against L's *omnes*, but L actually has *omnos* altered from *omnis*, and Talbot no doubt misread it as *omnis* (cf. above, p. xvi, n. 5).   Pertz is correct in giving *Geldefordia*, III, 4, 18, as L's reading against *Gildefordia*, P, C, but this is a special case, see p. xviii, n. 1.

edition is a decided improvement upon that of Pertz, although, while removing most of Pertz's errors, it introduces a few new ones. Gertz, furthermore, failed to see that C and B are ultimately derived from L only, and formed the curious opinion that C is an eclectic text based on L, P, and B. It is of course impossible that Duchesne used B, there is not the least reason to think he used P,[1] and it has been shown above that he did not use L at first hand. Gertz also proposes many emendations of which the average merit is remarkably low. Apart from slight and obvious corrections (in most of which he was anticipated by Pertz, Talbot, or L'), I have adopted only three of Gertz's emendations in the text of the present edition, and in one of these he was anticipated by Maseres.[2] I have considered two others worth mention in the Textual Notes,[3] and a few others are discussed in the Linguistic Notes.[4] Gertz's explanatory notes consist practically exclusively of references to passages in the Classics and the Vulgate, which have verbal correspondences with the *Encomium* : they are derived largely from the notes to his translation.

The method in which the text of the *Encomium* is presented in the present edition is described sufficiently in the note prefixed to it.[5] With regard to the divisions of the text, it may here be observed that L states where the second book begins and where the Argument ends (thus implying where the first book begins). The point where the Prologue ends and the Argument begins is to be inferred with certainty from the subject-matter. The beginning of the third book, however, is indicated only by a space and an ornamented initial, and hence it is not recognised as a separate book in the early editions or in V. Pertz and Gertz, however, divide the text into three books, and, since nothing would be gained by departing from this very natural arrangement, I do the same. Chapter divisions were first introduced by Pertz : Gertz somewhat modified the divisions of Pertz. Since references to the *Encomium* have practically always been made in modern times by the divisions of Pertz, I have retained these, though those of Gertz are somewhat better.[6]

The text had originally no title in L. The one usually used is due to Duchesne, who headed his text ' Emmæ Anglorum reginæ Richardi I. ducis Normannorum filiæ encomium''. The title adopted by Pertz [7] was suggested by the late inscription on L, fo. 1r, and this inscription was followed strictly by Gertz, who entitles the text ' Gesta Cnutonis Regis '. The title ' Encomium Emmae (Reginae) ' has become the one generally used in England, and I adopt it in the present edition, feeling that it is, after all, the most suitable for a work which is not a biography of Knút, but which is devoted, at least in the author's expressed intention, ' per omnia reginae Emmae laudibus '.

The only translation of the *Encomium* known to me is that by Gertz into Danish entitled ' Kong Knuts liv og gerninger eller æreskrift for dronning Emma oversat af M. Cl. Gertz ' (Copenhagen, 1896). It has a brief introduction, many citations of verbal

---

[1] No sound evidence that C used P can be advanced. P makes in the text, and C in the margin, the very obvious emendations *contingere*, I, 1, 2, and *oculos utrosque*, III, 6, 10, but they would occur to any reader, though they may not be correct. Similarly L's *Geldefordia*, III, 4, 18, may have been altered to *Gildefordia* (so T) by P and Talbot independently ; but the name in L has been rewritten by an early corrector, and it is possible that *Gil-* was the original form used by the Encomiast, and that P has preserved it, while Talbot reverted to it, as being the better known in his time. Both forms are found early, see Ekwall, *Dict. of Eng. Place-names*, p. 197.

[2] See Textual Notes on II, 4, 6 ; II, 7, 13 ; II, 10, 22.

[3] I, 1, 2 ; III, 9, 10.

[4] See Linguistic Notes on Prol., 14 ; Arg., 9 and 12 ; II, 7, 21 ; II, 9, 7 ; II, 10, 6 ; II, 16, 6 and 7 ; II, 18, 10 ; III, 5, 16 ; III, 6, 10 ; III, 10, 5. On Gertz's emendation in III, 12, 2, see below, p. xxxii, n. 1.

[5] See below, p. 3.

[6] In one case Gertz's arrangement is much better : see Linguistic Note on I, 1, 27.

[7] Quoted above, p. xvii.

parallels, and a few historical notes professedly derived from those of Langebek. I have quoted from it occasionally in the Linguistic Notes as representing the best which can be made of difficult passages.

The only discussion of the *Encomium* of any value is that of J. C. H. R. Steenstrup, *Normandiets Historie under de syv første Hertuger* (Copenhagen, 1925), pp. 21–4. The *Histoire Littéraire de la France*, vii. 573–4, limits itself to an appreciation of the writer's style. M. Manitius, *Geschichte der lateinischen Literatur des Mittelalters*, ii (Munich, 1923), pp. 329 ff., has a rather perfunctory account of the *Encomium*, which is not always accurate or intelligent.[1] Innumerable allusions to the *Encomium* (often rather impatient) occur in the pages of most writers on the English and Scandinavian history of the eleventh century.[2]

B. *The Encomiast*

Concerning the life of the author of the *Encomium* we know nothing except four facts which he himself tells us. The first is that he was commanded to write his work by Queen Emma ; the second, that he obeyed her at least partly out of personal gratitude ; the third, that he was an inmate either of St. Bertin's or of St. Omer's ; the fourth, that he personally saw Knútr on the occasion of his visit to these foundations on his way to Rome.[3] We may reasonably conjecture that his association with the queen originated during her exile in Flanders (1037–40), but we cannot assume that he was still an inmate of St. Bertin's or St. Omer's at that time. His latinity, as will appear below, shows that he was possessed of considerable learning,[4] and his selection by the queen to write a work in praise of herself and her family suggests that he enjoyed some reputation as a man of letters.

Our knowledge of the history of the two associated foundations at St. Omer in the early eleventh century is unfortunately poor. They were originally little more than branches of one foundation and were under one abbot. According to Folquin, the historian of St. Bertin's, this state of affairs persisted until the time of Abbot Fridogis (820–34), who substituted canons for monks at St. Omer's.[5] This was apparently considered equivalent to a separation of the two foundations,[6] and henceforth there was always much jealousy between them as to which was the superior. Folquin quotes a charter in two forms, which purports to define certain rights of supervision granted to

---

[1] Cf. above, p. xii, n. 7, and below, p. xxxvi.

[2] Milton already uses the *Encomium* freely in his *History of England*, and points out its value as a contemporary source for the murder of Ælfred. He gives a translation of the forged letter (*Enc.* III, 3).

[3] These facts are all recorded in the Prologue and II, 20–1. The assumption (which is as old as Duchesne) that the Encomiast was a monk of St. Bertin's is quite unjustified. He regarded the two foundations at St. Omer as being a unity (see below, p. xx), and gives no indication as to which he was the more closely attached. The word *uernula* does not necessarily mean ' monk ' in the Latin of the period : it often is simply ' servant '. We know of at least one canon of St. Omer's who engaged in historical studies ; see below, note 6. On the evidence of the drawing on fo. iv of MS. L, see Preface.

[4] See Introduction, § C.

[5] See *Cartulaire de l'abbaye de Saint-Bertin*, edited by M. Guérard (Paris, 1840), pp. 74–5.

[6] *Ibid.*, 84 : ' Hugo abbas condolens infelicissimæ et miserrimæ divisioni et discissioni venerabilis Sithiensis coenobii ab infando Fridogiso factæ . . .' Similarly Lambert, a canon of St. Omer's, who compiled lists of the heads of both foundations about 1120, says : ' iste Fredegisus a consortio monachorum Sancti Audomari segregavit aecclesiam anno Domini 830 '. Lambert, however, regards Hugo of St. Quentin, Fridogis's successor, as being actually the last abbot to preside over both houses. See *M.G.H.S.*, xiii. 390–1.

St. Bertin's over St. Omer's in the time of Abbot Hugo, the successor of Fridogis, by Folquin, Bishop of Thérouanne.[1] This charter is suspect,[2] but there is no reason to doubt that some connection between the houses survived the activities of Fridogis. In Alardus Tassart's version of the *Cartularium Sithiense*,[3] a few documents are given to fill the gap between 962, when Folquin's history ends, and 1021, where that of Simon begins. One of these[4] is dated 1015 and states that St. Bertin's and St. Omer's owned common property at that date. Whatever the date of the surviving form of the document may be, a version of it was already current in the time of John of Ypres (d. 1383), who summarizes it.[5] The Encomiast certainly speaks as if the two foundations were in some sense a unity in describing Knútr's visit to them.

The Encomiast refers to St. Bertin's and St. Omer's as *monasteria* (II, 21, 1 and 11) and *caenobia* (*ibid.*, 15). St. Omer's was strictly a collegiate church in his time : if monks had ever returned there, so important an event would not have escaped the chroniclers. The words *monasterium* and *caenobium* are, however, both freely used in medieval Latin in the sense ' collegiate church '.

The state of scholarship seems to have been good at St. Bertin's in the eleventh century ; concerning the affairs of St. Omer's we have no information in this period. In 1042 or 1043, Bovo became abbot of St. Bertin's. Our knowledge of his career is derived from the *Gesta Abbatum Sancti Bertini Sithiensium* of Simon (written 1095–1123).[6] We do not know if Bovo was educated at St. Bertin's or came there from elsewhere.[7] Simon speaks highly of him as a scholar, and Folcard addresses him with respect as his teacher and dedicates his life of St. Bertin to him.[8] Bovo's own extant tract on the *Inventio* of St. Bertin's bones is written in admirably clear Latin, and this may also be said of a few other works written at St. Bertin's in the same period.[9] Of Bovo's predecessor Rodericus, who was abbot from 1021, we know only that he had a reputation as a disciplinarian, and that he was originally a monk of Arras. If the Encomiast belonged to St. Bertin's, a large part of his career there must have been spent under the abbacy of Rodericus.

It might be temping to identify the Encomiast with Bovo, for the latter states in his above-mentioned tract that he had previously written an historical work, which dealt partly with events of which he had been a witness.[10] Bovo's style is, however, markedly different from that of the Encomiast, and correspondences in vocabulary and phrase are

---

[1] *Cartulaire de . . . Saint-Bertin*, 85–8.
[2] *Neues Archiv*, vi. 421–2, footnote.
[3] St. Omer MS. 750 (written about 1512).
[4] *Cartulaire de . . . Saint-Bertin*, p. xcix.
[5] Martène and Durand, *Thesaurus novus anecdotorum*, iii. 571.
[6] Ed. in *Cartulaire de . . . Saint-Bertin*, and in *M.G.H.S.*, xiii. 600 ff.
[7] It has sometimes been stated that Bovo was educated at St. Bertin's, but this is only derived from John of Ypres, who interpreted the statement of Simon, that Bovo imitated the virtues of his predecessor, as implying that he modelled himself on Rodericus, while the latter still presided over St. Bertin's. Simon's statement that Bovo was the *egregius imitator* of Rodericus may mean no more than that he discharged his office in same admirable manner as the latter. Simon also says that Bovo was reared from his youth under monastic discipline, but we cannot infer that this means at St. Bertin's.
[8] *Acta Sanctorum Septembris*, ii. 604. At least as the teacher of this eminent biographer of Englishmen, Bovo deserves to be remembered in this country.
[9] The works in question are a few eleventh-century additions to the *Libellus Miraculorum S. Bertini*, Erembold's *Libellus de Miraculo S. Bertini* (see *M.G.H.S.*, xv. 516 ff.), and a poem printed in *Neues Archiv*, ii. 228–30.
[10] ' Cum nonnullas rerum convenientias scribendis gestis antehac pervenisse meminerim, quorum plura ego ipse viderim, quaedam maiorum haud spernendorum virorum relatu didicerim . . .' (*M.G.H.S.*, xv. 526).

not greater than one would expect between two authors of the same period, who both employ rhymed prose. Nevertheless, the two works are different in subject and spirit, and this might account for the difference in style. The most that can be said is, that it is not totally impossible that Bovo was the writer of the *Encomium*. The hand of the Encomiast is not to be traced with certainty in the other St. Bertin's writings of the period, though he somewhat resembles Erembold in style.[1]

The *Encomium* was clearly written during the reign of Hörthaknútr (1040–2), when Queen Emma was at the height of her influence. She no doubt instigated the writing of a laudatory work on the history of the Danish dynasty in England during the last months of her stay in Flanders, after Hörthaknútr had been offered the English crown. She must then have felt a considerable degree of confidence in the future, and it is not surprising that she considered that the time was opportune for making a record of her trials and their fortunate outcome, set in a background of the feats of her husband. The *Encomium* is, accordingly, written purely for the personal glorification of Emma and her relatives. It is not in any sense a piece of political propaganda defending the Danish occupation of England, which is depicted as purely aggressive. The strength of the English resistance is not under-estimated, the peace of 1016 is regarded as due to the exhaustion of both sides, not to the superiority of Danish arms,[2] and it is hinted that Eadmund intended to renew the struggle.[3] Furthermore, the Encomiast regarded the hostility of the English to the Danes as justified, and their resistance as natural, if perhaps unwise.[4] The first two books of the *Encomium* provide, in short, a confused but unprejudiced account of the Danish conquest of England, and, as will appear below, they are studiously modest concerning Knútr's personal prowess,[5] and are generous to Eadmund,[6] while proper indignation at the treachery of Eadric for working in the Danish interest is expressed.[7] The third book is written entirely from Emma's point of view, and this was not exclusively either Danish or English. In fact, the one link between the two main subjects of the *Encomium*, the wars of the English with the Danes and the story of Emma, is that Emma's marriage is stated to have caused a racial reconciliation in England after the death of Eadmund.[8] That English and Danish statesmen continued to look askance at each other after 1016 we need not doubt, but the Encomiast's story is that there was no racial friction after his heroine's marriage, and he maintains this position with considerable consistency, although owing to his suppression of Emma's connection with the West-Saxon house, he would leave the uninformed reader wondering in what way the marriage of their conqueror to a Norman lady could possibly placate the English. We may suspect that the object of Knútr's marriage was a reconciliation with Normandy rather than with the English (cf. below, p. xlv), and we may doubt if the English regarded Emma with sufficient affection to feel any enthusiasm for her astonishing recovery of her former position in 1017, much less to change their feelings towards their conqueror on her account, but she evidently wished it to be thought that they did so, and instructed her Encomiast accordingly, for such

---

[1] See below, p. xl.
[2] II, 13 ; note also II, 16, where the war is said to have been one of ' pares paribus ui corporis uirtuteque animi '.
[3] II, 14 : ' ne forte si uterque superuiueret neuter regnaret secure, et regnum diatim adnihila[re]tur renouata contentione '.
[4] II, 1 : ' Angli siquidem memores, quod pater eius iniuste suos inuasisset fines . . .'
[5] See below, p. lx.
[6] Note especially the description of his gallantry at Ashingdon (II, 9) and his determination to renew resistence afterwards (II, 10).
[7] II, 15.
[8] This is clearly placed before the reader by the Encomiast in his Argument : he explains that he begins a work in praise of Emma with an account of Sveinn, because the war begun by that monarch might have had no end but for his son's marriage to Emma ; cf. II, 16 (at end).

a surprising view of the course of contemporary English politics can hardly have been the unprompted concoction of a Flemish ecclesiastic.[1] The Encomiast, having committed himself to the view that racial antagonism subsided with Emma's re-appearance in England, opens his third book with an account of the succession of Haraldr, in which that event is depicted as due to an ill-advised movement among the English,[2] and in which there is no suggestion that the new king would be more welcome to his Scandinavian than to his English subjects. Still less is it suggested that Emma's interests coincided with those of a Danish party. The wrong committed by Haraldr's supporters is not regarded as especially directed against the dynasty of Knútr, but against Hörthaknútr as a son of Emma, and, failing him, against Emma's other sons.[3] Emma was, evidently, quite willing to accept a reversion of the crown to the West-Saxon house, rather than to Danish rulers with whom she had no connection. Eadweard appears as lacking legal standing rather than a reasonable claim to succeed : the witan had sworn him no oath.[4] An English prelate appears as a supporter of the claims of Emma's sons.[5] One forms the impression that, if Emma really supported the claims of Magnús of Norway after the death of Hörthaknútr,[6] she did so in a wild attempt to avoid personal eclipse rather than in any preference for the continuance of Scandinavian rule as such.

There can be little doubt that, in commanding a history of the Danish conquest and its aftermath to be written, Emma was influenced by the example of her father, Richard the Fearless, who caused a history of himself and his predecessors to be written by Dudo of St. Quentin. It is very probable that she recommended Dudo's work as a model to the author of the *Encomium*. Although I am not of opinion that it can be mechanically demonstrated that the Encomiast knew Dudo's book, it is not to be denied that the two writers are markedly similar in style and method.[7] The style of the Encomiast will be compared with that of Dudo below,[8] but one example of their similarity of treatment may be given here : the method in which the Encomiast leads the ignorant reader to assume that all Emma's family were all the children of Knútr, but avoids making a direct statement on the matter with which the better-informed reader could quarrel,[9] is very similar to that in which Dudo, seizing upon the fact that the French chroniclers had often failed to distinguish the Northmen of the Loire from those of the Seine, claimed the deeds of the former for the latter and so created for future ages the problem of the *mouvance de Bretagne*.[10]

Although the *Encomium* is not without its value for pure history,[11] it is for the illumination of character and motive that it deserves the greatest attention. It is not its least merit, in view of the late date of the Norse Sagas, that it provides a nearly contemporary view of the characters of several of the heroes of Scandinavian history. Knútr appears as a politician rather than as a warrior, and Sveinn as a warrior king of the later viking age, who accepted Christianity as a belief, but not as an influence. The political wavering of Thorkell is covered, but not concealed,[12] while Eiríkr appears as a mighty warrior : the

---

[1] It has been argued on insufficient grounds that the Encomiast was English (see below, p. xxxvi) : if this were the case, he would be even less likely to have personally over-estimated Emma's capacity to cause a sudden wave of contentment with Danish domination among the English.

[2] III, 1 : ' ut quidam Anglorum . . . mallent regnum suum dedecorare quam ornare '.

[3] III, 1 : ' relinquentes nobiles filios insignis reginae Emmae '.

[4] III, 8.   [5] III, 1.   [6] See below, p. xlix.

[7] Steenstrup first pointed this out (*Normandiets Historie*, p. 21).

[8] Pp. xxxiv ff.

[9] Cf. below, pp. xlvi ff.

[10] See A. le Moyne de la Borderie, *Histoire de Bretagne*, ii. 355–98 and especially 496–504.

[11] See below, pp. lxviii ff.   [12] Cf. below, pp. liv ff.

romantic and knightly qualities which he displays in the Sagas do not appear, and are perhaps to be regarded as added to his character with little foundation by later tradition. Of the English characters, the persistent bravery of Eadmund and the treachery and insidiousness of Eadric appear as clearly as in the native records. Above all, the *Encomium* enables us to get behind the dry notices in which the *Old English Chronicle* records the political crisis which followed the death of Knútr to the feelings and view-points of the protagonists. It shows us Haraldr eagerly canvassing possible supporters,[1] and Emma alarmed but full of schemes.[2] We see Emma unwilling to absolve Godwine for his part in the murder of Ælfred, but disinclined to blame him for it directly, owing to his satisfactory attitude in Hörthaknútr's reign.[3] We feel Emma's repugnance for her rival, Ælfgifu of Northampton, in the favourable mention of the scandal concerning the birth of Haraldr, and the suppression of the fact that Ælfgifu was an active worker in her son's cause.[4] We are made to feel Emma's vanity : she did not desire posterity to know that she was in any way connected with the English house which had failed to stem the Danish onset, although the suppression of this fact makes her claim to have been the cause of an Anglo-Danish reconciliation little less than absurd. Her withdrawal to Flanders, reasonable as it was, has to be excused at length with Scriptural and Sallustian quotations.[5] Her ambition also appears plainly : the rejection of her sons is the rejection of Emma,[6] her son's obedience to her counsels is specially extolled.[7] Eadweard appears very conscious of his weak legal position and disinclined to undertake a dangerous enter-prise, Æthelnoth as loyally determined to fulfil what he had promised to Knútr, Godwine as the willing tool if not the accomplice of Haraldr in a brutal murder,[8] and Haraldr as a brutal and completely unscrupulous usurper. Whatever the precise justice of these last four judgments may be, they show us exactly how the persons in question appeared to Emma and her party. A work which throws so much light on the characters of eleventh-century English and Scandinavian history, and upon how they appeared to each other, is one of the most important documents preserved from the period.

C. *The Learning and Latinity of the Encomiast*

The only non-Biblical works mentioned in the *Encomium* are the *Aeneid* [9] and a pseudo-Virgilian epigram, from which two lines are quoted.[10] It is pointed out that the *Aeneid* is devoted to the praise of Octavian, because the praise given to his family glorifies him, though he is scarcely mentioned by name, and this suggests that the Encomiast knew some such account of Virgil's life and work as that by Junius Philar-

---

[1] See below, n. 6, and p. lxiv.   [2] See note 6 below.
[3] See below, p. lxv.
[4] See below, p. lxiv.   [5] III, 7.
[6] See the curious letter (III, 3) alleged to have been forged by Haraldr in the Queen's name. While this document shows us Haraldr canvassing support as he appeared to Emma's party, its picture of Emma shows her as she knew she must have appeared to her opponents, enraged to be *tantum nomine regina* and revolving all manner of schemes to secure a change on the throne. This view of the Queen is put skilfully by her Encomiast into a composition attributed to the villainous Haraldr : this is equivalent to saying that it was prevalent in some quarters, but was mere scandal. The Encomiast is careful to say that Emma actually passed the time in sorrowful expectation and daily prayer (III, 2). See further on the story of the letter below, p. lxvii.
[7] Arg., ' maternis per omnia parens consiliis '.   [8] See below, p. lxv.
[9] Arg., 7.
[10] II, 19 ; cf. *Poetae Latini Minores*, ed. A. Baehrens, iv. 156, and *Vitae Vergilianae*, ed. I. Brummer, p. 31.

gyrius.[1] There are also allusions to the classical myths about centaurs, and to the well-known story of the decimation of the Theban legion.[2] In view of the poverty of the information thus directly obtained, it is evident that, if any idea of the extent and direction of the Encomiast's reading is to be formed, this must be done by the close study of his language.

Although much of the present section of the Introduction will be concerned with the influence of classical authors on the Encomiast, it cannot be emphasised too strongly that this influence is a veneer upon his language, which remains of a basically medieval type, exhibiting that deep influence of late Latin syntax which characterizes practically all medieval narrative Latin. Most of the constructions which distinguish this language from classical Latin can be readily exemplified from the *Vulgate*, which is the greatest single influence upon medieval Latin prose. In the following paragraphs, attention will be drawn to a number of constructions, the free use of which shows the medieval character of the Encomiast's language, though many of them are occasionally found in the classical period.[3]

The Encomiast is particularly fond of the use of the ablative of the gerund with a force practically equivalent to that of a present participle active : e.g., Prol., *precipientem negligendo conticessere*, ' to be silent, disregarding thee, who commandest (me to write) ' ; II, 1, *non quod asperos euentus belli metuendo fugeret*, ' not because he was fleeing, fearing . . .' When the main verb and this participial gerund have the same object, this is expressed once only : e.g., Arg., *diuitiis ampliando regnum . . optinuit*, ' he held the kingdom, enriching it '. Other examples are I, 1, *preparando* ; *fingendo* ; I, 5, *tangendo* ; *festinando* ; *remittendo* ; *reddendo* ; II, 1, *despiciendo* ; II, 2, *relinquendo* ; II, 7, *inuadendo* ; III, 6, *narrando* ; *parcendo*.

The Encomiast makes very free use of the present participle active with the force of a past participle : e.g., III, 4, *ascendens in statione . . parabat*, ' having landed, he was preparing ' ; III, 13, *ut ueniens secum optineret regnum*, ' that having come, he should . . .' Other examples are II, 2, *audiens* ; *perpendens* ; II, 4, *ualedicens* ; II, 6, *diripientes* ; II, 7, *educens* ; II, 9, *requirens* ; *dicens* ; II, 10, *uertentes* ; II, 11, *redeuntes* ; *repetentes* ; III, 6, *rapientes*. Conversely, he sometimes uses the past participle passive with the force of a present participle : e.g. Prol., *si neglecta uenustate dictaminis . . . multiplici narratione usus fuero*, ' if, disregarding elegance of form, I adopt a prolix method of narration ' ; I, 4, *primo prelio usus . . . inuadit*, ' taking advantage of (the result of) the first battle, he invades '.

The Encomiast frequency uses the ablative absolute where the subject or the object is the same as that of the main verb : e.g., II, 2, *quibus uix extinctis . . refocillantur*, ' which having scarcely been extinguished are rekindled ' ; II, 7, *quo reuerso rex . . . prohibuit*, ' whom, after his return, the king forbade ' ; II, 13, *electisque internuntiis, premittit*, ' and he sends elected messengers ' ; III, 4, *hac fraude . . . . composita . . . est directa*, ' this forgery having been composed, it was directed '. He also sometimes places the ablative absolute after the main verb, to express an action subsequent to that

---

[1] See Brummer, *op. cit.*, p. 43 : ' (Virgilius) nouissime scripsit Aeneida in honorem Caesaris, ut uirtutes Aeneae, ex cuius genere cupiebat esse, suo carmine ornaret.' The Encomiast perhaps had a manuscript of Virgil with introductory matter, including a life of the poet.

[2] III, 5 ; cf. below, p. xxxiv.

[3] Ample Biblical example of most of these constructions are given by F. Kaulen, *Handbuch zur Vulgata* (Mainz, 1870 ; 2nd ed., Freiburg-in-Breisgau, 1904) ; H. Roensch, *Itala und Vulgata* (Marburg and Leipzig, 1869 ; 2nd ed., Marburg, 1875) ; W. E. Plater and H. J. White, *A Grammar of the Vulgate* (Oxford, 1926). In the present work, I use the term Classical Latin to include all writers later than Terence and earlier than Apuleius, and, when it is necessary to distinguish Late Latin from Medieval Latin, the line between them is regarded as falling about A.D. 600.

of the main verb, and thus continue the narrative : e.g., I, 4, *adiacentem regionem inuadit, fusis fugatisque hostibus,* ' he invades the adjacent region, and scatters the enemy and puts them to flight '.[1]

The Encomiast makes free use of the infinite of purpose [2] : e.g., Arg., *successorem esse constituit* ; III, 1, *missam audire subintrarent.*

The Encomiast is frequently content to construct long sentences out of a succession of main clauses joined by copulae : e.g., I, 1, *pater . . . fugit, et . . . . . obiit et Suein . . . . tenuit* ; III, 4, *est obuius factus, et eum . . . suscepit . . eiusque fit . . miles.*

The Encomiast is often inexact both in his use of the reflexive pronoun and its possessive adjective and his failure to use them [3] : e.g., I, 3, *quod ipsi* (= *sibi*) . . . . *in mentem uenerat* ; I, 3, *quid sibi* (= *illi*) *super hoc negotii uideretur, orsus est inquirere* ; II, 16, *sponsa . . . omnium eius* (= *suorum*) *temporum mulierum praestantissima* ; II, 16, *sed abnegat illa, se unquam Cnutonis sponsam fieri, nisi illi* (= *sibi*) . . *affirmaret.*

It should be observed that, although the Encomiast uses the ablative without preposition to express point of time, he also uses it to express duration, as is so frequent in the *Vulgate* : e.g., I, 5, *pauco superuixit tempore* (cf. Exod. xxi. 21) ; II, 2, *aliquanto tempore* ; II, 9, *tota quadragesima* ; III, 12, *toto exilii tempore.* As is usual in texts which use the ablative to express duration, we sometimes find a preposition added to it to indicate point of time : e.g., II, 11, *in nocte.*

The Encomiast sometimes uses the ablative with *in* after verbs of motion to indicate place whither : e.g., II, 7, *in ea confugerant* ; III, 4, *induxit eum in uilla* ; III, 5, *adducuntur . . in medio* ; III, 6, *eductusque in insula* ; III, 7, *fugite in alia* (cf. Textual Note).[4]

Although the Encomiast uses the accusative and infinitive construction freely, especially after verbs of command and implied command (e.g., II, 20, *oro* ; II, 21, *impetro*), he also has a very large number of noun clauses introduced by *quod, quia* and *quoniam* : e.g., I, 1, *affirmare ualeam, quod* ; II, 8, *dicentes quod* ; II, 3, *ut . . patefaceret, quia* ; Arg., *nosti, quoniam* ; I, 1, *liquet procul dubio, quoniam.* He also has the *Vulgate* use of *quoniam* to introduce direct quotations : e.g., III, 7, *tali responsione censeo utendum, quoniam* ; *insinuat, quoniam si persequuti uos.*

The following points should be noticed concerning the use of conjunctions introducing subordinate clauses. The temporal conjunctions *dum* and *ubi* are used with the subjunctive or the indicative, without the difference of mood implying a difference of meaning [5] : e.g., I, 5, *dum . . . . . hortaretur* ; II, 2, *dum . . . . inquireret* ; III, 1, *dum . . . . . subintrarent* ; III, 10, *dum . . . . . contemplaretur* ; II, 10, *dum ardebant* ; *dum intuentur* ; II, 16, *dum . . . transuehitur* ; III, 3, *dum . . . . . plangimus* ; III, 12, *dum . . . . . apparatur* ; I, 3, *ubi . . uisum esset* ; II, 2, *ubi . . . . . patefaceret* ; II, 10, *ubi . . . . adessent* ; II, 3, *ubi concessum est.* The historic present is rarely used after *dum* unless the main verb is historic present : an exception is II, 10, *ceperunt . . . . . dum intuentur.* *Dum* is also used with the subjunctive to mean ' seeing that ' [6] : e.g., II, 12, *dum . . scirem necesse esse me fugere, quid satius fuit,* ' seeing that I knew I must flee, which was the better . . . ? ' ; III, 3, *dum sciatis.* In II, 9, *dum esset,* the con-

---

[1] This seems the most natural way to take the passage, rather than to regard the absolute clause as referring to the flight of the enemy in the battle described in the previous sentence ; cf. *Vulg.*, Num. xiii. 1, ' profectusque est populus de Haseroth, fixis tentoriis in deserto Pharan '.
[2] The construction is, of course, frequent in verse in the classical period.
[3] Cf. Kaulen, *op. cit.*, 1st ed., p. 141.
[4] Cf. Suet., *Claud.* 40 : *inducta teste in senatu.*
[5] On the common late use of *ubi* with the subjunctive, see Stolz-Schmalz, p. 767.
[6] Recorded by Baxter in the eighth century, but only with the perfect indicative ; this sense of *dum* is, however, found with the subjunctive from Tertullian onwards, see Stolz-Schmalz, p. 744.

junction has a definitely concessive force, the point being that, although the banner was made of plain material, a figure appeared on it miraculously in time of war. In II, 10, *dum* . . . . . *eligerent*, the conjunction is causal in force,[1] the sense being that there was a severe battle because the Danes preferred death to flight. There is nothing requiring comment in the use of *cum*. *Postquam* is used with the pluperfect indicative, III, 5, *postquam manducauerant*, a use which is more frequent in late than in classical prose (e.g., *Vulg.*, Gen. xxxi. 10 ; Exod. ii. 11 ; etc.) *Quamquam, licet,* and *tametsi* are used with the subjunctive (II, 13 ; III, 9), and this is the invariable construction of concessive clauses in the *Vulgate* after *quamquam, licet,*[2] and *quamuis,* though *tametsi* takes the indicative. In II, 7, *quousque* . . . . . *conglobarent*, the late use of *quousque* for *quoad* appears : see Stolz-Schmalz, p. 769, and cf. *Vulg.*, Tob. vi. 6. A late usage, which does not occur in the *Vulgate*, is that of *quatinus* for final *ut* in I, 1, *quatinus . . . facilius sit*, and II, 10, *in hoc conspiratos, quatinus.*[3]

The Encomiast is particularly fond of the adverb *utpote*. He uses it in the usual classical construction before a relative, II, 1, *utpote qui iuuenis erat*,[4] and also directly before the verb, in a sense practically equivalent to that of *ut* : e.g., Arg., *utpote decebat* (cf. II, 2). He uses it, however, most freely in the sense ' seeing that ', ' being in truth ', ' inasmuch as ', before adjectives and nouns : e.g., II, 6, *ad bellandum, utpote iuuenem, feruentissimum,* ' very anxious to fight, inasmuch as he is a youth ' ; II, 9, *utpote formidolosi* ; II, 18, *utpote futurum heredem regni* ; III, 5, *utpote fessi.* There can accordingly be little doubt that II, 16, *utpote regina famosa*, means ' inasmuch as she was a famous queen '.[5]

The Encomiast twice uses *ac si* as an equivalent of *quasi* : II, 9, *ac si intextus* ; II, 15, *ac si* . . . . . *fecisset.* This usage is not common and is practically confined to late texts, although occasional early examples are found (see *Thes.*, s.v. *atque*, cols. 1083–4, and Stolz-Schmalz, pp. 658 and 784). Baxter records this use of *ac si* in insular Latin in the seventh and ninth centuries, and examples are to be found in writers of the Encomiast's period, as Syrus, *Vita S. Maioli*, ii. 22, *imperatrix . . acsi ancillarum ultima* ; Folquin, *Vita Folquini*, Prol., *uestrum . . . . successum acsi meum* ; *Miracula S. Bauonis*, i. 3, *acsi funditus infecta.* The Encomiast also uses *adeo* twice in the sense of *ideo*, ' therefore ' : II, 6, *si . . cecidero . . . . non Anglis gloriae erit adeo, quia* ; II, 13, *quamquam perplurimi interficerentur, numerus eorum non adeo minuebatur, quia.* This use of *adeo* is late and exceptionally rare : see *Thes.*, s.v. *adeo*, col. 616, lines 29–34, and Stolz-Schmalz, p. 497. Medieval instances are *Miracula S. Bertini*, 3, *sed mirum dictu . . . adeo nullam lesionem passus* ; Regino of Prüm, *Chronicon*, 836, 881 : *non adeo preualuit.*

The Encomiast's use of *denique* with a force practically equal to that of *namque* should be observed [6] : e.g., I, 1, *hic denique* . . . . . *duxit originem* ; II, 9, *hoc denique testatur.*

The three following verbal constructions may be observed. (1) The Encomiast uses

---

[1] Concessive and causal *dum* with the subjunctive is again a late Latin construction, not found before Tertullian, see Stolz-Schmalz, *loc. cit.*

[2] Except in 2 Cor. iv. 16, where *licet* takes the indic. in the best manuscripts, though not in the received text.

[3] Examples in Lewis and Short, and Kaulen, *op. cit.*, 1st ed., p. 211 ; history of the usage in Stolz-Schmalz, p. 770 ; see also Baxter for occurrences in insular Latin ; the usage is also frequent in medieval continental Latin.

[4] Note the indicative for classical subjunctive ; cf. Stolz-Schmalz, p. 713.

[5] Cf. below, p. xlvi. The Encomiast's use of *utpote* before verbs is unusual, but his use of it before nouns and adjectives is to be paralleled from the works of most of his contemporaries, and, of the classical writers, instances are frequent in Horace (see Lewis and Short). Some medieval writers (e.g., Ruotger and Folquin) use *utputa* in the same way.

[6] See E. Skard, *Målet i Historia Norwegiae* (Oslo, 1930), p. 11.

the typical *Vulgate* construction of *facere* with the accusative and infinitive in a causal sense : e.g., III, 5, *tortores uinctos* . . *sedere fecerunt* ; II, 3, *nauim* . . *fecit parari* ; and with the subject of the infinitive unexpressed : II, 7, *eam coangustare fecit* ; III, 2, *fecit epistolam* . . . . . *componere*.[1] (2) The Encomiast usually expresses the idea of giving orders that something be done to something, or somebody, when the actual recipient of the instructions is not named, with *iubeo* and an accusative and active infinitive : e.g., II, 15, *multos* . . . . *occidere* . . . . *iuberet* ; II, 16, *quam* . . . *iussit inquirere*.[2] (3) In II, 13, *media mihi libere erit regio*, we have the use of *esse* and an adverb as predicate, which is so frequent in the *Vulgate* (e.g., Psa. cxl. 10, *singulariter sum* ; see Kaulen, *op. cit.*, 1st ed., p. 241).

It will be convenient to present in alphabetical order the chief verbs which exhibit peculiarities of rection in the *Encomium* : *accelero* + inf., II, 3 (rare classically, e.g., Stat., *Theb.* i. 516 ; late Lat. and *Vulg.* frequent) ; *accuro* + inf., II, 6 ; *aduehor* + acc. of place whither, III, 14 (rare, e.g., Val. Fl. iii. 485 ; Sol., 53, 8 ; hardly *Aen.* viii. 136, where *Teucros = Troiam*) ; *apto* + acc. and inf., II, 9 ; *attineo* + dat., Prol. ; *circumfero* + acc. and dat., I, 4 (cf. Vell. ii. 92, 2, *circumferens* . . *orbi* . . . . . *bona*) ; *continuo*, ' join ', + *ad*, Arg. ; *dispono* + acc. and inf., III, 1 (late Amm., etc.) ; *egredior* + acc. of place whence, II, 7 (fairly common in classical writers, but later increasingly frequent, see Forcellini, s.v. *egredior*, 6, and *Thes.*, s.v. *egredior*, cols. 285–6) ; *elabor a*, II, 10 and 12 (not before Oros.) ; *eligo in* + acc., III, 1 (late, e.g., *Vulg.*, 1 Par. ix. 22 ; construction extended by Encomiast to *benedico in* and *laudo in*, III, 1 ; cf. Adalbold, *Vita Heinrici*, 15, *corono in*) ; *eligo* + inf., II, 7 (late, frequent from Ulpian onwards) ; *experior si*, II, 7 (rare, e.g., Val. Fl. v. 561 ; cf. *Vulg.*, Iudith viii. 31 ; 1 Ioan. iv. 1, *probo si*) ; *ferueo ad* + ger., II, 6 ; *gaudeo de*, III, 6 (rare classically, frequent from Tertull. onwards) ; *indignor* + dat. of person, II, 21, and + *de*, II, 22 (both late constructions, e.g., *Vulg.*, Ioan. vii. 23 ; Matt. xx. 24) ; *intendo in* + abl., I, 3 (rare, e.g., Caes., *B.G.* iii. 22) ; *intueor* + acc. and inf., II, 6 and 7 ; *mando*, ' announce ', + acc. and inf., II, 3 ; *patior*, ' allow ', + dat. of person, I, 1 ; *piget* + dat. and inf., III, 2 : *prestolor* + acc., II, 8, III, 4 (ante- and post-classical) ; *preualeo in* + acc., II, 10 ; *rebello* + dat., II, 5 ; *redarguo* + abl. of cause, I, 3, and + *de*, Prol. ; *sentio contra*, Arg. (*sentio* + adverbial *contra* is occasionally found, see *Thes.*, s.v. *contra*, col. 741). In I, 2, *onustas de* . . *bellatoribus primis*, we have a telescoped expression, ' loaded (with men) from among the best warriors ', rather than a construction of *onustus* with *de* ; in II, 8, where *sequuntur*, *obtemperant* and *fauent* have the same object (*eum*), this is in the acc., though this is proper only to the first of the three verbs ; in III, 4, *suscipio in fide* is used for the classical *recipio in fidem* (it may be noticed that *fide* is in rhyme).[3] Since the Encomiast adopted a deliberately poetical style, carefully enriched with Virgilian borrowings, all ordinary poetical constructions are to be regarded as normal in his work, and, accordingly, constructions peculiar only in that they are not found in classical prose are excluded from the above list.

It is clear from the above paragraphs that the syntax of the *Encomium* is characterised by a very large number of late Latin peculiarities, most of which are to be found in profusion in other medieval Latin works. Similarly, in choice of phrase, the Encomiast's language is deeply influenced by late Latin, particularly by that of the *Vulgate*. This

---

[1] This construction is very frequent in the *Vulgate*. It is not unknown in the classical period : e.g., *Aen.* ii. 538–9, *nati* . . . *cernere letum fecisti* ; cf. Stolz-Schmalz, p. 584.
[2] This construction is not common in the *Vulgate* : cf., however, 2 Mach. xiv. 27, *iubere* . . *Machabaeum* . . . *mittere Antiocham*. In such sentences, the Encomiast also uses the construction, usual in the *Vulgate*, of *iubeo* with acc. and inf. pass. : e.g., I, 3, *iussit suam patefieri uoluntatem* ; III, 4, *iussit naues* . . . *repelli*.
[3] William of Jumièges, vii. 11, ' in sua fide suscepit '.

is a feature which it shares with practically all the Latin of the Middle Ages, and in consequence it is impossible, in the case of many correspondences of phrase between the *Vulgate* and the *Encomium*, to say if they are due to direct influence, or to the phrases in question having become part of the fabric of medieval Latin. It is, of course, possible in the case of many Scriptural phrases to say that they are an integral part of medieval Latin, and that their use by a writer is no sign of direct Scriptural influence on his style, but, in the present state of Latin lexicography, it is not possible to do the contrary, and definitely affirm that a given Scriptural phrase had not become in any sense a cliché and that its use by a writer proves personal knowledge on his part of the book of the Bible from which it is ultimately derived.[1] Accordingly, I present the following list of correspondences between the language of the *Vulgate* and that of the *Encomium*, not to show that the Encomiast was a careful student of the Scriptures, but to illustrate, as one of the medieval peculiarities of the *Encomium*, the extent of the Scriptural element in its language. Many of the Scriptural phrases found in the *Encomium* occur in other west European Latin works of its period. I limit the list to the more striking correspondences, and do not attempt to give complete references to the Scriptural occurrences of the phrases : *Enc.*, Arg., *suo subiugauit imperio*—Iudith i. 1, *subiugauerat . . . imperio suo* ; *Enc.* I, 1, *formidine mortis*—Psa. liv. 5, *formido mortis* ; *Enc.* I, 2, *princeps miliciae*— *Vulg.*, frequent expression ; *Enc.* I, 2, *tibique uictoriam ascribi*—2 Reg. xii. 28, *nomini meo ascribatur uictoria* ; *Enc.* I, 3, *armis bellicis*—*Vulg.*, frequent collocation ; *Enc.* I, 3, *pro muro*—1 Reg. xxv. 16 ; *Enc.* I, 5, etc., *Deo gratias*—*Vulg.*, frequent expression ; *Enc.* I, 5, *natiuitatis . . . . terram*—*Vulg.*, frequent collocation ; *Enc.* II, 1, *terra quod esset opima*— Gen. xlix. 15, *terram quod (esset) optima* ; *Enc.* II, 2, *non preualebit*—*Vulg.*, favourite expression ; *Enc.* II, 3, *aromatibus condito*—Gen. l. 2, *aromatibus condirent* (both of a corpse) ; *Enc.* II, 6, *in prima fronte*—3 Reg. xx. 17 ; *Enc.* II, 6, *periculosa sit desperatio*— 2 Reg. ii. 26 ; *Enc.* II, 8, *uirum fortem fieri suadent*—1 Reg. xviii. 17, *esto uir fortis* ; *Enc.* II, 9, *innumerabili multitudine*—Iudith ii. 8, *multitudine innumerabilium* ; *Enc.* II, 9, *uiri cordati*—Iob xxxiv. 10 ; *Enc.* II, 10, *uera suspitione*—cf. Num. v. 14, *falsa suspicione* ; *Enc.* II, 13, *premittit . . . . qui dextras . . dent et accipiant*—2 Mach. xiv. 19, *praemisit . . . . . ut darent dextras atque acciperent* ; *Enc.* II, 13, *pacifice salutato*—1 Reg. xxx. 21, *salutauit . . pacifice* ; *Enc.* II, 13, *meridianae plagae*—*Vulg.*, such expressions with *plaga* frequently ; *Enc.* II, 16, *placuit . . . uerbum*—Iudith xi. 18, *placuerunt . . . uerba* ; *Enc.* II, 17, *rei postmodum probauit exitus* ; III, 9, *postmodum rei probauit euentus*— Gen. xli. 13, *postea rei probauit euentus* (cf. Ruth iii. 18, *quem res exitum habeat*) ; *Enc.* II, 18, *Saluatoris . . gratia*—Tit. ii. 11, *gratia . . Saluatoris* ; *Enc.* III, 1, *morte amara*—1 Reg. xv. 32, *amara mors* ; *Enc.* III, 2, *exitum rei expectabat*—Ruth iii. 18, *expecta . . . . quem res exitum habeat* (cf. *Enc.* II, 7, *euentum rei expectauit*, and quotations above relating to II, 17) ; *Enc.* III, 2, *in peccatis uiuens*—*Vulg.*, frequent combinations with verb + *in peccatis* ; *Enc.* III, 4, *prestolabantur eius aduentum*— Iudic. ix. 25, *illius praestolabantur aduentum* ; *Enc.* III, 5, *mane autem facto*—Matt. xxvii. 1 ; *Enc.* III, 6, *ocul[os] . . . . . erui*—Iudic. xvi. 21, *eruerunt oculos* ; *Enc.* III, 7, *cum . . gratiarum actione*—*Vulg.*, frequent expression ; *Enc.* III, 8, *ne . . . pigritaretur uenire*—Act. ix. 38, *ne pigriteris uenire* ; *Enc.* III, 9, *cuncta disponentis*—Sap. xv. 1, *disponens omnia* ; *Enc.* III, 9, *forti iubet esse animo*—Tob. v. 13, *forti animo esto* ; *Enc.* III, 10, *gaudio magno gaudebat*—Matt. ii. 10, *gauisi sunt gaudio magno* ; *Enc.* III, 10, *uiscera diuinae misericordiae*—Luc. i. 78, *uiscera misericordiae Dei*. It may be observed that the Encomiast knew the expression *uniuersae carnis uiam ingredi* (I, 5),[2]

---

[1] This unsound method is applied by Skard to the *Historia Norvegiae* (*op. cit.*, p. 67).
[2] See *N.E.D.*, s.v. *way*, sb.[1], p. 201, col. 1 ; it may be observed that the expression is of quite remarkable frequence in the Encomiast's period ; see, e.g., Odilo, *Epitaphium Adalheidae*, 6 ; Sig. Gem., *Vita Deoderici*, 3 ; Adalbert, *Vita Heinrici*, 3 ; Adalbold, *Vita Heinrici*, 29.

and that he has (III, 7) the phrase *secreta cordis*, which, in its English form, ' secrets of the heart ', was introduced into Psa. xliii. 22, by Coverdale.[1] In *Enc.* III, 14, *qui unanimes in domo habitare facit*, we seem to have a reminiscence of Psa. cxxxii. 1, *quam bonum . . . . habitare fratres in unum*, influenced in expression by Psa. lxvii. 7, *qui inhabitare facit unius moris in domo*.

The Encomiast alludes directly to four passages of Scripture : II, 7, *Deus itaque, qui omnes homines uult magis saluare quam perdere* (cf. Luc. ix. 56) ; II, 14, *Deus memor suae antiquae doctrinae, scilicet omne regnum in se ipsum diuisum diu permanere non posse* (cf. Marc. iii. 24) ; II, 21, *largitor hilaris monitu apostolico* (cf. 2 Cor. ix. 7) ; III, 7, *illud autenticum domincae exortationis preceptum . . . . . quo . . electis insinuat, quoniam si persequuti uos fuerint in una ciuitate fugite in alia* (cf. Matt. x. 23). 2 Cor. ix. 7, is also echoed in *Enc.* II, 21, *hilariter largitus est*. In II, 22, the reference to the king's inability to take his property with him in death recalls Iob xxvii. 19 ; the story of Hörthaknútr's vision in *Enc.* III, 9, appeared to Plummer [2] to be influenced by Act. xxvii, but the parallel is not particularly close.

No reader can fail to be struck by the considerable influence of the Latin poets and historians on the Encomiast's language, for there is not a page of the *Encomium* upòn which verbal correspondences with their works cannot be found. Considerable caution, however, must be exercised in drawing conclusions concerning the Encomiast's reading from these correspondences. Many of them are phrases found in a variety of classical authors, others had become clichés in the Middle Ages, and do not prove direct knowledge of the Classics in authors using them. (Examples of phrases of both these kinds, which occur in the *Encomium*, will be given in the Linguistic Notes.) A knowledge of a classical author on the part of the Encomiast can be proved only by the presence in his work of such a large number of verbal correspondences with the author in question that they cannot be accidental, or by the presence of a smaller number of correspondences, which are shown by their striking nature or their length to be derived directly from the author concerned. In the case of Virgil and Sallust, the first of these conditions prevails, and in that of Lucan the second. Accordingly, it can be definitely affirmed that the Encomiast knew these three authors. It can be suggested with probability that, of the Latin poets, he knew Horace, Ovid, and Juvenal and, of the historians, Caesar. It would, however, be hazardous to affirm definitely that he knew these four last-named authors.

The Encomiast's borrowings from Sallust are remarkable in that their number and their frequent length makes it certain that he made a close first-hand study of both the *Catilina* and the *Iugurtha*. The following are the most remarkable parallels between the Encomiast and Sallust : *Enc.*, Prol., *memoriam rerum gestarum—Iug.* iv. 6, *memoria rerum gestarum* ; *Enc.*, Prol., *mecum . . . me reputante—Cat.* lii. 2, *mecum reputo* ; *Enc.*, Prol., *sese humana consuetudo habeat—Iug.* liii. 8, *res humanae ita sese habent* ; *Enc.* I, 1, *nihilque . . . . . . patiebatur remissi—Iug.* liii. 6, *nihil . . . remissi patiebatur* ; *Enc.* I, 1, *sibi fecerat obnoxios et fideles—Cat.* xiv. 6, *obnoxios fidosque sibi faceret* ; *Enc.* I, 4, *melius est ut sileam, quam . . . pauca dicam—Iug.* xix. 2, *silere melius puto quam parum dicere* ; *Enc.* I, 4, *fusis fugatisque—Iug.* lii. 4, *fusi fugatique* (cf. lxxix. 4) ; *Enc.* II, 1, *si id parum processisset—Iug.* xlvi. 4, *sin id parum procedat* ; *Enc.* II, 6, *memoresque uirtutis—Iug.* xcvii. 5, *uirtutis memores* ; *Enc.* II, 9, *pro libertate et patria—Cat.* lviii. 11, *pro patria pro libertate* (both in a general's exhortation to troops) ; *Enc.* III, 4, *diem et tempus et locum— Iug.* cviii. 2, *diem locum tempus* ; *Enc.* III, 7, *sceleris nouitate—Cat.* iv. 4, *sceleris . . .*

---

[1] See *N.E.D.*, s.v. *secret*, a. and sb., p. 357, col. 3 ; the phrase occurs in the *Vita S. Bertini metrica prima*, 360–1, in the *Vita Oswaldi* (Raine, *Historians of the Church of York*, i, 405), and frequently in the early Christian poets ; cf. Erembold, *in cordis mei secreto*.

[2] *Two of the Saxon Chronicles*, ii. 217.

nouitate ; *Enc.* III, 7, *quid facto . . opus sit*—*Cat.* xlvi. 2, *quid facto opus esset* ; *Enc.* III, 7, *emori fortunis . . . honestus exitus*—*Iug.* xiv. 24 (both in excusing a flight) ; *Enc.* III, 7, *pro suo casu spes satis honestas reliquae dignitatis conseruandae exequitur*— *Cat.* xxxv. 4, *satis honestas pro meo casu spes reliquae dignitatis conseruandae sum secutus* ; *Enc.* III, 7, *frequentia negotiatorum*—*Iug.* xlvii. 2, *frequentiam negotiatorum* ; *Enc.* III, 7, *quae prima mortales ducunt*—*Iug.* xli. 1 ; *Enc.* III, 8, *uenire . . maturet*—*Iug.* xxii. 1, *maturantes ueniunt* ; *Enc.* III, 8, *ardebat . . animo*—*Iug.* xxxix. 5, *animo ardebat* ; *Enc.* III, 8, *iniurias ultum ire*—*Iug.* lxviii. 1, *ultum ire iniurias* ; *Enc.* III, 9, *quam maximas potest . . . parat copias*—*Iug.* xlviii. 2, *quam maxumas potest copias . . . parat* ; *Enc.* III, 9, *copia pugnandi*—*Iug.* lii. 3, etc., *copiam pugnandi* ; *Enc.* III, 9, *quod in tam atroci negotio solet fieri*—*Cat.* xxix, 2, *quod plerumque in atroci negotio solet* ; *Enc.* III, 10, *iuxta . . . consulere*—*Cat.* xxxvii. 8, *iuxta . . . consuluisse* ; *Enc.* III, 11, *cuncta . . . luctu compleri*—*Cat.* li. 9, *luctu omnia compleri* ; *Enc.* III, 11, *si pro singulis . . . parem disserere, prius me tempus quam rem credo deserere*—*Iug.* xlii. 5, *si singillatim . . . . parem disserere, tempus quam res maturius me deserat* ; *Enc.* III, 13, *optimum factu rati*—*Cat.* lv. 1, *optumum factu ratus.*

The above list could have been considerably increased by the inclusion of collocations, which, although they are used by Sallust, appear in too many other writers to have any distinctive flavour (e.g., I, 2, *cessissent prospere* ; II, 1, *euentus belli* ; II, 14, *diu multumque*). A number of expressions are also excluded, which are common to the Encomiast and Sallust, but might arise independently in any two writers (e.g., II, 1, *inuasisset fines* ; II, 9, *in medios . . hostes* ; II, 18, *supra repetam*), while *animus . . . . . . rapitur* and *pro muro*, though found in Sallust (*Iug.* xxv. 7 ; *Cat.* lviii. 17) are omitted, as they are included in respectively the Virgilian and the Biblical lists (see pp. xxxi and xxviii). There are also a number of passages in the *Encomium*, where thought or treatment have been influenced by Sallust in a more general way : we may, for example, compare parts of the Encomiast's *Prologue* with *Cat.* iii. 1–2, the remark on the bad effect of leisure on soldiers in *Enc.* I, 1, with *Cat.* xi. 5, and the Encomiast's description of the flight after Ashingdon with *Iug.* lii. 4 and xcvii. 3. In style, Sallust cannot be said to influence the Encomiast, who even removes the typical asyndeton of some of the Sallustian phrases which he borrows (see the instances quoted above from II, 9 ; III, 4). On the other hand, in III, 1 (*sceptrum, coronam*), an isolated adoption of Sallustian asyndeton occurs. Attention may also be drawn to the typically Sallustian use of *parare* for *conari* : e.g., II, 1, *parat retinere sceptrum* ; II, 9, *deturbare parauit* ; III, 4, *parabat adire* (cf. *Cat.* xviii. 5 ; *Iug.* xiii. 2 ; etc.).

The Encomiast's knowledge of the language of Latin history was by no means all provided by Sallust, but there is an absence of correspondences between his language and that of any particular Latin historian sufficiently close to prove direct influence of the one writer on the other. He has a few correspondences of phrase with Caesar (e.g., *Enc.* III, 7, *pro re atque tempore*—*B.G.* v. 8, *pro tempore et pro re*) and some of his knowledge of Latin historical phraseology may be due to a study of that writer. Gertz, however, is certainly unwise to suggest that the Encomiast's remarks on the diversity of the nations who submitted to Knútr (II, 17) echoes the opening of the *De Bello Gallico*, for similar passages occur in Dudo and elsewhere.

The debt of a medieval author to Virgil is always difficult to assess, because some Virgilian phrases, like *armato milite*, became part of the texture of the Latin tongue as it was written in the Middle Ages, and are not to be regarded as evidence that a writer who employs them studied Virgil at first hand. In the case of the *Encomium*, however, so many parallels with Virgil are to be found, that there is no room for doubt that its author had a good knowledge of the *Aeneid*, and some familiarity with the *Eclogues* and *Georgics*. The following list of collocations common to the Encomiast and Virgil will illustrate the debt of the former to the Latin poet : *Enc.*, Prol., *morti* . . *occumberem—Aen.* ii. 62, *occumbere morti* ; *Enc.* I, 2, *compositae pacis—Aen.* vii. 339, *compositam pacem* ; *Enc.* I, 3, *animo sederat*, and II, 12, *sederet animis—Aen.* iv. 15, *animo . . . sederet* and ii. 660, *sedet . . animo* ; *Enc.* I, 3, *instructique armis—Aen.* viii. 80, *instruit armis* ; *Enc.* I, 4, *armato milite—Aen.* ii. 20 ; *Enc.* I, 4, *turritas . . puppes* and II, 7, *turritis pupibus—Aen.* viii. 693, *turritis puppibus* ; *Enc.* I, 4, *erat cernere—Aen.* vi. 596, viii. 676, *cernere erat* ; *Enc.* I, 4, *uenientes austros—Ecl.* v. 82, *uenientis . . austri* ; *Enc.* I, 4, *aspera signis —Aen.* v. 267, ix. 263 ; *Enc.* I, 4, *equatis . . rostris—Aen.* v. 232 ; *Enc.* I, 4, *spumare cerula—Aen.* viii. 672, *spumabant caerula* ; *Enc.* I, 4, *pedestri pugnae . . . accingunt— Aen.* xi. 707, *pugnaeque accinge pedestri* ; *Enc.* II, 2, *difigunt oscula* and II, 21, *infixit oscula* ; *dulcia oscula infigeret—Aen.* i. 687, *oscula dulcia figet* ; *Enc.* II, 4, *curui litoris— Aen.* iii. 16, etc., *litore curuo* ; *Enc.* II, 5, *solutis . . . . . funibus—Aen.* v. 773, *soluique . . . funem* ; *Enc.* II, 6, *queque obuia metebat—Aen.* v. 513, *proxima quaeque metit* ; *Enc.* II, 14, *faedere . . firmato—Aen.* xi. 330, *foedera firment* (cf. xii. 212) ; *Enc.* II, 15, *aetate florens—Ecl.* vii. 4, *florentes aetatibus* ; *Enc.* II, 21, *defixus lumina—Aen.* vi. 156 ; *Enc.* II, 21, *cumulare altaria—Aen.* xi. 50, *cumulatque altaria* ; *Enc.* III, 1, *saltus canibus . . . cinxit—Aen.* iv. 121, *saltusque indagine cingunt* ; *Ecl.* x. 57, *canibus circumdare saltus* ; *Enc.* III, 2, *insidias moliebatur—Geor.* i. 271, *insidias . . moliri* ; *Enc.* III, 5, *uinctisque post tergum manibus—Aen.* ii. 57, *manus . . . post terga reuinctum* ; *Enc.* III, 5, *tanto discrimine—Aen.* iii. 629, *discrimine tanto* ; *Enc.* III, 5, *ruptis . . . obicibus— Geor.* ii. 480, *obicibus ruptis* ; *Enc.* III, 6, *effossis . . luminibus—Aen.* iii. 663, *luminis effossi* ; *Enc.* III, 7, *animus . . . diuersus huc illucque rapitur—Aen.* iv. 285-6, viii. 20-1, *animum nunc huc . . nunc . . illuc · . . . rapit . . perque omnia uersat* ; *Enc.* III, 8, *equ[u]m conscendit—Aen.* xii. 736, *conscendebat equos* ; *Enc.* III, 9, *spumas salis aere ruebant—Aen.* i. 35 ; *Enc.* III, 9, *maris facies—Aen.* v. 768 ; *Enc.* III, 9, *faeda tempestas uentorum nubiumque . . . glomeratur—Georg.* i. 323-4, *foedam glomerant tempestatem . . . . . . nubes* ; *Enc.* III, 9, *anchorae de proris iactae—Aen.* iii. 277, vi. 901, *ancora de prora iacitur* ; *Enc.* III, 9, *incepto desisteret—Aen.* i. 37, *incepto desistere* ; *Enc.* III, 10, *in medium consulere—Aen.* xi. 335, *consulite in medium* ; *Enc.* III, 11, *impulit aures—Georg.* iv. 349, *Aen.* xii. 618 ; *Enc.* III, 12, *uincit amor patriae—Aen.* vi. 823, *uincet amor patriae.*

Some collocations occur in the above list which are found in other classical writers besides Virgil, though ones like *nec mora* (I, 4) and *tergum dedero* (II, 6), which, although they occur in Virgil, are so frequent as to be part of the common stock of the language, are excluded, as are also ones which occur in Virgil, but in a different sense from that in which they are used by the Encomiast : e.g., *dolo reperto* (III, 2 ; *Aen.* iv. 128) ; *cupidine capti* (III, 5 ; *Aen.* iv. 194). I have not attempted to collect even the distinctively Virgilian collocations exhaustively, and, even if a complete list of them were made, it would still not indicate the extent of the Virgilian influence upon the *Encomium*, because, in addition to these identical collocations, there are many others in the *Encomium* which are undoubtedly echoes of Virgilian ones, in which the phraseology is somewhat modified. Examples are : *Enc.* I, 4, *armorum seges—Aen.* iii. 46, *telorum seges* ; *Enc.* I, 4, *eratis rostris—Aen.* ix. 121, *aeratae . . . . prorae* (in ix. 119, *rostris* occurs, and cf. viii. 675) ; *Enc.* II, 2, *uolitans fama—Aen.* vii. 392, etc., *fama uolat* ; *Enc.* II, 5, *intrat pelagus— Aen.* vi. 59, *maria intraui* ; *Enc.* II, 5, *uerrit . . fluctus—Aen.* v. 778, *aequora uerrunt* (in v. 776, *fluctus* occurs) ; *Enc.* II, 5, *puppibus . . . . rudentibus—Aen.* iii. 561-2, *rudentem . . . proram* ; *Enc.* II, 6, *rumpens morulas—Aen.* iv. 569, *rumpe moras* ; *Enc.* II, 7, *respirare copia—Aen.* ix. 813, *respirare potestas* ; *Enc.* III, 8, *copia data est . . loquendi—Aen.* i. 520, *data copia fandi* (cf. ix. 484) ; *Enc.* III, 9, *membris . . placidae quieti . . cedentibus* [1]*—Aen.* v. 836, *placida laxabant membra quiete* (cf. i. 691). There

---

[1] The influence of Virgil and Lucan are here mingled, see below, p. xxxii.

are also many decidedly Virgilian turns of expression in the *Encomium*, such as the formula *potior optata* . . (II, 6 and 14 ; *Aen.* i. 172), the mañy similarities to the description of the shield in *Aen.* viii which are found in the description of the ships in *Enc.* I, 4, the use of *accingo* with an accusative of the indirect object (II, 6 ; *Aen.* iv. 493), and the absolute *certum facio*, ' duly inform ' (III, 13 ; *Aen.* iii. 179). The reader will also observe many instances of the use of single words with a strong Virgilian flavour by the Encomiast.

After Virgil, the Encomiast shows more definite signs of a knowledge of Lucan than of any other Latin poet. In particular, practically the whole of the description of Emma's departure from Flanders in III, 12, is derived from Lucan's account of a similar event (viii. 147–58). The Encomiast has in this case derived so much of his thought as well as so many phrases from Lucan, that it is desirable to quote the whole passage, to enable the reader to make a comparison :

> Cunctos mutare putares
> Tellurem patriaeque solum : sic litore toto
> Plangitur, infestae [1] tenduntur in aethera dextrae.
> Pompeiumque minus, cuius fortuna dolorem
> Mouerat, ast illam, quam toto tempore belli
> Ut ciuem uidere suam, discedere cernens
> Ingemuit populus ; quam uix, si castra mariti
> Uictoris peteret, siccis dimittere matres
> Iam poterant oculis : tanto deuinxit amore·
> Hos pudor, hos probitas castique modestia uoltus,
> Quod submissa nimis, nulli grauis hospita turbae,
> Stantis adhuc fati uixit quasi coniuge uicto.

The Encomiast opens II, 7 with a slightly modified citation of Lucan iii. 762, *primus Caesareis pelagi decus addidit armis.* In *Enc.* III, 14, *hic fides habetur regni sociis*, there is a distinct reminiscence of Luc. i. 92, *nulla fides regni sociis.* Otherwise, the Encomiast does not draw so freely on Lucan's rich store of poetical language as might be expected, but the following parallels may be noticed : *Enc.* III, 9, *maris . . amfractu*—Luc. v. 416, *maris anfractus* ; *Enc.* III, 9, *suppara uelorum*—Luc. v. 429. *Enc.* III, 9, *membris . . placidae quieti somni cedentibus*, is a mixture of Lucan's *somno cedentia membra* (v. 511 ; cf. iii. 8) and the Virgilian passage quoted above, p. xxxi. The Horatian phrase *metuensque futuri* is borrowed by Lucan (ii. 233), but since the Encomiast shows traces of a knowledge of Horace (see below), he may be assumed to have borrowed it directly.

The traces of a knowledge of other Latin poets are less definite in the *Encomium*. The question whether the Encomiast knew the comedians is a difficult one, for, as is well known, there are many elements in their language which are not classical but re-appear in late Latin, and the Encomiast naturally has a number of such words.[2] Furthermore, his favourite, Sallust, was an archaist and there are points of contact between his language and that of the comedians. One may, however, perhaps draw attention to the parallel of *Enc.*, Prol., *erga me . . . meritam* and Plautus, *Amph.* 1101, *erga me merita*, and to the expression, *Enc.* III, 3, *quid captetis consilii*, which is a favourite with the comedians (Plaut., *Ass.* 358 ; Ter., *And.* 170, 404).

Lucretius was scarcely known in the Encomiast's period, but, whether by accident, or by direct or indirect influence, it may be noted that three distinctive Lucretian collocations occur in the *Encomium* : *Enc.* II, 11, *membris abradunt*—Lucr. iv. 1103, *abradere membris* ; *Enc.* III, 7, *sagaci ratione*—Lucr. i. 130 and 368, *ratione sagaci* ; *Enc.* III, 14, *inuiolabile uiget*—Lucr. v. 305, *inuiolabilia . . . . . uigere*.

---

[1] *Enc.* has *infensae*, which we may retain or emend to agree with Lucan. Gertz foolishly alters to *intensae*. [2] See below, p. xxxix.

It seems probable that the Encomiast had some knowledge of Ovid, for I, 1, *armatis* . . *manibus nudis* . . *occurreret*, appears to be an echo of *A.A.* iii. 5, *armatis* . . *concurrere nudas*, and II, 24, *caeli palatio*, is a famous Ovidian collocation (*Met.* i. 176). The following parallels may also be observed : *Enc.* II, 1, *uentis* . . . *commisit carbasa*—*Her.* vii. 171, *praebebis carbasa uentis* ; *Enc.* II, 1, *resumptis uiribus*—*Met.* ix. 59 and 193, *resumere uires* [1] ; *Enc.* II, 4, *radiantibus auro*—*A.A.* iii. 451 ; *Enc.* II, 12, *resisteretis armis* —*Met.* ix. 201, *resisti* . . . *armis* ; *Enc.* III, 7, *mente* . . *tacita*—*Met.* v. 427 ; *Enc.* III, 13, *correptus amore*—*Fast.* iii. 681. I exclude from this list III, 5, *ceca cupidine*, because the collocation *caeca cupido*, although found in Ovid (*Met.* iii. 620), occurs in many other poets, including Lucretius and Juvenal, and also II, 9, *brumali tempore*, II, 5, *flatu secundo* (cf. III, 9, *secundis flatibus*), and III, 6, *ocul*[*os*] . . . . *erui* because, though these collocations are Ovidian (*Am.* iii. 6, 95 ; *Met.* xiii. 418 ; xii. 269), the first two are extremely common elsewhere, and the third is also Biblical (see above, p. xxviii).

The influence of Horace upon the language of the *Encomium* is not great, but the author appears to have known his writings. He has the famous Horatian phrase *metuensque futuri* (III, 1 ; *Sat.* ii. 2, 110) and imitates it in I, 1, *periculi* . . . . *metuens*, and II, 2, *metuens bellorum*, while II, 4, *spetiosa spectacula*, is probably an echo of *A.P.* 144, *speciosa* . . *miracula*. Other parallels are : *Enc.* II, 10, *nescii cedere*—*Od.* i. 6, 6, *cedere nescii* ; *Enc.* II, 16, *esse* . . *in uotis*—*Sat.* ii. 6, 1, *erat in uotis*. *Enc.* I, 1, *duxit originem*, is a frequent expression in Latin authors, not to be regarded as distinctively Horatian, though it occurs in *Od.* iii. 17, 5 (*ducis originem*). In *Enc.* II, 22, the passage on Knútr's unwillingness to amass riches for a prodigal heir seems influenced in thought, though not in language, by *Od.* iii. 24, 61–2.[2] It may be observed that *adclinis* is used in a transferred sense by the Encomiast (II, 7) and Horace (*Sat.* ii. 2, 6), a usage which is otherwise exceptionally rare (see *Thes.*, *s.v.*).

The striking collocation *erroris* . . *nebula* (Arg.) occurs in Juvenal (x. 4), but is not sufficient in itself to enable it to be affirmed that the Encomiast knew Juvenal, for there are otherwise few correspondences in phrase between them. The expression *sinus pandit uelorum* (III, 10) recalls Juvenal (i. 149–50, *utere uelis, totos pande sinus*), but Virgil has *pandentemque sinus* (*Aen.* viii. 712), although *sinus* there does not mean ' sails '. The collocation *agere pacem* occurs in both Juvenal (xv. 163, *agit* . . . . *pacem*) and the Encomiast (I, 1, *pacem* . . . *ageret*), but it is a very common one (see *Thes.*, *s.v.* ' ago ', col. 1384). It cannot be affirmed that the Encomiast knew Juvenal, although there is no reason why he should not have done so : Dudo shows clear traces of a knowledge of Juvenal, and Folquin quotes him directly in the prologue to his *Vita Folquini*.

It is difficult to assess the extent of the Encomiast's knowledge of the vast Latin literature of the later Empire and the Middle Ages. This literature has received very inadequate lexicographical treatment, and accordingly any statement concerning its language must be made with the greatest caution. The language of the *Encomium* is full of phrases relating to matters concerning religion and the Church, all of which are to be found in an identical or similar form in other works, but this technical language is a part of the fabric of ecclesiastical Latin, and nothing can be learned from it of the influence of one author or another.[3] A certain number of striking and unusual collocations are

---

[1] This expression is, however, much used in Medieval Latin, e.g., Dudo, ed. Duchesne, p. 80 ; Odilo, *Epitaphium Adalheidae*, 21 ; John of Wallingford, ed. Gale, p. 548.

[2] The thought in the *Encomium* is not quite clear ; why should Knútr fear that his heir would be angry, if he were parsimonious (*de eius parcitate indignaretur*) ? Did the Encomiast take the Horatian *indignoque* . . . *heredi* as ' for an angry heir ' ?

[3] Examples of such phrases are : I, 1, *secundum Deum et seculum* ; II, 7, *iunxit quieti sempiternae* ; II, 7, *educens e corpore* (cf. II, 14) ; II, 14, *in celesti solio* (also in Dudo, ed. Duchesne, p. 91) ; II, 17, *diuina dispensatione* ; II, 21, *sanctorum* . . . *suffragia* ; II, 21, *superna clementia* ;

common to the *Encomium* and to earlier Christian Latin works, and some examples of these will be found in the Linguistic Notes, but there are not sufficient correspondences with any one writer to prove that the Encomiast studied his works. Furthermore, we have seen from the Encomiast's use of Virgil and Sallust that he usually borrows a phrase from his models when he needs it, but does not take in solid blocks of material, or mould his subject-matter to enable it to be treated in a succession of sentences derived from one source. The only departure from his usual method is the heavy borrowing from one passage in Lucan in the description of Emma's departure from Flanders, and here he has probably not modified his thoughts in order to use Lucan's words : there happened to be a quite remarkable similiarity between what Lucan said about Cornelia and what the Encomiast would in any event have said about Emma, that is to say, that the Flemings were sorry to see her go, even though she was returning in triumph, both because of her merits, and because she was not a burdensome guest. (In fact, he had already said that she was able in part at least to pay her way, III, 7.) The Encomiast, therefore, clothed thoughts, which he already had, in words conveniently provided by Lucan. Obviously, such an agreement between his ideas and those of another writer would seldom occur, and, since he did not shape his material in order to pillage his models, his borrowings would normally be limited to phrases and occasional clauses. Accordingly, influence of an author upon him can usually be traced by linguistic means only when such influence is very considerable and is exerted by an author with a style so individual that small fragments from his works can be recognised with certainty.

The *Encomium* is clearly influenced in form by the Antonian form of biography,[1] in which the writer begins by declaring that he is undertaking a task for which he is imperfectly fitted, not from choice, but at the command of a superior, and in which the account of the acts of the subject of the biography is declared to be abbreviated for lack of time, or some similar cause, rather than for lack of material (cf. *Enc.*, Prol. ; I, 4 ; II, 20 ; III, 11). This form of biography is exceptionally common in the Middle Ages, but the expression, *Enc.* III, 10, *nulla . . . explicabit pagina*, seems to echo the *nulla explicabit oratio* of Sulpicius Severus's *Vita Martini*, 26, the word *pagina* being substituted for *oratio* for the sake of rhyme, and accordingly we may assume that the Encomiast was familiar with that famous specimen of an Antonian life.

The Encomiast alludes (III, 5) to the decimation of the Theban legion, contrasting with it the more cruel murder of the companions of the ætheling Ælfred. It was a widely held belief, perhaps founded on fact, that Ælfred's men were decimated, as will appear in the discussion of the crime below (see p. lxvii), and this naturally turned the Encomiast's thoughts to the most famous story of decimation in all the literature available in the Middle Ages. He has not enough to say about the massacre of the Thebans to enable one to determine in what form he was most familiar with the story. He only mentions that the massacre took place on an open plain, a feature to be found in various versions (see, e.g., *Acta Sanctorum Septembris*, vi. 342, 345), and that the victims were not bound. The latter statement is a reasonable inference from the willing acceptance of death by the martyrs, which is a standing element in the legend.

It has been suggested above (Introduction, § B) that the Encomiast knew Dudo's history of the Norman dukes. It would, in fact, be very surprising if Emma's elected

---

II, 23, *transiit ad Dominum* ; II, 23, *coronandus in parte dextera* (also twice in *Vita Oswaldi*, in Raine, *Historians of the Church of York*, i. 412, 443) ; II, 23, *Domino auctore omnium* ; II, 23, *diuinae dispositioni* ; II, 24, *in aeterna requie* ; III, 1, *apostolica autoritate* ; III, 4, *Dei inimicis* ; III, 5, *divina miseratio* ; III, 7, *gratia superni respectus* (also Folquin, *Vita Folquini*, 4) ; III, 9, *Dei nutu* ; III, 11, *renascentibus in Christo* ; III, 13, *diuini muneris gratia*. Here may also be mentioned the common expressions, I, 5, *naturae persoluit debita*, and II, 24, *requiescat in pace*.

[1] See *Two Lives of Saint Cuthbert*, ed. B. Colgrave (Cambridge, 1940), p. 310.

apologist had failed to be acquainted with Dudo's work. It is not possible, however, to advance definite proof of influence of Dudo on the Encomiast. The resemblance of their works is great, but it is largely due to the following four causes. (1) They both employ rhymed prose. This, however, is a medium much used in their period.[1] (2) They both have a preface explaining their reasons for reluctantly obeying an order to write. This is due to their both being influenced by the Antonian form of biography. (3) They are strikingly similar in their methods of handling their material (cf. above, p. xxii). This is, however, due to a deeper cause than mere influence. Freeman [2] called Dudo one of ' a very bad class of writers, those who were employed, on account of their supposed eloquence, to write histories which were intended only as panegyrics of their patrons.' The Encomiast belongs undeniably to this class of writers, who have to find a middle way between obvious lies and truths unpalatable to their employers, and it is not to be wondered at that his methods at times remind us of Dudo's. (4) They both use the typical Latin of the period, with its great Biblical element, but adorn it with fragments from the Classics, and it is accordingly not remarkable that a good many phrases, especially Scriptural and Virgilian ones, are common to them both.   It is in fact surprising that such coincidences in choice of phrase are not more numerous than they are.[3]

Although Dudo has not influenced the Encomiast in a way which can be proved, I am strongly inclined to the view that the Encomiast knew his work. Decision in this matter can only be subjective, but I do not hesitate to suggest that any reader who will, for example, compare the Encomiast's accounts of the battle of Ashingdon (II, 10–11), of the excellencies of Emma (II, 16), and of the mourning for Knútr (II, 24), with almost any of Dudo's descriptions of battles, high-born maidens, and princely funerals,[4] will have little doubt that the Encomiast was familiar with Dudo's work.   If the influence of Dudo's language is not striking in the *Encomium*, this can be sufficiently explained by the fact that the Encomiast had nothing to learn from Dudo as a Latinist.   In variety of construction and phrase he is greatly superior to Dudo, whose periods are heavy and weighed down by an excessive use of the ablative absolute, and who repeats his favourite formulae with wearisome regularity.

I am inclined to think that the Encomiast was familiar with Asser's *Res Gestae Ælfredi*.   He has two glosses on English place-names, equating *Scepei* with *insula ouium* (II, 8) and *Aescenedun* with *mons fraxinorum* (II, 9).   Although these glosses are of an obvious nature, it is unlikely that the Encomiast fabricated them himself, because they are the only ones he attempts.   He offers no explanations, for example, of *Sanduich*, *Scorastan, Heli*, or *Geldefordia*, so it seems reasonable to conclude that he drew his glosses from a source which had the two glosses quoted above, but none for any other place-name which he had to mention.   Asser would be just such a source, for he has the glosses *Sceapieg, insula ouium* (ed. Stevenson, p. 5) and *Æscesdun, mons fraxini* (p. 28), and does not gloss any of the other place-names which occur in the *Encomium*.   It may here be remarked that if the Encomiast had heard the name of the site of the great battle of 1016

---

[1] See below, p. xxxix.   [2] *N.C.*, i. 148.
[3] The following similarities of expression between the Encomiast and Dudo may be mentioned. (I quote Dudo by Duchesne's pagination owing to the rarity of Lair's edition in England.) *Enc.* I, 1, *ueridica . . . relatione*—Dudo, p. 129, *ueridicae relationis* (but the expression is not unusual :   see, e.g., *Vita S. Cunegundis*, 6) ;   *Enc.* I, 1, *cogitationum aestus* — Dudo, p. 71, *cogitatione aestuans* ;   *Enc.* III, 5, *satis supraque*—Dudo, p. 121, *supraque satis*.   A selection of phrases which are common to Dudo and the Encomiast, but which occur frequently in their contemporaries also, will be mentioned in the Linguistic Notes.
[4] E.g., the battles in Dudo, pp. 70 and 94 (the leaving of the fallen enemy unburied is a frequent element in Dudo's battles) ;   the description of Gunnor, pp. 152–3 ;   the obsequies of Richard the Fearless, pp. 157–8.

as *Assandun* (its form in the *Old English Chronicle*), he certainly would not have glossed it in the way he does, whether he knew Asser or not. It is evident that he heard the name in the form *Æscendun*, and that he assumed the first element of this to be a plural of the first element of *Æscesdun*, and adopted Asser's gloss, modifying it in accordance with this assumption. The fact that the Encomiast's informants called the site of the battle *Æscendun* implies, either that they believed that the place in question was Ashdon (O.E. *Æscendun*), not Ashingdon (O.E. *Assandun*), or that the confusion of *Assan-* with *Æscen-*, which gave rise to the modern form of the latter name, had already taken place in the middle of the eleventh century.[1] The first element of the name as written by the Encomiast, *Aescene-*, is shown by the gloss *fraxinorum*, to be intended for a genitive plural. Such genitives are not proper to strong masculine nouns in either O.E. or O. Flemish, but, if the Encomiast made up his mind that the element *Æscen-* was a genitive plural, he might very probably write it with a dissyllabic termination corresponding to O.E. *-ena*, O. Flemish *-ona*, with the vowels weakened to *-e*, as might occur in either language by his period.[2]

Since the Encomiast very probably derived these two glosses from Asser, the view that they suggest that he was an Englishman[3] cannot be for a moment supported. Even if he fabricated them himself, they would only show that he had a knowledge of some Germanic tongue, and the same applies to his glosses of the first element of *Hardecnuto* as *uelox uel fortis*, and of *Athala* as *nobilissima* (II, 18 ; III, 7). The forms of the names of English and Scandinavian persons and of English place-names in his work throw little light on the question. The form *Alfridus* is Flemish, not English,[4] but the other English names retain their native form. The element *Ead-* is written *Aed-* or *Ed-*, reflecting the late O.E. pronunciation with monophthongization.[5] *Aelnotus* reflects an O.E. pronunciation of *Æþelnoþ* with loss of the intervocalic dental, which is often found in the eleventh century.[6] *Heli/Haeli* represents O.E. *Elig* (on the initial *H* see below, p. xxxviii). The forms *Goduinus*, *Sanduich*, *Scepei*, *Scorastan* represent the normal O.E. forms. On *Geldefordia*, cf. above, p. xviii. *Londonia* and *Wyntonia* (P) are normal latinised forms. (It may be noted that, of the various Latin forms of Winchester, Asser uses *Wintonia*.) Two forms of Scandinavian names suggest that the Encomiast heard them from an English witness : these are *Norduuega*, which represents an O.E. *Norþweg*[7] (cf. O. Danish *Norweg* already on the greater Jelling stone, about 980), and *Thurkil*, with *-u-*, for which

---

[1] The confusion referred to is certainly early, for it underlies *Nesenduna*, the form found in *Domesday Book* for Ashingdon : see the various early forms of the name collected by P. H. Reaney, in *The Place-names of Essex*, pp. 176–7 ; cf. the early forms for Ashdon, *id.*, pp. 502–3 ; on the question at which of the two places the battle was fought, see M. Ashdown, *English and Norse Documents*, pp. 298–9.

[2] Luick, *Historische Grammatik der englischen Sprache*, p. 489 ; J. Mansion, *Oud-Gentsche Naamkunde* (' s-Gravenhage, 1924), pp. 220 and 282. MS. P has, for L's *Aesceneduno*, the corrupt form *Kescesdume*. The medial *-es-* of this form is to be regarded as a purely scribal error, due to the presence of *-es-* in the preceding syllable. In view of the gloss *fraxinorum*, the form of P cannot be regarded as suggesting that the original form of the *Encomium* was *Aescesduno*.

[3] Manitius takes this view : reference above, p. xix.

[4] See various names in *Alf-* in Mansion, *op. cit.*, p. 298.

[5] Cf. Mansion, *op. cit.*, p. 255.

[6] See Napier and Stevenson, *Crawford Collection*, p. 150, n. 2.

[7] Although the forms used for Norway both in O.E. and early Anglo-Latin are usually without the dental, the form *Norþweg(as)* occurs in the Cottonian MS. of the O.E. Orosius (ed. H. Sweet, E.E.T.S., p. 19), and again in MS. F of the *Chronicle*, entry for 1028, so the evidence for both the existence of the form and its late survival is reasonably good. It is, of course, possible that the Encomiast heard a form with no dental, and that his *-d-* is due to the same interest in etymology which appears in his glosses.

O. Norse had -o- by a primitive change. *Eric* is a form found on Northumbrian coins, though *Yric* was the form in usual use in England in the eleventh century.[1] The forms *Cnuto* and *Suein* are derived from names the accented syllables of which did not differ in O.E. and O. Norse pronunciation in the eleventh century. The forms *Hardecnut* (with weakening of the medial vowel to -e-), and *Haroldus* (with medial -o-) are developments from the Scandinavian forms, which are equally possible in O.E. and O. Flemish in the eleventh century.[2] With the form *Danomarchia*, Florence of Worcester and William of Malmesbury's *Danemarchia* may be compared : the -o- is a mere fanciful spelling, for the genitive plural in O. Flemish was in -a, as in O.E. and O. Norse, in the eleventh century [3] (cf. *Hardocnuto*, II, 18). The form *Dani*, though the unmutated vowel is O. Norse, not O.E., occurs frequently in Anglo-Latin (e.g., in Æthelweard and Florence). Continental names (including the adverb *Theutonice*, II, 18) appear in forms quite usual in contemporary documents and do not in any way suggest that an Englishman wrote them. In matters of pure spelling there is nothing to enable us to decide the nationality of the Encomiast. The use of *sc* for Germanic *sk* is equally Flemish and English, and that of *ae* is not significant in a Latin text, for *e* and *ae* are equivalent graphs in the Latin spelling of the period. Similarly the interchange of *t* and *th* (*Aelnotus, Thurkil/Turkil, Athala, Scothia, Theutonice*) and of *ch* and *k* (*Turchil/Turkil*) is usual in the Latin spelling of proper names (cf. Henry of Huntingdon's *Turchetel/Turcetil*, Rolls Series, pp. 156, 178), and so is the use of *d* for *þ* (*Hardecnut, Norduuega*). The use of *g* for a spirantal sound (*Norduuega*), and that of *f* for a voiced spirant (*Alfridus*), were usual in English in the eleventh century, and frequent in Flemish.[4] The most that can be said concerning the Encomiast's nationality is that the use of the form *Alfridus* suggests a Flemish writer, and that the other English names and the Scandinavian ones might equally well have been written by an Englishman or by a Fleming. If he was a Fleming, one or two forms suggest that his informants were English rather than Scandinavian. His correct spelling of continental names would not be surprising, even were he English, if he resided in Flanders from the time when he saw Knútr there till that of Emma's exile.

If the Encomiast—as seems probable—knew Asser's work, it is a most remarkable fact that, in describing the magic banner of the Danes (II, 9), he agrees exactly with the account believed to have been interpolated into Asser by Parker from the *Annals of St. Neot's* with regard to the nature of the magical properties attributed to the banner.[5] The Encomiast is, as one would expect of him, the more poetical in his language, but the facts stated by the two writers are exactly the same. The passage given by Parker is clearly stated in Wise's edition of Asser not to have been present in the lost Cottonian MS., but I am inclined to think that the *Annals of St. Neot's* and the Encomiast used manuscripts of Asser in which the passage in question occurred. That there is a literary connection between the *Encomium* and the passage in the *Annals of St. Neot's* seems to me certain.

There is little that is noteworthy in the grammatical forms found in the *Encomium*, or in their use. The following points may be observed :

---

[1] See Napier and Stevenson, *op. cit.*, p. 143.

[2] The -a- of the first syllable of *Hardecnut* is not necessarily Norse or Flemish : this name usually retains -a- in O.E. documents, though the native -ea- is sometimes substituted for it : see the forms in Plummer's index, *Two of the Saxon Chronicles*, ii. 391. While *Harold* is a normal O.E. form, it would also be the form which the Scandinavian name would take in Flemish of the period : see Mansion, *op. cit.*, p. 154.

[3] Mansion, *op. cit.*, pp. 282 and 292. [4] *Ibid.*, pp. 136 and 138.

[5] See Stevenson's edition of Asser, p. 44. I quote the relevant words from Asser, for comparison with the Encomiast's account : ' Dicunt etiam, quod in omni bello ubi praecederet idem signum, si victoriam adepturi essent, appareret in medio signi quasi corvus vivens volitans : sin vero vincendi in futuro fuissent, penderet directe nihil movens '.

1. Examples of late transferences from one declension to another occur : *consultus* follows the fourth declension (I, 3 ; II, 12), a late usage of which the first genuine occurrence is in Isidore of Sevile (ix. 4, 9) ; note also the neuter forms, Prol., *blasphemium* (see Glossary) and, II, 3, *tumulum* (very rare, see Lewis and Short).

2. The following forms may be observed : II, 16 (twice), abl. s. *iusiurando* : cf. the regular form in III, 1 ; II, 10, *uoluntarius*, comp. from *uoluntarie*, see Linguistic Note ; II, 21, *mirificentior*, comp. from *mirificus*, cf. superl. *mirificentissimus*, Aug., *De Civ. Dei*, xviii. 42 ; II, 14, *misertus*, late form for *miseritus* ; III, 3, *priuate* for *priuatim* ; III, 1, perf. *odiuit*, a formation found already in a direct quotation in Cic., *Phil.* xiii. 19, 42, and used in the *Vulgate* (Psa. xxxv. 5, and frequently).

3. I, 1, *nullus* is used for *nemo*, a very frequent use in late Latin (see Stolz-Schmalz, p. 489) ; III, 8, *uersus* is used as a preposition, a late usage (*ibid.*, p. 518) ; II, 4, *a longe* is a compound adverb of late type (*ibid.*, p. 524). Notice the compound demonstrative pronoun, II, 18, *istum hunc* (cf. classical *hic iste*).

4. A confusion of the verbal suffixes *-esco* and *-esso* is reflected by Prol., *conticessere*, and II, 4, *capescerent*. Baxter records *capesco* in the thirteenth century.

5. On the use of *fueram* for *fui* or *eram* (e.g., III, 1, *non fas fuerat*) and in the pluperfect passive, II, 6, *fuerat congregatus*, see Stolz-Schmalz, pp. 561–2. On the use of the future perfect form as a simple future (e.g., II, 6, *si uictor fuero, regi ipsi triumphabo ; si autem cecidero siue tergum dedero*) and on future perfect tenses of the type seen in Prol., *usus fuero*, see *ibid.*, 563–4.

6. Late obscuring of classical distinctions of voice occurs in a few verbs and verbal forms : *Exosus*, 'hated', I, 5 ; frequent in late and Biblical Latin. *Incognitus*, 'ignorant', II, 10 ; to be found occasionally in medieval writers, e.g., *incognita uiarum*, Eulogius of Cordova (d. 859), *Memoriale Sanctorum*, iii. 10 (*Patrologia*, cxv. 810 ; *Acta Sanctorum Septembris*, v. 625). *Perscrutatus*, 'having been examined', Arg., late and medieval usage (Amm. xvii. 4, 6 ; *Vita S. Vulganii, Acta Sanctorum Novembris*, i. 572), but note *perscruto* for *perscrutor* is found in Plautus. *Suspectus*, 'suspecting', II, 8 ; so already Ammianus (xxix. 4, 5), and often in medieval writers, e.g., Gildas, *Historia*, 25. See also Linguistic Note on *contingi*, I, 1.

7. Note (*a*) the use of *deuio* as a transitive verb, III, 4 ; this is an exceptionally rare usage : it occurs in Corippus, *Ioh.* iv. 774, *clipeo . . deuiat hastam*, and is recorded by Ducange as occurring *c.* 1000 ; (*b*) the transitive use of *giro*, Arg., cf. Glossary.

8. *Credo* is used with the infinitive in a sense practically equivalent to 'expect' or 'hope' in Prol., *si in rem tibi prouenire crederem* ; on this late construction, see E. Löfstedt, *Beiträge zur Kenntnis der späteren Latinität* (Stockholm, 1907, pp. 59–61), and cf. Vict. Vit., i. 30, *credidit . . . . . sociare*.

The spelling of MS. L is the normal spelling of the eleventh century. There is practically nothing which requires comment with regard to it. The use of inorganic initial *h* should be observed : II, 4, *habundantissime* ; II, 7, *his* ; III, 4, *habundanter* ; III, 6, *Heli, Haeli* ; III, 11, *horas*. It is noteworthy that all these words except those in II, 4, and III, 4, have initial *h* in P also. Accordingly, unless P is derived from L, it is probable that some of these instances of inorganic initial *h* go back to an older stage in the transmission of the text of the *Encomium* than L, if not to the author.

The Encomiast has very few peculiarities of vocabulary : all words and meanings which are unusual will be found in the Glossary, where it will be seen that I have been able to parallel practically all of them, and the further lexicographical exploration of medieval Latin will doubtless do the same for the minute residue. It should be noticed that the Glossary and the Linguistic Notes are strictly supplementary to the present section of the Introduction, and information which has been given here is not repeated.

The vocabulary of the Encomiast resembles his syntax and his phraseology in that it avails itself of the resources of the classical poets and historians without abandoning those of late and ecclesiastical Latin. Accordingly, we find a very considerable number of non-classical words and meanings. Firstly, there are many words which express ideas peculiar to religion and the Church, and many special ecclesiastical senses of ordinary words : e.g., *agones*, ' pains of martyrs ', III, 6 ; *famulus*, II, 21 ; *intercessor*, III, 6 ; *martyrizo*, III, 6 ; *missa*, III, 1 ; *pascalis*, II, 9 ; *religio*, ' religion ', III, 7. Secondly, there are many words and meanings, which are not specifically ecclesiastical but merely non-classical. Some of these are found in early Latin, and disappear in classical times to reappear later : e.g., *animatus*, ' encouraged ', III, 11 ; *condignus*, II, 15 ; *repedo*, II, 1 ; *uictoriosus*, II, 7. Many others are found only in late writers : e.g., *humilio*, II, 22 ; *incurro*, ' incur ', I, 3 ; *insinuo*, ' make known ', III, 7 ; *obrizum*, I, 4 ; *persisto*, ' remain ', II, 11 ; *pompatice*, II, 8 ; *presumo*, ' dare ', III, 1 ; *uilla*, ' town ', III, 4.

It has been remarked in several places above that the Encomiast uses not pure prose but rhymed prose. This medium had not been consistently used in any insular work at the time when the *Encomium* was written, but on the Continent it was in its period of maximum popularity. The subject of medieval rhymed prose has been treated by K. Polheim in his admirable work, *Die lateinische Reimprosa* (Berlin, 1925), so it is not necessary to dwell at length here upon the technique of the writers who use it, but it may be remarked that its main principle is to end successive groups of words with the same termination, as, for example, in the opening of the *Encomium*, Book II, *sceptrum . . fidelium . . memores . . fines . . uires . . comperto . . reperto . . consilio . . iubet . . fugeret . . consuleret*. The greatest freedom is allowed as to the length of the word-groups and the number of times a rhyme is repeated. The language tends to be poetically coloured. Like his contemporaries, the Encomiast writes rhymed prose without the attention to the *cursus*, which complicates it in the twelfth century. The writers of this medium are as a rule little influenced by the peculiar latinity called by W. H. Stevenson ' Hesperic ',[1] with its involved style and strange vocabulary, which is so well known to students of insular Latin, and this is certainly true of the Encomiast, who has few peculiarities of syntax or vocabulary. Indeed, though many of the familiar figures of rhetoric could be exemplified from his work, they are of a kind into which any scholar with a tenth of his classical learning would fall naturally, and it is not necessary to assume that he gave any conscious attention to rhetorical studies of any kind.

In the extensive rhyme-prose literature of the tenth and eleventh centuries, the *Encomium* is by no means an isolated example of a panegyric on a royal person. In particular, the later *Vita Mahthildis* and Odilo's *Epitaphium Adalheidae* are eulogistic accounts of royal ladies which recall the *Encomium* in matter, tone, and style. Readers of the rhyme prose of the period will have no difficulty in observing how closely the writer of the *Encomium* adheres to its traditional style and choice of word and phrase, though this is only imperfectly shown by the parallels quoted in the present edition from such writers as Dudo, Odilo, Ruotger, and the biographers of the German emperors. His method of handling his subject-matter is also very much in the tradition of rhymed prose biography. The manner in which he anticipates criticism in his prologue, in which he changes his subject (I, 5, *ad alia festinando stilum adplicabo ad Sueini obitum*), recalls himself to his main theme (II, 18, *ne longius a proposito exorbitem, supra repetam historieque sequar ordinem*), inserts a document (III, 2, *cuius etiam exemplar non piget nobis subnectere*), and excuses himself from detailing the charities of Knútr (II, 20, *quae enim ecclesia adhuc eius non letatur donis ?*), will recall similar passages in the biographical

---

[1] In his edition of Asser, p. xcii ; Stevenson is, however, misleading when he says that Dudo is imbued with Hesperic influence. The prose of Dudo is neither obscure in syntax nor affected in vocabulary.

literature of the period to all who are even moderately familiar with it. The Encomiast's remarks on the duties of a historian in his preface also have a general similarity to passages in other writers of the period, as for example the prologue to Adalbold's *Vita Heinrici*. It may be observed that both his Sithiensian contemporaries, Bovo and Erembold, use rhymed prose, but it cannot be said that the Encomiast resembles them particularly closely in vocabulary, phrasing, or style.[1]

The alternative conclusion to the *Encomium* preserved in the Paris MS. is also in rhymed prose, and is, therefore, to be attributed to an early date. It is obviously unlikely that the scribe of P wrote it, adopting rhymed prose in imitation of the Encomiast, for he does not use rhyme in his summary of the first book. On the other hand, the summary in P of the bulk of III, 7, is in rhymed prose and is therefore not likely to be the work of the scribe of P, but is very probably from the hand responsible for the alternative conclusion. It is, therefore, likely that, when the *Encomium* was provided with a revised ending, it was decided that it would be better policy to pass rapidly over Emma's flight than to dwell on it with excuses.[2] P also reduces a long passage in III, 10, to a sentence, but this may be due to the scribe, and the fact that the sentence contains a rhyme may be an accident.

For vigour, facility, and variety of style, the Encomiast compares very favourably with most of those who used rhymed prose in his period. Furthermore, although it is dangerous as yet to express an opinion on the matter, it seems likely that the further study of these writers will show that the Encomiast holds a pre-eminent place among them both for the extent of his classical learning and his capacity to use it to good advantage,

D. *Queen Emma*

In the course of its entry for 1002, the *Old English Chronicle*[3] interrupts its record of the wars of King Æthelred and the Danes to insert the following sentence : ' And then, the same spring, the Queen, Richard's daughter, came to this country.'

Although the precise date of Æthelred's marriage with the lady who makes this abrupt entry into the annals of his country is not known, we can be sure that it took place soon after her arrival in England, for in the following year (1003) we find her possessed of sufficient property in Devonshire to appoint a French reeve named Hugh to look after it. The *Old English Chronicle*, perhaps not uninfluenced by insular prejudice, regards the fall of Exeter in 1003 as due to the shortcomings of this man.

The new queen bore a name which the English wrote *Imme* or *Imma*.[4] It was known to be equivalent to *Emma*, and Latin writers, from her own Encomiast onwards, nearly always used the latter form.[5] In conformity with the usual practice of modern historians, I propose henceforth to use the name-form *Emma* in referring to Imme, daughter of Richard.

Emma was a daughter of Richard I of Normandy[6] by a woman named Gunnor, who is said to have been at first his mistress, but whom he subsequently married, and by whom

---

[1] Erembold, like the Encomiast, explains the etymology of the name *Athala*.

[2] Cf. above, p. xxiii.

[3] When the *Old English Chronicle* is quoted without the mention of a manuscript, this implies that MSS. C, D and E, the main authorities for the annals dealing with the eleventh century, are in substantial agreement.

[4] The variation of *Y* and *I*, which occurs in the first syllable, is of no significance in the eleventh century. The Queen's name is fully discussed below, Appendix I.

[5] Florence of Worcester is the only exception : he uses *Ælfgifu* (in various modified forms) and *Emma* indifferently (cf. below, p. 56).

[6] He ruled 943-96, having succeeded as a child.

he had a numerous family.[1] We have the authority of William of Jumièges [2] that Richard II, who succeeded his father as duke of Normandy in 996, and Emma, wife of Æthelred, were among the children of Richard and Gunnor, and did not belong to their father's illegitimate family.[3] Nothing is known of Emma's life before she came to England, but, since she bore a child at least as late as 1019, she cannot have been very far advanced in years when she became Æthelred's bride.

It is evident that Emma, soon after her arrival in England, took the name *Ælfgifu*, which she afterwards used on all official occasions. No account of this proceeding is extant. Florence of Worcester, in reproducing the *Chronicle's* account of the queen's arrival in England, says that she was called Emma, but in English Ælfgifu, and both MS. F of the *Chronicle* (entry for 1017) and the *Chronicon Abbatiae Rameseiensis* (Rolls Series, p. 151) have similar remarks. The date of the change of name cannot be determined. Her signatures begin with a grant dated 1004 (K. 709), but this document is spurious. K. 714 and 1301, both from 1005, are better documents, and, since the queen signs them both as *Ælfgifu*, her change of name is to be safely dated in or before 1005. The object of the change was, no doubt, to give the queen a name in closer conformity than *Imme* with the traditional nomenclature of the family into which she had married, for the name *Ælfgifu* appears more than once in their genealogical tree, and, in particular, had been borne by Æthelred's grandmother, the sainted wife of Eadmund I. It appears, however, that the name *Imme* was still used privately by the queen, and that reference was popularly made to her by it.[4]

It will appear below (Appendix I) that, in witnessing documents with the title *Regina*, Emma was following the English custom of the period. The positions in which her signatures appear in lists of witnesses suggest that her status as Æthelred's queen was rather lower than that which his mother Ælfthryth had enjoyed during the earlier part of his reign.[5]

Æthelred's marriage with Emma undoubtedly marked a departure in English foreign policy. Although some historians have built too much upon evidence at once scanty and unsound in endeavouring to depict Eadweard the Elder and his sons as following a conscious and consistent anti-Norman policy,[6] it is undoubtedly the case that we look in vain for any signs of cordiality between England and Normandy before Emma's marriage. On the other hand, it is certain that the English and Norman courts were on

---

[1] See Dudo (ed. Duchesne, pp. 152-3).

[2] iv. 18. By a curious oversight, J.-M. Toll, *Englands Beziehungen zu den Niederlanden bis 1154* (Historische Studien, 145), p. 41, makes Emma a child of her father's first wife, Emma, daughter of Hugh of Paris.

[3] To whom Dudo, *loc. cit.*, alludes, saying that Richard *genuit duos filios, totidem et filias, ex concubinis.*

[4] See further on Emma's names, Appendix I.

[5] See Appendix II.

[6] Freeman (*N.C.*, I, chap. 4) and Green (*Conquest of England*, chaps. 5 and 6) are the chief offenders. The evidence which they advance for the assumption, that England and Normandy were antagonistic in the tenth century, is mainly the cordial attitude of England towards the Bretons, but it is now generally recognised that the Normans against whom the Bretons were then struggling were those of the Loire, not those of the Seine (see Stenton, p. 344, and detailed discussion by De la Borderie, referred to above, p. xxii, n. 10). Green also attempts in a most hazardous manner to see an anti-Norman policy in some of the English royal marriages of the tenth century. It is also unwise to regard the English support of Louis d'Outremer as inspired by an anti-Norman tendency in English policy, or to place undue weight on the fact that, when in 938 Arnulf of Flanders captured the wife and children of Herlwin of Montreuil, who appears to have been at the time in the same group as the Normans among the ever-changing French political combinations, they were sent to England for custody. The only recorded instance of direct contact between

very uneasy terms in 990, but that a reconciliation was arranged in 991.[1] It is reasonable to assume that relationships between the two courts were tolerably cordial at the time when Emma's marriage was arranged, and, since Æthelred was able to claim Norman hospitality in 1013, it appears likely that no serious friction developed between him and his brother-in-law after the marriage. Now William of Jumièges [2] has a story that Æthelred, at some time subsequent to his marriage with Emma, sent an unsuccessful expeditionary force against Normandy. It is very unlikely that this is a confused memory of the quarrel of 990–1, which apparently did not pass out of the diplomatic sphere. On the other hand, it seems improbable that Æthelred, at any time after his marriage, sent forces against his brother-in-law, the man to whom he turned for refuge in 1013. Therefore it would appear probable that the clash referred to by William of Jumièges, a writer whose chronology is notoriously vague, is to be placed before, rather than after, Emma's marriage, and that the latter event was a sign of a clearing of the air between England and Normandy, even if it were not a part of a formal settlement. This chronological re-arrangement has two further points in its favour. It places the English attack on Normandy in a period when Æthelred was possessed by a fit of restless energy (his Cumbrian expedition belongs to 1000), and when it is known that the Scandinavian invaders of England were making use of Norman harbours (see *Old English Chronicle*, 1000), a practice which would sufficiently explain Æthelred's action in sending forces against the Normans.[3] Accordingly, while certainty cannot be reached in this matter, it is not too much to say that it is highly probable that the marriage of Emma inaugurated a period of good relationships between the governments of two countries which had not long previously been at open war.[4]

The *Old English Chronicle* provides no information concerning Emma's activities after her arrival in England in 1002, until it records her withdrawal to Normandy in the serious emergency of 1013. In a document (K. 1311) obviously modified in its extant form, she is associated with her husband in confirming grants previously made to St. Paul's. She bore three children to Æthelred, the future Eadweard the Confessor, the ill-fated Ælfred, and a daughter, Godgifu. There can be no doubt that Eadweard was the elder of the brothers, in view not only of the direct statement of the Encomiast,[5] but also of the fact that his father selected him rather than his brother to accompany an embassy to the witan in 1014.[6] It is reasonable to assume that Eadweard was born soon after Emma's marriage, if even a theoretical responsibility was laid on his shoulders in

England and Normandy before Æthelred's reign is a letter written by an abbot of St. Ouen's and addressed apparently to King Eadgar : it is a request for help with restorations (*Memorials of St. Dunstan*, Rolls Series, pp. 363–4). In Æthelred's time, commerce between London and Normandy was apparently regular, for the dues to be paid by Norman merchants at London are mentioned in a legal code, which also shows that merchants from Rouen were especially privileged (Liebermann, *Gesetze*, i. 232).

[1] See Stenton, pp. 370–1. It is, however, only a theory, though a reasonable one, that the cause of the friction was that the Normans allowed the Scandinavian invaders of England to use their ports.

[2] v. 4.

[3] So, in essentials, *N.C.*, i. 302–3, and Steenstrup, *Normandiets Historie*, p. 162.

[4] See *N.C.*, i. 304 and note, on Gaimar's story that Æthelred crossed to Normandy in person to fetch his bride. Henry of Huntingdon (Rolls Series, p. 174) and Æthelred of Rievaulx (*Patrologia*, cxcv. 730) say that messengers were sent to Normandy. Æthelred's brother-in-law did not hesitate to conclude a treaty with Sveinn, permitting him to sell in Normandy the plunder won in one of his invasions of England (*N.C.*, i. 342), but this was at least not an act of open hostility. Henry of Huntingdon (Rolls Series, p. 176) says that Æthelred asked Richard for help and advice in 1009, when an attempt to improve the English resistance to the Danes was being made.

[5] See below, p. lxiv, n. 3. [6] See *Old English Chronicle*.

1014. Concerning Godgifu, the *Old English Chronicle* is curiously silent, but, since Ordericus Vitalis [1] tells us that she was an exile in Neustria during Knútr's invasion, it is evident that she must have withdrawn from England, when the Danish invaders triumphed. In all probability she accompanied either her mother, her brothers, or her father, when the royal family, one after the other, sought Norman hospitality in 1013.[2]

Emma is commonly assumed to have regarded her first husband and her family by him without affection.[3] The evidence for this is William of Malmesbury's statement that she transferred to Eadweard the dislike which she had previously felt for Æthelred, and that she gave the greater part of her love to Knútr during his life, and the greater part of her praise subsequently.[4] It is much to be doubted if these words of William's are more than a rhetorical expansion of the statement of the *Old English Chronicle* that Eadweard was ungenerously treated by his mother.[5] William's statement finds no confirmation in the *Encomium*. In order to prepare for his well-known implication that Knútr was Emma's first husband, the Encomiast omits Æthelred from his narrative almost entirely. There is no mention of an English king in his account of the invasion of Sveinn, and, in his description of Knútr's siege of London, he gives the impression that some local chief—*eum principem, qui interius ciuitati presidebat*—rather than the king of England died in the city. Again, in dealing with Eadmund's succession to the throne, the Encomiast says that the people said that they would choose Eadmund rather than the prince (*princeps*) of the Danes, but he carefully avoids calling Eadmund *rex*, or closely defining his status, and does not give a hint that the fact that the *princeps* who had died at London was Eadmund's father gave the latter a hereditary claim to the throne. On the other hand, he has not a word to say against either the *princeps* or Eadmund, and his peculiar manner of dealing with them is due simply to his desire to suppress the fact that Emma was the widow of Æthelred when she married Knútr : he felt, that the less he said about Æthelred, the better for his purpose. It will appear below that the suppression of Emma's first marriage was an artistic necessity to the Encomiast, and therefore nothing can be inferred from it as to the light in which Emma regarded her first husband. Similarly, there is no implication in the *Encomium* that Emma disliked Eadweard, who is depicted, perhaps unjustly,[6] as a somewhat unenterprising youth, but as nothing worse. It will appear below that Emma's agreement with Knútr, whereby Eadweard was excluded from the succession, was the best arrangement that she could make at the time, and that it certainly does not show any lack of affection towards him on his mother's part.[7] Similarly, in supporting Hörthaknútr's claims after Knútr's death, Emma did the best she could for her family : there was then no party for Eadweard, and she could therefore have done nothing to further his claims, even had she so desired. The most that can be said on this question is that Emma's lack of generosity towards Eadweard, which is vouched for by the *Chronicle*, may be taken to suggest that her attitude towards him was rather luke-warm, but that we have no knowledge whatever concerning her feelings towards Æthelred,[8] Ælfred and Godgifu.

---

[1] Ed. Duchesne, p. 655. [2] See below, pp. xliv–v.

[3] Examples are numerous : e.g., *N.C.*, i. 736 ; Oman, *England before the Norman Conquest*, p. 613 ; Bugge, *Smaa bidrag til Norges historie paa 1000-tallet* (Christiania, 1914), p. 10.

[4] *Gesta Regum*, ii. 196.

[5] Entry for 1043, C and D, mis-dated 1042, E. [7] See below, p. xlv.

[6] See below, p. lxvii.

[8] William of Malmesbury, *Gesta Regum*, ii. 165, has an unsupported theory that Æthelred alienated the affections of Emma by his infidelity. There is no need to be surprised that William, who tells so many stories of the moral imperfections of the kings of the West-Saxon house, desires to put Æthelred on a level with the rest, but it is noteworthy that he has no anecdotes of his usual kind to support his view. Palgrave (*Normandy and England*, iii. 111) seems to derive from a

Gaimar says that Emma received Winchester, Rockingham, and Rutland from her husband at the time of her marriage.[1] It is evident that he was not well informed concerning the property that Emma then received, for it is certain that this included an estate near Exeter.[2] He probably mentions Winchester in this connection simply because of Emma's well-known later association with that city, and Rutland because it was administered later for the benefit of various queens.[3] Rockingham may be a mere line-filler. In a charter dated 1012 (K. 720), Æthelred grants his wife land near Winchester, and her association with its neighbourhood cannot be shown to have begun before that time.

When Æthelred's fortunes were at a very low ebb in the winter of 1013, the Queen withdrew to Normandy, accompanied by Ælfsige, abbot of Peterborough,[4] and the king about the same time sent Eadweard and Ælfred abroad in charge of Ælfhun, bishop of London. Soon after Christmas, Æthelred also withdrew to Normandy. No doubt the two princes also went to Normandy, for Eadweard was there, and accompanied his father's messengers from thence, a few months later, after the death of Sveinn.

The movements of Emma after her flight in 1013 are difficult to determine. She is not mentioned again in the *Old English Chronicle* until 1017, when, it is stated, Knútr had her fetched and married her, before the beginning of August. The compilers of the *Chronicle* must have known that these words could only imply that she was fetched from Normandy, for, when last mentioned (1013), the queen was there. However, we know that her son Eadweard returned to England just before his father in 1014, and also that he was in Normandy during Knútr's reign.[5] It is therefore evident that he was able to withdraw again to Normandy after the war once more turned against the English. There is no reason why Emma, with or without Ælfred and Godgifu, should not also have returned to England with Æthelred in 1014, and have withdrawn again in 1015 or 1016. Therefore, there may be some truth underlying Thietmar's story, that Emma was in London when it was besieged by Knútr, and entered into communication with the Danes at that time.[6]

The clear implication of the *Old English Chronicle* and the direct statement of her own Encomiast are together sufficient to place it beyond doubt that Emma was in Normandy when Knútr ' had her fetched ' in 1017.[7] It is unlikely that he had ever previously seen her, though it is just possible that he did so in 1016, if the story that she opened negotia-

---

confused memory of William's words a belief that Emma fled back to Normandy soon after her marriage. Roger of Wendover (ed. Coxe, i. 427) misunderstands William so far as to explain Æthelred's quarrel with Richard I, who was six years dead when Emma came to England, as due to the Duke's disgust at the treatment meted out to his daughter.

[1] *Lestorie des Engles*, 4138 ff.   [2] See above, p. xl.

[3] Gaimar says that Ælfthryth had held the same property previously.

[4] MS. E of the *Chronicle* adds to the annal for 1013 that, while abroad, Ælfsige visited Bonneval, where he purchased the body of St. Florentine, which he afterwards brought back to England. Roger of Wendover (ed. Coxe, i. 448) has an unsupported story that Eadric Streona went abroad with Emma, and remained with her two years.

[5] See below, p. xlv, n. 3.

[6] *M.G.H.S.*, iii. 849. The details of Thietmar's account are very discreditable to Emma, for the Danish terms, to which she is said to have agreed, include the delivery of her stepsons Eadmund and Æthelstan for execution ; they need not, however, be taken seriously.

[7] William of Jumièges, v. 9, believed, like Thietmar's informant, that Emma was in London during Knútr's siege of the city ; he assumes, however, that Knútr in some way got her out of the city and married her as soon as Æthelred died. Gaimar, *Lestorie des Engles*, 4207, says that Emma was at Winchester when Æthelred died, but he does not make it clear what he thought her subsequent movements were. William of Malmesbury, *Gesta Regum*, ii. 180, says that Richard of Normandy gave his sister in marriage to Knútr, thus showing that he believed Emma was in Normandy when the marriage was arranged.

tions with the Danes in that year is true.   It is, however, unlikely that the politic Knútr would be greatly swayed by personal preferences in selecting a bride : we may be sure that reasons of prudence guided his choice.   It has been shown above [1] that the Encomiast depicts the marriage of Knútr and Emma as occasioning a reconciliation of the English and the Danes, but it is extremely unlikely that the restoration of their Norman queen could in the least placate the English.   William of Malmesbury offers a better reason, for, while he also suggests that the marriage would placate the English, he adds that Knútr had another reason for it : he hoped to reduce any enthusiasm which Richard of Normandy might have for the cause of Eadweard and Ælfred by giving him new nephews.[2]   There can be little doubt that here is an explanation of at least part of what Knútr had in his mind.   The two young princes were probably beyond his reach in Normandy, but even if that were not the case, to have dealt with them as he did with Eadmund's sons and with the ætheling, Eadwig, would have earned the hatred of a most formidable neighbour.[3]   It would, therefore, seem to him a good bargain to marry their mother under an agreement, that any son born of the marriage should succeed to the English throne, to the exclusion both of his own sons by his mistress, and of Emma's sons by Æthelred.   Such a bargain would also appeal to Emma : she would recover her position in England, if she bore a son he would succeed his father, and her older sons would be no worse off than if she declined the bargain.   The agreement, which the Encomiast says Knútr made with Emma, is essentially that which I suggest in the foregoing sentences would probably have appealed to them both, but, since the Encomiast suppresses Emma's first marriage, it does not appear in his work that both sides had to make concessions.   There can be no doubt that Emma did an excellent thing for herself in accepting this bargain, and it may be observed, that, when her son by Knútr ultimately secured the throne, he at once invited Eadweard, his surviving half-brother, to make his home in England.   Accordingly, it cannot be reasonably argued that Emma's children by Æthelred lost by their mother's second marriage.[4]   Knútr achieved his probable object, a reconciliation with Normandy, at least till the death of Richard II.[5]   It may be remarked that his choice of Emma as a bride was masterly.   Freeman [6] suggested that the young conqueror might have been expected to wed a young Norman princess, if he aimed at forming a link with Normandy. On the contrary, this would have been a quite different method of procedure, involving

---

[1] P. xxi.
[2] *Gesta Regum*, ii. 181.   Raoul Glaber, ii. 2, also suggests that Knútr's object was to improve relationships with Normandy.
[3] The Encomiast (ii. 18) says that the young princes were sent to Normandy after Hörtha-knútr's birth.   It is possible, therefore, that Ælfred returned, like Eadweard, in 1014, and that they both remained in England till after their mother married Knútr.   Ordericus Vitalis (ed. Duchesne, p. 655) says, however, that they fled when Knútr invaded England, so perhaps they escaped in 1015 or 1016, returned with their mother in 1017, and were sent back later.   (On a deed supposed to be enacted by Eadweard in Flanders in 1016, see below, p. lxiv.)   Ordericus (*loc. cit.*) adds that Godgifu was in Neustria with her brother (he fails to indicate which) during Knútr's invasion of England.   It is fairly certain that she would withdraw in 1013 (cf. above, p. xliv), and the words of Ordericus imply that, if she returned in 1014, she was able to escape in 1015 or 1016.   It would be possible to take the word *filios* in *Enc.* II, 18, to mean ' children ', and assume that Godgifu again returned to England with her mother in 1017, and was later sent away with her brothers.   William of Jumièges (vi. 10) obviously much over-simplifies the movements of Ælfred and Eadweard, when he says that they left England with their father during Sveinn's invasion, and were left behind by him on his return.   At least in the case of Eadweard, we know that this is untrue.
[4] Emma has been much blamed for her treatment of her older children by modern historians : examples occur in most treatments of the history of the period, so I do not give references.
[5] See below, p. xlviii.   [6] *N.C.*, i. 410.

first negotiations for a settlement with Richard, which, if successful, might have been sealed by a royal marriage. Knútr, by marrying a Norman princess who must have been herself eager, for the reasons suggested above, to become his bride, made a marriage which would cause a reconciliation, instead of first negotiating a reconciliation and then sealing it with a marriage.[1]

A word may here be said on the suppression of all reference to Emma's first marriage by the Encomiast. Though he would hardly have implied that Knútr was her first husband without her approval, it would certainly appeal to him strongly to do so on artistic grounds alone. His book is intended to be entirely devoted directly or indirectly to Emma's praise : he emphasises this in his *Argument*. Now a woman who married a man who had been her late husband's relentless foe, and who had driven her children from their country, could not be made to appear an entirely pleasing character[2] ; it was obviously best for the Encomiast's purpose to say as little as possible about Æthelred, so, as has been shown above, he reduces him to an unnamed and shadowy *princeps*. When he comes to describe Emma's marriage, the Encomiast says that, after Knútr had settled the affairs of his new kingdom, he lacked nothing but a noble wife, and had a search made for one. A suitable bride was found in Normandy, distinguished by wealth, descent, beauty and wisdom : she was in fact a famous queen (*utpote regina famosa*, cf. above, p. xxvi). The story of the bargain with Knútr follows, and concludes with the sentence : *Placuit ergo regi uerbum uirginis et . . . uirgini placuit uoluntas regis*. These words achieve the affect that the Encomiast wishes. They contain no syllable of untruth, yet what reader, ignorant of the facts, could fail to forget that *uirgo* need mean no more than ' woman ',[3] and that the Encomiast has already said that Emma was a famous queen when Knútr wooed her ? Indeed, he would probably assume, even if he remembered the latter remark, that *regina* had its well-attested sense of ' princess ' in the passage.[4]

When the Encomiast has mentioned that the birth of Hörthaknútr occurred soon after Emma's marriage, he goes on to say that his parents kept him with them as heir to the kingdom, but that they sent their other sons to Normandy to be brought up. Here again he avoids direct untruth. To one ignorant of the facts, he would give the impression that these other sons were younger children of Knútr and Emma, while a better-informed reader could hardly quarrel with the passage, but would assume that Knútr had practically adopted his wife's children : the case would be very different if the Encomiast has said that the royal pair sent their younger sons to Normandy, but this he carefully avoids doing, both in this passage and in III, 1, where, in explaining where Emma's sons were when Knútr died, he calls Hörthaknútr, not *natu maximus*, but simply *unus eorum*. The latter passage is illuminating, for the Encomiast is usually particular about relative ages, and emphasises that Knútr was Sveinn's elder son (I, 3), and that Ælfred was younger than Eadweard (III, 4).

At first Emma's status as Knútr's wife seems to have been a little lower than it had been as Æthelred's,[5] but this soon altered, and from 1020 onwards she always witnessed

---

[1] It is very noticeable that the Encomiast, in his account of the wooing of Emma, has no word about her relatives ; the lady herself is approached directly and exclusively.

[2] This is the aspect of the marriage which disgusts William of Malmesbury, *Gesta Regum*, ii. 180, who does not know whether the match was more disgraceful to Richard of Normandy, or to a woman ' quae consenserit ut thalamo illius caleret qui uirum infestauerit, filios effugauerit '

[3] Excellent examples of this sense will be found in Lewis and Short, *s.v.* ' virgo ', IIA.

[4] Steenstrup (reference above, p. xix) sees that the Encomiast's words are perfectly defensible, but fails to recognise his obvious intention to deceive. Similarly Langebek, in his note on the passage, suggests that Emma is called *virgo* in view of her chastity. Most historians have, however, emphasised the mendacity of the Encomiast, but have not noticed the skill with which he has refrained from verbal untruth. [5] See Appendix II.

documents immediately after her husband, before the archbishops. Her public appearance at the translation of St. Ælfheah's bones in 1023 was one of the remembered features of that occasion (see *Old English Chronicle*, MS. D) [1]. She bore two children to Knútr, Hörthaknútr and Gunnhildr. Hörthaknútr was born before 1023, when he appeared in public with his mother on the occasion just mentioned. It is probable that he was born soon after Emma's marriage, for the Encomiast states that this was the case, and already about 1023 the young prince was sent to Denmark, apparently to be initiated into statecraft by Thorkell Hávi.[2] The precise age of Gunnhildr, Emma's daughter, is not to be determined, nor is it known with certainty whether she was older or younger than her brother : it is, however, clear from the German authorities that she was very young when she married the future Emperor Henry III in 1036 ; and since we know that on one occasion Knútr and Emma recommended themselves and their son to the prayers of the monks of Bremen, without mentioning their daughter (see below, p. 57), it seems likely that this took place before her birth, and that she was the younger child.

Charters do not add anything very interesting or valuable to what we know of Emma's activities during Knútr's reign. She had some interest, the exact nature of which is not known, in the abbey of Evesham (see R. 81, with note, p. 405), and hence it is not surprising to find her associated with her husband in making a grant to that foundation by the fabricator of the clumsy forgery, K. 1316 (cf. below, p. 60). Stowe Charter 39, dated 1018, in which the queen is said to have requested her husband to make a grant to Ælfstan (or Lyfing), the archbishop of Canterbury, appears to be a genuine document. Similarly, there is nothing suspicious about R. 86, in which it is recorded that Knútr and Emma gave their priest Eadsige leave to dispose as he saw fit of certain property, when he became a monk. In a forged charter (K. 735), Knútr is alleged to have made a grant to St. Edmund's for the benefit of the souls of himself, Emma and their children. Lastly, two documents in writ form are addressed jointly to Knútr and Emma (W. 23, a forgery ; Earle, p. 232 ; Thorpe, p. 313).

Emma seems to have joined Knútr heartily in his generous ecclesiastical policy.[3] William of Malmesbury [4] mentions both her generosity to Winchester and her activity in spurring Knútr to display his liberality there. We have already seen that when Ælfheah's bones were translated in 1023, she graced the ceremony with her presence. A brief document drawn up in Eadweard the Confessor's reign records that Knútr gave an estate in Oxfordshire to Christ Church, Canterbury, on her behalf (R. 96) ; a forged document (K. 697, dated 997, when she was not yet in England) refers to the same grant. During Hörthaknútr's reign, Emma and the king granted an estate in Huntingdon to Ramsey (K. 1330 ; cf. on the later history of the land, K. 906), and the *Chronicon Abbatiae Rameseiensis* (Rolls Series, pp. 151–2) praises the generosity she showed to the Church, and the example she thereby set to Hörthaknútr. On her alleged generosity to the minster of St. Hilary at Poitiers, see *N.C.*, i. 442, and note 4. Emma's name is entered

---

[1] Raoul Glaber, ii. 2, states that Richard of Normandy and Emma persuaded Knútr to make peace with the king of Scots. It is impossible to say if a memory of some actual part played by Emma in Scottish affairs underlies this. Roger of Wendover (ed. Coxe, i. 463) curiously connects Knútr's marriage with his dismissal of his Danish fleet the next year, and attributes the latter action to Emma's persuasion. This can hardly have any foundation : such false inferences are frequent in second-hand chronicles.

[2] See below, p. 75.

[3] Prior Godfrey of Winchester dwells on Emma's generosity to the church and the poor in his epigram on her (Wright's *Satirical Poets*, Rolls Series, ii. 148). Godfrey's first line, *Splendidior gemma meriti splendoribus Emma*, may echo some popular verse known to Henry of Huntingdon, who calls the Queen *Emma, Normannorum gemma* (Rolls Series, p. 174).

[4] *Gesta Regum*, ii. 181 and 196.

in the *Liber Vitae* of both Thorney and Hyde ; the drawing in the latter, depicting Emma and Knútr presenting a golden cross to the New Minster, is well known.[1] A forged charter of St. Edmund's claims her as a benefactor of that community (K. 761 ; cf. K. 735, referred to above), and a St. Edmund's insertion in MS. Bodley 297 of Florence of Worcester states that she urged Knútr to restore the monastery.[2]

Emma seems to have been an enthusiastic collector of saints' relics. Eadmer [3] states that, in Knútr's time, she purchased and gave to Canterbury an arm of St. Bartholomew, and MS. F of the *Old English Chronicle* mentions that, on the death of Hörthaknútr, she gave the head of St. Valentine to the New Minster, Winchester, for the benefit of her son's soul.[4] Among the treasures of which she was deprived by Eadweard in 1043 was the head of St. Ouen : she had purchased his body when she was in Normandy after Æthelred's death, and had previously given the trunk to Canterbury.[5]

Emma's career from the death of Knútr till that of Hörthaknútr will be fully discussed in the next section of this Introduction. It need only be pointed out here that her choice of Flanders rather than Normandy as a place of exile from 1037 to 1040 was no doubt occasioned by the fact that her nephew Robert, who seems to have been favourable to the cause of her sons,[6] had died in 1035, and Normandy was in the disorders of a minority rule. This must also have been an added inducement to Eadweard to leave Normandy, when Hörthaknútr invited him to return to England in 1041. Baldwin V of Flanders, according to both the *Old English Chronicle* and the Encomiast, received Emma kindly, though his feelings towards her family must have been somewhat mixed, as, when he succeeded about 1030 in displacing his father, the older ruler had been restored by Robert of Normandy, who seems to have acted with some barbarity on this occasion.[7]

It has already been mentioned that Emma had property at Exeter already in 1003, that Æthelred granted her land near Winchester in 1012, that Knútr granted her an estate in Oxfordshire for immediate transference to Christ Church, and that Gaimar alleges that Æthelred gave her Winchester, Rutland, and Rockingham as a marriage gift. To this it may be added, that one writ of Eadweard the Confessor (K. 876) approves that she should have the benefit of an East-Anglian estate, which one of her followers had previously enjoyed,[8] and that a number of others (K. 874, 883–4, 905) deal with the history of an estate at Bury St. Edmunds, upon which she had had rights of jurisdiction, which were discharged for her by the well-known landowner, Ælfric, son of Wihtgar, apparently with the help of one, Ordger (see R., p. 426). Two forged documents (R. 114, 118) allege that Emma granted estates at Hayling Island and Wargrave to the Old Minster, Winchester, but it is very doubtful if any truth underlies their statements.[9]

After her return to England in 1040, Emma seems to have taken up residence at

---

[1] See the Viking Society's *Saga-Book*, xii. 131 ; and Birch's ed. of Hyde *Liber Vitae*, frontispiece and p. 57.

[2] *Memorials of St. Edmund's Abbey* (Rolls Series, i. 341).

[3] *Historia Novorum* (Rolls Series, pp. 107 ff.).

[4] F's Latin version (contradicting the English) says the Old Minster, but the sacred object seems to have been preserved at the New Minster (see Plummer, *Two of the Saxon Chronicles*, ii. 222).

[5] William of Malmesbury, *Gesta Pontificum* (Rolls Series, pp. 419–20).

[6] See *N.C.*, i. 473 ff.

[7] William of Jumièges, vi. 6. Toll, *Englands Beziehungen zu den Niederlanden*, p. 29, regards Baldwin V's mother as a sister of Emma : this is a double error. Baldwin IV's second wife was a *niece* of Emma (William of Jumièges, v. 13), but she was not the mother of Baldwin V, who was a son of his father's first wife, Otgiva of Luxemburg.

[8] This writ is addressed to Earl Ælfgar : since he was not an earl before the exile of Godwine in 1051, the document must belong to the last year of Emma's life.

[9] See Miss Robertson's notes on the documents.

Winchester.[1] At least, she was there when Eadweard in 1043 descended upon her and deprived her of her lands and loose property.[2] She was allowed to reside in the town. The possible reasons for Eadward's action have been discussed at length by Freeman,[3] but it cannot yet be said that they are entirely clear. The only reason offered by the *Chronicle* is resentment on Eadweard's part that his mother had been ungenerous towards him, and MS. D adds that this was before and after he became king. The Latin chroniclers follow this account, William of Malmesbury (*Gesta Regum*, ii. 196) adding a good deal of embroidery, while Florence of Worcester and Roger of Wendover adhere closely to the *Chronicle*. Nevertheless, the facts that the great earls supported the king in his action against his mother, and that Stigand was at the same time deposed from his bishopric, because he had been an influence on the queen, make it certain that the king's action was prompted by something more important than bad feeling within the royal family.[4]

Emma signed a few documents dated after the reduction of her status in 1043 : K. 771, 773, 774, 775, 779. All these are dated 1044, except the last, which is spurious. The English document R. 101, dated 1044 by a late endorsement, seems rather to belong to 1045 (see Miss Robertson's notes), and, if so, it is the last occurrence of Emma's signature.[5]

Emma's death occurred 6 March 1052, and she was buried at Winchester beside Knútr in the Old Minster.[6] It is not possible today to point to the place where she lies, for the bones in early Winchester tombs have been much disturbed at various times and are now so confused that those of individuals cannot be identified.[7]

It is well known that Emma's three sons Eadweard, Ælfred, and Hörthaknútr, were all childless. Through her daughter Gunnhildr, who married the future Emperor Henry III, she had one granddaughter, Beatrix, abbess of Quedlinburg. Her daughter Godgifu, whose movements during the Danish invasions have been discussed above (pp. xliii and xlv), married Drogo of Mantes. Ordericus Vitalis (ed. Duchesne, p. 655) gives as her children by him Walter of Mantes, the opponent of the Conqueror, Ralph, earl of Hereford, so famous in the history of the Confessor's reign, and Fulk, bishop of Amiens. To these, modern authorities have added their contemporary, Amauri of Pontoise. Although his existence is proved by at least one charter, his claim to be a son of Drogo is negligible, resting only on a statement in a romance.[8] Ralph is stated in the *Chronicon*

---

[1] Her residence at Winchester was still known as *domus Emmae reginae* in William I's reign ; see *N.C.*, iv. 59, n. 2.

[2] *Old English Chronicle* ; MS. C and E describe the incident in identical words, but D has another version, the only one which mentions the part played by the great earls. C adds a notice of Stigand's deposition and its cause. [3] *N.C.*, ii. 60 ff.

[4] A. Bugge, reference as above, p. xliii, n. 3, attempts to defend as serious history the story of the *Translatio S. Mildrethae*, that Emma's fall was due to her having urged Magnús of Norway to invade England, offering him her hand and wealth. It is not impossible that Emma dreamed in her dotage of repeating her recovery of her position in 1017 by similar means. I think it very unlikely that she had any strong preference for one dynasty as such against another, though this view is advanced, Stenton, pp. 420–1 : cf. above, p. xxii.

[5] She signs K. 788, which is dated 1049 by a late endorsement, but the signatures show that it belongs to an earlier period : Ælweard signs as bishop of London, and he died in 1044, and, as Stigand signs as a priest, the document presumably belongs to 1043–4, during the period of his deposition from the bishopric of Elmham.

[6] Dated 1051 by MS. C. of the *Chronicle*, which starts the year at Easter or at the Annunciation in some annals in this period (see *E.H.R.*, xvi. 719–21) ; cf. MSS. D and E. C is the only manuscript to mention the Queen's place of burial.

[7] See *Victoria History of Hampshire*, v. 56.

[8] See F. Lot, *L'élément historique de Garin le Lorrain*, in *Études . . . . dédiées a Gabriel Monod* (Paris, 1896), p. 205.

Abbatiae Rameseiensis [1] to have come to England with his uncle Eadweard in 1041, and this may very reasonably be accepted. Drogo died when accompanying Robert of Normandy on his pilgrimage in 1035,[2] and Godgifu subsequently married Eustace of Boulogne. The *Old English Chronicle*, MS. D (1052 = 1051), mentions that Eustace was married to the king's sister. Florence of Worcester [3] and William of Malmesbury [4] add to this her name in the form *Goda*, and know that Ralph was her son, but William says that she had been the wife of Walter of Mantes, thus confusing her husband with her son. Godgifu's second marriage appears to have been childless : this would explain why it is not mentioned in the *Genealogia Comitum Buloniensium*.[5] *L'art de vérifier les dates* [6] suggests that two sons of Eustace, who were not sons of his second wife Ida, were children of Godgifu, but their existence is very uncertain. Godgifu must have died soon after 1051, when the *Chronicle* speaks of her as if she were alive, for Eustace began the wooing of his second wife in 1056.[7] Many estates are stated in *Domesday Book* to have been at one time in Godgifu's possession.[8] Ordericus calls her *Godioua*, all other authorities *Goda*. (*Domesday Book* uses this form both for her and for Godgifu, wife of Leofric of Mercia.) She seems to have followed her mother's example in taking a name familiar in her husband's country, though it is not very clear what this was. The evidence, for what it is worth, is her signature as *Ehtde comitissae* (gen.) to a charter published in the *Cartulaire de l'abbaye de Saint-Père de Chartres*,[9] and a reference to her by her husband Drogo as *Etiae vel Emmae* (dat.) in another charter printed in Ducange's *Histoire de l'état de la ville d'Amiens et de ses comtes*.[10] In a text of the latter document in Mabillon, *Acta Sanctorum*, iii. 2, 624–5, the reading, however, is *Evæ* (*vel Emmæ*).

Godgifu's sons were all childless except Ralph, concerning whose son and descendants see *N.C.*, ii. 683 ff. These were Queen Emma's only descendants more remote than grandchildren.

I have excluded from the above account of Queen Emma mere foolish stories like that of the ploughshares (see *N.C.*, ii. 585 ff.), that of Gaimar (*Lestoire des Engles*, 4493 ff.) that she incited Knútr against the sons of Eadmund, and that of various late authorities (see *N.C.*, i. 786) that she was involved in the murder of her son Ælfred.

E. *The Historical Content of the ‘ Encomium ’*

The Encomiast opens his first book with a brief account of the youth of Sveinn, who is said to have been a young prince who enjoyed such popularity that his father became jealous and wished to expel him from the kingdom (the reader has already gathered from the *Argument* that this kingdom is Denmark) and deprive him of the succession. The army, however, took the side of Sveinn : a battle followed, and the king fled wounded to the Slavs, and died soon after, leaving Sveinn in peaceful possession of the throne. This account of Sveinn's clash with his father, Haraldr Blátönn, is of very considerable interest, for it agrees very closely with that of Adam of Bremen (ii. 25–6). According to Adam, Sveinn schemed to deprive his father of the kingdom, when he saw him to be advanced in years, and his supporters were persons whom Haraldr had forced to become Christians. The upshot, however, is the same in Adam's account, as in that of the Encomiast : Haraldr is defeated in battle and flees wounded *ad ciuitatem Sclauorum, quae Iumne*

---

[1] Rolls Series, p. 171.   [2] *Ord. Vit.*, ed. Duchesne, p. 487.
[3] Ed. Thorpe, i. 204–5.   [4] *Gesta Regum*, ii. 199.   [5] *M.G.H.S.*, ix. 301.
[6] ii. 762.   [7] *Ibid.*   [8] *N.C.*, iv. 743.
[9] Ed. Guérard, i. (Paris, 1840), 173.
[10] Amiens, 1840, p. 160.

dicitur, where he dies within a few days.[1] This close agreement between the two oldest accounts of the war of Haraldr and Sveinn leaves little room for doubt that it is substantially correct and to be preferred to the various other versions.[2] The Encomiast's confirmation of Adam's account is of very great value, for, although Adam had the advantage of discussing Sveinn's career with the latter's grandson, Sveinn Úlfsson, his information concerning the early part of it is by no means always reliable.[3]

The Encomiast now depicts Sveinn as ruling in peace, while giving every attention to the defences of his country, till his warriors rouse him to an invasion of England, a project which he had himself been silently considering. This invasion will be shown below to be Sveinn's final and successful attack on England in 1013–14, and the Encomiast shows singularly little regard to historical accuracy, when he depicts the period of Sveinn's reign between the fall of Haraldr Blátönn and 1013 as one of continuous peace. In the interval Sveinn had conducted two vigorous campaigns in England,[4] and had been the central figure in the combination which defeated Óláfr Tryggvason and made Norway in a great degree subject to Denmark.[5] Some time in 994, perhaps before his English campaign of the same year, which began in the autumn, he ravaged the Isle of Man.[6] At some time in this period he probably challenged the encroaching power of the German empire in Sleswick, but this may possibly have been before his father's fall.[7] Furthermore, although Adam's story of his war with Sweden is no longer credited,[8] he seems to have had various troubles of which we no longer know the precise nature, except that he was at some time seized by his enemies and held to ransom.[9] The Encomiast may not have known of all these events, but, since he was so well informed about the circumstances under which Sveinn became king, it would be absurd to assume that he was ignorant of them all. Since he was aware of Thorkell Hávi's activities in England, as will appear below, he can hardly have failed to know something of those of Sveinn. Also, since he was aware that

---

[1] These events are placed by Adam at the very end of Archbishop Adaldag's life (*nouissimis archiepiscopi temporibus*), and Adaldag died 29 April 988. The year of Haraldr's death cannot, therefore, be exactly determined ; . Adam gives 1 November as the day.

[2] Other accounts are given by Sven Aggeson (*En ny text af Sven Aggesøns værker*, ed. M. Cl. Gertz [Copenhagen, 1916], pp. 78 ff. ; also in Langebek, *Scriptores*, i. 51 ff.), whose story is quite different ; by Saxo Grammaticus (ed. Holder, p. 331), whose version has points of contact with Adam and Sven, and with the Icelandic story also ; by the five extant versions of the Icelandic Saga of the Jómsvíkings, by *Heimskringla* in its version of the Jómsvíking story, and by Oddr in his Saga of Óláfr Tryggvason (pp. 109 ff. in ed. referred to below, p. 68, n. 1), with differences of detail, but agreement in substance. When *Fagrskinna* (p. 80), makes Haraldr die of sickness, this implies a rejection of the usual Icelandic story of his death as improbable by the compiler, rather than the existence of a divergent tradition (see G. Indrebø, *Fagrskinna* [Christiania, 1917], pp. 152–3).

[3] For example, Adam, expressly claiming Sveinn Úlfsson as his informant, alleges that a conquest of Denmark by the Swedes took place just after Haraldr Blátönn's death. This story is rejected today by all scholars : see especially L. Weibull, *Kritiska undersökningar i Nordens historia* (Copenhagen, 1911), pp. 90 ff.

[4] In 994 and 1003–5. [5] See below, p. 68.

[6] This event is noticed in the Welsh Latin annals on the fly-leaves of the Breviate of *Domesday Book* in the Record Office, and in the Welsh vernacular chronicles.

[7] The best introduction to the intricate problems connected with the history of Sleswick in the tenth and eleventh centuries is Vilh. la Cour, ' Kong Haralds tre storværker ', in *Aarbøger for nordisk oldkyndighed og historie*, 1934, pp. 55–87.

[8] See above, n. 3.

[9] Stories of this sort, differing widely in detail, are found in Thietmar (*M.G.H., SS.*, iii. 848), Adam of Bremen (ii. 27), Saxo Grammaticus (ed. Holder, p. 333), Sven Aggesøn (*loc. cit.*), and the Icelandic Sagas about the Jómsvíkings. Some element of truth must lie under such a widely spread tradition.

Eiríkr ruled Norway in the Danish interest (II, 7), he must have known something of how Norway came to be in some degree under Danish rule. In a work devoted to the praise of Sveinn and his family, it would, of course, be natural to suppress any undertakings in which they did not meet with success, and accordingly it is not surprising that the Encomiast does not mention the undignified episode of Sveinn's capture, widely known as it appears to have been. On the other hand, the two English expeditions were reasonably successful, and the Encomiast, if he had wished to mention them, could easily have implied that they were even more so. The omission of them is, therefore, to be attributed to dramatic motives : the Encomiast thought it better to depict Sveinn as attacking England once with immediate and complete success, than as going there repeatedly with ultimate success. The omission of the brilliant success against Norway in 1000 is to be attributed to the severely selective method of the Encomiast. He limits his account of the victories of both Sveinn and Knútr to their conquests of England, neglecting both the former's success in battle against Óláfr Tryggvason, and that gained by the latter by more insidious means over Óláfr Haraldsson. Accordingly, even if he knew something of affairs in Sleswick, we would not expect him to mention either the military successes of Sveinn, or the diplomatic ones of Knútr,[1] in that region.

The Encomiast sets out in the form of a speech the reasons in favour of an invasion of England urged on Sveinn by his warriors. They remind the king that Thorkell, whom they call his general (*princeps miliciae tuae*), formerly went to England, with Sveinn's permission, to avenge his brother, who had been killed there. He took a large part of the army with him and conquered the south of the country. He made peace with the English, and remained in their country, glorying in his success, instead of returning and ascribing his victory to the royal support. He thus deprived the Danish forces of forty ships manned with the finest warriors. The warriors urged Sveinn to set out and bring him to heel. They consider that Thorkell and his supporters, English and Danish, will be deserted by their Danish troops. They recommend that, if Thorkell and his Danish supporters submit, they should be treated generously.

It is, of course, well known that Thorkell Hávi conducted a vigorous campaign in England just before Sveinn's final invasion, and that he concluded peace with Æthelred in 1012, and entered his service with forty-five ships.[2] It is also confirmed by an early Icelandic tradition that he avenged a brother in England some time before the death of Sveinn, although, since the brother in question seems not to have arrived in England till just after Thorkell, the Encomiast is not correct in stating that vengeance was the original object of Thorkell's invasion.[3] It is highly improbable that Thorkell was ever in Sveinn's service, or took any forces with him to England which could be considered part of Sveinn's army, but, on the other hand, it is more than likely that his progress was regarded by Sveinn with disquiet, for the latter had himself long cherished designs upon England.

The Encomiast lavishes his rhetoric on Sveinn's preparations and voyage [4] without much concrete information, beyond stating that he took his elder son, Knútr, with him, but left the younger one in charge of his kingdom, with a military force and a few selected councillors. It is, of course, true that Knútr accompanied his father in 1013, and it will appear below that he seems to have had a brother who remained behind. It will be necessary to return to the Encomiast's statement that Knútr was the elder son.

The Encomiast professes only to touch lightly upon Sveinn's conquest of England, and he certainly adds nothing to our knowledge of it. He states that the fleet touched at an unnamed point and that a landing was made. The local resistance was overcome

---

[1] See Adam of Bremen, ii. 54.   [2] See below, pp. 73–4.   [3] See below, p. 73.
[4] On the elaborate description of Sveinn's fleet, and the similar one of Knútr's fleet in II, 4, see Appendix V.

and the adjacent region invaded with success. This procedure was applied at a number of ports in succession, until, at the cost of much labour, the whole country was subdued and Sveinn became king. Resistance had practically ceased when, very shortly afterwards, Sveinn died, having previously committed the sceptre to Knútr, at the same time admonishing him concerning statecraft and due attention to the practice of Christianity. He had also asked his son, if the opportunity arose, to take his body to Denmark, for he knew that the English hated him as the invader of their country. The Danes received the new king gladly, and rejoiced that he had been made king while his father still lived.

Brief as it is, the Encomiast's account of Sveinn's conquest of England is misleading. Sveinn did not sail from point to point, conquering a little at a time. His fleet appeared at Sandwich before the beginning of August 1013, but the *Old English Chronicle* does not suggest that there was any fighting there, but rather emphasises the rapidity with which Sveinn proceeded thence to the Humber and up the Trent to Gainsborough. There his ships lay during a campaign which laid Northumbria, the East Midlands and Wessex at his feet in the course of a few months, and at the end of which all held him for full king, while London, which had just before resisted him successfully, surrendered to him. In fact, the fleet was still at Gainsborough when Knútr decided to leave England after his father's death. Accordingly the Encomiast's account of Sveinn's conquest is very imperfect. It will appear below that his account of that of Knútr is almost as bad. On the other hand, his definition of Sveinn's position at the end of his campaign deserves attention. He does not say that resistance ceased entirely, but that hardly anyone continued to resist. Now, this is perfectly true : we know that Thorkell's fleet, at least, remained unsubdued and loyal. With regard to the position finally reached by Sveinn in England, he says that he was *tota Anglorum patria* . . *intronizatus*. Although Freeman was wrong in considering the last word vague in sense (see Glossary), it is not necessary to press it unduly, and to regard it as implying a legal English coronation. The Encomiast's words can be regarded as precisely equivalent to those of the *Old English Chronicle*, which states that the whole people considered Sveinn ' full king ', a phrase which regularly implies kingly power without perfect constitutional standing.[1] The manner in which the Encomiast makes Sveinn personally name his successor as king shows that he did not consider that he had attained a royal position in England by the constitutional processes of an elective monarchy. In fact, he carefully says that the *Danes* rejoiced when Knútr was made their king.

We have no means of telling if there is any truth in the story that Sveinn nominated Knútr as his successor, but we know from the *Chronicle* that the latter was chosen king by the Danish fleet as soon as his father died, and this may well have been a ratification of Sveinn's choice. It will appear below that Sveinn's body was ultimately removed to Denmark, and this may have been in accordance with his expressed wish. It may also be remarked that there is nothing absurd in the advice concerning Christian observances placed by the Encomiast on the lips of the dying king. The story of Sveinn's baptism on the occasion of a legendary invasion of Denmark by the Emperor Otto I, which has found its way from Adam of Bremen (ii. 3) into the Icelandic Sagas, is without foundation, but there is no doubt that a son of Haraldr Blátönn would be baptised in infancy. Both Adam of Bremen and Saxo Grammaticus attribute the fall of Haraldr Blátönn at least in part to a heathen reaction, but it does not follow that Sveinn himself turned his back on Christianity, because he may have secured his throne with heathen support. Adam's story is that he did so, and met with many misfortunes in consequence, being expelled from his kingdom by the Swedes (see above, p. li, n. 9), but this is a wild legend with no foundation. Even Adam (ii. 37, 39) has to admit that Sveinn, after his period of

---

[1] Cf. below, p. lxiii, n. 3.

apostasy, became a vigorous supporter of the faith, and furthered it to the best of his ability in Denmark and, after 1000, in Norway.[1] Adam mentions only one intervention on Sveinn's part in ecclesiastical affairs. He says (ii. 39, and Schol. 27) that he was responsible for appointing a Bishop of Skáney.[2] Skáney had not previously been a bishopric. The Encomiast believed that the minster of Roskilde, which actually was founded by Sveinn's father, was built by Sveinn.[3] Sveinn may, however, have extended the buildings, as Jørgensen suggests.[4]

The second book of the *Encomium* begins with Knútr's return to Denmark after his father's death. The English had mustered, hoping to be able to expel him since he was as yet but a youth, and, feeling his forces to be unequal to holding the country, he withdrew to discuss the position with his brother. This, of course, is very much what actually happened after the death of Sveinn. When Æthelred returned and advanced against him, Knútr fled, leaving such of the English as had joined him to the mercy of his enemies. We need not be surprised that the Encomiast omits this aspect of Knútr's withdrawal, and also his barbarous treatment of the hostages in his hands. The Encomiast says that Thorkell did not return with Knútr, but remained behind, having concluded peace with the English, and adds that it was the opinion of some that his motive in so doing was to be able to assist Knútr on the return of the latter from England, either by persuading the English to surrender or by attacking them unexpectedly from behind. The Encomiast considers that this is proved to be the correct view of Thorkell's motives for remaining in England by the fact that the bulk of the Danish forces remained with him, the king permitting only sixty ships to accompany himself. This is equivalent to declaring that Thorkell must have had an understanding with Knútr, since it would not have been possible for him to retain such large forces as he did, except with the king's approval.[5] Now, in the rhetorical speech attributed to Sveinn's warriors in I, 2, they imply that they consider it likely that Thorkell and his supporters will rally to Sveinn's cause when he appears in England, by urging Sveinn to be merciful to them if they should do so.[6] This passage and the one at present under discussion, in which it is implied that Thorkell made peace with the English after Sveinn's death, and that he had an understanding with

---

[1] See below, p. 71.

[2] Adam states that Sveinn, after the fall of Óláfr Tryggvason, appointed a certain Gotebald, who had just come from England, Bishop of Skáney, and adds that Gotebald is said to have preached sometimes in Sweden and often in Norway. Gotebald was commemorated at Lund on 21 August, together with his successors Bernard and Henry (see *Necrologium Lundense*, in Langebek, *Scriptores*, iii. 454). Jørgensen, *Den nordiske kirkes grundlæggelse*, p. 249, speaks of an English tradition that Gotebald died in 1004, quoting Alford, *Fides Regia Britannica* (iii = *Fides Regia Anglicana*, p. 437). Alford, however, took this date from a highly imaginative account of Gotebald in an anonymous work, *The English Martyrologe* (1st ed., 1608), p. 88, where it is merely offered as an approximation. A number of other erroneous or unfounded statements concerning Gotebald have found their way from the *Martyrologe* into various works.

Saxo (ed. Holder, pp. 338–9) and the *Annals of Roskilde* credit Sveinn with the making of various ecclesiastical appointments, some of which Adam, no doubt more correctly, refers to Knútr (see *N.C.*, i. 680–1), while others belong to a period long before the beginning of Sveinn's reign.

[3] See below, p. lvii.   [4] *Op. cit.*, p. 407.

[5] The Encomiast is vague about the size of Thorkell's forces. In I, 2, Sveinn's warriors say that Thorkell has forty ships with him ; in II, 1, the Encomiast says that all the forces brought to England by Sveinn and Knútr did not return with the latter, and clearly implies that they joined Thorkell, and in II, 2, Knútr complains that Thorkell has retained a large part of his fleet ; yet in II, 3, Thorkell brings nine ships to Denmark, and says that he has left only thirty in England.

[6] I, 2, end.

Knútr at the time of the latter's withdrawal,[1] work neatly together to give the impression that the expectations of Sveinn's warriors were, in fact, fulfilled and that Thorkell joined Sveinn and concluded peace with the English (while having a tacit understanding with Knútr) after his death.   We, of course, know that Thorkell fought for the English against Sveinn,[2] and the Encomiast, whatever his motives, is plainly anxious to deceive when he implies the contrary.[3]   (Intention to deceive in the Encomiast is generally to be recognised by his care to avoid verbal untruth : the supreme example of this is discussed above, p. xlvi.   When he falls into error through faulty or incomplete information, as in his bad descriptions of the military course of the Danish conquests of England, he tells his story in a manner which leaves no doubt as to what his words mean.)   Since the Encomiast has been detected as handling the story of Thorkell in a dishonest manner, it will be necessary to use great circumspection in considering all his further references to him.

The Encomiast proceeds to describe the arrival of Knútr in Denmark and his consultation with his brother Haraldr, king of the Danes.   Knútr regards his brother, who, it is emphasised, was the younger,[4] as holding a kingdom belonging to Knútr himself by right of heritage, but he nevertheless proposes that they should provisionally divide it and attempt the re-conquest of England jointly.   If they should succeed, then let Haraldr take England or Denmark, and Knútr will be content with the other.   He ends his speech with a complaint that Thorkell has deserted him, as he had previously deserted Sveinn, and expresses the expectation that he will oppose the Danes in the event of another invasion of England, while adding an expression of confidence that he will not meet with success.   Haraldr rejects Knútr's proposals, and Knútr does not press the matter, but spends some time with his brother, while his fleet is undergoing repairs and his army restored to efficiency.   The brothers visit ' Slavia ' together, and bring their mother home from there.   After noting that at this time an English matron brought the bones of Sveinn to Denmark, where his sons laid them to rest in a tomb prepared by himself in the minster which he had built to the honour of the Holy Trinity, the Encomiast goes on to describe how Knútr prepared to invade England as summer drew near.   While he was thus occupied, Thorkell suddenly appeared with nine ships.   He remembered his behaviour to Sveinn, and how he had remained in England without Knútr's permission, and he was anxious to assure the latter of his good intentions.   He placates Knútr with difficulty, stays with him a month, and urges an invasion of England, saying that he has left thirty ships there, and that their crews will join the invading forces.   Knútr says farewell to his brother and his mother and departs with a fleet of two hundred sail,[5] which is described with some elaboration.   The composition of the crews is also touched upon.[6]

There is much that is interesting and important in this account of Knútr's visit to

---

[1] The Encomiast is careful not to make a plain statement on either point.   The words *pace confecta* might be taken to refer to the peace originally made by Thorkell before Sveinn arrived, but no reader not conversant with the history of the time would fail to infer from them that Thorkell again concluded peace after Sveinn's death, and hence that he had fought for Sveinn. Similarly, it is not declared that Knútr and Thorkell had an agreement, but it is clearly hinted.

[2] See below, p. 74.

[3] The Encomiast's probable motives for depicting Thorkell as a loyal supporter of Sveinn and Knútr are discussed below, p. 84.

[4] See Linguistic Note on II, 2, 12.

[5] This is a much more reasonable estimate of Knútr's fleet than the thousand ships of Adam of Bremen (II, 50).   An early interpolater of the *Old English Chronicle* estimated that Knútr had one hundred and sixty ships, but it is not clear if this is meant to include the forty ships seduced by Eadric in 1015 from the English service (see Plummer, *Two of the Saxon Chronicles*, ii. 195).

[6] See Appendix V.

Denmark. The fact of the visit itself is amply established by the *Old English Chronicle* and Adam of Bremen (ii. 50). Knútr's brother Haraldr, however, is known practically only from the *Encomium* and from Thietmar.[1] The latter states that after the death of Sveinn, Æthelred, whom he had expelled, returned to England, and purposed to desecrate the corpse of his enemy, but an English matron disinterred it and took it to the North, where his sons received it and buried it. They prepared to avenge the disgrace proposed against their father. Thietmar then says that he will report their proceedings on the authority of a certain person, who, it emerges later, was one Sewald. Haraldr and Knútr (the names are given in that order) attacked London in July 1016, after the death of Æthelred. The queen and her sons, Æthelstan and Eadmund, were in the city. The queen opens negotiations with the enemy (see above, p. xliv), but the princes contrive to leave the city. In a subsequent brush Eadmund and Thurgut, a supporter of Sveinn's sons, is killed. (This unknown Thurgut is certainly not Thorkell, whom Thietmar mentions by his right name just below.) Æthelstan succeeds in forcing the Danes to raise the siege. Thietmar then goes back to tell, still on the authority of Sewald, how Thorkell's men had previously martyred Ælfheah, whom by an extraordinary error he calls Dunstan. It has been suggested that Thietmar or his informant has confused the two English princes, and that Eadmund's brother Æthelstan took part in the fighting round London in 1016, and was killed.[2] In any event, it is clear that, while these passages of Thietmar contain a considerable amount of truth, they are so full of confusion that nothing can be built upon their unsupported statements, and we cannot prefer their story, that Haraldr came to England, to that of the Encomiast. On the other hand, the Encomiast would have a good motive for suppressing any active part which Haraldr may have taken in the expedition, for he would wish to give Knútr as much credit as possible. Accordingly, he cannot be regarded as being necessarily a reliable source on this matter. The question must be left open, whether Haraldr came to England, or merely allowed his kingdom to be used as the base for the expedition. Practically nothing is to be learned about Haraldr from other sources. In mentioning Sveinn's marriage to a Polish princess, various Icelandic sources state that he had two sons by her, and, in contradiction to the *Encomium*, Knútr is said to have been the younger.[3] It has been noted that Thietmar places Haraldr's name before Knútr's, which perhaps suggests the same thing. It would, on the whole, appear more likely that Sveinn entrusted his established kingdom to his elder son, and took the younger one with him to England. The otherwise worthless account of Haraldr in the Danish *Chronicon Erici* [4] suggests that he was the elder, and therefore succeeded his father.[5] The *Knytlinga Saga*, chap. 8, assumes that he died before Sveinn and that Knútr therefore succeeded his father. The *Chronicon Erici* and the *Encomium* can be regarded as providing sufficient evidence that Haraldr succeeded Sveinn

---

[1] The passage of Thietmar now to be discussed will be found in *M.G.H., SS.*, iii. 849 ff.

[2] So Freeman, *N.C.*, i. 700 ; a rather different view, W., p. 168.

[3] The two sons are named by Oddr in his Saga of Ólafr Tryggvason (p. 148 in ed. referred to below, p. 68, n. 1), by *Fagrskinna* (p. 83, derived from Oddr), *Heimskringla* (*Óláfs Saga Tryggvasonar*, chap. 34, derived from Oddr), *Knytlinga Saga* (chap. 5, derived from *Heimskringla*). All these sources derive the statement ultimately from Oddr. *Fagrskinna* adds that Haraldr was the eldest, and it is possible that this is from the text of Oddr which it uses. The relevant passage of Oddr is extant only in two manuscripts of the Icelandic translation of his (lost) Latin Saga, and the names of Sveinn's two sons are given by the one in the opposite order to the other. *Heimskringla* states that Knútr ruled Denmark three years longer than England, so Snorri clearly did not know of Haraldr's reign in Denmark (*Magnús Saga Góða*, chap. 5).

[4] In Langebek, *Scriptores*, i. 159.

[5] On the absurd account of Haraldr in the *Chronicon Erici*, see Steenstrup, *Normannerne*, iii. 435 ff. This text is the source of all the many references to Haraldr in later Danish chronicles : see, e.g., *Gammeldanske Krøniker*, ed. by M. Lorenzen (Copenhagen, 1887-1913), *passim*.

as king of Denmark. Haraldr disappears after this entirely from history. It has been reasonably conjectured that he died soon afterwards, and that the journey of Knútr to Denmark in 1019 (*Old English Chronicle*) was made to claim the vacant throne. It is noticed in a copy of the Gospels belonging to Christ Church, Canterbury, that Haraldr and Knútr both entered into the brotherhood of that foundation. This, however, does not imply that Haraldr was ever in England : his brother probably gave his name to the monks.[1]

The statement that Haraldr and Knútr visited ' Slavia ' and fetched their mother thence is of considerable interest, for we are able to infer from other sources that she was a Polish princess, and had been the wife of Eiríkr of Sweden before her marriage to Sveinn.[2]

The story of the removal of Sveinn's body to England is practically identical in the *Encomium* and in Thietmar,[3] and is, no doubt, to be accepted, especially as Icelandic, Danish, Norman and English tradition knew of the removal, though not of the matron.[4] There can be no doubt that the minster, which the Encomiast believed to have been built by Sveinn to the honour of the Holy Trinity, was that of Roskilde, the dedication of which was to the Holy Trinity.[5] The Icelandic and Danish accounts, though they are both late and poor, confirm that Sveinn was buried at Roskilde.[6]

It is scarcely necessary to point out the suspicious nature of the allusions to Thorkell which occur in the Encomiast's account of Knútr's visit to Denmark. In II, 1, the Encomiast has been at pains to suggest that Thorkell acted in agreement with Knútr in remaining in England, yet, when Knútr arrives in Denmark, he expresses anxiety concerning the probable behaviour of Thorkell in the event of a Danish invasion of England. Then the Encomiast suddenly makes Thorkell rush to Denmark to placate Knútr, and only succeed in doing so with difficulty. The glaring inconsistency between the suggestion of II, 1, that Thorkell was working in agreement with Knútr, and the two passages in question is the greatest artistic failure in the *Encomium*, but it at least makes it obvious that the Encomiast was not honest in his account of Thorkell.

The Encomiast's account of Knútr's conquest of England may be summarised as follows. After the Danes touch at Sandwich, and ascertain that the English are preparing to resist, Thorkell proposes to take an advance party against the enemy, and Knútr and his chiefs agree. Thorkell takes the crews of more than forty ships, and wins a victory

---

[1] See Steenstrup, *op. cit.*, p. 309.

[2] See Adam of Bremen, ii. 37, and Schol. 25 ; Thietmar, *M.G.H.*, *SS.*, iii. 848–9 ; and, on the question of Sveinn's marriages, see Bjarni Aðalbjarnson's ed. of *Heimskringla* i. (Reykjavík, 1941, pp. cxxiv ff.), where further references are given. To judge from Saxo Grammaticus (ed. Holder, p. 343), Knútr's peaceful expedition to visit his mother grew in Danish tradition into two military campaigns.

[3] When the Encomiast (I. 5) makes the dying Sveinn anxious not to be buried in England, because the people hated him, he is undoubtedly hinting at the possibility of desecration of the corpse ; Thietmar openly declares that the motive of the matron was to save the corpse from desecration. Remembering how Hörthaknútr treated his half-brother's corpse in 1040, we cannot doubt that such fears were justified.

[4] See the Icelandic text printed in Appendix IV ; *Chronicon Erici* (Langebek, *Scriptores*, i. 159) ; William of Jumièges, v. 8 ; Heremannus (in *Memorials of St. Edmund's Abbey*, Rolls Series, i. 39) ; Gaimar, *Lestorie des Engles*, 4163. The Encomiast, William, and Heremannus all stress the care taken to preserve the body in transit. Sveinn's temporary grave in England was at York ; so Gaimar, and also the northern editor of Florence of Worcester, who would certainly be well-informed on such a point (Symeon of Durham, Rolls Series, ii. 146). Gaimar places the removal of the bones ten years or more after Sveinn's death. Langebek (*Scriptores*, ii. 480) suggests that Knútr instructed the matron before he left England ; Freeman (*N.C.*, i. 682) wonders if she was Sveinn's mistress.

[5] See above, p. liv ; and, on the foundation of Roskilde by Sveinn's father, Adam of Bremen, ii. 26.   [6] See Appendix IV, and *Chronicon Erici*, *l.c.*

over superior English forces at Sherston.[1] They rejoin the main body again. It is stated that Thorkell afterwards received a large part of the country as a reward for his services on this occasion. Fired by his example, Eiríkr, the ruler of Norway in the Danish interest, undertakes a similar expedition, and on his return is entrusted with the siege of London. It need hardly be said that the battle of Sherston belongs to a much later stage in the campaign, and that it is ridiculous to depict it as a sort of trial of the enemy's strength at the very beginning. Furthermore, there is no reason to believe that Thorkell commanded the Danes at Sherston, even if it be assumed, which is quite uncertain, that he fought on the Danish side during the 1015–16 campaign or part of it. One would infer from the *Old English Chronicle* that Knútr commanded at Sherston in person, and his panegyrist Óttarr Svarti alleges that he did so.[2] There is again no satisfactory evidence that Eiríkr undertook independent raids in England early in the campaign.[3] The statement that Eiríkr was in charge of the siege of London is interesting, for there is an Icelandic tradition of fair antiquity,[4] that Eiríkr was present when Knútr besieged the city. A Norse verse is also extant, which is believed to refer to Eiríkr and to allege that he fought Úlfkell in the London neighbourhood in the course of Knútr's conquest.[5] Therefore, it seems probable that the Encomiast is right, and that Eiríkr continued to accompany Knútr's army after his appointment as earl of Northumbria, which took place before the siege of London began. There is, therefore, no reason why the Encomiast should not be right when he says that Eiríkr was in charge of the siege. The Encomiast shows himself to be well informed on political matters, when he says that Eiríkr was ruler of Norway under Danish suzerainty, and that Thorkell ultimately received a large part of England from Knútr.

In place of an account of the extensive operations of the earlier part of Knútr's campaign (up to April 1016), we have seen that the Encomiast offers us only a description of some apocryphal independent raids by Thorkell and Eiríkr. With the opening of the siege of London, however, he begins to be reasonably correct in describing the course of the campaign. He states that Eiríkr invested the city closely, and he mentions the operation of circumvallation to which the *Old English Chronicle* also refers. Soon after the siege began, the *princeps* in charge of the city died ; this evidently refers to Æthelred, as just below Eadmund is said to be a son of the *princeps* in question.[6] The citizens bury him [7] and then submit. Knútr enters the city in triumph, and sits in the throne of the kingdom.[8] But on the previous night the son of the deceased *princeps* had left the city, and had begun to organise resistance again. Knútr does not trust the citizens of London sufficiently to risk being besieged in the city, so he decides to winter in Sheppey and to repair his fleet. Eadmund—his name is now given—reoccupies London and winters there. The Encomiast mentions a report that Eadmund made Knútr an offer of single combat at this time, which was refused. The fact that the treacherous Eadric Streona was with Eadmund is also mentioned.

---

[1] The Encomiast seems quite unaware of the position of Sherston. In warning his men of the impossibility of flight, Thorkell tells them, not that they are far from their ships, but that their ships are far from the shore. If this is not mere loose writing (not a usual fault in the *Encomium*), it can only mean that the shore was near, but that the ships were not at it, and hence that Sherston was reached by going along the coast from Sandwich.

[2] M. Ashdown, *English and Norse Documents*, p. 138.   [3] See below, p. 71.
[4] See below, p. 71.   [5] See below, p. 70.
[6] See above, p. xliii.
[7] The burial of Æthelred in London is not mentioned by the *Chronicle*, but it was a well-known fact : Florence of Worcester (ed. Thorpe, i. 173), William of Malmesbury (*Gesta Regum*, ii. 180) and Gaimar (*Lestorie des Engles*, 4199) all say he was buried in St. Paul's.
[8] No doubt a mere rhetorical flourish : the Encomiast can hardly have thought such an action without due election could have any significance.

This account of the fighting at London is fairly near to the truth.   Actually Æthelred died just before, not just after, the arrival of the Danish forces at London.   The departure of Eadmund to gather forces outside the city is a well-known fact, and it is also the case that the Danes abandoned the siege of London soon afterwards.[1] The Encomiast, however, diverges slightly from the truth in order to give Knútr the credit of entering the city, and abandoning it for reasons of caution, instead of being dislodged from his siege-lines by force.   The Encomiast is correct in saying that Eadric was with Eadmund at the time when Knútr was in Sheppey,[2] and that there was a story that Knútr was challenged to single combat by Eadmund, though no other writer places this incident so early as the retreat to Sheppey.[3]   The Encomiast's chronology of these operations will be discussed below,[4] but it may be observed here that he omits a long campaign, including two further sieges of London, between the raising of the first siege and the Danish retreat to Sheppey.

The Encomiast goes on to describe how Eadmund, who had been collecting forces all Lent, advanced in the spring to attempt to drive the Danes from England.   The Danes leave their retreat and give action at Ashingdon.   The battle and the treachery of Eadric are described at length, and a common belief that the latter was in league with the Danes is mentioned.   Thorkell is said to have been present at the battle (or, at least, just before it) on the Danish side.   The completeness of the Danish victory is emphasised.

In this account of the end of the campaign the Encomiast again over-simplifies events, for a great Danish raid into Mercia intervened between Knútr's leaving his retreat at Sheppey and the battle of Ashingdon.   In depicting Ashingdon as a great Danish victory and the culmination of the campaign, the Encomiast is undoubtedly justified. It is, however, doubtful how far the details of his description of the battle are not merely imaginative,[5] except that the Old English Chronicle confirms his story that Eadric played an unworthy part.[6]   As for Thorkell's alleged presence, we have seen that the Encomiast's statements concerning that chief are always'suspect, and this is particularly the case with the one under consideration, for Thorkell is introduced at this point as a vehicle for comments on a magic banner.

The Encomiast, like the Old English Chronicle, attributes the opening of negotiations after Ashingdon to Eadric Streona.   He gives practically the same terms for the territorial settlement as does MS. D of the Chronicle,[7] and also mentions the payment made

---

[1] Stenton describes these operations clearly, pp. 385–6.

[2] He had deserted Knútr for Eadmund when the former was driven to Sheppey : on Eadric's movements at this time, and errors in some sources concerning them, see Plummer, Two of the Saxon Chronicles, ii. 197.

[3] A single combat or an offer of one is well known to occur in many stories of the war of Knútr and Eadmund, though it is usually placed after Ashingdon (N.C., i. 705 ff.).   The Encomiast is not at all explicit about the election of Eadmund as king : his followers encourage him, dicentes quod eum magis quam principem Danorum eligerent.   But below (ii. 12 and 13), Eadric and Knútr call him rex.   The Chronicle is definite that Eadmund was duly elected by such of the witan as were at hand when his father died (N.C., i. 689).

[4] See below, p. lxi.

[5] Freeman accepts them largely into his text, N.C., i. 394.

[6] The Encomiast mentions a report that Eadric's treachery at Ashingdon was prearranged with the Danes ; cf. Florence of Worcester (ed. Thorpe, i. 177).

[7] The English delegates offer Knútr a kingdom in australi parte, and Eadmund is to remain with the bounds meridianae plagae.   There can be little doubt that australi is an error for boreali (cf. Textual Note on II, 13, 10), and that the Encomiast here described the division very much as the Chronicle, MS. D, which gives Wessex to Eadmund, the norðdæl to Knútr.   But just below, Knútr, in accepting their terms, says that, as they have suggested, he will take the media regio. We find precisely the same inconsistency of language in the Chronicle, where all the other manuscripts give Knútr Mercia, instead of the norðdæl of D. Cf. N.C., i. 708.

to the Danish forces.[1] He does not mention the personal meeting of the kings, and since he incorrectly makes the victorious Danes retire to London after Ashingdon, he creates the impression that Knútr was at London during the peace negotiations.[2]

The Encomiast now mentions that the death of Eadmund followed soon after the peace, and states that Knútr was chosen king by the whole country. Unfortunately, the Encomiast throws no light on the vexed question whether Knútr had a right to succeed automatically under his treaty with Eadmund.[3] It may be noted that the widely spread story that Eadmund died by treachery is not mentioned by the Encomiast.[4] This practically proves that it was not yet current in his time in a form in which Eadric was the culprit. Of course, the Encomiast would automatically suppress it if he knew it in a form which blamed Knútr.

It will be seen from the above paragraphs that the Encomiast makes the siege of London the centre of the war of 1015-16 [5] : the alleged raids of Thorkell and Eiríkr are a prelude, the retreat to Sheppey and the battle of Ashingdon an epilogue. It is evident that the Encomiast had no informant with more than a vague memory of the course of the war. Whoever supplied his information remembered the siege of London, the retreat to Sheppey, and the culmination of the war at Ashingdon. The battle of Sherston was a name to him : he had not the vaguest idea of its place in the campaign. Of the siege of London itself he remembered the outstanding incidents : the death of the king in the city (which, however, he placed after instead of just before the siege began), Eadmund's withdrawal to raise forces elsewhere, and Knútr's withdrawal from London. He knew something of the activities of Eadric, and of the terms and circumstances of the peace. From these inadequate materials, the Encomiast has had to patch up his story.

The Encomiast's account of the war of 1015-16 is by no means devoid of value. It can add practically nothing to the facts we learn from other sources,[6] but it is valuable to have its confirmation of the *Old English Chronicle* on one or two matters in which prejudice might have affected the compilers of that work. Accordingly, it is interesting to notice that the treacherous Eadric and the gallant Eadmund bear much the same character in both the *Chronicle* and the *Encomium*, and that both sources agree in suggesting that Eadmund received ready support from the English, when he left London to collect forces. Lastly, the impression of Knútr's character given by the Encomiast is interesting. In his whole account of the campaign he never once gives a hint that his hero displayed the least sign of personal courage, and twice he speaks as if his caution was so great as to call for a word of explanation.[7] Since he would assuredly have been delighted to attribute some personal prowess to his hero, if there were the least ground for doing so, one can hardly fail to conclude that Knútr left behind him no trace of fame for strength

---

[1] II, 13, last words ; cf. *N.C.*, i. 709.

[2] The mistake is no doubt due to the fact that Knútr wintered in London after the settlement ; Henry of Huntingdon has a similar error : he makes Knútr take London between Ashingdon and the peace of Olney (Rolls Series, pp. 184-5).

[3] See *N.C.*, i. 709-10.

[4] On the many stories of this nature, see *N.C.*, i. 711 ff.

[5] Foreign writers tend to do this, for the siege made a great impression at the time, and London was, in fact, ' the key-point in the struggle ' (Stenton, p. 386) : accordingly, the accounts of the war given by Thietmar and William of Jumièges (v. 8-9) are concerned almost exclusively with the siege.

[6] It does show us that the Norse tradition that Eiríkr took part in the fighting round London is sound ; and that the story that Eadmund offered single combat to Knútr is early.

[7] II, 1, *non quod . . . metuendo fugeret*, the Encomiast carefully insists ; II, 7-8, it is carefully emphasised that Knútr was *prudens* and *sapiens* in withdrawing to Sheppey, and declining single combat. In II, 6, Thorkell says his king is very eager to fight, but this is no doubt courtesy : in fact, the king appears very willing to let Thorkell test the strength of the resistance for him.

or courage in battle. The Encomiast does not even place a rhetorical speech on his lips at Ashingdon to offset that of Eadmund. Eiríkr and Thorkell quite overshadow their king in the Encomiast's account of the conquest.

The Encomiast supplies an artificial chronology of the campaign to suit his own purposes. He evidently knew that it ended in the year following the one in which Knútr landed in England. He does not seem, however, to be aware how late Knútr began the campaign of 1015 : he says (II, 4) that Knútr was busy with his preparations as the summer drew near, and that Thorkell then appeared and stayed more than a month with the king; he then proceeds to describe the invasion. Therefore, he can hardly have thought of the landing at Sandwich as taking place later than midsummer. (It actually took place about 8 September.) The Encomiast, therefore, has to fill up a great deal of time, and his difficulty in so doing is considerable, because he did not know many of the incidents of the war. He therefore places the supposed raids of Thorkell and Eiríkr, the siege of London, the death of Æthelred, the relief of London, and Knútr's retreat to Sheppey before the beginning of the winter of the year in which Knútr landed. Actually Æthelred did not die until 23 April 1016, and the siege of London had not then begun. The Encomiast gets himself out of his difficulty by taking a hint from the Latin historians and sending his heroes into winter quarters. Knútr's stay in Sheppey, a mere brief incident in the campaign of the summer and autumn of 1016, is magnified to include the whole winter 1015–16, and Eadmund is made to remain in London at the same time. Since the Encomiast has put all the fighting that he knew about into the year of the invasion except the battle of Ashingdon, he has to place that action soon after Easter of the following year (II, 9) for, even if he knew that it did not take place till the autumn, he obviously had no knowledge to enable him to describe another summer campaign.

The Encomiast proceeds to state that his hero ruled England in peace till his death (*fine tenus*), thus confirming that absence of domestic incident which we infer from the silence of the *Chronicle* on home affairs during Knútr's reign. The Encomiast is perhaps pointed in saying that Knútr held England in peace : his hero's Northern adventures are purposely excluded from his story (cf. p. lii above). The words *et nobiliter duces et comites suos disposuit* no doubt refer, among other things, to the fourfold division of England in 1017. He mentions that Knútr commenced his reign with a number of executions, which he attributes to the monarch's distaste for those who had been false to Eadmund, and it may be observed that Florence of Worcester [1] gives a similar reason for certain executions with which he credits Knútr. The Encomiast gives only one example of these executions, that of Eadric Streona, and, in so doing, he offers the earliest of the many embroideries of the undoubted fact that Knútr had Eadric executed.[2]

We now come to the Encomiast's account of the marriage of his hero and heroine, the birth of their son, and the dispatch of Eadweard and Ælfred to Normandy. This has been discussed elsewhere in some detail.[3] The Encomiast goes on to say that when Hörthaknútr grew up (*adulto denique puero*, an expression which need not be pressed, for he was only a child in 1023), his father gave his entire dominion to him by oath, and sent him to hold the kingdom of Denmark. It is an undoubted fact that Knútr sent his son to Denmark about 1023,[4] and Norse tradition confirms the statement of the Encomiast, that he was permitted a position of sub-kingship there.[5] We have no means of telling if Knútr really promised him ultimate succession to England at the same time, but, if we

---

[1] Ed. Thorpe, i. 179.
[2] On the many stories of Eadric's end, see C. E. Wright, *The Cultivation of Saga in Anglo-Saxon England*, pp. 206 ff.
[3] See above, pp. xliv ff.   [4] See below, p. 75.
[5] See *Fagrskinna*, p. 185.

accept the probable story of the bargain of Knútr and Emma,[1] there is no reason against assuming that he did so. (He had not acquired Norway at this time, and it would therefore be outside anything he promised to Hörthaknútr ; hence the fact that he afterwards gave it to one of his illegitimate sons is not inconsistent with the Encomiast's statement that he made Hörthaknútr heir to his entire dominions when he sent him to Denmark.)

The Encomiast goes on to say that, when once Knútr became king of Denmark, he found himself king of five realms, Denmark, England, Wales, Scotland and Norway. Knútr's claims on Wales and Scotland were vague, but it is certainly true that Malcolm of Scotland and certain lesser northern kings submitted to him (*Chronicle*, MS. E, 1031) in some measure. In any event, the Encomiast's estimate of the extent of his dominions compares very favourably with some others for truth and modesty.[2] It would perhaps be unwise to press the statement of the Encomiast that Knútr had five realms when once he had acquired Denmark. He knew, however, that Knútr became king of England before the death of his brother, and he may have regarded the *de jure* sovereignty of Norway as going with that of Denmark, despite Óláfr Helgi's *de facto* kingship of the former country. On the date of Knútr's becoming in some sense king of Wales and Scotland he was probably quite vague.

The Encomiast now passes on to praise Knútr's generosity to the Church and his other good works, including his suppression of unjust laws, a point which would have come more fittingly in the course of his preceding remarks on the king's secular affairs. He does not detail the king's generosity in his own land, but tells how Gaul, Italy and especially Flanders, through which countries he went to Rome,[3] have cause to pray for his soul. He exemplifies this by his famous account of Knútr's visit to St. Omer's and St. Bertin's, when he was an eye witness of the monarch's liberality and exuberant penitence. There is no reason to doubt the substantial truth of his description of Knútr's behaviour, upon which Sir Charles Oman's comments require neither addition nor improvement.[4]

The Encomiast says that Knútr lived only a short time after his return from Rome. The date of Knútr's pilgrimage is an old and difficult problem, but it may be said that the *Old English Chronicle* (MS. E, 1031), the *Encomium*, Adam of Bremen,[5] and the Norse Sagas,[6] agree in placing it late in his life. Accordingly, the customary modern view that this pilgrimage is to be identified with the visit to Rome made by Knútr in 1027, when he attended the coronation of the Emperor Conrad, is not to be accepted with any confidence. It would seem that Knútr was in Rome twice. Florence of Worcester already confuses the two visits, when he says that Lyfing accompanied Knútr on the later one and became a bishop just afterwards, for Lyfing's appointment more probably belongs to 1027 (cf. below, p. 59, n. 5). The well-known letter which Knútr wrote from Rome to his people is quoted by Florence under 1031, but this is obviously also a confusion : the letter clearly belongs to the visit of 1027 (cf. below, p. 82, n. 4). Freeman correctly emphasises that it is of no chronological significance that the Encomiast mentions the pilgrimage after his statement that Knútr finally became king of five realms, including Scotland.[7] This is due, not to a belief on the part of the Encomiast that the pilgrimage followed the

---

[1] See above, p. xlv.   [2] See *N.C.*, i. 766.

[3] *Knytlinga Saga*, chap. 17, mentions that Knútr went to Rome, passing through Flanders, and it is, of course, well known that St. Bertin's lay on the normal route from England to Rome.

[4] *England before the Norman Conquest*, p. 592.

[5] II, 63 : he places the visit in the time of Archbishop Libentius, 1029–32.

[6] Both *Fagrskinna* (in the insertion dealing with Knútr, see below, p. 83) and *Knytlinga Saga*, chaps. 17–18. Although the latter work is largely derivative in its account of Knútr (cf. below, p. 91), it has some scraps of independent information.

[7] *N.C.*, i. 751.

submission of the Scottish kings in 1031, but to his treatment of Knútr's affairs in two divisions, the secular and the ecclesiastical.

The third book of the *Encomium* opens by mentioning that Knútr was buried at Winchester,[1] and points out that Emma was alone in England, Hörthaknútr being in Denmark and her other two sons in Normandy. All these princes were rejected by the English, who made Haraldr king, although his claim to be Knútr's son was very uncertain. All these statements are fully confirmed by the *Old English Chronicle*. All manuscripts notice the burial of Knútr at Winchester. MSS. C and D add that Emma was in the city and that Haraldr, who claimed falsely to be a son of Knútr, had her deprived of all Knútr's best treasures. She remained, however, in the city as long as she could ; that is, till her exile two years later. MS. E does not mention the robbery of Emma, but it defines the political position more exactly. The witan met at Oxford after Knútr's death, and Leofric of Mercia, supported by practically all the thanes from north of the Thames, and by the representatives of the seafaring population of London, chose Haraldr as guardian of all England on behalf of himself and his brother Hörthaknútr. Godwine and the Wessex representatives opposed this in vain. It was, however, agreed that Emma should hold Wessex on behalf of her son, and should have her seat in Winchester, and retain about her the royal bodyguard. Godwine was her most faithful supporter. This arrangement did not prejudice the general regency granted to Haraldr over the whole country : it is said expressly that Godwine and his party might not in the least prevail against the proposal that Haraldr should have such a regency. It is also plain that Emma's position in Wessex was, in actual fact, ineffective : MSS. C and D show that she was unable to resist when Haraldr's men came to carry off her treasures.[2] MS. E, in fact, concludes its notice of these events by saying that Haraldr was now full king over all England,[3] even though his claim to be a son of Knútr was considered by many to be poor. Again, in noticing Haraldr's death in 1040, it remarks that he controlled England for four years and sixteen weeks, practically the whole period from the death of Knútr.[4] There can, accordingly, be no doubt that the Encomiast describes the *de facto* position correctly when he says that Haraldr was made king after Knútr's death. On the other hand, he has two passages further on which show that he was alive to the *de jure* position.[5]

The Encomiast now tells his well-known story of how Haraldr asked Archbishop Æthelnoth to crown him and, upon being refused, attempted to avenge himself on the Church by neglecting his religious observances. It is difficult to say if there is any truth in this story. Obviously, if Haraldr ever made such a request, he would be refused, since the archbishop could not crown as king one who had not been duly elected.[6] (The

---

[1] See Textual Note on III, 1.

[2] MS. C distinctly says that Harold had the treasures taken *þe heo ofhealdan ne mihte.* Stenton, p. 414, interprets the evidence on Emma's position similarly. I disagree strongly with Plummer (*Two of the Saxon Chronicles*, ii. 209) when he takes the words of the *Chronicle* to mean that Emma attempted to rule Wessex by force in defiance of the witan's election of Haraldr as regent.

[3] *Full cyng ofer eall Englaland* : cf. the *Chronicle's* use of the phrase *full cyning* of Sveinn's standing late in 1013, and cf. above, p. liii.

[4] See Plummer, *op. cit.*, p. 218. It should be observed that no *Chronicle* manuscript implies that Haraldr became a constitutional king in 1035. It is true that MS. D, after noticing the death of Knútr, adds the words *ond Harold his sunu feng to rice*, but these words are shown to be a clumsy interpolation by the fact that the pronouns in the following sentences still refer to Knútr. The original form of the entry may be seen in MS. C.

[5] See below, pp. lxiv and lxviii.

[6] It is beside the point that Haraldr does seem to have been crowned ultimately : this would be after he was elected King in 1037 (see for evidence of his coronation, *N.C.*, i. 778). On the course of events in Haraldr's period, see Stenton, p. 414 (where the evidence is admirably inter-

Encomiast rhetorically makes the archbishop refuse out of loyalty to the sons of Emma, but there is not the least reason to think that he would have refused to crown Haraldr if he had been elected.) Furthermore, it will appear below that Haraldr and his party were quite aware that what they must do was to canvass support and thus secure election by the witan, not try to persuade an unwilling churchman to perform an empty ceremony. Accordingly, the whole story is to be rejected, and with it goes the allegation that Haraldr was childish enough to neglect his religious observances (especially by indulging in Sunday sport) out of pique.[1]

We now come to the Encomiast's much-discussed account of the murder of Emma's son Ælfred. He says that after Haraldr's usurpation Emma awaited the upshot of events quietly. Haraldr was not permitted to injure her, so he plotted with his supporters to secure his position by killing her sons. He had a letter forged, purporting to be from the queen to the two princes in Normandy. In this letter—which is quoted in full—he made Emma complain that she is queen in name only ; her sons were daily being more and more deprived of the kingdom, which was their heritage ; the usurper was perpetually going round seeking the support of the magnates of the kingdom by gifts, threats and prayers ; they, however, would prefer Ælfred or Eadweard as king ; let one of the princes come to discuss with the queen how the matter can best be managed ; let them send a reply by the present messenger. The interest of this document hardly requires emphasis. It describes the activities of Haraldr as they would appear to Emma and her friends, and it shows that, although the Encomiast states that Haraldr was chosen king after the death of Knútr, he was perfectly well aware that he had not yet secured legal kingship, but was working for it with increasing success. Incidentally, a picture of Haraldr's party going about to canvass support has reached us from another and totally independent source.[2]

The letter was sent to the princes, who fell into the trap. They replied that one of them would come, and gave a day, a time and place. Ælfred [3] set out with his brother's approval. He was accompanied by an unspecified number of troops, and, as he passed through Flanders, he added a few men of Boulogne to these, refusing Baldwin's offer of larger forces. He did not land in England at the first point at which he touched, for he

---

preted), and Plummer (op. cit., pp. 208-11, where the statements of the different manuscripts of the Chronicle are carefully considered). Older treatments (especially Freeman's) are hopelessly confused by assuming that Haraldr was elected king of part of the country in 1035 ; but the statement that his supporters wished to choose him as warden of all England on behalf of himself and his brother, and that his opponents could not in the least prevent them from doing so, implies that a division was contemplated when Hörthaknútr returned. Haraldr's party (especially his mother, see reference in note 2, below) canvassed support vigorously, and, as Hörthaknútr did not appear, Haraldr secured constitutional election to the throne in 1037.

[1] Such evidence as there is does not suggest that Haraldr was particularly irreligious or even anticlerical : see N.C., i. 504-5.

[2] See E.H.R., xxviii. 115-16.

[3] He is stated to be the younger of the two. The Encomiast is the only writer early enough to be of any value who pronounces on this point, but it has been suggested above (p. xlii) that Eadweard's selection to lead his father's delegation to the witan in 1014 confirms the Encomiast. P. Grierson, Transactions of the Royal Historical Society, xxiii. 95, quotes as throwing light on this point a Ghent charter dated 25 December 1016, in which Eadweard promises to restore the English possessions of St. Peter's if he should become king. This document does not prove Eadweard to be older than Ælfred : if he chose to anticipate his election over the heads of his half-brother Eadwig and any other of Æthelred's elder family who may have been alive, and of the sons of Eadmund Ironside, he might also have imagined circumstances under which he would become king, even if he were younger than Ælfred. Eadweard was so remote from any likelihood of becoming king in 1016, that I greatly doubt if the charter in question is anything more than an imaginative forgery, drawn up after Eadward became king. (A facsimile of the document may be seen in Messager des sciences historiques de Belgique, 1842, facing p. 238.)

observed that he was being awaited, and would be attacked if he went ashore. Landing elsewhere, he attempted to go to his mother. When, however, he was near her, Godwine met him, and swore loyalty to him, but diverted him from London (the Encomiast was apparently unaware that Emma resided at Winchester) to Guildford, where he arranged a night's lodging for him and his men. Godwine departed, promising to return in the morning. As soon as Ælfred and his men had retired to bed, Haraldr's men appeared, seized their weapons, and bound them. In the morning they mocked them and butchered nine out of every ten ; of the residue, they sold some, reserving others for further mockery or to be their own slaves. Nevertheless, the Encomiast himself had seen some who escaped. Ælfred himself was taken to Ely, and was there mocked, tried, blinded, tortured and killed. The monks buried him, and some say that they have seen miracles at his tomb.

There are three independent early accounts of the murder of Ælfred. One is that of the Encomiast ; another is the ballad inserted with a brief prose introduction in MSS. C and D of the *Old English Chronicle* under 1036 ; a third is the Norman version, which is given most fully and clearly by William of Poitiers.[1] The story of the ballad [2] and its introduction is that Ælfred came to England, and said he was going to his mother, who was at Winchester. Godwine and other powerful men were unwilling to permit this, because feeling was running in Haraldr's favour, and Godwine, accordingly, intercepted the ætheling. (This is equivalent to an admission that the ætheling's visit was regarded as being not without political significance.) Godwine killed some of Ælfred's companions, and ill-treated others in various ways. The ætheling himself was removed to Ely : he was blinded on board ship on the way. He remained with the monks till he died. He was buried at Ely.

The closeness of this account to that of the Encomiast in outline and in many details is obvious. The main difference is that, in the Encomiast's account, Godwine merely intercepts the ætheling, while Haraldr's men commit the crime. The Encomiast clearly knew a version of the story in which Godwine intercepted Ælfred and guided him to a convenient place for Haraldr's men to do the rest. He has told this story, but he has let Godwine's motives appear from the events without comment : he leaves it open to anyone foolish enough to do so to fail to infer that Godwine was acting in agreement with Haraldr in guiding Ælfred's party to Guildford. The Encomiast's reason for this was, no doubt, that he was writing at a time when Godwine was officially assumed to be comparatively innocent [3] and was making himself useful to Hörthaknútr.[4] The Encomiast also adds two major details to the ballad : he makes it clear that Ælfred had a political object, and he names the place of interception as Guildford. On this latter point a number of later versions confirm him.[5]

---

[1] William of Poitiers and William of Jumièges (vii. 11), as frequently elsewhere, are in very close agreement in their accounts of the murder, and it is disputed whether one of them is derived from the other, or whether they have a common source : see William of Jumièges, *Gesta Norman-norum Ducum*, ed. J. Marx (Rouen and Paris, 1914), pp. xvii. ff., for a discussion of this problem and further references. Practically the same story appears in the later Norman chronicles : Wace, *Roman de Rou* (ed. Andresen, ii. 218 ff.), Benoît de Sainte-Maure, *Chronique des ducs de Normandie* (ed. Michel, iii. 74 ff.).

[2] Plummer, *Two of the Saxon Chronicles*, ii. 212 ff., has conclusively shown that the text of the ballad and introduction in MS. C of the *Chronicle* is the original version, while that in MS. D, which omits all reference to Godwine, has been tampered with. Accordingly, I use the C text of this source only.

[3] His trial and acquittal for the murder in Hörthaknútr's time is well known.

[4] See Florence of Worcester (ed. Thorpe, i. 194–5).

[5] See below. Wace and Benoît drag a mention of Guildford into the Norman version of the story, though they do not make it the point of interception.

The version of William of Poitiers [1] makes Ælfred sail from Wissant (a port on the Flemish coast) to Dover, apparently with considerable forces,[2] and lay claim to the throne. He advances inland, and is met by Godwine, who swears fealty, and enters into discussions of an unspecified nature with him over a meal. At night, however, Godwine makes the ætheling captive, and sends him to Haraldr in London, who blinds him and sends him by sea to Ely, where he soon dies of his injuries. Outrages against his companions are committed by both Godwine and Haraldr. Here there are many correspondences of detail with the other versions : the ætheling comes through Flanders as in the *Encomium*, his landing at Dover agrees with the versions which make Guildford the point of interception, he is captured at night as in the *Encomium*, and he is sent to Ely by sea as in the *Chronicle*. The Encomiast makes Ælfred come to discuss with his mother how to get rid of Haraldr ; William makes him come to claim the throne ; the *Chronicle* makes his coming alarm the chief men, for feeling was strongly in Haraldr's favour, and this is equivalent to an admission that Ælfred's proposed visit to his mother was not to be a mere act of filial affection. All three sources also agree that Godwine intercepted the ætheling. The *Chronicle* attributes the subsequent outrages to Godwine, William to the king, to whom Godwine delivers the captive ætheling. The Encomiast has not accused Godwine in words of acting for Haraldr, but he has left it open to the reader to assume that he intercepted the ætheling in order to give Haraldr's men an opportunity to seize him. The Encomiast is a master of the art of giving the impression he desired without words : he must have been perfectly aware that his reader would assume Godwine's guilt from his narrative, and, accordingly, he must have been willing to let Godwine be thought guilty, or else he would have made it clear that he was innocent. Therefore, it may be said that all three sources point to Godwine as involved in the murder. The Encomiast and William, however, regard Haraldr (or at least his men) as even more deeply involved than Godwine. The *Chronicle* puts the entire blame on Godwine, while making it clear that he was acting in the interests of the political party which supported Haraldr. If this version be preferred to the agreement of the other two, it is possible to absolve Haraldr of personal complicity, but all three versions agree in convicting Godwine, and implying that he was now on Haraldr's side. Therefore this view of his political position and of his guilt must be accepted.

A failure to appreciate the political circumstances of the time has reduced the value of many discussions of Ælfred's murder. It has been assumed that Emma, supported by Godwine, was ruling Wessex in Hörthaknútr's interest at the time, and hence that Godwine was probably not involved in the murder of Emma's son (so Freeman), or was involved in it, but was acting not in Haraldr's interest, but, in some mysterious way, in that of Hörthaknútr (so Plummer). It cannot be too clearly emphasised that the only source which tells the story of Emma's supervision of Wessex, and of Godwine's support of her, emphasises that Haraldr, in spite of this arrangement, was ' full king ' over all England already in 1035, and was officially regent of the whole country.[3] Emma's regency of Wessex was intended to be limited from the outset, and was never sufficiently effective to enable her to prevent the robbery of her personal property. This being the case, it is unlikely that the astute Godwine would remain long faithful to her cause, or would fail to make his peace with Haraldr's party. We have seen that, of the three main accounts of Ælfred's murder, two place Godwine on the king's side openly, and the

---

[1] Duchesne, *Historiae Normannorum Scriptores*, pp. 178–9.

[2] On this point William of Jumièges is definite ; William of Poitiers says that Ælfred was *accuratius quam frater antea aduersus uim præparatus*. The Norman chroniclers place an attempt on England by Eadweard with a fleet of forty ships just before that of Ælfred (see below), so presumably William of Poitiers means to imply that Ælfred had more than forty ships.

[3] See above, p. lxiii.

third by implication. Therefore, one must assume (with Stenton, p. 415) that Godwine had joined Haraldr's party by 1036. Florence of Worcester (ed. Thorpe, i. 195) gives what purports to be the form of oath with which Godwine excused himself at his trial for the murder during Hörthaknútr's reign. According to this, Godwine did not deny complicity, but claimed that he did what he did on the orders of his lord and king. This is in perfect agreement with what has already been concluded.

The later versions of the story are of little value, except that they repeat a few of the details given by the earlier versions, and hence suggest that these are of an historical nature. The versions of Henry of Huntingdon, William of Malmesbury and Gaimar are historically of little value, because they place the murder at the wrong time, after the death of Haraldr, but all three blame Godwine, which is significant. They confirm the detail given by the Encomiast that Ælfred's men were decimated, and they all take this to mean that one in ten was spared, not that one in ten was executed. Henry and Gaimar place the interception at Guildford, William at Gillingham. The biographer of Eadweard blames Haraldr exclusively, but he is prejudiced, and even he has to take notice of the fact that Godwine was suspected. (He removes the accusation of Godwine from the reign of Hörthaknútr into that of Eadweard, a curious confusion.)

The version of Florence of Worcester is a curious piece of work. Its basis is the ballad and its prose introduction in the uncorrupted form in which Godwine is blamed. It attempts to combine with this a corrupted version of the Norman story. In William of Poitiers and the Norman chroniclers, Ælfred's expedition is preceded by a definitely military one undertaken by Eadweard, which has to be abandoned.[1] Florence evidently knew a version of the Norman story in which Eadweard's expedition was combined with Ælfred's, but which followed the same general lines as the version as we know it in William of Poitiers. Hence, in Florence, Eadweard and Ælfred come to England at the same time, with strong forces. Eadweard succeeds in joining Emma, but Ælfred's adventures proceed as in the *Chronicle*, with touches from the Norman story. After Ælfred's death, Eadweard withdraws.

A final word must be said on the Encomiast's curious story about the forged letter. It is obviously not to be taken seriously. A Norse source shows that some tale was current in which Emma was concerned with a forged letter.[2] Probably the Encomiast saw fit to tell this story in a form completely creditable to his patroness in the hope that his version would supersede others less favourable to her.

The Encomiast tells the rest of his story briefly. He describes how Emma withdrew to Flanders after Ælfred's death, and her kindly reception there.[3] No doubt he was influenced by respect for the queen's feelings in saying that she withdrew on her own initiative : we know from the *Chronicle* that she was exiled in 1037. He depicts the queen as being not entirely without friends to accompany her, and as having sufficient means to pay her way at least in part and even to implement her sympathy for the poor by almsgiving. She summoned Eadweard from Normandy to consult with her, but he declined to act, on the ground that the English chiefs had sworn him no oaths, and that therefore it would be more fitting to look to Hörthaknútr. He himself returned to Normandy. Although Eadweard's visit to Flanders may be apocryphal, the reason, which the Encomiast makes him offer for his unwillingness to act, shows a sound grasp of the

---

[1] If there is anything in this story, it explains why Ælfred—apparently the younger brother—made the journey of 1036 alone : Eadweard had failed in one attempt and was discouraged. Gaimar (*Lestoire des Engles*, 4785–90) is so surprised that Ælfred, whom he believed to be the younger, came to England, that he invents a fantastic explanation.

[2] See below, p. 83.

[3] P. Grierson (p. 97 in article referred to above, p. lxiv, n. 3) suggests that the *castellum* near Bruges, where Emma landed, was Oudenbourg.

political situation. Although the Encomiast in III, 1, says the English made Haraldr king, he was evidently aware that some *de jure* position had been officially accorded to Hörthaknútr.[1] Emma now sends messengers to Hörthaknútr, who comes to Flanders with ten ships, having left a powerful fleet mobilised, apparently in Denmark, which could come to his assistance if need arose. Although Emma's message to Denmark is not mentioned by the *Chronicle*, it is evident that some word must have been sent to Hörthaknútr, or he would not have known that his mother was in Flanders. He certainly sailed to Flanders to join her in 1039 (*Chronicle*, MS. C). In Flanders, Emma and her son hear of the death of Haraldr, and that the English are anxious to make Hörthaknútr king. They are preparing to depart for England, when a more formal embassy than the messengers who brought the news arrives to offer the allegiance of England. Hörthaknútr crosses to England in triumph.

This account of the events immediately before and after the death of Haraldr agrees very closely with the *Old English Chronicle*. The one addition is the powerful fleet mobilised by Hörthaknútr, and here the Encomiast has the confirmation of Adam of Bremen, though that authority makes him congregate his ships in Flanders (ii, 71).[2] The *Chronicle* merely says that Hörthaknútr was sent for after Haraldr's death, but, when the Encomiast declares that a deputation of important men crossed to Flanders, he has the support of the *Chronicon Abbatiae Rameseiensis*.[3]

The only event of Hörthaknútr's reign mentioned by the Encomiast is that he invited his brother Eadweard to England to hold the kingdom with him. In the *Argument* he is more explicit : he says that Haraldr divided the glory and wealth of the kingdom with his brother. The *Chronicle* says that Eadweard had long been an exile, but was nevertheless sworn into the kingship (*to cinge gesworen*, MSS. C and D). The precise position taken up by Eadweard in England is difficult to decide, but it may be said that the *Encomium* and the *Chronicle* agree that it was of a royal nature. One may reasonably conjecture that it was that of acknowledged heir to an ailing monarch, who knew his days were numbered.[4] We know from William of Poitiers that Hörthaknútr's death was not unexpected by himself, and, if the Sagas are to be believed, this was not the first time he had received a less fortunate brother with kindness and generosity.[5] The return of Eadweard is attributed to a direct invitation from his brother both by the Encomiast and by William of Jumièges (vii. 11) and it is obviously probable that such an invitation was sent, in view of the warm reception the exile clearly received.

The value of the *Encomium* as a historical document may now be briefly assessed. It is evident that its author had some very good informant on Scandinavian affairs. This is shown by his knowledge of the circumstances of the death of Haraldr Blátönn, of the connection of Knútr's mother with ' Slavia ', of Eiríkr's position in Norway, and participation in Knútr's wars, of Sveinn's interest in the minster of Roskilde and burial there, and of the appointment of Hörthaknútr as king of Denmark by his father. Though all these matters are known to us from other sources, the Encomiast is by far the earliest authority for them, except in a few points, where he is confirmed by Thietmar or by

---

[1] Cf. above, pp. lxiii–iv.

[2] It would appear certain that the fleet mobilised by Hörthaknútr ultimately joined him in Flanders, for the *Chronicle*, MSS. C and D, notices that he came from there to England with sixty ships.

[3] Rolls Series, pp. 149–50.

[4] Saxo (ed. Holder, p. 361) suggests less disinterested motives for Hörthaknútr's generosity.

[5] Sveinn, Knútr's illegitimate son, fled to Denmark on the return of Magnús Óláfsson to Norway, and was well received : according to *Heimskringla* (though the older versions of the Saga of Magnús and the Norwegian compendia do not mention this), Hörthaknútr associated Sveinn with himself in the government.

skaldic verse.   In view of his general reliability on Scandinavian affairs, it is probably advisable to accept the Encomiast's account of the reign of Haraldr Sveinsson in Denmark in preference to those of Thietmar and the *Chronicon Erici*, except that we may suspect that Knútr was younger than his brother.

On the Danish invasion of England, the Encomiast is less good.   He confirms a Scandinavian tradition that Thorkell avenged a brother in England, but he had no good source of information on the campaigns of Sveinn and Knútr, and he makes matters worse by giving a dishonest account of the behaviour of Thorkell.   However, even here, his work is of some value, for its view of the characters of Eadmund and Eadric confirms the impression of them given in the *Chronicle*, and so removes any suspicion of bias in the latter work.

The Encomiast's account of Knútr's reign is meagre.   He mentions the executions of 1017, the king's good rule, generosity and piety, and the extent of his dominions.   For the rest, he reserves his space for accounts of the marriage of Knútr and Emma, and of Knútr's visit to St. Omer.   In dealing with the former matter he wrote to orders, and told a strange tale while avoiding verbal untruth.   In dealing with the St. Omer visit, he gives us a picture of Knútr by an eyewitness for which we must be grateful, even if we suspect it of some exaggeration of detail.

Concerning events after the death of Knútr the Encomiast is well informed. Although he does not add anything essential to the *Chronicle*, he is here very valuable as a confirmatory source, in view of the meagre and desultory nature of the entries in all manuscripts of the *Chronicle* in this period.

Finally, three points concerning the Encomiast's methods may be emphasised. Firstly, if he decides to tell an untruth, he generally contrives to do so by implication only.   His handling of Emma's marriage is the supreme example of this, but there are others in his version of the story of Thorkell.[1]   Secondly, he delights to decorate his narrative with anecdotes : the chief examples are Eadmund's challenge to Knútr, the magic banner of the Danes, the execution of Eadric by Eiríkr, Haraldr and the archbishop, the forged letter, and Hörthaknútr's dream in III, 9.   Some or all of these tales may have had a foundation in popular report, but they are to be regarded as ornamental additions to the narrative.   Thirdly, the Encomiast is so severely selective a writer that nothing can ever be argued from his silence.

---

[1] See above, pp. liv–v.   A different use of implication occurs in the story of Ælfred's murder : there the complicity of Godwine is implied without definite statement, because, though it was universally believed that Godwine was involved, the Encomiast evidently thought it better not to emphasise this.

ENCOMIUM EMMAE REGINAE

ON THE TEXT AND TEXTUAL NOTES

L = British Museum, MS. Add. 33241.
L' = matter in L not in the hands of the original scribes.
P = Bibliothèque Nationale, MS. Fonds Lat. 6235.
V = National Library of Wales, MS. Hengwrt 158 (= Peniarth 281).
C = *Historiae Normannorum Scriptores Antiqui*, edited by A. Duchesne, Paris, 1619.
T = the agreement of V and C.
B = British Museum, MS. Add. 6920.

The text follows L, save for minor grammatical corrections which are signalised in the Textual Notes. All matter not present or erroneously cancelled in L is enclosed in square brackets, with the exception of marks of punctuation and expansions of contractions of an obvious character. Initial *p̄* is expanded as *pre-*, since L prefers that form to *prae-*, when the prefix is written out. *ae* and *ę* are regarded as equivalent symbols, and *ae* is printed for them both. Letters added in the margins or above the lines by the original scribes of L are enclosed in parentheses ( ), except when a correction has been made by one of these scribes by writing above a cancelled letter or letters. Letters printed in caret brackets ⟨ ⟩ are present in L, but are to be neglected in reading. A modern system of punctuation, capitalisation and word-division is substituted for that of the manuscript.

The passage in II, 16, which is now lost in L, is given according to T, in the spelling of C, but with the substitution of *u* for the initial *v* of C.

Pertz's division into three books is retained, although the beginning of the third book is not indicated in L by a heading : there is, however, a blank space and an ornamented initial. The division of the books into chapters is also that of Pertz.

In the Textual Notes, the self-corrections of the original scribes of L are recorded, but corrections in late hands (L') are not noticed (even when the same correction is made in the present text), except when they have rendered the original reading obscure. The comments and conjectures of L' are excluded, with one exception (see on III, 1, 2). From P only the major variants are given, together with a few readings which support doubtful readings of L, suggest how L is to be corrected, or throw light on the relationship of L and P. Readings of V and C are given only in a few cases, where they are of special interest, and B is neglected entirely.

INCIPIT PROLOGUS

Salus tibi sit a Domino Iesu Christo, o regina, que omnibus in hoc sexu positis prestas morum eligantia.

Ego seruus tuus nobilitati tuae digna factis meis exhibere nequeo, quoque pacto uerbis saltem illi placere possim nescio. Quod enim cuiuslibet peritiae loquentis de 5 te uirtus tua preminet, omnibus a quibus cognosceris ipso solis iubare clarius lucet. Te igitur erga me adeo bene meritam magnifacio, ut morti intrepidus occumberem, si in rem tibi prouenire crederem. Qua ex re, mihi etiam ut precipis, memoriam rerum gestarum, rerum inquam tuo tuorumque honori attinentium, litteris meis posteritati mandare gestio, sed ad hoc faciendum me mihi sufficere posse dubito. 10 Hoc enim in historia proprium exigitur, ut nullo erroris diuerticulo [1] a recto ueritatis tramite [2] declinetur, quoniam, cum quis alicuius gesta scribens ueritati falsa quaedam seu errando, siue ut sepe fit ornatus gratia, interserit, profecto unius tantum comperta admixtione mendatii auditor facta uelut infecta ducit. Unde historicis magnopere cauendum esse censeo, ne ueritati quibusdam falso interpositis contraeundo nomen [3] 15 etiam perdat, quod uidetur habere ex offitio. Res enim ueritati,[4] ueritas quoque fidem facit rei. Hec mecum aliaque huiusmodi me reputante rubor animum uehementer excruciat, cum pariter considero, quam pessime in talibus sese humana consuetudo habeat. Uidens enim aliquis quempiam pro exprimenda rei ueritate uerbis indulgentem, uanae loquacitatis eum mordaciter redarguit,[a] alium uero, 20 quem dixi blasphemium fugientem et aequo modestiorem in narratione, cum operta denudare debeat, aperta oc[c]uluisse dicit. Tali itaque angustia circumseptus [b] ab inuidentibus loquax dici timeo, si neglecta uenustate dictaminis historiam scripturus multiplici narratione usus fuero. Quoniam uero, quin scripturus sim, euadere me non posse uideo, unum horum quae proponam eligendum esse autumo, scilicet aut 25 uariis iudiciis hominum subiacere, aut de his, quae mihi a te, domina regina, precepta sunt, precipientem negligendo conticescere. Malo itaque a quibusdam de loquacitate redargui, quam ueritatem maxime memorabilis rei per me omnibus occultari. Quocirca, quandoquidem iubentem dominam magni pendens hanc mihi elegi uiam, excusabiles [5] deinceps occasiones posthabens hinc narrationis contextionem [6] faciam.

---

[a] redarguit: Ta *erased after this word, doubtless because the scribe was about to omit the words* alium . . . dicit, *but observed his error after writing the first two letters of the next sentence,* L.
[b] circumseptus: circumceptus, L, *corrected by* L'.

---

[1] *erroris diuerticulo*: the expression is found elsewhere, as Paul. Nol., *Ep.*, Appendix, 2, 11, and Boeth., *Porphyr.* (Vienna Corpus, xlviii, p. 10).
[2] *a recto ueritatis tramite*: practically the same phrase occurs Amm., xxii. 10, 2, but similar expressions are frequent in the Encomiast's period.
[3] *nomen*: that is, presumably, the name of 'historian' (*scriptor rerum gestarum*). Gertz emends *historicis* to *historico*, which improves both the grammatical smoothness of the sentence and the rhyme.
[4] *Res enim ueritati*, etc. Gertz explains rather than translates: 'Er det nemlig saa, at Kendsgerningen selv skaffer den sanddru Fremstilling Tiltro, saa er det ogsaa omvendt saa, at den sanddru Fremstilling skaffer Kendsgerningen Anerkendelse som Kendsgerning.' Cf. Ruotger, *Vita Brunonis*, 9: 'euentus rei non multo post dictis fidem fecit'.
[5] *excusabiles . . . occasiones*: probably 'affairs from which one can excuse oneself'; the Encomiast proposes to neglect all non-essential business in order to attend to his undertaking.

4

PROLOGUE

May our Lord Jesus Christ preserve you, O Queen, who excel all those of your sex in the admirability of your way of life.

I, your servant, am unable to show you, noble lady, anything worthy in my deeds, and I do not know how I can be acceptable to you even in words. That your excellence transcends the skill of any one speaking about you is apparent to all to whom you are known, more clearly than the very radiance of the sun. You, then, I esteem as one who has deserved of me to such a degree, that I would sink to death unafraid, if I believed that my action would lead to your advantage. For this reason, and, furthermore, in accordance with your injunction, I long to transmit to posterity through my literary work a record of deeds, which, I declare, touch upon the honour of you and your connections, but I am in doubt concerning my adequacy for doing this. This quality, indeed, is required in history, that one should not deviate from the straight path of truth by any divergent straying, for when in writing the deeds of any man one inserts a fictitious element, either in error, or, as is often the case, for the sake of ornament, the hearer assuredly regards facts as fictions, when he has ascertained the introduction of so much as one lie. And so I consider that the historian should greatly beware, lest, going against truth by falsely introducing matter, he lose the very name which he is held to have from his office. The fact itself, to be sure, wins belief for the veracious presentation, and the veracious presentation does the same for the fact. Having reflected upon these and similar matters, shame powerfully afflicts my spirit, when I likewise consider how very imperfect the customary behaviour of mankind is in such matters. In fact, when a man sees somebody giving the rein to words to express the truth of a matter, he blames him bitterly for loquacity, but another, whom I describe as one avoiding reproach, and too restrained in his account, he declares, indeed, to hide what was open, when he ought to uncover what was concealed. And so, hedged in by such difficulty, I fear to be called loquacious by the envious, if neglecting elegance of form, I adopt a prolix method of narration when addressing myself to writing history. Since, indeed, I see that I cannot avoid writing, I aver that I must choose one of the alternatives which I am about to enunciate, that is either to submit to a variety of criticisms from men, or to be silent concerning the things enjoined upon me by you, Lady Queen, and to disregard you, who enjoin me. I prefer, accordingly, to be blamed by some for loquacity, than that the truth of so very memorable a story should be hidden from all through me. Therefore, since I have chosen this way for myself, greatly esteeming the lady who commands me, I will set aside one after the other affairs from which I can excuse myself, and proceed to the composition of my narrative.

This explanation involves the assumption that *occasio* had already in the eleventh century developed the sense ' affair ', in which its English derivative *occasion* is first used in the sixteenth century (see *N.E.D.*, s.v. *occasion*, sb[1]., sense 6). I cannot parallel this usage, but the only other explanation possible of the phrase is to take it as ' pretexts which excuse one ', giving to *excusabilis* an active force of extreme rarity, of which *Thes.*, *s.v.*, col. 1297, quotes only one example, Claud. Don., *Aen. Prooem.*, p. 3, 10 ; cf., however, A. S. Napier, *Old English Glosses*, i. 2793.

[6] *narrationis contextionem* : the expression occurs also in Macr., *Somn. Scip.* i. 2, 11.

5

[ARGUMENTUM]

Fortasse, o lector, ambiges, meque scriptorem erroris [a] aut inscitiae redargues,
cur in huius libelli capite actus laudesque Sueini [b] strenuissimi regis promulgauerim,
cum in suprascripta epistola ipsum codicellum laudi huius dominae me spoponderim
facturum. Quod ita esse ipse fatebere, meque ab eius laudibus nusquam accipies
5 deuiare, si prima mediis, atque si extima sagaci more conferas primis. Atque ut ad
hoc intuendum nulla erroris impediaris nebula, a similibus atque a penitus ueris hoc
tibi habeas theorema. Aeneida conscriptam a Uirgilio quis poterit infitiari ubique
laudibus respondere Octouiani ,[1] cum pene nihil aut plane parum eius mentio uideatur
nominatim interseri ? Animaduerte [2] igitur laudem suo generi asscriptam ipsius
10 decori claritudinis claritatisque in omnibus nobilitare gloriam. Quis autem hoc [c]
neget, laudibus reginae hunc per omnia respondere codicem, cum non modo ad eius
gloriam scribatur, uerum etiam eius maximam [3] uideatur optinere partem ? Id tibi
si probabile non uidetur, euidenti [d] alterius rei inditio [e][4] approbetur. Nosti,
quoniam, ubicumque giraueris [5] circulum, primo omnium procul dubio principium
15 facies esse punctum, sicque rotato continuatim orbe reducetur circulus, quo reductu
ad suum principium eius figurae continuetur ambitus. Simili igitur continuatione
laus reginae claret (in primis [f]), in mediis uiget, in ultimis inuenitur, omnemque
prorsus codicis summam complectitur. Quod esse mecum sentiens sic collige.
Sueinus, rex Danorum, uirtute armis quoque pollens et consilio Anglicum regnum ui
20 suo subiugauit imperio, moriensque eiusdem regni Cnutonem filium successorem esse
constituit. Hic postmodum eisdem Anglis contra se sentientibus atque acriter uim
inferenti ui quoque repugnantibus multa confecit bella [6] ; et fortasse uix aut
numquam bellandi adesset finis, nisi tandem huius nobilissimae reginae iugali copula [7]
potiretur, fauente gratia Saluatoris. Uiuens [g] adhuc de hac eadem regina suscepto
25 filio, Hardecnut scilicet, quicquid suae parebat ditioni tradidit. Qui defuncto patre
Anglicis absens erat, regnum siquidem Danorum procuraturus ierat ; quae absentia
imperii sui fines inuadendi iniusto peruasori locum dedit, qui accepto regno fratrem
regis nefandissima proditione interemit ; sed diuina ultio subsecuta impiumque
percutiens, regnum cui debebatur restituit ; quod totum in textu planius liquebit.
30 Hardecnut itaque recepto regno, maternis per omnia parens consiliis, diuitiis

---

[a] erroris : *corrected from* terroris, L.   [b] Sueini : *corrected from* Surini, L.
[c] hoc : hic, L.
[d] euidenti : *altered to* uidenti *by superpunctuation of* e, *owing to following corruption* inditium, L'.
[e] inditio : inditium, L.   [f] in primis *added in margin*, L.
[g] uiuens : aduc *erased after this word*, L.

---

[1] *Octouiani* : a genuine medieval spelling, e.g., William of Malmesbury, *Gesta Regum*, ii. 170.
[2] *Animaduerte*, etc. : Gertz tampers with the sentence unnecessarily, though the construction
ipsius decori, ' to his honour ', is somewhat forced ; cf. II, 2, *quae meae repetam gloriae*, ' which
I will seek again to my glory '.
[3] *eius maximam* : the thought is clear ; Gertz clarifies the syntax by adding *mentio* after *eius*,
but perhaps *eius* goes with *partem* (' part of it ', i.e., of the book), and *gloria* is to be understood
from the previous clause as the subject.

ARGUMENT

Perchance, O Reader, you will wonder, and will accuse me of error or incompetence because at the beginning of this book I bring to attention the deeds and glory of Sveinn, that most active king, since in the above epistle, I pledge myself to devote this book to the praise of the Queen. But you will admit that this is the case, and allow that I nowhere deviate from her praises, if you wisely compare the beginning with the middle, and the end with the beginning. And that no cloud of error may hinder your understanding of this, you may take the following as an illustration from similar and entirely true matters. Who can deny that the Aeneid, written by Virgil, is everywhere devoted to the praises of Octavian, although practically no mention of him by name, or clearly very little, is seen to be introduced? Note, therefore, that the praise accorded to his family everywhere celebrates the glory of their fame and renown to his own honour. Who can deny that this book is entirely devoted to the praise of the Queen, since it is not only written to her glory, but since that subject occupies the greatest part of it? If that does not seem satisfactory to you, let it be established by the clear proof afforded by another matter. You are aware that wherever you draw a circle, first of all you certainly establish a point to be the beginning, and so the circle is made to return by continuously wheeling its orb, and by this return the circumference of the circle is made to connect itself to its own beginning. By a similar connection, therefore, the praise of the Queen is evident at the beginning, thrives in the middle, is present at the end, and embraces absolutely all of what the book amounts to. Agreeing with me that this is the case, consider what follows. Sveinn, king of the Danes, mighty alike in courage and arms and also in counsel, brought the English kingdom under his rule by force, and, dying, appointed his son Knútr to be his successor in the same kingdom. The latter, when he was opposed by the English, and vigorously using force was resisted by force, afterwards won many wars; and perhaps there would scarcely or never have been an end of the fighting if he had not at length secured by the Saviour's favouring grace a matrimonial link with this most noble queen. He had a son, Hörthaknútr by this same queen, and, while still living, he gave him all that was under his control. He was absent from England at his father's death, for he had gone to secure the kingdom of the Danes. This absence gave an unjust invader a chance to enter the bounds of his empire, and this man, having secured the kingdom, killed the king's brother under circumstances of most disgraceful treachery. But divine vengeance followed, smote the impious one, and restored the kingdom to him to whom it belonged. All this will become more clearly evident in the narrative. And so Hörthaknútr, having recovered the kingdom, and being in all things obedient to the counsels of his mother, held the kingdom

---

[4] *rei inditio* : expression found in various writers, as Nep., *Att.* 16.

[5] *giraueris*, etc. : the writer has in mind some such description of a circle as that of Boeth., *Arith.* ii. 30 : ' Est enim circulus posito quodam puncto et alio eminus defixo, illius puncti qui eminus fixus est aequaliter distans a primo puncto circumductio, et ad eundem locum reuersio unde moueri coeperat '.

[6] *confecit bella* : a fairly common collocation, see *Thes.*, s.v. *conficio*, col. 196, and add Lucan ix. 658, to the references there given.

[7] *iugali copula* : more usual is *coniugalis copula*, as Aug., *De Civ. Dei*, xiv. 22, etc. Cf., however, *Aen.* iv. 16, *uinclo . . . iugali*, and many similar phrases.

ampliando regnum imperialiter optinuit ; usus [1] quin etiam egregia liber[ali]tate, fratri, utpote decebat, secum regni decus atque diuitias impertiuit. His enim animaduersis, o lector, uigilique, immo etiam perspicaci, oculo mentis [2] perscrutato textu, intellige, huius libelli seriem per omnia reginae Emmae laudibus respondere.

EXPLICIT ARGUMENTUM

[I]

[1] Regem [a] Danorum Sueinum, inquam [3], ueridica comperi relatione omnium sui temporis regum ferme fortunatissimum extitisse, adeo ut, quod raro contingi [b][4] solet, principiis felicibus secundum Deum et seculum multo felicior responderet exitus. Hic denique a nobilissimis, quod primum est inter homines, duxit originem,
5 magnumque sibi decus secundum seculum peperit imperii quod amministrabat regimen. Tantam deinde illi gratiam diuina concessit uirtus, ut etiam puerulus intimo affectu diligeretur ab omnibus, tantum patri proprio inuisus, nulla hoc promerente pueruli culpa, sed sola turbante inuidia. Qui factus iuuenis [5] in amore cotidie crescebat populi ; unde magis magisque inuidia augebatur patri, adeo ut eum
10 a patria non iam clanculum sed palam uellet expellere, iurando asserens [6] eum post se regnaturum non esse. Unde dolens exercitus relicto patre herebat filio, et eum defensabat sedulo. Huius rei gratia congrediuntur in praelio ; in quo uulneratus fugatusque pater ad Sclauos fugit, et non multo post ibi obiit, et Suein eius solium quiete tenuit. Quam strenue [c] uero prudenterque interim secularia disposuerit
15 negotia, paucis libet ad memoriam reducere, quatinus his interpositis facilius sit gradatim per haec ad subsequentia descendere. Denique cum nullo hostium incursu trepidus pacem in securitate ageret, periculi semper ac uelut instantis metuens in castris muniebat [7], quod hostibus si adessent nullatenus fortasse resisteret, nihilque suis quae bello necessaria forent preparando patiebatur remissi, scilicet ne per otium,
20 ut assolet, uiriles emollirentur animi [8]. Nullum tamen adeo difficile inuenire poterat negotium, ad quod inuitos inpulisset milites, quos multa liberali munificentia sibi

----

[a] Regem : P *begins here under the following title,* Ex eodem Gilda in Historia de Sueyno et Knuctone, quam in gratiam scripsit ad reginam Emmam.

[b] contingi : contingere, P ; coniungi *conjectures Gertz with hesitation (cf. Introduction, p. xviii, and Linguistic Note below).*

[c] Quam strenue . . . positi (31) : regnum prudenter et strenue in rebus omnibus gubernans et suos in armis ad quoscunque euentus exercens et clementia liberalitateque artissime sibi deuinciens, P.

----

[1] *usus . . . egregia liber[ali]tate* : cf. Odilo, *Epitaphium Adelheidae,* 12, ' usa . . . perfecta liberalitate '.

[2] *oculo mentis* : this expression, which is as old as Cicero, is a favourite in the Encomiast's period : e.g., Dudo (ed. Duchesne, p. 53), Sig. Gemblac., *Vita Deoderici,* 22 ; Folquin, *Vita Folquini,* 8.

[3] *inquam . . comperi* : the Encomiast generally makes his own observations in the 1st person sing., but sometimes in the 1st plur. (cf. III, 6) ; cf. Stevenson's Asser, pp. 199–200. ' ueridica comperi relatione ' : cf. *Miracula S. Bertini,* 44 : ' ueridicorum uirorum . . . sedula compertum est relatione '.

[4] *contingi* : MS. P has *contingere,* which Duchesne also suggests in the margin. Obvious as this proposal is, it is wiser to retain the reading of L, and to assume that *contingi* is used with deponent force ; cf. E. Löfstedt, *Philologischer Kommentar zur Peregrinatio Aetheriae* (Uppsala and Leipzig, 1911), p. 215. See Textual Note for porposal by Gertz.

imperially and increased it with riches. Yea and furthermore, exercising admirable liberality, he shared, as was fitting, the honour and wealth of the kingdom between his brother and himself. Noticing these matters, O Reader, and having scanned the narrative with a watchful, nay more, with a penetrating eye, understand that the course of this book is devoted entirely to the praise of Queen Emma.

BOOK I

1. Sveinn, king of the Danes, was, I declare, as I have ascertained from truthful report, practically the most fortunate of all the kings of his time, so that, as seldom occurs, his happy beginning was followed by an end much happier from both the spiritual and the worldly point of view. He, then, derived his descent from a most noble source, a thing of foremost importance among men, and the government of the empire which he administered brought him great worldly honour. The divine power granted him such great favour, that even as a boy he was held by all in close affection, and was hated only by his own father. No fault of the boy deserved this : it was due only to envy. When he grew to be a young man, he increased daily in the love of his people, and, accordingly, his father's envy increased more and more, so that he wished, not in secret, but openly, to cast him out, affirming by oath that he should not rule after him. The army, grieved by this, deserted the father, adhered to the son, and afforded him active protection. As a result they met in a battle, in which the father was wounded, and fled to the Slavs, where he died shortly afterwards. Sveinn held his throne undisturbed. I wish to indicate briefly how truly actively and wisely he conducted his worldly affairs in the meanwhile, in order that, after this digression, it may be easier to pass on in succession from these matters to what followed. When Sveinn was at peace, and in no fear of any attack by his foes, acting always as if in fear of danger, and indeed of pressing danger, he attended to the strengthening of any positions in his fortresses, which might not have resisted hostile forces, should they have appeared, and, preparing everything necessary for war, he permitted no remissness in his men, lest their manly spirit should, as often happens, be softened by inactivity. Nevertheless, he could have found no activity so irksome, that his soldiers would have been unwilling, if he impelled them to it, for he had rendered them submissive and faithful to himself by manifold and generous munificence. So that you may realise how highly he was regarded by his men, I can strongly affirm that not one of them would have recoiled from danger owing to fear of

⁵ *iuuenis* : a very vague term in Medieval Latin ; cf. A. Hofmeister in *Papsttum und Kaisertum* (Munich, 1926), p. 316.

⁶ *iurando asserens* : we should perhaps read *sub iureiurando asserens*, a phrase used below, III, 1, 16, with which *Vita Oswaldi* (Raine, *Historians of the Church of York*, i. 468), ' sub iureiurando . . . promiserunt ' may be compared ; *iurando*, however, is used in similar phrases, e.g., Wipo, *Vita Chuonradi* 4, ' iurando . . subiciebantur '.

⁷ *in castris muniebat*, etc. : ' he fortified whatever there was among the defensive positions, which would perhaps not have withstood an enemy '. Gertz reads *id* for *in*, but this is unnecessary, for *quod* = (*id*) *quod*. The Encomiast frequently omits the antecedent of a relative, even though it is not in the same case as the relative, as in the clause following that under discussion, *quae bello necessaria forent preparando*, ' preparing the things which would be necessary in the event of war '.

⁸ *emollirentur animi* : the collocation *animos emollire* occurs Greg. Mag., *Moral.* iii. 20 ; Monk of St. Gall, *Gesta Karoli*, i. 4.

fecerat obnoxios et fideles. Atque ut scias, quantus suorum fuerit in precordiis, pro certo affirmare ualeam, quod nullus formidine mortis periculum refugeret, eiusque pro fidelitate hostibus innumeris solus, armatis etiam manibus nudis, inperterritus
25 occurreret, si euntibus tantum regale premonstraretur signum. At ne me credat aliquis hec falsa fingendo alicuius amoris gratia compilare : recte animaduertenti in subsequentibus patebit, utrum uera dixerim an minime. Omnibus enim [1] liquet procul dubio, quoniam humanitatis ita sese habeat consuetudo, ut plerumque ex rebus prospere cedentibus mentes quorumdam plus equo exagitet cogitationum
30 aestus, atque ex nimia in ocio licentia aggrediuntur aliqui, quod uix cogitare nedum facere audent in aduersitate positi.

[2] Ita etiam [a] prelibati regis militibus, cum in compositae pacis diuturnitate cuncta cessissent prospere, firma sui pro benefactis domini fretis stabilitate eadem ipsi agitanti placuit suadere, terram Anglicam inuadendo sorte bellica imperii sui finibus adicere. " Turchil ",.inquiunt, " princeps miliciae tuae, domine rex, licentia
5 a te accepta [2] abiit, ut fratrem suum inibi interfectum ulcisceretur, et magnam partem exercitus tui abducens uicisse se gaudet, et nunc meridianam partem prouinciae uictor obtinet, ac mauult ibi exul degens amicusque factus Anglorum, quos tua manu uicit, gloriari, quam exercitum reducens tibi subdi tibique uictoriam ascribi. Et nunc fraudamur sociis et quadraginta puppibus, quas secum duxit
10 onustas de Danorum bellatoribus primis. Non tam graue dominus noster patiatur dispendium, sed abiens cupientem ducat exercitum, et illi Turchil contumacem adquiremus cum suis satellitibus, eis quoque federatos Anglos cum omnibus eorum possessionibus. Scimus enim.diu eos non posse resistere, quia nostrates uiri ad nos transibunt facile. Quod si eos uelle contigerit, rex duci suo Danisque parcens eos
15 honoribus ampliabit. Si autem noluerint, quem despexere sentient ; hac illaque patria priuati inter primos hostes regis paenas luent."

[3] Huius rei adhortationem rex ubi audiit, primum secum mirari non mediocriter caepit, quia, quod ipsi diu dissimulanti celantique in mentem uenerat, itidem militibus cogitationem eius ignorantibus animo sederat. Accersito itaque Cnutone, filio suo maiore, quid sibi super hoc negotii uideretur, orsus est inquirere. Inquisitus
5 autem ille a patre, metuens ne redargueretur, si placito contrairet, tegna socordiae, non tantum terram adeundam esse approbabat, uerum etiam instigat hortaturque, ne mora ulla inceptum detineat. Ergo rex consulto optimatum firmatus militumque beniuolentia fisus classem numerosam iussit parari et uniuersam militiam Danorum undique moneri, ut statuto die armata adesset, et regis sententiam audiens quaeque
10 imperarentur deuotissime expleret. Cursores mox prouintiae ex iussu domini sui cunctam pergirant regionem, quietam quoque commonefaciunt gentem, ne quis ex

---

[a] Ita etiam . . . finibus (4, 20): Tandem suadentibus amicis et proceribus statuit ualidum exercitum in Angliam traiicere, maxime quod pridem illuc precesserat Turchil princeps milicie cum ualida manu, de cuius fide dubitabat, quod nihil de suis inibi gestis renunciasset. Instruitur igitur preualida et ornatissima classis. Ipse interim regni custodie prefecit filium natu minorem, cui nomen Haraldus, maiorem uero Knutum siue Canutum secum ducens. Omnibus igitur paratis et cum exercitu conscensis nauibus dextera uelificatione tandem ad oras Britannicas appulit, P.

---

[1] *Omnibus enim*, etc. : Gertz begins the second chapter here, and with reason, for these general observations are intended to introduce and explain the actions of Sveinn's warriors described in chapter 2.

death, but, unafraid, would have gone out of loyalty to him against innumerable enemies alone, and even with bare hands against armed men, if only the royal signal should be given to them as they went. And lest any man think that I am lying, and concocting what I say from regard for any person's favour, in what is to follow, it will be plain to any one paying due attention, whether I am telling the truth or not. For it is abundantly plain to all, that it is the habit of human nature that fervour of mental activity, arising from favourable circumstances, unduly stimulates the spirits of some, and that some will undertake matters owing to the excessive liberty which they enjoy in time of leisure, which they would hardly contemplate, much less perform, if placed in unfavourable circumstances.

2. And so when in the continuity of a settled peace all matters were turning out favourably, the soldiers of the above-mentioned king, confident that they would profit by the firm steadfastness of their lord, decided to persuade him, who was already meditating the same plan, to invade England, and add it to the bounds of his empire by the decision of war. " Thorkell," said they, " your military commander, Lord King, having been granted licence by you, has gone to avenge his brother, who was killed there, and leading away a large part of your army, exults that he has conquered. Now, as a victor, he has acquired the south of the country, and living there as an exile, and having become an ally of the English, whom he has conquered through your power, he prefers the enjoyment of his glory to leading his army back, and in submission giving you the credit of his victory. And we are cheated of our companions and forty ships, which he led with him, manned from among the best Danish warriors. Let not our lord suffer so grave a loss, but go forth leading his willing army, and we will subdue for him the contumacious Thorkell, together with his companions, and also the English who are leagued with them, and all their possessions. We are certain that they cannot resist long, because our countrymen will come over to us readily. If they are willing to do so, the king, sparing his commander and the Danes shall advance them with honours ; but if they are unwilling, they shall know whom it is that they have despised. Deprived of country both here and there, they shall pay the penalty among the foremost enemies of the king."

3. When the king heard their exhortation in this matter, he began to wonder not a little, that what had long before entered his mind, though he had dissimulated and concealed, had been present in the hearts of his soldiers, who did not know his thoughts. And so having summoned Knútr, his elder son, he began to inquire what were his views concerning this matter. He, questioned by his father, fearing to be accused, if he opposed the proposal, of wily sloth, not only approved of attacking the country, but urged and exhorted that no delay should hold back the undertaking. Therefore, the king, supported by the counsel of his chief men, and relying upon the goodwill of his soldiers, ordered that a numerous fleet should be prepared, and that warning should be given on all sides to the entire military power of the Danes to be present under arms at a fixed date, and in obedience to the king's wish, to perform with the utmost devotion whatever they were commanded. Messengers soon traversed the whole country at the command of their king, and admonished the tranquil people, in order that no member of so great an army should escape the choice

² *accepta . . . licentia* : a frequent expression in Medieval Latin, e.g., the ' Astronomer ', *Vita Hludowici*, 4 and 49 ; *Miracula S. Bertini*, 42.

A

tanto exercitu deesset, quin omnis bellator terrae aut iram regis incurreret, aut iussioni eius aduolaret. Quid ergo ? Absque contradictione adunantur, instructique armis bellicis gregatim regi suo presentantur, ostentantes se paratos ad periculum
15 et ad mortem, si tantum domini sui queant perficere uoluntatem. Rex autem uidens populum innumerabilem uoce preconaria iussit suam patefieri uoluntatem, se uelle scilicet classem aduersum Anglos armare ditionique suae omnem hanc patriam ferro dolisue [1] subicere. Quod ubi omnibus uisum esset laudabile, elegit primum qui regnum suum deberent custodire, ne [a], dum alienum incaute appeteret, illud quod
20 securus tenebat amitteret, et intentus in utroque neutri imperaret. Habebat enim filios duos bonae indolis [2], ex quibus primogenitum suo iunxit comitatui, natu [b] uero minorem prefecit uniuersi regni dominatui, adiuncta ei copia militari paucisque primatum, qui puerulum sagaciter instituerent, et qui huic consiliis armisque pro muro essent.

[4] Omnibus ergo rite dispositis [3] recensuit comites expeditionis, relictoque minore filio sua [c] in sede adiit nauigium uallatus armato milite. Nec mora : concurritur undique ad littora, circumfertur passim armorum seges multigena. Aggregati tandem turritas ascendunt puppes, eratis rostris duces singulos uidentibus dis-
5 criminantes. Hinc enim erat cernere leones auro fusiles in puppibus, hinc autem uolucres in summis malis uenientes austros suis [4] signantes uersibus aut dracones uarios minantes incendia de naribus, illinc homines de solido auro argentoue rutilos uiuis quodammodo non inpares, atque illinc tauros erectis sursum collis protensisque cruribus · mugitus cursusque uiuentium simulantes. Uideres quoque delphinos
10 electro fusos, ueteremque rememorantes fabulam de eodem metallo centauros. Eiusdem preterea celaturae multa tibi dicerem insignia, si non monstrorum quae sculpta inerant me laterent nomina. Sed quid nunc tibi latera carinarum memorem, non modo ornatitiis depicta coloribus, uerum etiam aureis argenteisque aspera signis ? Regia quoque puppis tanto pulcritudine sui ceteris prestabat, quanto rex
15 suae dignitatis honore milites antecedebat ; de qua melius est ut sileam, quam pro magnitudine sui pauca dicam. Tali itaque freti classe dato signo repente gaudentes abeunt, atque uti iussi erant, pars ante, pars retro, equatis tamen rostris, regiae puppi se circumferunt. Hic uideres crebris tonsis uerberata late spumare cerula, metallique· repercussum fulgore solem duplices radios extendere in aera. Quid
20 plura ? Tandem quo intendebant animi appropiabant finibus, cum finitimos mari patrienses eius rei sinister commouit nuntius. Nec mora : quo regia classis anchoras fixit, incolae eius loci concurrunt ad portum, potentiori se frustra parati defendere intrandi aditum. Denique relictis nauibus regii milites ad terram exeunt, et pedestri pugnae intrepidi sese accingunt. Hostes primo duriter contra resistentes dimicant, postea
25 uero periculi form(id)ine uersi in fugam sauciandi occidendique copiam persequentibus

---

[a] ne : *corrected from* nec, L.   [b] natu : *corrected from* natum, L.
[c] sua : *corrected from* suo, L or L'.

---

[1] *ferro dolisue* : cf. Sall., *Iug.* 25, 9, *aut ui aut dolis* ; for the rare antithesis *dolus-ferrum* cf. Amm., xvii. 13, 3, Sen., *Herc. Oet.* 438.
[2] *bonae indolis* : this old expression is a favourite in the period : e.g., Dudo (ed. Duchesne, p. 113) ; Sig. Gemblac., *Vita Deoderici*, passim ; Ruotger, *Vita Brunonis*, 4 ; Wipo, *Vita Chuonradi*, 23.
[3] *Omnibus . . rite dispositis* : again below, II, 16, 1 ; cf. Stat., *Theb.* vii. 390–1.

by which every warrior of the land must either incur the king's anger or hasten to obey his command. What then ? They mustered without any objection, and, having been provided with the arms of war, were presented troop by troop to the king and showed themselves prepared for danger or death if only they could perform the will of their lord. The king, seeing this innumerable host, ordered his wishes to be made known by means of heralds, that is to say, that he desired to arm a fleet against the English, and to bring all their country under his rule by force or stratagem. When this had appealed to all, he first selected persons to take charge of his own kingdom, lest while he was incautiously seeking a foreign one, he should lose the one which he held securely, and intent upon both, should rule neither. He had two sons of excellent qualities, and he took the elder in his own company, placing the younger at the head of the government of his whole kingdom, and attaching to him 'a military force and a few of his chief men, to instruct the boy wisely, and be a wall to him by their counsel and arms.

4. And so, everything being duly arranged, he reviewed the comrades of his expedition, and leaving his younger son in his place, went to his ship surrounded by armed soldiery. There was no delay : on all sides men were proceeding to the shore, and a variety of armed men were on every side. When at length they were all gathered, they went on board the towered ships, having picked out by observation each man his own leader on the brazen prows. On one side lions moulded in gold were to be seen on the ships, on the other birds on the tops of the masts indicated by their movements the winds as they blew, or dragons of various kinds poured fire from their nostrils. Here there were glittering men of solid gold or silver nearly comparable to live ones, there bulls with necks raised high and legs outstretched were fashioned leaping and roaring like live ones. One might see dolphins moulded in electrum, and centaurs in the same metal, recalling the ancient fable. In addition, I might describe to you many examples of the same celature, if the names of the monsters which were there fashioned were known to me. But why should I now dwell upon the sides of the ships, which were not only painted with ornate colours, but were covered with gold and silver figures ? The royal vessel excelled the others in beauty as much as the king preceded the soldiers in the honour of his proper dignity, concerning which it is better that I be silent than that I speak inadequately. Placing their confidence in such a fleet, when the signal was suddenly given, they set out gladly, and, as they had been ordered, placed themselves round about the royal vessel with level prows, some in front and some behind. The blue water, smitten by many oars, might be seen foaming far and wide, and the sunlight, cast back in the gleam of metal, spread a double radiance in the air. What more ? At length they approached the territories whither they were bound, and an ill-omened rumour of the matter disturbed the natives who dwelt nearest the sea. There was no delay : where the royal fleet cast anchor, the inhabitants of the place flocked to the port, prepared in vain to refuse access to a force stronger than themselves. Then, leaving their ships, the royal soldiers landed, and boldly made ready for an encounter on foot. At first the enemy gave battle, and put up a severe resistance, afterwards,

---

⁴ *austros suis*, etc. : it appears to be beyond doubt that the meaning is that the vanes indicated the way from which the wind was coming by their movements, cf. *Glossary*, s.v. *uersus*.

praestant. Ita rex ex affectu [1] primo prelio usus adiacentem regionem inuadit, fusis fugatisque hostibus. Tunc tali successu factus audentior ad naues redit, et reliquos portus, qui plures eam terram cingunt, eadem ratione inuadit. Postremo uniuersam patriam tanto labore perdomuit, ut, si quis omnem historiam eius ad plenum per-
30 currere uelit, non modicum auditores fatigabit, et sibimet iniurius erit, dum ut uoluit omnia perstringere minime ualebit.

[5] At ego [a] hec alteri narranda relinquens tangendo transire percupio, et ad alia festinando stilum adplicabo ad Sueini obitum, ut festiui regis Cnutonis regni elucidare queam exordium. Namque, ubi iam sepedictus rex tota Anglorum patria est intronizatus, et ubi iam pene illi nemo restitit, pauco superuixit tempore, sed tamen
5 illud tantillum gloriose. Presciens igitur dissolutionem sui corporis [2] imminere filium suum Cnutonem quem secum habuit aduocat, sese uiam [3] uniuersae carnis ingrediendum [b] indicat. Cui [4] dum multa de regni gubernaculo multaque hortaretur de Christianitatis studio, Deo gratias illi uirorum dignissimo sceptrum commisit regale. Huius rei facto maxime Dani quibus legitime preesse debuit fauent, eumque
10 patre adhuc uiuente regem super se constitui gaudent. Hoc ita facto pater orat filium, ut, si quando natiuitatis suae rediret ad terram, corpus paternum reportaret secum, neue pateretur se ali⟨g⟩enigenam in externis tumulari terris ; nouerat enim, quia pro inuasione regni illis exosus erat populis. Nec multo post postrema naturae persoluit debita, animam remit[t]endo caelestibus, terrae autem reddendo membra.

EXPLICIT LIBER I

INCIPIT SECUNDUS

[1] Mortuo patre Cnuto regni parat retinere sceptrum, sed ad hoc minime sufficere potuit deficiente copia fidelium. Angli siquidem memores, quod pater eius iniuste suos inuasisset fines, ad expellendum eum, utpote qui iuuenis erat, omnes [c] regni pariter collegerunt uires. Quo comperto rex clam per fideles amicos reperto
5 honoris sui consilio [5] classim sibi preparari iubet, non quod asperos euentus belli metuendo fugeret, sed ut fratrem suum Haroldum, regem scilicet Danorum, super tali negotio consuleret. Paterna itaque classe repetita instauratoque remige uentis marique regalia commisit carbasa, sed tamen non omnem militiam secum reduxit, quae cum patre suo secumque patriam introiuit. Nam Thurkil, quem principem

[a] At ego . . . ubi iam (3) : Itaque ubi, P.
[b] ingrediendum : so, *with confused syntax*, L ; *omitted*, P.
[c] omnes : omnis, L ; omnos L' ; omnis, P.

---

[1] *ex affectu* : the expression seems to be used in the sense of *ex uoto*.
[2] *dissolutionem corporis* : frequent in Christian Latin from Tertullian (*Adv. Marc.* v. 10) onwards ; combined with *immineo* in *Vita Mahtildis*, 8.
[3] *sese uiam*, etc. : the syntax is obviously confused, and *sese . . . . ingrediendum indicat* seems to be used to mean ' he indicates that he must enter '. The syntax might be eased by reading *sibi* for *sese*. A possibility would be to retain *sese* and to read *ad ingrediendum*, and to

fleeing in fear of peril, they afforded their pursuers the opportunity to inflict casualties both in wounded and slain. So the king, exploiting the first battle at will, invaded the adjacent region and scattered the enemy and put them to flight. Then, rendered bolder by such a victory, he returned to his ships, and invaded in the same way the many other ports which are all round that country. Finally, he conquered the whole country with so much exertion, that, if any one should wish to narrate his whole history in full, he would weary his hearers not a little, to his own detriment, without in any degree succeeding in touching upon everything, as was his intention.

5. But I, leaving these affairs for another to narrate, desire, merely touching upon them, to hasten on to other matters, and to turn my pen to the death of Sveinn in order to illuminate the beginning of the happy reign of King Knútr. For, when the king who has been often referred to was enthroned over the whole country of the English, and when already scarcely anyone resisted him, he survived for a period which was short, although it was glorious. Feeling, therefore, that the dissolution of his body was threatening him, he summoned his son Knútr, whom he had with him, and said that he must enter upon the way of all flesh. He exhorted him much concerning the government of the kingdom and the zealous practice of Christianity, and, thanks be to God, committed the royal sceptre to him, the most worthy of men. The Danes, over whom he had the lawful right to rule, very strongly approved this matter, and rejoiced that he was established as king over them, while his father was still alive. When this was so arranged, the father prayed the son, that if he should ever return to the land of his birth, he should carry back with him the body of his father, and should not let him be buried a stranger in a foreign land ; for he knew that he was hateful to those people owing to the invasion of the kingdom. Soon afterwards he paid the last dues to nature, returning his soul to the heavens, and giving back his body to the earth.

BOOK II

1. After the death of his father, Knútr attempted to retain the sceptre of the kingdom, but he was quite unequal to so doing, for the number of his followers was insufficient. The English, being mindful that his father had unjustly invaded their country, collected all the forces of the kingdom in order to expel him, inasmuch as he was a youth. When this became known, the king, whose faithful friends had found a plan to preserve his honour, ordered a fleet to be got ready for him, not because he was fleeing afraid of the harsh outcome of war, but in order to consult his brother Haraldr, the king of the Danes, about so weighty a matter. Accordingly, having returned to his father's fleet and re-manned it, he spread the royal sails to the wind and sea, but nevertheless he did not lead back with him the whole force which

regard that expression as an adverbial modification of *esse* understood : ' he points out that he is entering upon the way of all flesh ' : cf. *Vulg.*, *Tob.* xiii. 20, ' si fuerint reliquiae seminis mei ad uidendam claritatem '.

⁴ *Cui* : as the text stands, under the government of *commisit*, and defined by *illi uirorum dignissimo* ; it may, however, be that the writer, when he began his sentence, intended to use a verb of speaking which would take dival rection, but by an oversight used *hortor*, which normally governs the accusative.

⁵ *reperto sui honoris consilio* : the collocation *consilium reperire* is frequent, see *Thes.*, s.v *consilium*, col. 449 ; *sui honoris*, i.e., *sui honoris conseruandi*, cf. III, 7, 16-17.

10 militiae prediximus, terra quod esset optima inspecta maluit conuersari in tam fertili
patria cum patriensibus pace confecta ¹, quam uelut expulsus demum redire ad
propria. Et, ut quidam aiunt, hoc non fecit despiciendo dominum, sed uti, cum
resumptis uiribus fratrisque auxilio repedaret ad debellandum regnum, is aut
optimates regni consilio suo ad deditionem flecteret, aut, si id parum processisset,
15 dimicantes contra dominum suum hostes incautos a tergo cederet. Cuius rei patet
ueritas ex eo, quod secum maximam partem militum retinuit ᵃ, quodque rex non
amplius quam sexaginta ᵇ naues secum abire ᶜ permisit.

[2] Prospero itaque cursu ² rex natales ad fines. . . .ᵈ Cum mirarentur omnes
solitarium reditum eius, quantum ad regem, patri antea fideles, Haroldi regis subito
compleuit uolitans fama palatia, fratrem eius maiorem, Cnutonem scilicet, sua
aduenisse litora. Miratur rex omnisque pariter exercitus, atque adhuc nescii duros
5 ipsius presagibant casus. Igitur a latere regis milites diriguntur delecti, paratique
in occursum transmittuntur equi. Fraternus siquidem amor fratris eum monebat
inseruire decori. Cumque tandem honorifice, utpote regem decet, fraterna sub-
intraret limina, frater ipse in primo aditu occurrit, mutuoque brachiorum conexione
pressis corporibus sibi inuicem pia quam saepe defigunt oscula. Collum utriusque
10 partim pro amore partimque pro patris morte fusae madefecere lacrimae ; quibus
uix extinctis, mutuo refocillantur ³ affamine. Ubi, dum quisque fortunam fratris
inquireret, propriam quoque patefaceret, Cnuto, qui ᵉ⁴ natu maior fuerat, sic
Haroldum fratrem alloquitur : " Adueni, frater, partim causa tui amoris, partim
uero ut declinarem inprouisam temeritatem barbarici furoris, non tamen metuens
15 bellorum, quae meae repetam gloriae, sed ut tuo consultu edoctus presidioque
suffultus redeam certus uictoriae. Est autem primum quod mihi facies, si non
gloriae meae inuides, ut diuidas mecum regnum Danorum, meam scilicet hereditatem
quam solus tenes, deinde regnum Anglorum, si communi opera poterimus, nostrae
hereditati adicere : unum horum, quodcumque elegeris, feliciter teneto ⁵, et ego aliud
20 similiter tenebo. Huius rei gratia tecum hiemabo, ut tempus tuo sufficiat consilio,
et ut expedit reparentur naues et exercitus, ne deficiant necessaria, dum pugnae
ingruerit tempus. Thurkil noster nos relinquendo, ut patrem, in terra resedit, et
magnam partem nauium nostrarum retinuit, et ut reor nobis aduersarius erit, sed
tamen non preualebit."
25 Haroldus rex audito quod noluit his fratrem uerbis excepit : " Gaudeo, frater, de
tuo aduentu, habeoque gratias tibi, quod me uisitasti, sed est graue auditu quod

---

ᵃ retinuit : et *on an erasure*, L'.
ᵇ sexaginta : sexag *on an erasure*, L.
ᶜ abire : *corrected from* habire, L ; abire, P.
ᵈ Prospero . . . fines : *a word or words are evidently lost*, L, P.
ᵉ qui : quoniam, P, *perhaps rightly* (cf. *Linguistic Note*).

---

¹ *pace confecta* : the collocation *pacem conficere* is a favourite with the Encomiast, cf. below,
II, 7 and 13 ; it is not common in the classical period, see *Thes.*, s.v. *conficio*, col. 199.
² *Prospero . . cursu* : the collocation is very common (see *Thes.*, s.v. *cursus*, col. 1532) ; it
occurs again below, II, 3, III, 9. The verb of the sentence is lost.
³ *extinctis . . refocillantur* : bold metaphors.
⁴ *qui* : P's *quoniam* is much better, for it is otiose to repeat here that Knútr was the elder
(cf. I, 3), but reasonable to point out that, as the elder, he spoke first ; cf. Nithard, iii. 5,
'Lodhuuicus, quoniam maior natu erat, prior . . . . . testatus est'.

had entered the country with his father and himself. For Thorkell, whom we have already mentioned as a military commander, observed that the land was most excellent, and chose to take up his residence in so fertile a country, and make peace with the natives, rather than to return home like one who had, in the end, been expelled. And according to some, he did not do this because he despised his lord, but in order that when Knútr returned with renewed forces and his brother's help to subdue the kingdom, he might either incline the chief men of the kingdom to surrender by his counsel, or if this plan were not a success, attack the incautious enemy from behind as they fought against his lord. And the truth of this is apparent from the fact that he kept with him a very great part of the soldiers, and that the king did not let more than sixty ships depart in company with himself.

2. And so, after a prosperous voyage, the king (reached) his native land. When all the people, his father's former subjects, were wondering at his return, which was, for a king, unaccompanied, a swiftly-spreading rumour suddenly filled the palace of King Haraldr, saying that his elder brother, Knútr, had reached his shores. The king and also the whole army wondered, and though they did not yet know anything, they felt a presentiment that he had met with adverse fortune. Accordingly, chosen soldiers were sent from attendance on the king, and horses ready for use were dispatched to meet him, for brotherly love prompted the king to regard the dignity of his brother. When at length Knútr, exhibiting the respect due to a king, entered his brother's doors, his brother himself met him at the very entrance, and they, with their bodies mutually locked in an embrace, impressed tender kisses upon each other many times. Tears shed partly for love, and partly for their father's death moistened the neck of each, and when these were scarcely dry, the exchange of words brought on more. When each was describing his own fortune and asking about that of his brother, Knútr, who was the elder, addressed his brother thus : " I have come, oh brother, partly out of my love for you, and partly to avoid the unforeseen audacity of barbarous fury, not however because I feared war, which to my glory I will seek again, but in order that instructed by a pronouncement from you and supported by your protection I may go back certain of victory. But there is one thing which you will first do for me, if you begrudge me not the glory which is mine, that is to divide with me the kingdom of the Danes, my heritage, which you hold alone, and afterwards we will add the kingdom of the English to our heritage, if we can do so by our joint efforts. Keep one of these, whichever you choose, and enjoy your success ; I similarly will keep the other. To the end that there may be sufficient time for you to take counsel, I will winter with you, and also in order that the ships and army may be renewed, as is expedient, so that our requirements may not be wanting when the hour of battle is upon us. Thorkell, our compatriot, deserting us as he did our father, has settled in the country, keeping with him a large part of our ships, and I believe that he will be against us, but nevertheless he will not prevail." King Haraldr, having heard these unwelcome remarks, answered his brother in these words : " I rejoice, brother, at your arrival, and I thank you for visiting me, but what you say about the division of the kingdom is a serious thing to hear. It is my

---

⁵ teneto : the Encomiast is fond of the imper. sing. act. in -to : cf. II, 15, persoluito, occidito ; III, 1, inuadito.

loqueris de diuisione regni. Hereditatem, quam mihi pater te laudante tradidit, guberno, tu uero hac maiorem si amisisti doleo, teque iuuare paratus regnum meum partiri non sustinebo."

30   Hoc Cnuto audiens fratremque recte loquutum tacite perpendens, " Hoc tempore de hoc sileamus," inquit, " Deus enim rectius fortasse hoc solus ordinabit." Talibus aliisque diuersis sermonibus colloquentes conuiuiisque regalibus conuiuantes aliquanto tempore (simul) *a* manserunt, et naues meliorantes exercitum restaurauerunt. Pariter uero Sclauoniam adierunt, et matrem suam, quae illic morabatur, reduxerunt.

[3] Translatio *b* corporis Sueini in Danomarchiam. Interea quaedam matronarum Anglicarum nauim sibi fecit parari, et assumpto corpore Sueini regis sua in patria sepulti illoque aromatibus condito palliisque uelato, mare adiit, et prospero cursu appulsa ad portus Danorum peruenit. Mittens ergo utrisque
5 fratribus nuntium mandat corpus adesse paternum, ut hoc maturent suscipere, tumuloque quod *c* sibi parauerat locare. Illi hilares adsunt, honorifice corpus suscipiunt, honorificentiusque illud in monasterio in honore Sanctae Trinitatis ab eodem rege constructo, in sepulchro quod sibi parauerat, recondunt.

[Q]uo perfecto iamque appropiante sole aestiuo accelerat Cnuto redintegrato
10 exercitu redire suasque iniurias uindicare. At illi circa litora deambulanti subito apparescunt carbasa non multa in medio mari. Nam Thurkil memor quod Sueino fecerat, et quod tunc in terra absque licentia domini sui Cnutonis inconsulte remanserat, cum nouem nauibus earumque exercitu dominum suum requisiuit, ut ei patefaceret, quia non contra eius salutem se recedente remanserit. Qui ueniens non
15 presumpsit litora iniussus subire, sed eiectis anchoris premissisque nunciis poscit *1* se portus subintrare licere. Quod ubi concessum est, ascendit, misericordiamque domini sui quesiuit, et illi multo labore conciliatus,*d* dat fidei sacramentum, se illi deinceps fideliter seruiturum. Cum quo mense plus integro moratur, et ut ad Anglos redeat hortatur, dicens eum leuiter illos posse superare, quorum fines longe
20 lateque notificarentur utrisque. Presertim aiebat se triginta naues in Anglorum patria cum exercitu fidissimo reliquisse, qui uenientes sus⟨s⟩ciperent honorifice, ducerentque per fines totius patriae.

[4] Tunc rex ualedicens matri et fratri curui litoris repetiit confinia, qua iam adunauerat ducentarum nauium spetiosa spectacula. Nam hic erat tanta armorum copia, ut una earum nauium, si omnibus reliquis defecissent, sufficeret habundantissime tela. Erant autem ibi scutorum tanta genera, ut crederes adesse omnium
5 populorum agmina. Tantus quoque *e* decor inerat pupibus, ut intuentium hebetatis luminibus *a* flammeae magis quam [l]igneae *f* uiderentur a longe aspicientibus. Si quando enim sol illis iubar inmiscuit radiorum, hinc resplenduit fulgur armorum, illinc uero flamma dependentium clipeorum. Ardebat aurum in rostris, fulgebat quoque argentum in uariis nauium figuris. Tantus siquidem classis erat apparatus,

---

a simul *added in margin,* L ; *in text,* P.
b Translatio, *etc. : this heading is wanting in* P.
c quod : *so* L, P (*cf. Introduction,* p. xxxviii).
d conciliatus : *corrected from* consiliatus, L.
e quoque . . . Talis (5, 1) : *omitted, so reading* Tantus itaque milicies, P.
f [l]igneae : *admirable conjecture of Gertz.*

---

1 poscit, etc. : the combination of *licet* + acc. and inf. with *posco* + inf. makes a rather violent though syntactically regular clause.

part to rule the heritage which our father gave me with your approval ; as for you, if you have lost a greater one, I regret it, but though prepared to help you, I will not endure that my kingdom be divided." When Knútr had heard this, and had silently weighed his brother's reasonable words, he said : " Let us be silent concerning this for the moment, for God alone may perchance arrange the matter more equitably." Communing in such words and in other discussions of various kinds, and feasting at kingly banquets, they remained together for some time, and while mending the ships, they re-established the army. They also, in fact, went to the land of the Slavs, and brought back their mother, who resided there.

3. *The removal of Sveinn's body to Denmark.* In the meantime, a certain English matron had a ship prepared for her, and taking the body of Sveinn, who had been buried in her country, and having embalmed it and covered it with palls, she went to the sea, and making a successful voyage, arrived at the ports of the Danes. Sending a messenger to the two brothers, she indicated that the body of their father was there, in order that they might hasten to receive it, and place it in the tomb which he had prepared for himself. They came gladly, and received the body with honour, and with yet more honour placed it in the monastery which the same king had built in honour of the Holy Trinity, in the sepulchre which he had prepared for himself.

When this had been done, the summer sun was drawing near, and Knútr, having restored the army, hastened to return and avenge his injuries. But as he was strolling round the beaches, he observed a small number of ships out at sea. For Thorkell, remembering what he had done to Sveinn, and that he had also unadvisedly remained in the country without the leave of Knútr, his lord, sought his lord with nine ships and their crews, in order to make it clear to him that he was not acting against his safety in remaining, when he went away. When he arrived, he did not presume to approach the shore unbidden, but casting anchor, he sent messengers, and asked leave to enter the ports. When this was granted, he landed and asked his lord's mercy, and having become with great difficulty reconciled to him, he gave an oath of fidelity, to the effect that he would serve him continuously and faithfully. He remained with him more than a whole month, and urged him to return to England, saying that he could easily overcome people whose country was known far and wide to both of them. In particular, he said that he had left thirty ships in England with a most faithful army, who would receive them with honour when they came, and would conduct them through the whole extent of the country.

4. Then the king said farewell to his mother and brother, and returned to the area of the winding coast, where he had already assembled the fair spectacle of two hundred ships. For here was so great a quantity of arms, that one of those ships would have very abundantly supplied weapons, if they had been lacking to all the rest. Furthermore, there were there so many kinds of shields, that you would have believed that troops of all nations were present. So great, also, was the ornamentation of the ships, that the eyes of the beholders were dazzled, and to those looking from afar they seemed of flame rather than of wood. For if at any time the sun cast the splendour of its rays among them, the flashing of arms shone in one place, in another the flame of suspended shields. Gold shone on the prows, silver also flashed

---

¹ *hebetatis luminibus* : cf. *hebetare uisus, Aen.* ii. 605, and the expression *oculos hebetare,* in various authors, first Plin., *N.H.* viii. 129.

10 ut, si quam gentem eius uellet expugnare dominus, naues tantum aduersarios
terrerent, priusquam earum bellatores pugnam ullam capescerent [1]. Nam quis
contrariorum leones auri fulgore terribiles, quis metallinos homines aureo fronte
minaces, quis dracones obrizo ardentes, quis tauros radiantibus auro cornibus necem
intentantes in puppibus aspiceret, et nullo metu regem tantae copiae formidaret ?
15 Praeterea in tanta expeditione nullus inueniebatur seruus, nullus ex seruo libertus,
nullus ignobilis, nullus senili aet⟨t⟩ate debilis ; omnes enim erant nobiles, omnes
plenae aetatis robore ualentes, omnes cuiuis pugnae satis habiles, omnes tantae
uelocitatis, ut despectui eis essent equitantium pernicitates.

[5] Talis itaque milicies fastuosis scansis ratibus intrat pelagus solutis a litore
anchoris [2] et funibus, talique uerrit impetu fluctus, ut alatis [3] puppibus hanc super-
uolare undas putares uix tanto mari rudentibus. Regalis autem nauis reliquis
erat honor et intentio, quia nulla aliis inerat optio, nisi tantum ut regis sui fasces [a]
5 ampliarent toto studio. Exspectabili itaque ordine flatu secundo Sanduich, qui est
omnium Anglorum portuum famosissimus, sunt appulsi, eiectisque anchoris, batulis
exploratores se dedunt littori, et citissime finitima tellure explorata ad nota recurrunt
nauigia, regique edicunt, adesse resistentium parata milia. Patrienses enim regi
Danisque feruentissime rebellare ardentes, quas sibi ad luctam sufficere credebant
10 adunauerant phalanges, conglobatique et in unum conspirati [4] aduolitabant dextris
nobilium morituri.

[6] [T]unc [b] Turkil tempus intuens instare, quo fidelitatem suam domino suo
ualebat patefacere, " Ego ", inquit, " hoc certamen domino meo accurabo cum meis
euincere, nec regem meum ad bellandum, utpote iuuenem, feruentissimum huic
misceri patiar pugnae.[c] Nam, si uictor fuero, regi ipsi triumphabo ; si autem cecidero
5 siue tergum dedero, non Anglis gloriae erit adeo, quia rex supererit, qui et prelium
restaurabit et fortasse uictor meas iniurias uindicabit." Hoc dictum cum sanae mentis
esse uideretur omnibus, annuente rege ascendit cum suis e nauibus dirigens aciem
contra Anglorum inpetum [5], qui tunc in loco Scorastan dicto fuerat congregatus.
Quadranginta denique nauium et eo amplius Danorum exercitus ascenderat, sed
10 adhuc hic numerus medietati hostium minime par fuerat. At dux eorum, magis
fisus uirtute quam multitudine omnes rumpens morulas classica insonuit, gradiens in
prima fronte et mente semper Dei auxilium exorans queque obuia metebat mucronis
acie. Angli uero in primis fortiores dira cede Danos obtruncarunt, in tantum ut paene
uictoriam adepti aduersarios fugere cogerent, si non ducis alloquio retenti memoresque
15 uirtutis fugam erubescerent. Namque memorabat ille abesse diffugium, in terra
scilicet hostes, et a litore longe remotas pupes, ideoque, si non uincerent, quod pariter
occumbere deberent. Unde illi animosiores effecti in prelio ilico manifestant, quam

---

[a] fasces : *corrected from* facces, L.
[b] [T]unc : *illuminator failed to insert initial*, L ; *so above*, 3, 9.
[c] pugnae : nae *written over illegible erasure*, L'.

[1] *pugnam . . capescerent* : a frequent collocation in Livy and Tacitus.
[2] *solutis . . . anchoris* : a phrase used also by Cicero, *Att.* i. 13, 1.
[3] *alatis* : unusual as an epithet of ships ; cf. Cassiod., *Var.* i. 35, *ratis . . alata uelis.*
[4] *in unum conspirati* : ' acting as one man ' ; cf. Sen., *Ep.* 84, 10, *in unum conspirata*, of
a mind in which innumerable items of knowledge are blended into one.
[5] *inpetum* : to be taken in the unusual sense ' army ', which would arise naturally from
passages where *impetus* means practically ' army in attack '.

on the variously shaped ships. So great, in fact, was the magnificence of the fleet, that if its lord had desired to conquer any people, the ships alone would have terrified the enemy, before the warriors whom they carried joined battle at all. For who could look upon the lions of the foe, terrible with the brightness of gold, who upon the men of metal, menacing with golden face, who upon the dragons burning with pure gold, who upon the bulls on the ships threatening death, their horns shining with gold, without feeling any fear for the king of such a force ? Furthermore, in this great expedition there was present no slave, no man freed from slavery, no low-born man, no man weakened by age ; for all were noble, all strong with the might of mature age, all sufficiently fit for any type of fighting, all of such great fleetness, that they scorned the speed of horsemen.

5. And so the force which has been described, having unfastened the anchors and ropes from the shore, boarded the lofty ships and put to sea, and swept the waves with such impetus, that you would have thought that they were flying over the water in winged ships, which hardly creaked, heavy as the sea was. To the royal ship, however, the rest did honour and paid attention, for the others had no freedom of action, except to extend the sway of their lord with all their zeal. And so in good order and with a favourable wind they touched at Sandwich, which is the most famous of all the ports of the English, and after they had dropped anchor, scouts went ashore in boats, and having made a very rapid examination of the immediate neighbourhood, returned to the familiar ships, and reported to the king that thousands of opponents were present in readiness. For the natives, burning most fiercely to renew the war against the king and the Danes, had assembled squadrons which they believed to suffice them for the struggle, and gathered together and acting as one pressed on, doomed to die at the hands of the nobles.

6. Then Thorkell, observing the time to have come when he could demonstrate his fidelity to his lord, said : " I will undertake to win this fight for my lord with my troops, and will not permit my king to be involved in this battle, very eager to fight as he is, inasmuch as he is a youth. For if I be victorious, I will win on the king's own behalf ; but if I fall or turn my back, it will not be to the glory of the English, for the reason that the king will be left, and he will give battle again, and perhaps as a victor will avenge my injuries." Since this seemed to all to be good reasoning, he disembarked with the king's approval, and directed his force against the army of the English, which was then assembled at the place called Sherston. The Danish army had disembarked from forty ships and more, but still this number was by no means equal to half the enemy. But the leader, relying on courage rather than numbers, sounded the trumpets without delay, and advancing in the forefront and ever praying in his heart for the help of God, laid low all that came in his way with the sword's point. The English, indeed, were the more bold at first, and cut down the Danes with terrible slaughter, to such an extent that they nearly won the victory and would have compelled their enemies to flee, if the latter, held back by their leader's words and being mindful of their own bravery, had not regarded flight with shame. For he mentioned that there was no place to which they might flee, that they were, of course, foes in the land, and that their ships were far from the shore, and that accordingly, if they should not conquer, they would necessarily fall together. After they had been rendered of better courage by this, they forthwith showed in battle how

periculosa sit desperatio. Enimuero de refugio fugae desperati tanta in hostes
debachati sunt insania, ut non tantum [1] mortuorum aspiceres corpora cadentia,
20 uerum etiam uiuorum ictus declinantia. Tandem ergo potiti optata uictoria suorum
quae reperire poterant tumulabant menbra.[a] [2] Ab aduer[sar]iis quoque diripientes
spolia reuertuntur, et adiacentem [3] regionem inuadendam accinguntur.

[7] Hoc primum decus Turchil armis Cnutonis auxit, et magnam partem patriae
pro hoc postmodum promeruit. At tunc ad dominum regressus ei et sotiis suos
indicat euentus, facitque eos spoliis quae attulit ardentiores ad pugnam manubiis
letus et palmae successibus. Quo exemplo, Eric quidam, dux et princeps prouintiae
5 quae Norduuega dicitur, incitatus—nam et his [b] [4] Cnutonis regis intererat officialibus,
iam diu illi subditus, uir armis strenuus, omni honorificentia dignus—accepta licentia
cum suis est egressus, et partem terrae aggressus spolia diripuit, uicos inuadendo
destruxit, occurrentes sibi hostes domuit, et multos ex eis captiuauit, tandemque
uictoriosus ad socios cum spoliis redit. Quo reuerso rex parcens patriae prohibuit
10 ultra eam predari, sed iussit ciuitatem Londoniam, metropolim terrae, obsidione
teneri, quia in ea [c] confugerant optimates et pars exercitus et maximum, ut est
populosissima, uulgus. Et quia hoc pedites equitesque nequibant explere, undique
enim mari quodammodo non [in]pari [d] uallatur flumine, turritis pupibus eam
coangustare fecit, et firmissima uallatione tenuit.

15   Deus itaque, qui omnes homines uult magis saluare quam perdere, intuens has
gentes tanto periculo labor[ar]e, eum principem, qui interius ciuitati presidebat,
educens e corpore iunxit quieti sempiternae, ut eo defuncto liber Cnutoni ingressus
pateret, et utrique populo confecta pace paulisper respirare copia esset. Quod et
factum est. Nam ciues suo honorifice sepulto principe initoque salubri consilio [5]
20 elegerunt internuntios mittere et regi placita mandare, uidelicet ut dexteram illis
daret et ciuitatem pacifice susciperet. Hoc ubi Cnutoni [6] satis uideretur probabile
facto, faedus firmatum est, ingressui eius die constituto. At pars interioris exercitus
spreuere statutum ciuium, latenterque nocte illa, cuius sequenti die ingressus est rex,
cum filio defuncti principis egressi sunt ciuitatem, ut experirentur rursus collecta
25 innumerabili manu, si forte a finibus suis ualerent arcere ingressum regem. Nec
quieuerunt, quousque omnes penae Anglos sibi magis adhuc adclines quam Cnutoni
conglobarent. Cnuto autem ciuitatem intrauit, et in solio regni resedit. Sed tamen
Londonienses non sibi adhuc esse fideles credidit : unde et nauium stipendia [7] illa

[a] menbra : so L (cf. Linguistic Note).
[b] his : so L, P ; but P treats as ablative plural, distorting the sentence.
[c] in ea : so L, P (cf. Introduction, p. xxv).
[d] [in]pari : conjectured independently by Maseres and Gertz : pari, L, P.

---

[1] ut non tantum, etc. : the idea seems to be that some fell dead, but others threw themselves
on the ground to avoid the blows of their adversaries.
[2] menbra : a genuine medieval spelling (e.g., the 'Astronomer', Vita Hludowici, 34 ;
Miracula S. Bauonis, i. 5 ; Folquin, Gesta Abbatum, frequently).
[3] adiacentem : I hesitate to read [ad] adiacentem : see Introduction, p. xxxii.
[4] his : i.e., is, see Introduction, p. xxxviii.
[5] initoque salubri consilio : the expression consilium inire is frequent, while consilium salubre
(which occurs again below, III, 3), is an old cliché, found first in Cicero, much used in late and
medieval writers (see Archivum Latinitatis medii aevi, ix. 101–2), and beloved by Dudo.
[6] Hoc ubi Cnutoni, etc. : ' this was done at a time when it appealed sufficiently to Knútr ',
i.e., the peace proposals came at a time when Knútr was quite willing to end hostilities. The

dangerous a thing is desperation. For despairing of a refuge to which to flee, they raged on against the enemy with such madness, that you would have seen not only the bodies of the dead falling, but also of the living, as they avoided the blows. Accordingly they ultimately gained the victory which they desired, and buried such of the remains of their comrades as they could find. After they had also seized the spoils from their foes, they returned and made themselves ready for an invasion of the adjacent country.

7. This was the first honour which Thorkell brought to the arms of Knútr, and for this he afterwards received a large part of the country. But then, returning to his lord, he told him and his followers what had happened, and rejoicing in booty and the success of victory, he rendered them more eager for battle by the spoils he carried. Roused by this example, one, Eiríkr, leader and prince of the province which is called Norway—for he also was one of Knútr's officials, had already been long subject to him, and was a man active in war, and worthy of all honour—having received leave, set out with his followers, fell upon a part of the country, seized booty, attacked and destroyed villages, overcame the enemies who met him, captured many of them, and at length returned to his comrades victorious with the spoil. When he returned, the king, sparing the country, forbade him to plunder it further, but ordered the city of London, the capital of the country, to be besieged, because the chief men and part of the army had fled into it, and also a very great number of common people, for it is a most populous place. And because infantry and cavalry could not accomplish this, for the city is surrounded on all sides by a river, which is in a sense equal to the sea, he caused it to be shut in with towered ships, and held it in a very strong circumvallation.

And so God, who wishes to save all men rather than to lose them, seeing these natives to be pressed by such great danger, took away from the body the prince who was in command of the city within, and gave him to everlasting rest, that at his decease free ingress might be open to Knútr, and that with the conclusion of peace the two peoples might have for a time an opportunity to recover. And this came to pass. For the citizens, having given their prince honourable burial, and having adopted a sound plan, decided to send messengers and intimate their decision to the king, that is to say, that he should give them his pledge of friendship, and should take peaceful possession of the city. This occurred at a time when it seemed acceptable enough to Knútr, and a treaty was made, a day being arranged for his entry. But part of the garrison spurned the decision of the citizens, and in the night preceding the day on which the king made his entry, left the city secretly with the son of the deceased prince, in order to collect a very large force again, and try if they could perhaps expel the invading king from their country. And they did not rest till they had assembled nearly all the English who were still inclined to them rather than to Knútr. Knútr, however, entered the city and sat on the throne of the kingdom. But he, nevertheless, did not believe that the Londoners were yet true to him, and,

Encomiast has not Dudo's enthusiasm for the split ablative absolute, but there is no reason against assuming that he used one here. Gertz proposes *factu*, but this spoils the rhyme with *constituto*, does not greatly ease the construction, and gives a less satisfactory sense. Cf. II, 13, below, where the willingness of the Danes to conclude peace is again emphasised.

7 *nauium stipendia*: ' the equipment of his ships ', not ' the wages of his crews ', for it would be absurd to suggest that Knútr could have thought for a moment of discharging his crews while Eadmund was still in the field ; cf. *Glossary*, s.v. *stipendia*.

aestate restaurare fecit, ne, si forte exercitus aduersariorum ciuitatem oppugnaret,
30 ipse ab interioribus hostibus exterioribus traditus interiret. Quod cauens rursus ad
tempus ut prudens cessit, et ascensis ratibus [1] ac ciuitate relicta insulam Scepei
dictam cum suis petiit, ibique hiemans pacifice euentum rei expectauit.

[8] Aedmund itaque—sic enim iuuenis qui exercitum collegerat [a] dictus est—
recedente Cnutone cum populo non mediocri sed innumerabili ueniens ciuitatem
pompatice ingreditur, et mox eum uniuersi sequuntur, obtemperant, et fauent, et
uirum fortem fieri suadent, dicentes quod eum magis quam Danorum principem
5 eligerent. Erat quoque eius partis [b] comes primus Edricus, consiliis pollens sed
tamen dolositate uersipell[is] [c], quem sibi ad aurem posuerat Aedmund in omni[bus] [d]
negotiis. Fertur autem ipse iuuenis illo tempore domino Cnutoni recedenti
singularem pugnam [2] obtulisse; sed rex sapiens dicitur sic respondisse: "Ego
tempus luctae prestolabor congruae, dum non casum suspectus [e] certus fuero
10 uictoriae; tu uero, qui aues duellum in hieme, caue ne deficias etiam aptiori tempore."
Sic rex ut dictum est in S[c]eepei, quod est dictum Latine "insula ouium", ut poterat
hiemauit. Aedmund autem in Londonia dimisso exercitu ultimam hiemem [f] duxit.

[9] Recedente uero brumali tempore tota quadragesima rursus militiam adu-
nauit, et mox post pascales dies regem et Danos a finibus Anglorum deturbare
parauit, et ueniens cum innumerabili multitudine eos subito cogitauit inuadere.
At sermo non latuit Danos, qui puppibus posthabitis [3] petunt arida, aptantes se
5 excipere quaeque obuia. Erat namque eis uexillum miri portenti, quod licet cre-
dam posse esse incredibile lectori, tamen, quia uerum est, uerae inseram lectioni.
Enimuero dum esset simplissimo [4] candidissimoque intextum [g] [5] serico, nulliusque
figurae in eo inserta esset [i]mago, tempore belli semper in eo uidebatur coruus ac
si intextus, in uictoria suorum quasi hians ore excutiensque alas instabilisque pedibus,
10 et suis deuictis quietissimus totoque corpore demissus. Quod requirens Turchil,
auctor primi prelii, "Pugnemus", inquit, "uiriliter, sotii, nihil enim nobis erit
periculi: hoc denique testatur instabilis coruus presagientis uexilli." Quo audito
Dani audentiores effecti ferratisque induuiis indurati occurrunt Anglis in Aesceneduno [h] loco, quod nos Latini [i] [6] "montem fraxinorum" possumus interpretari.
15 Ibique nondum congressione facta Edric, quem primum comitum Edmundi [j] diximus, hec suis intulit affamina: "Fugiamus, o sotii, uitamque subtrahamus morti

---

[a] collegerat: colligerat, L; collegerat, P.
[b] partis: *corrected from* partes, L; partis, P.
[c] uersipell[is]: is *on an erasure*, L'; uersipellis, P.
[d] omni[bus]: bus *added*, L'; omnibus, P.
[e] suspectus: *so* L, P (*cf. Introduction, p.* xxxviii).
[f] hiemem: *corrected from* hiemaem *by subpunctuation of* a, L.
[g] intextum: *so* L, P (*cf. Linguistic Note*).
[h] Aesceneduno: Kescesdume, P.
[i] Latini: *so* L, P (*cf. Linguistic Note*).
[j] Edmundi: *altered from* Aedmundi, L.

---

[1] *ascensis ratibus*: the collocation occurs also Flor. i. 43, 3, and Iuuenc. iii. 124. Cf. below,
III, 4, *ascensis puppibus*.
[2] *singularem pugnam*: so Macr., *Sat.* v. 2, 15, for 'single combat'.
[3] *posthabitis*: 'left behind'; cf. the 'Astronomer', *Vita Hludowici*, 15, 'omnibus, quae
castrensis habitatio habuit, posthabitis'.
[4] *simplissimo*: superlative from *simplus* (see Lewis and Short).

accordingly, he had the equipment of his ships renewed that summer, lest if the army of his foes happened to besiege the city, he should be delivered by the foes within to those without and perish. Guarding against this, he again retired for the moment like a wise man, and having gone on board his ships, he left the city and went to the island called Sheppey with his followers, and wintered there, peacefully awaiting the outcome of the matter.

8. And so Eadmund—for so the youth who had collected the army was called—when Knútr retired, came with an army not insignificant but immense, and entered the city in state. Soon all followed him, obeyed him, and bestowed their favour upon him, and urged him to be a bold man, declaring that he rather than the prince of the Danes was their choice. On his side, furthermore, Eadric was the chief supporter, a man skilful in counsel but treacherous in guile, and Eadmund afforded him hearing in all affairs. It is told, moreover, that the youth himself at that time offered single combat to Knútr, as the latter was retiring ; but the king, being a wise man, is said to have answered thus : " I will await a time, when contest will be fitting, and when anticipating no misfortune, I shall be sure of victory ; but as for you, who desire combat in the winter, beware lest you fail to appear even when the time is more appropriate." Thus the king, as has been narrated, wintered as well as he could in Sheppey, that is to say in Latin ' insula ovium '. Eadmund, however, dismissed his army, and passed his last winter in London.

9. Now when winter was drawing to an end, he assembled forces during the whole of Quadragesima, and soon after Eastertide attempted to expel the king and the Danes from the country of the English, and advancing with a great multitude, planned a sudden attack upon them. But a report of this did not fail to become known to the Danes, who left their ships and went ashore, preparing to receive whatever they should encounter. Now they had a banner of wonderfully strange nature, which though I believe that it may be incredible to the reader, yet since it is true, I will introduce the matter into my true history. For while it was woven of the plainest and whitest silk, and the representation of no figure was inserted into it, in time of war a raven was always seen as if embroidered on it, in the hour of its owners' victory opening its beak, flapping its wings, and restive on its feet, but very subdued and drooping with its whole body when they were defeated. Looking out for this, Thorkell, who had fought the first battle, said : " Let us fight manfully, comrades, for no danger threatens us : for to this the restive raven of the prophetic banner bears witness." When the Danes heard this, they were rendered bolder, and clad with suits of mail, encountered the enemy in the place called Ashingdon, a word which we Latinists can explain as ' mons fraxinorum '. And there, before battle was joined, Eadric, whom we have mentioned as Eadmund's chief supporter, addressed these remarks to his comrades : " Let us flee, oh comrades, and snatch our lives from imminent death, or else we will fall forthwith, for

---

⁵ intextum : Gertz unnecessarily reads contextum against both L and P ; cf. Aen. x. 785, intextum tauris opus ; Luc. v. 516–17, domus . . . . . iunco cannaque intexta.

⁶ nos Latini : ' we Latinists '. Gertz reads Latine, spoiling the rhyme with interpretari. P, like L, reads Latini (not Latinis as Gertz alleges). Cf. Bede, Hist. Eccl. iv. 13, ' qualis locus a Latinis paeninsula, a Grecis solet cherronesos uocari ', and good instances of Latinus, ' Latin scholar ', quoted by L. Traube, Einleitung in die lat. Philologie des Mittelalters, 89–91, especially ' esse uelim Graecus, cum uix sim, domna, Latinus '.

imminenti, alioquin occumbemus ilico ; Danorum enim duritiam nosco *a*." Et
uelato uexillo, quod dextra gestabat, dans tergum hostibus magnam partem militum
bello fraudabat *b*. Et ut quidam aiunt hoc (non) *c* causa egit timoris sed dolositatis,
20 ut postea claruit ; quia [1] hoc eum clam Danis promisisse, nescio quo pro beneficio,
assertio multorum dicit. Tunc Aedmund hoc intuitus et undique angustiatus, " O
Angli," inquit, " aut hodie bellabitis, aut omnes una in deditionem ibitis. Pugnate
ergo pro libertate et patria, uiri cordati ; hi quippe qui fugiunt, utpote formidolosi,
si non abirent, essent impedimento exercitui." Et haec dicens in medios ingreditur
25 hostes circumquaque caedens Danos, nobiles hoc exemplo suos reddens ad bellandum
proniores.

[10] Commissum est ergo prelium pedestre grauissimum, dum Dani licet
pauciores nescii cedere magis eligerent internetionem quam fugae periculum. Resis-
tunt itaque uiriliter, et prelium hora diei nona ceptum ducunt in uesperam, se
gladiis [2] haud sponte opponentes, sed gladiorum aculeis uoluntarius alios urgentes.
5 Cadunt utriusque partis armati, plus tamen eius quae erat numero eminentiori. At
ubi iam aduesperante [3] noctis adessent tempora, uincit amor uictoriae tenebrarum
incommoda, quia neque horrebant tenebras instante cura maiore, neque etiam nocti
dignabantur cedere [4], in hostem tantum dum ardebant preualere. Et nisi luna
clarescens ipsum monstraret hostem, cederet quisque suum commilitonem ut inimi-
10 cum resistentem, nullusque utriusque partis superuiueret nisi quem fuga saluasset.
Interea ceperunt Angli fatigari paulatimque fugam meditari [5], dum intuentur
Danos in hoc conspiratos, quatinus aut uincerent aut usque ad unum omnes una
perirent. Uidebantur enim eis tunc numerosiores et in tam diutina conflictatione *d*
fortiores. Fortiores namque eos estimabant uera suspitione, quia iam stimulis ferri
15 commoniti casuque suorum turbati, magis uidebantur seuire quam bellare. Unde
Angli terga uertentes hac et illac fugitant absque mora semper ante aduersarios
cadentes, adduntque decus honori Cnutonis et uictoriae, [de]decorato *e* Aedmundo
fugiente principe. Qui *f*, licet deuictus ualentioribus cedens recederet, tamen adhuc
non penitus desperans tutis se commisit locis, ut demum fortiori multitudine collecta
20 iterum experiretur, si quid forte sibi boni succedere posset. At Dani fugientes non
longe sunt persecuti, quia incogniti locorum noctis obscuritate sunt retenti. Angli
uero loci non inscii cito a manibus hostium sunt elapsi, eos relinquentes ad spolia
seseque dantes ad inhonesta refugia.

---

a nosco : *corrected from* nasco, L'.   *b* fraudabat : *corrected from* fraudebat, L'.
c non *added above the line*, L ; *in text*, P.   *d* conflictatione : *corrected from* conflectatione, L'.
e [de]decorato : *conjectured by Gertz* ; decorato, L, P.
f Qui : *the hand changes* (*see Introduction*, *p. xi*), L.

---

[1] *quia* : not causal in force, but a mere connective ; cf. Stolz-Schmalz, p. 726.
[2] *se gladiis*, etc. : the sense clearly demands that *uoluntarius* be taken as a comparative
adverb, and similarly formed comparatives from adjectives in *-ius* are found, though they are
rare (e.g. *industrior*, Plaut., *Most.*, 150). The sentence apparently means that the warriors were
unwilling to oppose themselves to the swords (i.e. accept attack passively), but more ready
to attack others with the points of their own swords. It is not possible to ease the construction
by taking *haud sponte* as ' not alone ' ; it must be taken as ' not willingly ', in contrast to
uoluntarius, ' more willingly ', in the next clause. Gertz translates : ' det var ikke med deres
gode Vilje, naar de blot stillede sig til Modværge mod de andres Sværd, nej, meget mere stod deres
Lyst til selv at trænge ind paa de andre med Odden af deres egne Sværd '.

I know the hardihood of the Danes." And concealing the banner which he bore in his right hand, he turned his back on the enemy, and caused the withdrawal of a large part of the soldiers from the battle. And according to some, it was afterwards evident that he did this not out of fear but in guile ; and what many assert is that he had promised this secretly to the Danes in return for some favour. Then Eadmund, observing what had occurred, and hard pressed on every side, said : " Oh Englishmen, to-day you will fight or surrender yourselves all together. Therefore, fight for your liberty and your country, men of understanding ; truly, those who are in flight, inasmuch as they are afraid, if they were not withdrawing, would be a hindrance to the army." And as he said these things, he advanced into the midst of the enemy, cutting down the Danes on all sides, and by this example rendering his noble followers more inclined to fight.

10. Therefore a very severe infantry battle was joined, since the Danes, although the less numerous side, did not contemplate withdrawal, and chose death rather than the danger attending flight. And so they resisted manfully, and protracted the battle, which had been begun in the ninth hour of the day, until the evening, submitting themselves, though ill-content to do so, to the strokes of swords, and pressing upon the foe with a better will with the points of their own swords. Armed men fell on both sides, but more on the side which had superiority in numbers. But when evening was falling and night-time was at hand, longing for victory overcame the inconveniences of darkness, for since a graver consideration was pressing, they did not shrink from the darkness, and disdained to give way before the night, only burning to overcome the foe. And if the shining moon had not shown which was the enemy, every man would have cut down his comrade, thinking he was an adversary resisting him, and no man would have survived on either side, unless he had been saved by flight. Meanwhile the English began to be weary, and gradually to contemplate flight, as they observed the Danes to be of one mind either to conquer, or to perish all together to a man. For then they seemed to them more numerous, and to be the stronger in so protracted a struggle. For they deemed them stronger by a well-founded suspicion, because, being made mindful of their position by the goading of weapons, and distressed by the fall of their comrades, they seemed to rage rather than fight. Accordingly the English, turning their backs, fled without delay on all sides, ever falling before their foes, and added glory to the honour of Knútr and to his victory, while Eadmund, the fugitive prince, was disgraced. The latter, although he withdrew defeated, giving way to the stronger side, was not, however, yet entirely without hope, and betook himself to safe positions, in order that ultimately he might assemble a more powerful force, and try again if by chance any measure of good fortune could turn in his favour. The Danes, on the other hand, did not pursue the fugitives far, for they were unfamiliar with the locality, and were held back by the darkness of night. The English, being familiar with the locality, quickly escaped from the hands of their enemies, whom they left to seize the spoil, as they themselves withdrew to places of dishonourable refuge.

[3] *aduesperante* : this one word absolute construction is unusual with a present participle, and Gertz is probably right in adding *die* and comparing *Vulg.*, *Prov.* vii. 9.

[4] *nocti . . cedere* : an expression used by Livy (III, 17, 9, etc.) and also found in verse (Sil. v. 677).

[5] *fugam meditari* : an extremely common expression ; see *Thes.*, s.v. *fuga*, col. 1469.

[11] Tunc uictores sua leti uictoria, transacta iam nocte plus media [1], pernoctant quod supererat inter mortuorum cadauera. Non autem in nocte spolia dirimunt, sed interim suos requirunt, seseque adunantes, ut securiores esse possent, simul omnes uno in loco perstiterunt [a]. Inlucescente uero iam mane suorum agnoscunt 5 multos in prelio cecidisse, quorum cadauera ut poterant tumulauere. Ab aduersariorum quoque membris abradunt spolia bestiis et auibus eorum relinquentes morticina, et ad naues redeuntes Londoniamque repetentes saniora sibi querunt consilia.[2] Similiter et Angli suo cum principe sibi consulunt, et super hoc negotii Dei auxilium querunt, ut qui totiens armis sunt deuicti saltem aliquo consilio 10 ualerent remanere [3] suffulti.

[12] Iam etiam Edric, qui antea a bello recessit profugus, ad dominum suum et ad socios rediit, et susceptus est, quia uir boni consilii fuit. Is surgens in medio agmine omnes tali alloquutus est sermone : " Licet omnibus pene uobis sim inuisus quia bello cessi, tamen, si uestris sederet animis dictis parere mei consilii, uictorio-5 siores effici meo consultu possetis, quam si totius terrae his uiris resisteretis armis. Satis enim Danorum uictorias expertus frustra nos reniti omnino scio, et ob hoc me subtraxi a prelio, ut uobis postmodum prodessem consilio, non, ut uos estimatis, perculsus timore aliquo. Dum enim scirem necesse esse me fugere, quid satius fuit, aut uulneratum aut sanum recedere ? Est procul dubio certa uictoria interdum ab 10 fortiori hoste elabi fuga, cui nequit resisti [4] per arma. Omnes enim qui adsumus proh dolor [5] fugimus ; sed ne hic casus uobis eueniat ulterius, dextras Danis demus, ut ipsos faederatos habentes fugam periculumque bellorum sic saltem declinemus. Attamen hoc aliter nequit fieri nisi diuisione regni nostri. Et melius esse iudico, ut medietatem regni rex noster cum pace habeat, quam totum pariter inuitus 15 amittat."

[13] Placuit sermo optimatibus, et licet inuitus hoc tamen annuit Ae[d]mundus, electisque internuntiis, premittit ad naues Cnutonis, qui dextras Danis dent et accipiant ab eis. Quos ubi primum Dani uenientes intuentur, exploratores eos esse suspicantur. Sed postquam propius eos uident accedere [b], accersitis eis quidnam 5 quaesierint orsi sunt rogitare. Discentes uero ab eis pro conficienda pace eos uenire letantes eos sistunt conspectibus [6] regis ; erant enim obnixe optantes prospera pacis iam lassi bellorum et continuatione nauigationis. Tunc missi, rege pacifice salutato, " Miserunt nos ", inquiunt, " ad te, o rex, princeps noster et procerum nostrorum

[a] perstiterunt : *I emend thus rather than to* persistunt *in view of* pspicerunt, P, *and the rhyme ;* persisterunt, L.   [b] accedere : aceedere, L.

---

[1] *transacta iam nocte plus media* : cf. above, II, 3, *mense plus integro.* The qualification of an adjective by adverbial *plus* is not usual except with numeral adjectives, as in Verg., *Georg.* iv. 207, *plus septima . . aetas* ; but cf. Oros., i. 10, 19, etc., *plus solitus.* (The late use of *plus* with the positive adjective to express the comparative degree is, of course, another idiom entirely.)

[2] *saniora . . querunt consilia* : the collocation *consilium sanum* is old and frequent ; an example with comparative adjective and plural noun is Curt., iv. 1, 9 ; *consilium quaerere* is also frequent, Sall., *Iug.* 70, 5 ; etc. (see *Thes.*, s.v. *consilium*, col. 488).

[3] *remanere* : practically equivalent to *esse* ; on the similar use of *manere* in late Latin, see Stolz-Schmalz, p. 610.

[4] *cui nequit resisti* : the only natural translation is ' whom it is not possible to resist ', taking *nequit* as an impersonal verb, which is not usual (e.g., Plaut., *Truc.* 553 ; cf. Löfstedt, *Philologischer Kommentar zur Peregrinatio Aetheriae*, pp. 43–7) and *resisti* with impersonal force, as in Caes., *B.G.* i. 37 ; *B.C.* iii. 63.

11. Then, when it was already past midnight, the victors, rejoicing in their triumph, passed the remainder of the night among the bodies of the dead. They did not, however, divide the spoil in the night, but in the meantime sought their companions, and gathering together in order to be more secure, remained all together in one place. At the coming of the morning light they became aware that many of their men had fallen in the battle, and so far as they could, they buried their bodies. They also stripped the spoil from the limbs of their enemies, but left their bodies to the beasts and birds, and returning to London, went back to their ships and sought wiser counsels. In the same way, the English and their prince also consulted their own interests, and sought the help of God in this matter, in order that they, who had been so often conquered in battle, might at least be capable of deriving support from some plan of action.

12. Eadric, who had previously withdrawn in flight from the fighting, now returned to his lord and his companions, and was received for he was an able counsellor. This man arose amid the host, and addressed all as follows : " Although I am hateful to nearly all of you, because I withdrew from the fighting, nevertheless if it were in your minds to follow my advice, you would be empowered by my counsel to become more victorious, than if you resisted these men with the forces of the whole country. For having had sufficient experience of Danish success, I know that we resist utterly in vain, and I retired from the battle to benefit you afterwards by my advice, although I was not, as you think, shaken by any fear. For since I knew that I had to flee, which was the better, to withdraw wounded or whole ? There is, admittedly, a measure of victory in escaping for the time being by flight from a stronger enemy, whom it is not possible to resist with arms. Alas, we, who are here, are all fugitives ; but to avoid this again befalling you, let us establish friendship with the Danes, in order that having them as allies, we may thus at least avoid flight and the risks of fighting. But this cannot come to pass otherwise than through a partition of our kingdom. And I consider it better that our king should have half the kingdom in peace, than that he should in despite of himself lose the whole of it at the same time."

13. These words appealed to the chief men, and although unwilling, Eadmund also signified his approval, and having chosen intermediaries, dispatched them to the ships of Knútr to conclude mutual friendship with the Danes. When the Danes first saw these men coming, they suspected that they were scouts. But after they saw that they were coming nearer, they summoned them and began asking them what they wanted. When they learned from them that they came, in point of fact, to conclude peace, they gladly conducted them to the king's presence, for they were extremely desirous of the favours of peace, being by then tired of wars and protracted seafaring. Then the messengers saluted the king pacifically and said : " Our prince and a great number of our chiefs sent us to you, oh king, that you may come to an

---

[5] *proh dolor* : this exclamation, of which, since it is an inferior reading in Liv., xxii. 14, 6, the first genuine occurrence is probably Stat., *Theb.* i. 77, is of quite remarkable frequence in Medieval Latin. It occurs again below, III, 4.

[6] *conspectibus* : for the plural of one person, cf. Mart. Cap., ix. 891, *tuisque conspectibus*, Heges., i. 42, 5, *eius conspectibus*, etc. Instances are all late. A medieval instance is *Vita Minor Stephani Regis*, 6.

multitudo, ut consentias eis de pace, et datis nobis dextris et obsidibus a nobis itidem
10 recipias cum regni medietate.   Dominare in australi *a* parte cum quiete, e regione
autem sit noster Aedmundus in finibus meridianae plagae.   Huius rei gratia ad te
sumus legati ; tu uero bene faciens placito consenti ; alioquin, licet simus semel et
iterum a uobis bello deturbati, adhuc tamen maiori uiolentia roborabimur uobiscum
bellaturi."   Quibus rex non temere respondit, sed ipsis amotis consilium a suis
15 quaesiuit, et sic eis postmodum pacifice consensit.   Audierat enim a suis, quod multi
suorum defecissent, nec erat qui locum morientium suppleret, cum longe remoti
a propria patria essent.   Anglorum quoque quamquam perplurimi interficerentur,
numerus eorum non adeo minuebatur, quia in propriis positi[s] *b* semper qui morientis
locum restauraret inueniebatur.   Reuocatis itaque internuntiis, "Uestris," inquit
20 rex, "o iuuenes, legationibus consentio, et uti dixistis media mihi libere erit regio ;
sed tamen uectigal etiam suae partis uester rex, quicumque ille fuerit, exercitui dabit
meo.   Hoc enim illi debeo, ideoque aliter pactum non laudo."

[14] Faedere itaque firmato obsides dantur ab utraque parte, et sic exercitus
solutus bel(l)orum inportunitate optata letus potitur pace.   Uerumtamen Deus
memor suae antiquae doctrinae, scilicet omne regnum in se ipsum diuisum diu
permanere non posse, non longo post tempore Aedmundum eduxit e corpore Anglorum
5 misertus imperii, ne forte si uterque superuiueret neuter regnaret secure, et regnum
diatim adnihila[re]tur renouata contentione.   Defunctus autem regius iuuenis regio
tumulatur sepulchro, defletus diu multumque a patriensi populo ; cui Deus omne
gaudium tribuat in celesti solio.   Cuius rei gratia eum Deus iusserit obire, mox
deinde patuit, quia uniuersa regio ilico Cnutonem sibi regem elegit, et cui ante omni
10 conamine [1] restitit, tunc sponte sua se illi et omnia sua subdidit.

[15] Ergo miseratione diuina monarchiam regni Cnuto uir strenuus suscepit, et
nobiliter duces et comites suos disposuit, et fine tenus deinceps regnum Anglorum
pacifice tenuit.   Erat autem adhuc primaeua aetate [2] florens sed tamen indicibili
prudentia pollens.   Unde contigit, ut eos quos antea Aedmundo sine dolo fideliter
5 militare audierat diligeret, et eos quos subdolos scierat atque tempore belli in utraque
parte fraudulenta tergiuersatione pendentes odio haberet, adeo ut multos principum
quadam die occidere pro huiusmodi dolo iuberet.   Inter quos Edricus, qui a bello
fugerat, cum praemia pro hoc ipso a rege postularet, ac si hoc pro eius uictoria
fecisset, rex subtristis, "Qui dominum", inquit, "tuum decepisti fraude, mihine
10 poteris fidelis esse ?   Rependam tibi condigna premia, sed ea ne deinceps tibi placeat
fallatia."   Et Erico duce suo uocato, "Huic", ait, "quod debemus persoluito,
uidelicet, ne nos decipiat, occidito."   Ille uero nil moratus bipennem extulit, eique

---

a australi : *so* L, P ; boreali, T (*cf. Introduction, p. lix*).
b positi[s] : *finql letter erased*, L ; positis, P, T.

---

[1] *omni conamine* : also *Miracula S. Bertini,* 44, and *Historia Norvegiae* (Storm, p. 122), for
older and more frequent *toto conamine.*
[2] *primaeua aetate* : expression used also by Odilo, *Epitaphium Adelheidae,* 8 ; Adalbold,
Vita Heinrici, 1.

agreement with them about peace, and that having given us your friendship and hostages, you may receive the same from us together with half the kingdom. Rule in the north in tranquillity, but on the contrary let our Eadmund be in the bounds of the southern area. It is to this end that we have been sent to you ; act worthily yourself, and concur with what has been agreed ; otherwise, although we have been confounded by you more than once in war, we will nevertheless be strengthened by yet greater ferocity, when we fight you in the future." The king did not answer them rashly, but sent them away and sought advice from his companions, and accordingly he afterwards came pacifically to agreement with them. For he had heard from his companions that many of their troops had been lost, and there were none to fill the place of the dead, because they were far distant from their own land. Furthermore, although many of the English had been killed, their number was not reduced by this, because on the side of those who were in their own country some one was always found to fill a dead man's place. And so, having recalled the intermediaries, the king said : " I concur, young men, with what you have communicated, and as you have said, the midlands shall be at my disposal ; but nevertheless, your king, whoever he may be, shall in addition pay tribute to my army for his part of the kingdom. For I owe him this punishment, and accordingly I do not otherwise approve the settlement."

14. Thus a treaty was concluded, and hostages were given by both parties, and so the army, being released from the troubles of war, entered gladly upon the peace which they desired. But yet God, who remembered His own ancient teaching, according to which a kingdom divided against itself cannot long stand, soon afterwards, pitying the realm of the English, took away Eadmund from the body, lest it should chance that if both survived neither should rule securely, and that the kingdom should be continually wasted by renewed conflict. The dead prince, however, was buried in a royal tomb, and was wept long and sorely by the native people ; to him may God grant every joy in the heavenly kingdom. Soon thereafter it became evident to what end God commanded that he should die, for the entire country then chose Knútr as its king, and voluntarily submitted itself and all that was in it to the man whom previously it had resisted with every effort.

15. Accordingly, by the divine mercy, Knútr, that active man, assumed the absolute rule of the kingdom, gave splendid appointments to his commanders and followers, and held the kingdom of the English until his death peacefully and uninterruptedly. He was, however, as yet in the flower of youth, but was nevertheless master of indescribable wisdom. It was, accordingly, the case that he loved those whom he had heard to have fought previously for Eadmund faithfully without deceit, and that he so hated those whom he knew to have been deceitful, and to have hesitated between the two sides with fraudulent tergiversation, that on a certain day he ordered the execution of many chiefs for deceit of this kind. One of these was Eadric, who had fled from the war, and to whom, when he asked for a reward for this from the king, pretending to have done it to ensure his victory, the king said sadly : " Shall you, who have deceived your lord with guile, be capable of being true to me ? I will return to you a worthy reward, but I will do so to the end that deception may not subsequently be your pleasure." And summoning Eiríkr, his commander, he

ictu ualido caput amputauit [1], ut hoc exemplo discant milites regibus suis esse fideles, non infideles.

[16] Omnibus itaque rite dispositis nil regi defuit absque nobilissima coniuge ; quam ubique sibi iussit inquirere, ut inuentam hanc legaliter adquireret, et adeptam imperii sui consortem faceret. Igitur per regna et per urbes discurritur, et regalis sponsa perquiritur ; sed longe [a] lateque quaesita, uix tandem digna repperitur.
5 Inuenta est uero haec imperialis sponsa in confinitate Galliae et praecipue in Normandensi regio [ne [b], stirpe [2] et opibus ditissima, sed tamen pulcritudinis et prudentiæ deleotamine omnium eius temporum [c] [3] mulierum præstantissima, utpote regina famosa. Propter huiuscemodi insignia multum appetebatur a rege, et pro hoc præcipue quod erat oriunda ex uictrici gente, quæ sibi partem Galliæ uendicauerat
10 inuitis Francigenis et eorum principe. Quid multis immoror ? Mittuntur proci ad dominam, mittuntur dona regalia [4], mittuntur etiam uerba precatoria. Sed abnegat illa, se unquam Cnutonis sponsam fieri, nisi illi [d] iusiurando affirmaret, quod numquam alterius coniugis filium post se regnare faceret nisi eius, si forte illi Deus ex eo filium dedisset. Dicebatur enim ab alia quadam rex filios habuisse ; unde illa suis
15 prudenter prouidens sciuit ipsis sagaci animo profutura præordinare. Placuit ergo regi uerbum uirginis, et iusiurando facto uirgini placuit uoluntas regis,] et sic Deo gratias domina Emma mulierum nobilissima fit coniunx regis fortis[s]imi Cnutonis. Leta⟨e⟩tur Gallia, letatur etiam Anglorum patria, dum tantum [e] decus transuehitur per aequora. Letatur, inquam, Gallia, tantam tanto regi dignam se enixam,
20 Anglorum uero letatur patria, talem se recepisse in oppida. O res millenis milies petita uotis, uixque tandem effecta auspicante [f] gratia Saluatoris. Hoc erat quod utrobique uehementer iam dudum desiderauerat exercitus, scilicet ut tanta tanto, digna etiam digno, maritali conuinculata iugo, bellicos sedaret motus. Quid enim maius ac desiderabilius esse posset in uotis quam dampnosos ingratosque labores
25 belli placida finiri tranquillitate pacis, cum pares paribus ui corporis uirtuteque animi concurrerent, cumque nunc hi nunc uero illi alternanti [g] [5] casu belli non sine magno detrimento sui uincerent ?

[17] Uerum ubi diuina dispensatione multisque alterutrum diu habitis inter-

---

[a] longe : *corrected from* longae *by subpunctuation of* a, L.
[b] [ne . . . regis] : *this passage is present in P and T, but the leaf on which it stood has been lost in* L. *The text follows* C, *from which* V *differs in details of spelling only. I print* u *for the initial* v *of* C.
[c] temporum : *so* P, T (*cf. Linguistic Note*).
[d] illi : *so* P, T (*cf. Textual Note on 7*). iusiurando : *so* (*here and* 16) P, T (*cf. III*, 1, 16).
[e] tantum : tantus, L, *corrected by* L′.
[f] auspicante : aspirante, P, *perhaps rightly, cf.* II, 17, 12.
[g] alternanti : alternante, L′; alternatim, P.

---

[1] eique . . . caput amputauit : so Suet., *Galb.* 20, but *amputo* is constructed with dat. of disadvantage in the *Vulgate*, as 2 *Mach.* vii. 4.
[2] stirpe, etc. : Gertz unnecessarily adds *nobilissima* after *stirpe* ; but cf. Cic., *Off.* ii. 16, 57, *cum cognomine diues tum copiis.*
[3] temporum : Gertz reads *temporis* here and *ille.*below to soften the neglect of reflexive forms, but this is not unusual in the *Encomium*, see Introduction, p. xxv.
[4] dona regalia : a set medieval collocation, e.g., Thegan, *Vita Hludowici*, 42.

said : " Pay this man what we owe him ; that is to say, kill him, lest he play us
false." He, indeed, raised his axe without delay, and cut off his head with a mighty
blow, so that soldiers may learn from this example to be faithful, not faithless, to
their kings.

16. Everything having been thus duly settled, the king lacked nothing except a
most noble wife ; such a one he ordered to be sought everywhere for him, in order to
obtain her hand lawfully, when she was found, and to make her the partner of his rule,
when she was won. Therefore journeys were undertaken through realms and cities and
a royal bride was sought ; but it was with difficulty that a worthy one was ultimately
found, after being sought far and wide. This imperial bride was, in fact, found within
the bounds of Gaul, and to be precise in the Norman area, a lady of the greatest
nobility and wealth, but yet the most distinguished of the women of her time for
delightful beauty and wisdom, inasmuch as she was a famous queen. In view of her
distinguished qualities of this kind, she was much desired by the king, and especially
because she derived her origin from a victorious people, who had appropriated for
themselves part of Gaul, in despite of the French and their prince. Why should I
make a long story of this ? Wooers were sent to the lady, royal gifts were sent,
furthermore precatory messages were sent. But she refused ever to become the bride
of Knútr, unless he would affirm to her by oath, that he would never set up the son
of any wife other than herself to rule after him, if it happened that God should give
her a son by him. For she had information that the king had had sons by some
other woman ; so she, wisely providing for her offspring, knew in her wisdom how to
make arrangements in advance, which were to be to their advantage. Accordingly
the king found what the lady said acceptable, and when the oath had been taken,
the lady found the will of the king acceptable, and so, thanks be to God, Emma
noblest of women, became the wife of the very mighty King Knútr. Gaul rejoiced,
the land of the English rejoiced likewise, when so great an ornament was conveyed
over the seas. Gaul, I say, rejoiced to have brought forth so great a lady, and one
worthy of so great a king, the country of the English indeed rejoiced to have received
such a one into its towns. What an event, sought with a million prayers, and at
length barely brought to pass under the Saviour's favouring grace ! This was what
the army had long eagerly desired on both sides, that is to say that so great a lady,
bound by a matrimonial link to so great a man, worthy of her husband as he was
worthy of her, should lay the disturbances of war to rest. What greater or more
desirable thing could be wished than that the accursed and loathsome troubles of war
should be ended by the gentle calm of peace, when equals were clashing with equals in
might of body and boldness of heart, and when now the one side and now the
other was victorious, though at great loss to itself, by the changing fortunes of
war ?

17. But when by the divine dispensation they at length after frequent and
protracted interchange of emissaries decided to be joined by the marital link, it is

---

⁵ *alternante* : The Encomiast uses both -*e* and -*i* in the abl. sing. of participles in -*nt*- and
comparatives in -*ior*- : examples with -*e* are frequent, cases with -*i* are II, 7, *sequenti* ; II, 8,
aptiori ; II, 10, *eminentiori, fortiori* ; II, 12, *fortiori* ; II, 23, *maiori*. He would find authority
for such forms in his favourite poets Virgil and Lucan (e.g., *Aen.* i. 71, *praestanti* ; Luc. vii. 161,
maiori ; ix. 996, *priori*), and they are of course common in medieval writers.

nuntiis [1] maritali se tandem copula placuit confederari, difficile creditu est, quanta repente in utrisque alteri de altero exorta sit magnitudo gaudii [2].   Gaudebat enim rex, nobilissimis insperato se usum thalamis ;   haec autem hinc prestantissima 5 uirtute coniugis, hinc etiam spe gratulabunda acce(n)debatur futurae prolis. Ineffabiliter quoque uterque gaudebat exercitus opes suas communibus sperans augendas uiribus, ut rei postmodum probauit exitus.   Quam plures enim populi domiti bello, gentesque complures longe distantes uita, moribus, etiam et lingua, aeternaliter regi regiaeque poster[i]tati [a] annua compulsi [b] [3] sunt soluere uectigalia ! 10 Sed quid mirum, si tantus talisque rex repugnantes sibi dimicando deuinceret, cum quam plurimos partim liberali largitione partim patrocinandi gratia imperio suo ultroneos submitteret ?   Profecto non mirum, quoniam illic diuina aspirat gratia, ubi [i]ustitiae [c] probitatisque aequa libratur trutina.

[18] Sed quid multis immoror [4] ?   Gaudium magnum in coniugatione tantorum dixi fuisse, multo autem amplius dico, suscepta masculae prolis [d] oportunitate.   Non multo post siquidem Saluatoris annuente gratia filium peperit nobilissima regina. Cuius cum uterque parens intima atque ut ita dicam singulari gauderet dilectione, 5 alios uero liberales filios educandos direxerunt Normanniae, istum hunc retinentes sibi, utpote futurum heredem regni.   Itaque dilectissimum pignus, uti mos est Catholicis, sacro abluunt [e] fonte baptismatis, imponuntque ei uocabulum quodammodo optinens indicium futurae uirtutis.   Uocatur siquidem Hardocnuto, nomen patris referens cum additamento, cuius si ethimologia Theutonice perquiratur, 10 profecto quis quantusue fuerit dinoscitur.   ' Harde ' [5] quidem ' uelox ' uel ' fortis ' [6], quod utrumque, multoque maius his, in eo uno cognosci potuit, quippe qui omnes sui temporis uiros om[n]ium uirtutum prestantia anteiuit.   Omnes igitur eius uirtutes enumerare nequeo ;   quapropter, ne longius a proposito exorbitem, supra repetam historieque sequar ordinem.

[19] Adulto denique puero de quo sermo agitur pater adhuc in omni felicitate degens omne regnum suae dicioni subiectum sacramento deuinxit, eumque postmodum ad optinendam monarchiam regni Danorum cum delectis militibus misit. Cum autem rex Cnuto solum in primis [7] Danorum optineret regimen, quinque 5 regnorum, scilicet Danomarchiae, Angliae, Britanniae, Scothiae, Norduuegae uendicato dominio, imperator extitit.   Amicus uero et familiaris factus est uiris ecclesiasticis, adeo ut episcopis uideretur coepiscopus pro exibitione totius religionis,

---

[a] poster[i]tati : postestari, L ; potestati, P.
[b] compulsi : *so* L, P (*cf. Linguistic Note*).
[c] [i]ustitiae : ustitiae, L.
[d] prolis : *corrected from* proles, L ; proles, P.
[e] abluunt : *second* u *corrected from letter now illegible,* L ; abluunt, P.

---

[1] *habitis internuntiis* : ' messengers having been exchanged ' ;   for the force of *habitis*, cf. Cic., *Rep.* vi. 9, *multisque uerbis ultro citroque habitis.*
[2] *magnitudo gaudii* : also Hier., *In Ier.* xxx. 4.
[3] *compulsi* : in agreement with the more remote subject, *populi.*
[4] *quid multis immoror* : an expression of great frequency in Christian Latin ;   it occurs also above, II, 16.
[5] ' *Harde* ' :   for a discussion of the etymology of this name-element here offered by the Encomiast, and of the reason which he gives for the name chosen for the prince see the Additional Notes in Appendix V.

hard to credit how vast a magnitude of delight in one another arose in them both. For the king rejoiced that he had unexpectedly entered upon a most noble marriage ; the lady, on the other hand, was inspired both by the excellence of her husband, and by the delightful hope of future offspring.   Both armies also rejoiced indescribably, looking forward to increasing their possessions by joining forces, which was how events afterwards turned out.   For very many peoples were subdued in war, and very many nations extremely diverse in habits, customs and speech were permanently compelled to pay annual tribute to the king and to his royal issue.   But what wonder if so great a king as we describe should conquer in war those resisting him, since he brought under his sway very many peoples of their own free will, partly by his munificent bounty, and partly because they desired his protection ?   None indeed, for the divine grace bestows its favour where the scale of justice and uprightness is evenly adjusted.

18. But why should I protract the matter ?   I have said that there was great joy at the union of such great persons ; but I declare that there was much greater at the achievement of the advantage of a male offspring.   For indeed soon afterwards it was granted by the Saviour's grace that the most noble queen bore a son.   The two parents, happy in the most profound and, I might say, unparalleled love for this child, sent in fact their other legitimate sons to Normandy to be brought up, while keeping this one with themselves, inasmuch as he was to be the heir to the kingdom. And so they washed this very dear child, as is the custom of all Christians, in the sacred baptismal font, and gave him a name which conveyed in a measure an indication of his future excellence.   For indeed he was called Hörthaknútr, which reproduced his father's name with an addition, and if the etymology of this is investigated in Germanic, one truly discerns his identity and greatness.   ' Harde ', indeed, means ' swift ' or ' strong ', both of which qualities and much more could be recognised in him above all others, for he excelled all the men of his time by superiority in all high qualities.   Therefore I cannot enumerate all his excellencies ; accordingly, lest I wander too far from my theme, I will revert to where I was before and follow the course of my story.

19. When at last the boy to whom we refer grew up, his father, who was still living in the enjoyment of every happiness, pledged to him the whole realm which was subject to his command, and subsequently sent him with chosen troops to secure the rule of the kingdom of the Danes.   When, however, King Knútr first obtained the absolute rule of the Danes, he was Emperor of five kingdoms, for he had established claim to the rule of Denmark, England, Wales, Scotland and Norway.   He indeed became a friend and intimate of churchmen, to such a degree that he seemed to be a brother bishop for his maintenance of perfect religion, to monks also

---

⁶ ' uelox ' uel ' fortis ' : Gertz supplies *ualet* after these words, but this spoils the rhyme with *his* : it seems more likely that the Encomiast has here left the verbal idea to be supplied. *in eo uno* : ' in him above all others ' ; *Aen.* v. 704, *unum Tritonia Pallas quem docuit.*

⁷ *in primis* : Gertz in his translation assumes that the idea of the passage is, that at first Knútr held Denmark only, but that he ultimately secured the various other realms.   The Encomiast, however, knew perfectly well that Knútr became king of England while his brother was still king of Denmark, and, in any event, the sentence will not bear the meaning given to it by Gertz, but in fact implies that when Knútr first became king of Denmark, he found himself ruler of five countries.   On the historical aspect of the matter, see Introduction, p. lxii.

monachis quoque non secularis sed caenobialis pro continentia humillimae deuotionis. Defensabat sedulo pupillos et uiduas, sustentabat orphanos et aduenas, leges
10 oppressit iniquas earumque sequaces, iustitiam et equitatem extulit et coluit, ecclesias extruxit et honorauit, sacerdotes et clerum dignitatibus ampliauit, pacem et unanimitatem om[n]ibus suis indixit, ut de eo illud Maronicum dici posset, nisi extra Catholicam fidem (hoc) *a* fuisset :

> Nocte pluit tota, redeunt spectacula ma̧(ne) ;
> Diuisum imperium cum Ioue Cesar habes.

[20] Deo omni(modis) *b* placita studuit, ideoque quicquid boni agendum esse didicerat non negligentiae sed operationi committebat. Quae enim ecclesia adhuc eius non letatur donis ? Sed ut sileam quae in suo regno positis egerit, huius animam cotidie benedicit Italia, bonis perfrui deposcit Gallia, et magis omnibus hanc in caelo
5 cum Christo gaudere orat Flandria. Has enim prouintias transiens Romam petiit et, ut multis liquet, tanta hoc in itinere misericordiarum [1] opera exibuit, ut, si quis haec describere omnia uoluerit, licet innumerabilia ex his fecerit uolumina, tandem deficiens fatebitur, se uix etiam cucurrisse per minima. Nam quid singulis in locis fecerit sileo ; uerumtamen, ut credibiliora fiant quae assero, quid in una urbe
10 Sancti Audomari [2] fecerit dicam pro exemplo, quod etiam oculis meis me uidisse recordor.

[21] Ingressus monasteria et susceptus cum magna honorificencia humiliter incedebat, et mira cum reuerentia in terram defixus lumina et ubertim fundens lacrimarum ut ita dicam flumina [3] tota intentione [4] sanctorum expetiit suffragia. At ubi ad hoc peruentum est, ut oblationibus regiis sacra uellet cumulare altaria, o quotiens primum
5 pauimento lacrimosa infixit oscula, quotiens illud pectus uenerabile propria puniebant uerbera, qualia dabat suspiria, quotiens precabatur ut sibi non indignaretur superna clementia ! Tandem a suis ei innuenti sua porrigebatur oblatio, non mediocris, nec quae aliquo clauderetur in marsupio, sed ingens allata est palleati *c* extento in gremio, quam ipse rex suis manibus altari imposuit, largitor hilaris monitu
10 apostolico. "Altari" autem cur dico, cum uidisse me meminerim, eum omnes angulos monasteriorum circuisse, nullumque altare licet exiguum preterisse, cui non munera daret et dulcia oscula infigeret ? Deinde adsunt pauperes, munerantur etiam ipsi protinus singulatim omnes. Haec et alia his mirificentiora a domno Cnutone gesta uidi ego, uester uernula, Sancte Audomare, Sancte Bertine, cum
15 fierent uestris in caenobiis ; pro quibus bonis tantum regem impetrate uiuere in caelestibus habitaculis, ut uestri famuli canonici et monachi sunt orantes orationibus cotidianis.

a hoc *added above the line,* L ; *in text,* P.
b omni(modis) : *corrected from* omnibus, L ; omnibus modis, P.
c palleati : *so* L, P.

[1] *misericordiarum* : this plural, like those of other abstract nouns, is common in the *Vulgate*.
[2] *urbe Sancti Audomari* : this expression is, no doubt, already fully a place-name : L. Deschamps de Pas, *Histoire de . . . . Saint-Omer* (Arras, 1880), p. 1, quotes *castellum S. Audomari* as a form of the name already from the tenth century, and in the *Vita Aeduuardi* (Luard, *Lives of Edward the Confessor,* p. 424) the town is said to be named after the saint ; cf. *Old English Chronicle,* C 1065, D 1067, *æt* (*to) Sce Audomare.*

not a secular but a monk for the temperance of his life of most humble devotion. He diligently defended wards and widows, he supported orphans and strangers, he suppressed unjust laws and those who applied them, he exalted and cherished justice and equity, he built and dignified churches, he loaded priests and the clergy with dignities, he enjoined peace and unanimity upon his people, so that if it were not an infringement of the Catholic faith, that Virgilian saying might be quoted with reference to him :

> It rains all night, but the public games duly take place in the morning ;
> You, Caesar, hold divided empire with Jove.

20. He gave his attention entirely to things pleasing to God, and therefore he did not abandon to neglect any good thing which he had found to require doing, but set it in train. Consequently what church does not still rejoice in his gifts ? But to say nothing of what he did for those in his own kingdom, Italy blesses his soul every day, Gaul begs that it may enjoy benefits, and Flanders, above all, prays that it may rejoice in heaven with Christ. For he went to Rome by way of these countries, and as appears from many things, he displayed on this journey such great charitable activities, that if anyone should wish to describe them all, although he might make innumerable volumes out of these matters, at length he will admit in failure that he has not covered even the least ones. For I will not speak of what he did in separate places, but in order that what I assert may become more credible I will as an example tell what he did in the city of St. Omer alone, and I place on record that I saw this with my own eyes.

21. When he had entered the monasteries, and had been received with great honour, he advanced humbly, and with complete concentration prayed for the intercession of the saints in a manner wonderfully reverent, fixing his eyes upon the ground, and freely pouring forth, so to speak, rivers of tears. But when the time came when he desired to heap the holy altars with royal offerings, how often did he first with tears press kisses on the pavement, how often did self-inflicted blows punish that revered breast, what signs he gave, how often did he pray that the heavenly mercy might not be displeased with him ! At length, when he gave the sign, his offering was presented to him by his followers, not a mean one, nor such as might be shut in any bag, but a man brought it, huge as it was, in the ample fold of his cloak, and this the king himself placed on the altar with his own hand, a cheerful giver according to the apostolic exhortation. But why do I say on the altar, when I recall that I saw him going round every corner of the monasteries, and passing no altar, small though it might be, without giving gifts and pressing sweet kisses upon it ? Then poor men came and were all forthwith given gifts one by one. These things and others more wonderful were seen done by the lord Knútr by me, who am your servant, St. Omer and St. Bertin, when they came to pass in your monasteries ! And for these benefits, cause so great a king to live in the heavenly dwellings, as your inmates, both canons and monks, pray in their daily supplications.

---

[3] *lacrimarum . . . . flumina* : this expression, for which the Encomiast, despite his wealth of poetical language, offers an apology, is frequent, but late : see *Thes.*, s.v. *flumen*, col. 966 ; medieval occurrences are the ' Astronomer ', *Vita Hludowici*, 63, and Odilo, *Epitaphium Adalheidae*, 15.

[4] *tota intentione* : cf. Odilo, *Vita Maioli* (*Patrologia*, cxlii. 950), *tota mentis intentione*.

manoeuvre

[22] Discant igitur reges et principes huius domini imitari acciones, qui ut ualeret scandere sublimia sese humiliauit in infima, et ut posset adipisci caelestia hilariter largitus est terrestria. Non enim fuerat oblitus propriae conditionis modum, quod moriturus erat in mundo et relicturus quaeque possunt concupisci in seculo ; 5 et ob hoc diuicias, quas secum nequiuit moriens auferre, uiuens Deo et sanctis eius locis partitus est honorifice, ne forte, si auariciae studeret, omnibus inuisus uiueret, nullusque esset qui eius animae aliquid boni oraret, et alius ei succederet, qui in eius regno largus *a* uiueret et de eius parcitate indignaretur. Uerum hoc ne fieret satis cauit, et suis posteris bonum exemplum largitatis totiusque bonitatis reliquit, quod 10 et ipsi adhuc Deo gratias seruant, optime pollentes in regni moderamine et in uirtutum decore.

[23] Tantus itaque rex, postquam Roma est reuersus, et in proprio regno aliquantisper demoratus, omnibus bene dispositis transiit ad Dominum, coronandus in parte dextera ab ipso Domino auctore omnium. Turbabantur itaque eius obitu omnes qui audierant, maximeque qui eius solio deseruierant, quorum maxima pars 5 cuperet ei commori, si hoc non displiceret diuinae dispositioni.

[24] Lugebat domina Emma eius regina cum patriensibus, ulu(labant) pauperes cum potentibus, flebant episcopi et clerici cum monachis et sanctimonialibus ; sed quantum lugebatur [1] in mundo, tantum letetur in caeli palatio. Isti flebant hoc quod perdiderant, illi gratulentur de eius anima quam suscipiant. Isti sepelierunt 5 corpus exanime, illi spiritum deducant in sublime letandum [2] in aeterna requie. Pro eius transitu soli flebant terreni, sed pro eius spiritu interueniant cum terrenis etiam ciues caelici. Ut eius gloria crescat cotidie, oremus Deum intente ; et, quia hoc promeruit sua bonitate, cotidie clamemus, " Anima Cnutonis requiescat in pace. Amen."

[III]

[1] Mortuo Cnutone rege honorificeque sepulto in monasterio in honore Sancti Petri constructo [Wyntonie] *b* [3], domina regina Emma sola remansit in regno dolens de domini sui morte amara et sol(l)icita pro filiorum absentia. Namque unus eorum, Hardecnuto scilicet, quem pater regem Danorum constituit, suo morabatur in regno, 5 duo uero alii in Normanniae finibus ad nutriendum traditi cum propinquo suo degebant Rotberto. Unde factum est, ut quidam Anglorum pietatem regis sui iam defuncti obliti mallent regnum suum dedecorare quam ornare, relinquentes nobiles filios insignis reginae Emmae et eligentes sibi in regem quendam Haroldum, quem

a largus : *corrected from* largos, L.
b [Wyntonie] : *so* P ; *one and a half lines erased,* L ; *blank sufficient for about four words,* V ; *loss not indicated,* C ; *the erasure in L was evidently made before Talbot copied the text, but probably later than the activity of the earlier of the two annotators, who writes in the margin* Cnutus iacet apud Wyntoniam.

---

[1] *lugebatur . . . . letetur :* in view of the *isti . . . illi* of the sentences which follow, these verbs are not to be taken personally, ' let him rejoice as much as he was lamented ', but impersonally. This is a normal use of the passive of *lugeo* (e.g., Cat., 39, 5), but is a trifle uneasy with the deponent *letor.*

[2] *spiritum . . . . letandum :* ' let them lead his spirit aloft, to be rejoiced over in everlasting rest '. For the gerundive of *letor* used with the accusative of the direct object, cf. Sall., *Iug.* xiv. 22, *laetandum . . . . . casum tuum* ; on the late use of the gerundive to supply the wanting

22. Therefore let kings and princes learn to imitate the actions of this lord, who lowered himself to the depths that he might be able to climb the heights, and who cheerfully gave earthly things in order to be able to obtain heavenly ones. For he was not forgetful of the nature of his own condition, that he was to die in the world, and to leave whatever things can be desired in mortal life ; and because of this while alive he distributed honourably to God and his holy places the wealth which he could not take with him at death, lest perhaps if he acted avariciously, he should live hateful to all, and there might be no man who would pray for any good thing for his soul, and another would succeed him, who would live prodigally in his kingdom, and be disgusted at his parsimony. Truly he took good care that this should not happen, and left his posterity a good example of munificence and all benevolence, which they also, thanks be to God, still follow, being in a high degree mighty in their management of the kingdom and by the grace of their virtues.

23. And so this great king, after he had returned from Rome, and had lingered in his own kingdom some little time, having well arranged all matters, passed to the Lord, to be crowned upon his right hand by God himself the creator of all. Therefore all who had heard of his death were moved, and especially his own subjects, of whom the majority would have wished to die with him, if this would not have been at variance with the divine plan.

24. The Lady Emma, his queen, mourned together with the natives, poor and rich lamented together, the bishops and clerics wept with the monks and nuns ; but let the rejoicing in the kingdom of heaven be as great as was the mourning in the world ! These wept for what they had lost, but let those rejoice over his soul, which they take to themselves. These buried his lifeless body, but let those lead his spirit aloft to be rejoiced over in everlasting rest. Mortals alone wept for his departure, but for his spirit let the heavenly citizens as well as mortals intercede. Let us earnestly pray God that his glory may increase from day to day ; and since he has deserved this by his benevolence, let us pray every day : ' May the soul of Knútr rest in peace. Amen.'

BOOK III

1. When Knútr was dead and honourably buried in the monastery built at Winchester in honour of St. Peter, the lady, Queen Emma, remained alone in the kingdom, sorrowing for the bitter death of her lord and alarmed at the absence of her sons. For one of them, namely Hörthaknútr, whom his father had made king of the Danes, was in his own kingdom, and two others were residing with their relative Robert, for they had been sent to the country of Normandy to be brought up. And so it came to pass that certain Englishmen, forgetting the piety of their lately deceased king, preferred to dishonour their country than to ornament it, and deserted the noble sons of the excellent Queen Emma, choosing as their king one Haraldr, who is declared,

future participle passive, see Stolz-Schmalz, pp. 447, 556, 597. *corpus examine* : the expression, which occurs again below, III, 6, 17, is as frequent in the medieval as the classical period : e.g., Dudo (ed. Duchesne, p. 105) ; *Vita Mahthildis*, 8 ; Ruotger, *Vita Brunonis*, 48.

³ [*Wyntonie*] : it would be better for rhyme to place this word before *constructo*, but a whole clause may be lost : cf. Textual Note.

esse filium falsa aestimatione asseritur cuiusdam eiusdem regis Cnutonis concubinae;
10 plurimorum uero assertio eundem Haroldum perhibet furtim fuisse subreptum
parturienti ancillae, inpositum autem camerae languentis co(n)cubinae, quod
ueratius credi potest. Qui electus metuensque futuri aduocat mox archiepiscopum
Aelnotum, uirum omni uirtute et sapientia preditum, imperatque et orat se benedici
in regem, sibique tradi cum corona regale suae custodiae commissum sceptrum, et se
15 duci ab eodem, quia ab alio non fas fuerat, in sublime regni solium. Abnegat archiepiscopus *a*, sub iureiurando asserens se neminem alium in regem filiis reg(i)nae
Emmae uiuentibus laudarè uel benedicere [1]: " Hos meae fidei Cnuto commisit ;
his fidem *b* debeo, et his fidelitatem seruabo. Sceptrum, coronam sacro altari
impono, et hec *c* tibi nec denego nec trado ; sed episcopis omnibus, ne quis eorum
20 ea tollat tibiue tradat teue benedicat, apostolica autoritate interdico ; tu uero, si
presumis, quod Deo mensaeque eius commisi inuadito ! " Quid miser ageret, quo
se uerteret, ignorabat. Intentabat minas et nihil profecit, spondebat munera et nil
lucratus doluit, quoniam uir apostolicus nec ualebat minis deici nec muneribus
(flecti) *d*. Tandem desperatus abcessit *e 2*, et episcopalem benedictionem adeo
25 spreuit, ut non solum ipsam odiret benedictionem, uerum etiam uniuersam fugeret
Christianitatis religionem. Namque, dum alii aecclesiam Christiano more missam
audire subintrarent, ipse aut saltus canibus ad uenandum cinxit, aut quibuslibet aliis
uilissimis rebus sese occupauit, ut tantum declinare posset quod odiuit. Quod Angli
uidentes dolebant ; sed, quia hunc sibi regem elegerant, hunc erubuerunt deicere,
30 ideoque disposuerunt hunc sibi regem fine tenus esse.

[2] Domina autem regni Emma tacite exitum rei exspectabat, et aliquantisper
sollicita auxilium Dei cotidie exorabat. At ille clam, quia nondum palam audebat,
reginae insidias moliebatur, sed ut illi noceret a nemine permittebatur. Unde ille
cum suis iniquo excogitato consilio [3] natos dominae suae uolebat interficere, ut sic
5 securus deinceps in peccatis uiuens posset regnare. Uerumtamen nullum in hoc
omnimodis effectum acciperet [4], nisi fraudulentorum dolo adiutus hoc quod narra-
bimus adinueniret. Namque dolo reperto fecit epistolam in persona [5] reginae ad
filios eiusdem, qui in Nordmannia morabantur, componere, cuius etiam exemplar
non piget nobis subnectere :

[3] Emma tantum nomine regina filiis Aeduardo et Alfrido materna
impertit salutamina. Dum domini nostri regis obitum separatim plangimus,
filii karissimi [6], dumque diatim magis magisque regno hereditatis uestrae

---

a archiepiscopus : *written twice, the first writing of it erased,* L.
b fidem : *erasure after this word,* L.
c hec : hoc, L, P.
d (flecti) : *in lower margin,* L ; *in text,* P.
e abcessit : *so* L, P, V (*see Linguistic Note*).

---

[1] *laudare uel benedicere* : infinitives present for future ; Gertz eases the construction by
inserting *uelle* after *laudare,* but cf. below, III, 11, where *deserere* is for *deserturum esse.*
[2] *abcessit* : a genuine spelling (see, e.g., Monk of St. Gall, *Gesta Karoli,* ii, 12, Sig. Gemblac.,
Vita Deoderici, 16), though Duchesne and Gertz normalise.
[3] *iniquo . . consilio* : a rare collocation, cf. Aug., *De Civ. Dei,* xx. 19, 4, *iniquo malignoque
consilio,* which was perhaps echoing in Pertz's mind when he mis-copied *iniquo* as *maligno* in the
passage under discussion.

owing to a false estimation of the matter, to be a son of a certain concubine of the above-mentioned King Knútr; as a matter of fact, the assertion of very many people has it that the same Haraldr was secretly taken from a servant who was in childbed, and put in the chamber of the concubine, who was indisposed; and this can be believed as the more truthful account. Soon after being chosen, this man, fearing for the future, summoned Archbishop Æthelnoth, a man gifted with high courage and wisdom, and commanded and prayed to be consecrated king, and that the royal sceptre, which was committed to the archbishop's custody, should be given to him together with the crown, and that he should be led by the archbishop, since it was not legal that this should be done by another, to the lofty throne of the kingdom. The archbishop refused, declaring by oath that while the sons of Queen Emma lived he would approve or consecrate no other man as king: " Them Knútr entrusted to my good faith; to them I owe fidelity, and with them I shall maintain faith. I lay the sceptre and crown upon the holy altar, and to you I neither refuse nor give them; but by my apostolic authority, I forbid all bishops that any one of them should remove these things, or give them to you or consecrate you. As for you, if you dare, lay hands upon what I have committed to God and his table." He, wretched man, did not know what to do or whither to turn. He used threats and it did not avail him, he promised gifts and sorrowed to gain nothing, for that apostolic man could not be dislodged by threats or diverted by gifts. At length he departed in despair, and so despised the episcopal benediction, that he hated not only the benediction itself, but indeed even turned from the whole Christian religion. For when others entered church to hear mass, as is the Christian custom, he either surrounded the glades with dogs for the chase, or occupied himself with any other utterly paltry matters, wishing only to be able to avoid what he hated. When the English observed his behaviour they sorrowed, but since they had chosen him to be their king, they were ashamed to reject him, and accordingly decided that he should be their king to the end.

2. But Emma, the queen of the kingdom, silently awaited the end of the matter, and for some little time was in her anxiety daily gaining God's help by prayer. But the usurper was secretly laying traps for the queen, since as yet he dared not act openly, but he was allowed to hurt her by nobody. Accordingly, he devised an unrighteous scheme with his companions, and proposed to kill the children of his lady, that henceforth he might be able to reign in security and live in his sins. He would, however, have effected nothing whatever in this matter if, helped by the deceit of fraudulent men, he had not devised what we are about to narrate. For having hit upon a trick, he had a letter composed as if from the queen to her sons, who were resident in Normandy, and of this I do not hesitate to subjoin a copy:

3. ' Emma, queen in name only, imparts motherly salutation to her sons, Eadweard and Ælfred. Since we severally lament the death of our lord, the king, most dear sons, and since daily you are deprived more and more of the kingdom, your inheritance, I wonder what plan you are adopting, since you are

---

[4] *nullum . . . . effectum acciperet*: i.e., *nihil efficeret*; for this late use of *accipere* + abstract noun to form periphrastic tenses; see Stolz-Schmalz, p. 790.

[5] *in persona*: ' in the name of '.

[6] *karissimi*: this superlative is often spelled with *k* in the period, especially when vocative: e.g., *Vita Mahthildis*, 14, etc.; Odilo, *Epitaphium Adalheidae*, 18; *Miracula S. Bertini*, 44.

priuamini, miror quid captetis consilii, dum sciatis intermissionis uestrae
5 dilationem inuasoris uestri imperii fieri cotidie soliditatem [a]. Is enim incessanter
uicos et urbes circuit, et sibi amicos principes muneribus, minis et precibus facit ;
sed unum e uobis super se mallent regnare, quam istius qui nunc eis imperat
teneri ditione. Unde, rogo, unus uestrum ad me uelociter et priuate [b] ueniat,
ut salubre a me consilium accipiat, et sciat quo pacto hoc negotium, quod uolo,
10 fieri debeat. Per presentem quemquam internuntium, quid super his facturi
estis, remandate. Ualete, cordis mei uiscera.

[4] Hac fraude iussu Haroldi tyranni composita, regiis adulescentulis est directa
per pellaces cursores eisque ex parte [1] matris ignarae oblata et honorifice ab eis, ut
munus genitricis, suscepta. Legunt dolos eius nescii, et proh dolor nimis falsitati
creduli inconsulte remandant genitrici, unum eorum ad eam esse uenturum, con-
5 stituuntque ei diem et tempus et locum. Regres[s]i itaque legatarii intimant Dei
inimicis quae sibi responsa reddita sint a iuuenibus nobilissimis. Hinc illi prestolabantur eius aduentum, et quid de eo facerent ad suum inuenerunt detrimentum.
Statuto ergo die Alfridus, minor natu, laudante fratre elegit sibi commilitones, et
arripiens iter [2] Flandriae uenit in fines ; quo paululum cum marchione Balduino
10 moratus et ab eo rogatus, ut aliquam partem suae miliciae secum duceret propter
insidias hostium, noluit ; sed tantum Bononiensium paucos assumpsit et ascensis
puppibus mare transfretauit. At ubi litori uenit contiguus mox ab aduersariis est
agnitus. Qui occurrentes uolebant eum adgredi, sed statim ille agnoscens iussit
naues a litore illo repelli. Alia autem ascendens in statione matrem parabat adire,
15 estimans se omnem insidiarum [c] pestem euasisse. Uerum ubi iam erat proximus,
illi [3] comes Goduinus est obuius factus, et eum in sua suscepit fide, eiusque fit mox
miles cum sacramenti affirmatione. Et deuians eum a Londonia induxit eum in
uilla [Geldefordia] [d] nuncupata, inibique milites [e] eius uicenos et duodenos
decenosque [f] singula duxit per hospicia, paucis relictis cum iuuene, qui eius seruitio
20 deberent insistere. Et largitus est eis habundanter cibaria et pocula, et ipse ad sua
recessit hospicia, mane rediturus, ut domino suo seruiret cum debita honorificentia.

[5] Sed postquam manducauerant et biberant, et lectos, utpote fessi, libenter
ascenderant, ecce complices Haroldi infandissimi tiranni adsunt, et singula hospicia
inuadunt, arma innocentum [g] [4] uirorum furtim tollunt et eos manicis ferreis et
compedibus artant, et ut crucientur in crastinum seruant. Mane autem facto
5 adducuntur insontes in medio et non auditi dampnantur scelerose. Nam omnium

---

[a] soliditatem : *erasure between sixth and seventh letters,* L.
[b] priuate : *so* L, P (*cf. Introduction, p. xvi*).
[c] insidiarum : *corrected from* insidiorum, L. Uerum ubi : *erasure between these words,* L ;
blank space, V.
[d] [Geldefordia] : *so* L, *but in a different hand and ink* ; Gildefordia, P, T.
[e] milites : *corrected from* millites *by deletion of the second* l, L'.
[f] duodenos decenosque : denos et duodenos, P.
[g] innocentum : *so* L, P (*cf. III,* 6, 21, *and Linguistic Note*).

---

[1] *ex parte* : used for the classical *ex persona*.
[2] *arripiens iter* : a frequent collocation, perhaps first Stat., *Theb.* i. 100.
[3] *proximus, illi,* etc. : I place the comma after *proximus* with Pertz, rather than after *illi*
with Gertz, as it is better for the rhyme for *proximus* to end a clause. Gertz's punctuation gives
better syntax, however, for it supplies a word for *proximus* to govern, and there is no objection
to the absolute use of *obuius fieri* which it involves, for this occurs again below, III, 13.

aware that the delay arising from your proscrastination is becoming from day to day a support to the usurper of your rule. For he goes round hamlets and cities ceaselessly, and makes the chief men his friends by gifts, threats and prayers. But they would prefer that one of you should rule over them, than that they should be held in the power of him who now commands them. I entreat, therefore, that one of you come to me speedily and privately, to receive from me wholesome counsel, and to know in what manner this matter, which I desire, must be brought to pass. Send back word what you are going to do about these matters by the present messenger, whoever he may be. Farewell, beloved ones of my heart.'*

4. This forgery, when it had been composed at the command of Haraldr the tyrant, was sent to the royal youths by means of deceitful couriers, presented to them as being from their unwitting mother, and received by them with honour, as a gift from their parent. They read its wiles in their innocence, and alas too trustful of the fabrication, they unwisely replied to their parent that one of them would come to her, and determined upon day and time and place for her. The messengers, accordingly, returned and told the foes of God what answer had been made to them by the most noble youths. And so they awaited the prince's arrival, and schemed what they should do to him to injure him. Now on the fixed day Ælfred, the younger prince, selected companions with his brother's approval, and beginning his journey came into the country of Flanders. There he lingered a little with Marquis Baldwin, and when asked by him to lead some part of his forces with him as a precaution against the snares of the enemy, was unwilling to do so, but taking only a few men of Boulogne, boarded ship and crossed the sea. But when he came near to the shore, he was soon recognised by the enemy, who came and intended to attack him, but he recognised them and ordered the ships to be pushed off from that shore. He landed, however, at another port, and attempted to go to his mother, deeming that he had entirely evaded the bane of the ambush. But when he was already near his goal, Earl Godwine met him and took him under his protection, and forthwith became his soldier by averment under oath. Diverting him from London, he led him into the town called Guildford, and lodged his soldiers there in separate billets by twenties, twelves and tens, leaving a few with the young man, whose duty was to be in attendance upon him. And he gave them food and drink in plenty, and withdrew personally to his own lodging, until he should return in the morning to wait upon his lord with due honour.

5. But after they had eaten and drunk, and being weary, had gladly ascended their couches, behold, men leagued with the most abominable tyrant Haraldr appeared, entered the various billets, secretly removed the arms of the innocent men, confined them with iron manacles and fetters, and kept them till the morrow to be tortured. But when it was morning, the innocent men were led out, and were iniquitously condemned without a hearing. For they were all disarmed and delivered

---

⁴ *innocentum* : the Encomiast would easily find authority for such forms in the classical poets, e.g., *Aen.* vi. 200, *sequentum*, and they are, of course, the rule in Plautus, who actually has *Rud.* 619, *innocentum*.

---

* I borrow some expressions from Milton's translation of this letter.

exarmatis uinctisque post tergum manibus atrocissimis traditi sunt carnificibus, quibus etiam iussum est, (ut nemini) *a* parcerent nisi quem sors decima offerret. Tunc tortores uinctos ordinatim sedere fecerunt, et satis supraque eis insultantes illius interfectoris Thebeae legionis *b* exemplo usi sunt, qui decimauit primum 10 innocentes multo his mitius. Ille enim rex paganissimus Christianorum nouem pepercit, occiso decimo ; at hi profanissimi falsissimique Christiani bonorum Christianorum nouem peremerunt *c*, decimo dimisso. Ille, licet paganus Christianos trucidaret, patulo tamen in campo eos nexibus non inretitos decollari iussit, ut gloriosos milites. At isti, licet nomine Christiani, actu tamen paganissimi *d*, 15 la[n]ceolarum suarum ictibus non merentes heroas catenatos mactabant ut sues. Unde huius⟨s⟩cemodi tortores canibus deteriores digne omnia dicunt *e 1* secula, qui non miliciae uiolentia sed fraudium suarum insidiis tot militum honesta dampnauerunt corpora. Quosdam ut dictum est perimebant, quosdam uero suae seruituti mancipabant ; alios ceca cupidine capti *2* uendebant, nonnullos autem artatos uinculis 20 maiori inrisioni reseruabant. Sed diuina miseratio non defuit innocentibus in tanto discrimine consistentibus, quia multos ipsi uidimus quos ex illa derisione eripuit caelitus sine amminiculo *f* hominis ruptis manicarum compedumque obicibus.

[6] Ergo, quia militum agones succintim transcurrimus, superest ut et eorum principis, gloriosi scilicet Alfridi, martyrium narrando seriem locutionis adbreuiemus, ne forte, si singulatim omnia quae ei acta sunt perstringere uoluerimus, multis tibique precipue dominae reginae dolorem multiplicemus. Qua in re rogo te, domina, ne 5 requiras amplius quam hoc, quod tibi parcendo breuiter dicturi sumus. Possent enim multa dici, si non tuo parceremus dolori. Est quippe nullus dolor maior matri quam uidere uel audire mortem dilectissimi filii. Captus est igitur regius iuuenis clam suo in hospicio, eductusque in insula Heli *g* dicta a milite primum inrisus est iniquissimo. Deinde contemptibiliores eliguntur, ut horum ab insania flendus 10 iuuenis diiudicetur. Qui iudices constituti decreuerunt, illi debere oculi utrique *h 3* ad contemptum primum erui. Quod postqu[am] *i* parant perficere, duo illi super brachia ponuntur, qui interim tenerent illa, et unus super pectus unusque super crura, ut sic facilius illi inferretur paena. Quid hoc in dolore detineor ? Mihi ipsi scribenti tremit calamus, dum horreo quae iuuenis passus est beatissimus. Euadam 15 ergo breuius tantae calamitatis miseriam, finemque huius martyrii fine tenus perstringam. Namque est *j* ab inpiis tentus, effossis etiam luminibus inpiissime est

a (ut nemini) : *added in margin*, L ; *in text*, P.
b legionis : *corrected from* legionionis *by deletion of the second* ion, L'.
c peremerunt : perimerunt, L, P.
d paganissimi : *corrected from* paganississimi *by deletion of first* ssi, L.
e dicunt : *so* L, P (*cf. Linguistic Note*).
f amminiculo : *altered to* adminiculo, L'.
g Heli : Hely, P.
h oculi utrique : *so, with confused syntax*, L ; oculos utrosque, P (*cf. Linguistic Note*).
i postqu[am] : *completed by* L' ; postquam, P.
j est : *so* L, P, *though the word is redundant.*

---

1 *dicunt* : Gertz proposes to read *dicent* or *dicant*, but this is unnecessary in view of the fairly frequent use of the present for the future in the *Vulgate* (e.g., *Matt.* xxvii. 42, *descendat nunc . . . et credimus ei* ; *Ioan.* xxi. 23, *non moritur*).

2 *ceca cupidine capti* : the expression *caeca cupido* is frequent, see Introduction, p. xxxiii. The collocation *cupido capit/cupidine capitur* is a favourite with Livy (e.g., I, 6, 3), and occurs also Iust., xi. 7, 4, and in the poets (e.g., *Aen.* iv. 194 ; Ov., *Met.* xiii. 762).

with their hands bound behind their backs to most vicious executioners, who were ordered, furthermore, to spare no man unless the tenth lot should reprieve him. Then the torturers made the bound men sit in a row, and reviling them beyond measure, followed the example of that murderer of the Theban Legion, who first decimated guiltless men, though more mercifully than they did. For that utterly pagan ruler spared nine of the Christians and killed the tenth, but these most profane and false Christians killed nine of the good Christians and let the tenth go. That pagan, though he massacred Christians, nevertheless ordered that they should be beheaded on an open plain unfettered by bonds, like glorious soldiers. But these, though they were in name Christians, were nevertheless in their actions totally pagan, and butchered the innocent heroes with blows from their spears bound as they were, like swine. Hence all ages will justly call such torturers worse than dogs, since they brought to condemnation the worthy persons of so many soldiers not by soldierly force but by their treacherous snares. Some, as has been said, they slew, some they placed in slavery to themselves ; others they sold, for they were in the grip of blind greed, but they kept a few loaded with bonds to be subjected to greater mockery. But the divine pity did not fail the innocent men who stood in such peril, for I myself have seen many whom it snatched from that derision, acting from heaven without the help of man, so that the impediments of manacles and fetters were shattered.

6. Therefore, since I am dealing briefly with the sufferings of the soldiers, it remains that I should curtail the course of my narrative in telling of the martyrdom of their prince, that is to say the glorious Ælfred, lest perchance if I should choose to go over all that was done to him in detail, I should multiply the grief of many people and particularly of you, Lady Queen. In this matter I beg you, lady, not to ask more than this, which I, sparing your feelings, will briefly tell. For many things could be told if I were not sparing your sorrow. Indeed there is no greater sorrow for a mother than to see or hear of the death of a most dear son. The royal youth, then, was captured secretly in his lodging, and having been taken to the island called Ely, was first of all mocked by the most wicked soldiery. Then still more contemptible persons were selected, that the lamented youth might be condemned by them in their madness. When these men had been set up as judges, they decreed that first of all both his eyes should be put out as a sign of contempt. After they prepared to carry this out, two men were placed on his arms to hold them meanwhile, one on his breast, and one on his legs, in order that the punishment might be more easily inflicted on him. Why do I linger over this sorrow ? As I write my pen trembles, and I am horror-stricken at what the most blessed youth suffered. Therefore I will the sooner turn away from the misery of so great a disaster, and touch upon the conclusion of this martyrdom as far as its consummation. For he was held fast, and after his eyes had been put out was most wickedly slain. When this

---

³ *oculi utrique* : if emendation be attempted, it is quite certain that it must not be to the obvious *oculos utrosque* of P and Duchesne (see Introduction, p. xviii), because the sentence is a carefully constructed succession of words ending in -*i*. Gertz's *ut illi deberent oculi utrique* is in every way to be preferred, but, since the meaning is obvious, the text may stand as in L, and one of the Encomiast's rare syntactical lapses may be assumed.

occisus. Qua nece perfecta relinqu[u]nt corpus exanime, quod fideles Christi, monachi scilicet eiusdem insulae Haeli [a], rapientes sepelierunt honorifice. In loco autem sepulcri eius multa fiunt miracula, ut quidam [b] aiunt, qui etiam se haec 20 uidisse saepissime dicunt. Et merito : innocenter enim fuit martyrizatus, ideoque dignum est ut per eum innocencium exerceatur uirtus. Gaudeat igitur Emma regina de tanto intercessore, quia (quem) [c] quondam in terris habuit filium nunc habet in caelis patronum.

[7] At regina [d] tanti sceleris nouitate perculsa quid facto sibi opus sit mente considerat tacita. Animus igitur eius diuersus huc illucque rapitur, et se amplius tantae perfidiae credere cunctatur, quippe quae perempti filii inconsolabiliter confundebatur merore, [1] uerum multo amplius ex eiusdem consolabatur certa requie. 5 Hinc duplici, ut diximus, angebatur causa, necis uidelicet filii miserabili mestitia, tum uero reliquae suae uitae dignitatisque diffidentia. Sed fortassis hic mihi quilibet clamabit, quem liuor huiuscae dominae liuidum onerosumque reddit, "Cur eadem nece mori refutabat, quae sub hac proditione necatum filium aeterna requie frui nulla tenus dubitabat ? " Ad quod destruendum tali responsione censeo utendum, 10 quoniam, si persecutor Christianae religionis fideique adesset, non uitae discrimen subire fugeret. Ceterum nefarium et execrabile cunctis Ortodoxis uideretur, si ambitione terreni imperii talis famae matrona uita priuaretur, neque profecto emori fortunis tantae dominae honestus exitus haberetur. Haec et his similia ante oculos ponens, et illud autenticum dominicae exortationis preceptum suis fortunis con- 15 ducibile censens, quo uidelicet electis insinuat, quoniam si persequuti uos fuerint in una ciuitate fugite in alia [e], pro suo casu spes satis honestas reliquae dignitatis conseruandae exequitur, et tandem gratia superni respectus consilio sollerti utitur [2]. Exteras nationes petere sibi utile credit, quod sagaci ratione fine tenus perducit. Tamen quas petit non externas sibi experta est fore, quis immorans haud secus ac 20 suis colitur decentissime. Igitur pro re atque tempore quam plurimos potest sibi fidos optimates congregat. His presentibus secreta cordis sui enucleat. A quibus etiam inito dominae probato consilio, commeatus classium eorum apparatur exilio. Itaque prosperis usi flatibus [3] transfretant, et cuidam stationi haud longe a castello Bruggensi distanti sese applicant. Hoc castellum Flandrensibus colonis incolitur, 25 quod tum frequentia negotiatorum tum affluentia omnium quae prima mortales ducunt famosissimum habetur. Hic equidem a marchione (eiusdem prouintiae) [f] Balduino, magni et inuictissimi principis filio, eiusque coniuge Athala, quae interpretatur "nobilissima", Francorum regis Rodberti et reginae Constantiae filia,

---

[a] Haeli : Helye, P.   [b] ut quidam . . . patronum : *omitted*, P.
[c] (quem) : *added in margin*, L.
[d] At regina . . . famosissimum habetur (26) : Regina uero tanti sceleris nouitate perculsa atque doloris telo saucia cum fidis proceribus mentis archana communicat atque cum iisdem clam nauigant (*so*) et stationi haud longe a castello Brugensi distanti sese applicant, P.
[e] alia : aliā, *but the stroke appears to be a late addition*, L ; alia, T ; *cf. II*, 7, *11*.
[f] (eiusdem prouintiae) : *added in margin*, L ; *in text*, P.

---

[1] *confundebatur merore* : the expression *maerore confundi* is early, e.g., Liv. xxxv. 15, 9.
[2] *consilio . . utitur* : the expression *consilio uti* is of very great frequence in both classical and later times.
[3] *prosperis usi flatibus* : Cic., *Off.* ii. 19, *prospero flatu . . utimur* ; the expression *flatus prosperus* occurs also Dict. Cret., i. 23, and *Cod. Theod.* cxxxv. 34.

murder had been performed, they left his lifeless body, which the servants of Christ, the monks, I mean, of the same Isle of Ely, took up and honourably interred. However, many miracles occur where his tomb is, as people report who even declare most repeatedly that they have seen them. And it is justly so : for he was martyred in his innocence, and therefore it is fitting that the might of the innocent should be exercised through him. So let Queen Emma rejoice in so great an intercessor, since him, who she formerly had as a son on earth, she now has as a patron in the heavens.

7. But the queen, smitten by so unheard-of a crime, considered in silent thought what it was needful that she should do. And so her mind was carried this way and that in uncertainty, and she was chary of trusting herself further to such perfidy, for she was dazed beyond consolation with sorrow for her murdered son, although she derived comfort in a much greater degree from his assured rest. And so she was, as we have said, distressed for a twofold reason, that is to say, because of misery and sadness at her son's death, and also because of uncertainty concerning what remained of her own life and her position. But perchance at this point some one, whom ill-will towards this lady has rendered spiteful and odious, will protest to me : " Why did she refuse to die the same death, since she in no way doubted that her son, who had been slain under these conditions of treachery, enjoyed eternal rest ? " To rebut this I consider that one must use such a reply as : " If the persecutor of the Christian religion and faith had been present, she would not have shrunk from encountering mortal danger. On the other hand it would have appeared wrong and abominable to all the orthodox, if a matron of such reputation had lost her life through desire for worldly dominion, and indeed death would not have been considered a worthy end to the fortunes of so great a lady." Keeping these and similar arguments in mind, and considering advantageous to her fortunes that authentic injunction of the Lord's exhortation, in which, to wit, He says to the elect, " If they should persecute you in one city, flee into another," she acted upon a hope of saving what was left of her position, which was under the circumstances in which she was placed sufficiently sound, and at length followed a sagacious plan by the grace of the divine regard. She believed it expedient for her to seek foreign nations, and she brought this decision to consummation with shrewd judgment. However, she did not find that those nations which she sought were to be foreign to her, for while she sojourned among them she was honoured by them in a most proper manner, just as she was by her own followers. And so she assembled as many nobles who were faithful to herself as she could, in view of the circumstances and the time. When these were present, she told them her inmost thoughts. When they had proceeded to approve the plan put in train by their lady, their ships' supplies are prepared for exile. And so, having enjoyed favourable winds, they crossed the sea and touched at a certain port not far from the town of Bruges. The latter town is inhabited by Flemish settlers, and enjoys very great fame for the number of its merchants and for its affluence in all things upon which mankind places the greatest value. Here indeed she was, as she deserved, honourably received by Baldwin, the marquis of that same province, who was the son of a great and totally unconquered prince, and by his wife Athala (a name meaning ' most noble '), daughter of Robert, king of the French, and Queen Constance. By them, furthermore, a house in the above-named town, suitable for

honorifice, uti se dignum erat, recipitur. A quibus etiam in predicto oppido domus
30 regali sumptui apta eidem reginae tribuitur, ceterum obsonium benigne offertur.
Quae partim illa cum maxima gratiarum actione suscipit, partimque sese non
indigere *a* quodammodo ostendit.

[8] In tanta igitur posita securitate legatos suo filio mittit Eduardo postulatum,
ne uersus se pigritaretur uenire. Quibus ille obaudiens, equ[u]m conscendit et ad
matrem usque peruenit. Sed, ubi eis copia data est mutuo loquendi, filius se matris
fortunas edocet miserari, sed nullo modo posse auxiliari, cum Anglici optimates
5 nullum ei fecerint iusiurandum, quae res indicabat a fratre auxilium expetendum.
His ita gestis Eduardus Normanniam [1] reuehitur, et mens reginae quid sibi foret
agendum etiam nunc cunctatur. Post cuius reditum nuntios Hardecnutoni filio suo
legat, qui tunc temporis regimen Danorum optinebat, per quos sui doloris nouitatem
aperit, et ut ad se uenire quantotius maturet petit. Cuius aures ut tanti sceleris
10 horror incussit [2], primo omnium mens eius intolerabili obtusa *b* dolore [3] in consulendo
fatiscit [4]. Ardebat enim animo fratris iniurias ultum ire, immo etiam matris
legationi parere.

[9] Hinc utrique rei preuidens quam maximas potest nauium militumque parat
[copias] *c*, quorum ampliorem numerum quodam maris in amfractu collocat, qui, si
inter e(u)ndum sibi copia pugnandi seu etiam necessitas repugnandi accideret,
presidio aduentaret. Ceterum non amplius decem nauibus se comitantibus ad
5 matrem proficiscitur, quae *d* non minima doloris anxietate fatigabatur [5]. Dum
igitur prospero cursui intenti non modo certatim spumas salis aere ruebant, uerum
etiam su(p)para uelorum [6] secundis flatibus attollebant, ut maris facies non umquam
certa sed semper mobilitate flatuum dubitanda habetur et infida, repente faeda
tempestas uentorum nubiumque a tergo glomeratur et ponti superficies iam
10 superuen[ien]tibus *e* austris turbabatur. Itaque, quod in tam atroci negotio solet fieri,
anchorae [7] de proris iactae harenis affiguntur fundi. Quae res, tametsi tum illis
fuerit inportuna, tamen non absque Dei nutu cuncta disponentis esse creditur acta,
ut postmodum rei probauit euentus, membris omnium placidae quieti somni cedentibus. Nam postera nocte eodem Hardecnutone in stratu quiescente diuinitus
15 quaedam ostenditur uisio, quae eum confortans et consolans forti iubet esse animo.
Hortatur preterea ne ab incepto desisteret, quia paucarum *f* dierum [8] interuallo
iniustus regni inuasor, Haroldus scilicet, occideret, et regnum patriis uiribus domitum
sibi iusto heredi iustissima successione incolume rediret.

a indigere : indigern, L.
b obtusa : *corrected from* dbtusa, L.
c [copias] : *so* P ; *omitted*, L.
d quae non . . . cedentibus (14) : *omitted*, P.
e superuen[ien]tibus : *conjectured by* T, *adopted by* Pertz ; *Gertz prefers* superruentibus, *but
this verb is rare and cf. I, 4, 6.*
f paucarum : *so* L, P (*cf: Linguistic Note*).

---

[1] *Normanniam* : the poetical construction of the accusative of names of countries without
preposition after verbs of motion to express motion whither (as *Aen.* i. 2, *Italiam* . . . . *uenit*),
is sometimes adopted in medieval prose : e.g., *Historia Norvegiae* (Storm, p. 219), *uenit Flandream.*
For the use of the construction in earlier prose, see Stolz-Schmalz, p. 387.
[2] *incussit* : this use of *incutio* for *concutio* or *percutio*, though rare, is classical (e.g., Val. Fl.,
v. 550).

royal outlay, was allotted to the queen, and in addition a kind offer of entertainment was made. These kindnesses she partly accepted with the greatest thanksgiving, partly she shewed that up to a point she did not stand in need.

8. And so, being placed in such great security, she sent messengers to her son Eadweard to ask that he should come to her without delay. He obeyed them, mounted his horse and came to his mother. But when they had the opportunity for discussion, the son declared that he pitied his mother's misfortunes, but that he was able in no way to help, since the English nobles had sworn no oath to him, a circumstance indicating that help should be sought from his brother. Thereupon Eadweard returned to Normandy, and the queen still hesitated in her mind as to what she ought to do. After her son's departure, she dispatched messengers to her son Hörthaknútr, who then held sway over the Danes, and through them revealed to him her unheard-of sorrow, and begged him to hasten to come to her as soon as possible. The horror of so great a crime made his ears tremble, and first of all as he deliberated his spirits sank stunned by intolerable sorrow. For he burned·in his heart to go and avenge his brother's injuries, nay more, to obey his mother's message.

9. Accordingly, providing for either eventuality, he got ready the greatest forces he could of ships and soldiers, and assembled the greater number of them in a certain inlet of the sea, to come to his support if on his journey the opportunity to give battle or the need for defence should befall him. For the rest, he set out accompanied by not more than ten ships to go to his mother, who was labouring under the very great distress of sorrow. When, therefore, they were absorbed in their prosperous voyage, and were not only eagerly ploughing the salt foam with brazen prows, but also raising their topsails to the favourable winds, whereas the surface of the sea is never dependable, but is always found to be unreliable and faithless, suddenly a murky tempest of winds and clouds was rolled up from behind, and the surface of the sea forthwith was agitated by overtaking south winds. And so the anchors were dropped from the prows, and caught in the sands of the bottom, which is what is wont to be done in such desperate straits. This incident, although it was distressing to them at the time, is not believed to have taken place without the consent of God, who disposes all things, as the issue of the affair afterwards proved, when the limbs of all yielded to quiet rest and sleep. For on the next night, when Hörthaknútr was at rest in his bed, by divine providence a vision appeared, which comforted and consoled him and bade him be of good cheer. Furthermore, it exhorted him not to desist from his undertaking, for after a space of a few days the unjust usurper of his kingdom, Haraldr, would perish, and the kingdom conquered by his father's strength would return safely·by most rightful succession to himself, the rightful heir.

---

[3] *intolerabili . . dolore* : frequent collocation, see *Thes.*, s.v. *dolor*, col. 1851.

[4] *mens . . . . . fatiscit* : this collocation occurs Stat., *Theb.* iv. 187, and is elsewhere extremely rare.

[5] *doloris anxietate fatigabatur* : the collocation *dolor fatigat* is fairly frequent, see *Thes.*, s.v. *dolor*, col. 1844.

[6] *suppara uelorum* : usually *alta suppara uelorum*, but cf. Sen., *Herc. Oet.* 699.

[7] *anchorae*, etc. : references to the anchor of a ship catching in the sand are not infrequent, *Thes.*, s.v. *harena*, col. 2529.

[8] *paucarum dierum* : only three instances of the plural of *dies* in the fem. are given by *Thes.*, s.v. *dies*, col. 1023, lines 70-2.

[10] Euigilans igitur somniator talibus inditiis certior fit [1], et Deo omnipotenti tantae consolationis causa gratias reddidit, simulque [a] futura nulla tenus dubitat, quae sibi memorata uisio predixerat. Denique maris ira pacata omnique tempestate sedata prosperis flatibus sinus pandit uelorum ; sicque secundo usus cursu [2] ad
5 Brugensem sese applicuit portum. Hic anchoris rudibusque [3] nauibus affixis et nautis qui eas seruarent expeditis recta se uia cum delectis ad hospicium dirigit matris. Qualis ergo meror qualisque letitia in eius aduentu fuerit exorta, nulla tibi umquam explicabit pagina. Dolor haud modicus habebatur, dum in uultu eius faciem perempti mater quadam imaginatione contemplaretur ; item gaudio magno gaude-
10 bat, dum superstitem saluum adesse sibi uidebat. Unde uiscera diuinae misericordiae se sciebat respicere, cum nondum tali fru[s]traretur solamine. Nec longe [b] post filio cum matre morante et memoratae uisionis promissa expectante nuntii leta ferentes nuntia aduentant, qui uidelicet Haroldum mortuum nuntiant, qui etiam referunt, Anglicos ei principes nolle aduersari, sed multimodis iubilationibus sibi conletari ;
15 unde regnum hereditario iure [4] sibi debitum non dedignetur repetere et suae dignitati eorumque saluti iuxta in medium consulere.

[11] His Hardecnuto materque animati repetere statuunt horas [c] auiti regni [5]. Cuius rei [d] fama ut populares impulit aures, mox cuncta dolore et luctu compleri cerneres. Dolebant enim diuites eius recessione, cuius semper amabili fruebantur conlocutione ; dolebant pauperes eius recessione, cuius diutinis largitionibus [e] ab
5 aegestatis defensabantur onere ; dolebant uiduae cum orphanis, quos illa extractos sacro fonte baptismatis non modicis ditauerat. Quibus igitur hanc laudibus efferam nescio, quae ibidem numquam abfuit renascentibus in Christo. Hic eius fides patet laudanda, hic bonitas omnimodis celebranda. Quod si pro singulis eius benefactis parem disserere, prius me tempus quam rem credo deserere. Unde ad seriem nostrae
10 locutionis propero redire.

[12] Dum reginae filiique eius reditus apparatur, omne litus planctu gemituque confunditur, omnes dextrae caelo attollebantur infensae. Flebant igitur, a se dis(c)edere illam, quam toto exilii tempore ut ciuem uidere suam. Nulli diuitum grauis hospita, nulli pauperum in quolibet onerosa. Omnes igitur natale solum
5 mutare putares, cunctas [6] secum exteras petere uelle diceres regiones. Sic toto plangebatur littore, sic ab omni plorabatur populo astante. Licet ei quodammodo

---

[a] simulque . . . expectante (12) : emensoque mari ad matrem peruenit eidemque uisum exponit. Nec longe post, P.
    [b] longe : longo *with erasure* (*of* et ?) *before it*, L ; longe, P (*see previous note*).
    [c] horas : *so*, L, P, *but* h *is erased in* L (*by* L' ?) ; oras, T ; *cf. Introduction, p.* xxxviii.
    [d] Cuius rei . . . ubertate (12, 10) : *omitted*, P.   [e] largitionibus : *altered from* largitione, L.

---

[1] certior fit : ' is duly informed '; Gertz is in error in suggesting that certior here means securior. For the absolute use of certiorem facere, cf. Plaut., Bacch., 841, *ex me quidem hodie numquam fies certior.* Note also below, III, 13, where certum facere is similarly used (cf. Aen. iii. 179). Cf. Thes., s.v. certus, col. 922.
[2] secundo . . cursu : an old and favourite collocation : e.g., Caes., B.C. iii. 47 ; Liv., xlv. 41, 8.
[3] rudibusque : Gertz makes the tempting emendation to rudentibusque, but I have preferred not to emend, assuming that the Encomiast imagined that ' rods ' of some kind were used in mooring the vessels, or even that confusion may have sometimes taken place in the senses of rudis and rudens : in a fifteenth-century glossary (Wülcker's revision of Wright's Anglo-Saxon and Old English Vocabularies, i. 608), the meaning ' cable ' is assigned to both words.

10. The dreamer accordingly, when he awoke, was enlightened by the signs described above, and returned thanks to Almighty God for such great consolation, and had at the same time not the slightest doubt about the coming events which the vision above described had foretold. Thereupon, the wrath of the sea having subsided, and the storm having dropped, he spread his bellying sails to the favourable winds ; and thus, having enjoyed a successful voyage, he touched at Bruges. Here, having moored his ships with anchors and rods, and having commissioned sailors to look after them, he betook himself directly with chosen companions to the lodging of his mother. What grief and what joy sprang up at his arrival, no page shall ever unfold to you. There was no little pain when his mother beheld with some stretch of her imagination, the face of her lost one in his countenance ; likewise she rejoiced with a great joy at seeing the survivor safe in her presence. And so she knew that the tender mercy of God had regard to her, since she was still undeprived of such a consolation. And soon afterwards, while the son was lingering with his mother expecting the events promised by the vision above described, messengers arrived bearing glad tidings, and announced, to wit, that Haraldr was dead, reporting furthermore that the English nobles did not wish to oppose him, but to rejoice together with him in jubilation of every kind ; therefore they begged him not to scorn to return to the kingdom which was his by hereditary right, but to take counsel for both his own position and their safety with regard to the common good.

11. Encouraged by these things, Hörthaknútr and his mother decided to return to the shores of the ancestral realm. When word of this matter smote the ears of the people, soon you would have seen pain and grief to be universal. For the rich mourned her departure, with whom they had ever enjoyed pleasant converse ; the poor mourned her departure, by whose continual generosity they were relieved from the burden of want ; the widows mourned with the orphans, whom she had freely enriched when they were taken from the holy baptismal font. Therefore I do not know with what praises to exalt her, who never failed to be immediately present with those being re-born in Christ. Her faith clearly calls for praise and at the same time her kindness is in every way to be extolled. If I should propose to discuss this matter with regard to her individual good deeds, I believe that my time would be exhausted before my subject, so I hasten to return to the course of our narrative.

12. While preparations were being made for the return of the queen and her son, the whole shore was perturbed by lamentation and groaning, and all raised angry right hands to the sky. They wept, in short, that she, whom during her whole exile they had regarded as a fellow citizen, was leaving them. She had not been a burdensome guest to any of the rich, nor had she been oppressive to the poor in any matter whatever. Therefore you would have thought that all were leaving their native soil, you would have said that all the women intended to seek foreign lands along with her. Such was the lamentation on the whole shore, such was the wailing of all the people

---

[4] *heredetario iure* : this expression is exceptionally common in Medieval Latin ; it is of early origin, occurring perhaps first in Florus, i. 24, 7, as the text is not reliable in Cic., *Har. Resp.* 14.

[5] *auiti regni* : an expression which occurs already Cic., *Manil.* 8 ; Liv. i. 15, 6. *populares . . aures* : also Odilo, *Miracula Adalheidae*, 7.

[6] *cunctas* : apparently, the *matronae* of the sentence after next by a rather violent use of *e sequentibus praecedentia*.

congauderent prist(i)num gradum repetere dignitatis, non tamen eam matronae
siccis dimittere poterant oculis. Tandem uincit amor patriae, et omnibus uiritim
osculatis et flebili eis dicto uale, cum filio suisque altum petit mare non absque magna
10 lacrimarum utrimque fusa ubertate.

[13] Igitur principes Anglici parum praemissae fidentes legationi, antequam ab
illis transfretaretur, obuii sunt facti optimum factu rati, ut et regi reginaeque satis-
facerent, et se deuotos eorum dominationi subderent. His Hardecnuto cum matre
certus *a* factus et transmarini littoris tandem portum nactus, a cunctis incolis eiusdem
5 terrae gloriosissime recipitur, sicque diuini muneris gratia regnum sibi debitum
redditur. His ita peractis et omnibus suis in pacis tranquillitate compositis, fraterno
correptus amore nuntios mittit ad Eduardum, rogans ut ueniens secum optineret
regnum.

[14] Qui fratris iussioni obaudiens Anglicas partes aduehitur, et mater amboque
filii regni paratis commodis nulla lite intercedente utuntur. Hic fides *b* habetur regni
sotiis, hic inuiolabile uiget faedus materni fraternique amoris. Haec illis omnia
prestitit, qui unanimes in domo habitare facit, Iesus Christus, Dominus omnium,
5 cui in Trinitate manenti inmarcessibile floret imperium. Amen.

a certus : certius, L, tertius, P.
b Hic fides . . . Amen : His itaque fratribus concorditer regnantibus mors media intercidit
et regem Hardechnutonem uitalibus auris abstulit. Regem mater et frater maximo cum luctu
honorifice sepeliunt. Mortuo Ardechnutone in regnum successit Edwardus, heres scilicet legit-
timus, uir uirium eminentia conspicuus, uirtute animi consiliique atque etiam ingenii uiuacitate
preditus et, ut omnia breuiter concludam, omnium expetendorum summa insignitus, P.

standing by. Although they rejoiced with her to some extent at her recovery of her old position, nevertheless the matrons could not let her go with dry eyes. At last love of the homeland prevailed, and having kissed all severally and having said a tearful farewell to them, she sought the deep sea with her son and her followers after a great abundance of tears had been shed on both sides.

13. Under these circumstances the English nobles, lacking confidence in the legation previously sent, met them before they crossed the sea, deeming that the best course was for them to make amends to the king and queen, and to place themselves devotedly under their dominion. When Hörthaknútr and his mother had been apprised by these men, and when he had at length reached a port on the other side of the sea, he was most gloriously received by all the inhabitants of that country, and thus by the grace of the divine favour the realm which was properly his was restored. After the events described, he arranged all his affairs in the calm of peace, and being gripped by brotherly love, sent messengers to Eadweard and asked him to come and hold the kingdom together with himself.

14. Obeying his brother's command, he was conveyed to England, and the mother and both sons, having no disagreement between them, enjoy the ready amenities of the kingdom. Here there *is* loyalty among sharers of rule,* here the bond of motherly and brotherly love is of strength indestructible. All these things were granted them by Him, who makes dwellers in a house be of one mind, Jesus Christ, the Lord of all, who, abiding in the Trinity, holds a kingdom which flourishes unfading. Amen.

* The allusion is to Lucan's *nulla fides regni sociis* (i. 92).

APPENDIX I

QUEEN EMMA'S NAME, TITLE, AND FORMS OF ASSENT

It is evident that *Ælfgifu* was the name always used officially by the Queen. We find it used in her signatures to the following English documents : R. 81, 94, 98, 101 ; K. 788. It is used with reference to her in R. 86, 96, Earle, p. 232, and also in the forgery, R. 114. On the other hand, the double form *Ælfgifu Imma* occurs, with orthographical variations, in R. 85 in signature, and in R. 118 in reference, while in W. 23 *Emma* is used in reference. These last three documents are, however, all either complete forgeries or much modified in their extant form. Emma is referred to by Eadweard the Confessor simply as his mother, without a name being given, in K. 874, 876, 883, and in the Latin document, K. 905.

Similarly, in most Latin documents the Queen signs as *Ælfgifu*. The double form is found only in K. 779 and 962, of which the former is certainly, the latter probably, a forgery (see R., p. 417), and in the Latin version of the forged R. 85 referred to above (Stowe Charter 41, Thorpe, p. 326). K. 761 and 727 have the Queen's signature respectively in the forms *Ymma* and *Emma*, but the former is a forgery, and the latter has latinised signatures in its extant form. The Queen is regularly referred to as *Ælfgifu* in Latin documents : K. 720, 735, 906, 1316, 1330 ; also in Stowe Charter 39, referred to above, p. xlvii, and in the Hyde *Liber Vitae*.[1] The only exceptions are K. 697, which has the double form, K. 761, already referred to, which has *Ymma* in reference as well as signature, and K. 1311, which has *Emma*. The first two of these are obvious forgeries, and the last is much modified in its extant form.

In the *Old English Chronicle* Emma is at first referred to simply as *seo hlæfdige*, as if the compilers were uncertain under what name reference to her should be made. She is so referred to in MSS. C, D and E in 1002, 1003, 1013, and in D in 1043. In C, D, E, 1017, she is (with minute variations) *þæs cyniges lafe Æþelrædes . . . . Ricardes dohtor*. She is first named in D, 1023, where she is *Imma seo hlæfdige*. In C, D, 1035, she is *Ælfgyfu seo hlæfdige*, but C adds *Imme* as a gloss above the line ; the corresponding entry in E has *Ælfgifu, Hardacnutes modor*. In 1037, C, D, and E all have *Ælfgyfe* (acc.), but while E calls her Knútr's widow and Hörthaknútr's mother, C and D call her *ða cwene*, the first undoubted use of *cwen* as a title of a queen of the West-Saxon house since a remote period. E uses the name *Ælfgifu* in 1040. In the records of her death in 1052, C calls her *Imme*, D *Ælfgyfu*, and E *Ælfgiue Ymma* ; C gives her the exact title *seo ealde hlæfdige*, ' the Queen Dowager ', but D calls her *seo hlæfdige*, and E gives no title.

The double form *Ælfgifu Imme* no doubt arose in cases where the one name was added to gloss the other, as in MS. C of the *Chronicle*, 1035. MS. F of the *Chronicle* adds *Ymma* as a gloss on the *Ælfgifu* of the E-type manuscript which was its source in 1040, and in 1002 and 1017, where its source gave no name, it has, respectively, *Ymma* ' *Ælfgiua* ', and *Ælfgiue* ' *on Englisc* ' *Ymma* ' *on Frencisc* '. In a genealogy, Florence of Worcester (i. 257) has *Ælfgiua uel Imme*. In the St. Edmund's additions in MS. Bodley 297 of Florence of Worcester, the Queen's English name twice has *Emme* (gen. sing.) written above it as a gloss.[2] From such passages the double name *Ælfgifu Imme* arose : we have seen that the *Chronicle* has it in MS. E, 1052, and that it is found in a number of charters

---

[1] References as above, p. xlviii, note 1.
[2] *Memorials of St. Edmund's Abbey* (Rolls Series, i. 341, 343).

of doubtful authenticity. It also probably occurred in the Thorney *Liber Vitae* (see the Viking Society's *Saga Book*, xii. 131), though the scribe of the extant manuscript has misunderstood it as two names, and has written *Imma et Ælfgifa*. In the *Chronicon Monasterii de Abingdon* (Rolls Series, i. 434), the queen is called *regina binomia* . . . *Ælfgiua Imma*. The double form is also used in the twelfth-century text known as the *Laws of Eadweard the Confessor*,[1] but Hoveden (Rolls Series, ii. 235) inserts *id est* between the two names in incorporating the text into his history.

We may conclude from all the above evidence that *Ælfgifu* was the name officially used by the queen, and that instructed persons used it in referring to her. On the other hand, her original name, *Imme*, was widely known, and continued in popular use, appearing in the *Chronicle*, D, 1023, C, 1052, and in the forged charter, K. 761. It became the form used in referring to Emma in official documents of the Norman period : references will be found below (p. 57). This indicates that her old official name fell into disuse after her death.

Of the Anglo-Latin writers, Henry of Huntingdon, William of Malmesbury, Symeon of Durham (when he is not merely transcribing Florence), Æthelred of Rievaux, Heremannus [2], Walter Map, Roger of Wendover, and the tract *De primo Saxonum adventu* [3] refer to the queen exclusively as *Emma*. It has already been noticed that *Emma* occurs in signature in K. 727, and in reference in K. 1311 : the extant forms of both documents are much modified, and in both *Emma* may be regarded as substituted for *Ælfgifu*. It would seem reasonable to conclude that, when *Ælfgifu* ceased to be used, it was felt that the correct Latin form was *Emma*. Florence of Worcester uses *Emma* and *Ælfgifu* (the latter in various spellings) indifferently, while in his notice of the Queen's death he has *Ælfgiua Imme*, following the *Chronicle*, MS. E, and in a genealogy (i. 257) he has *Ælfgiua uel Imme*. The form *Imma* rarely appears in Latin writers, except in the official documents of the Norman period, where, as has been noticed, it replaces *Ælfgifu*. Otherwise, it is limited to the spurious charter K. 761, referred to above, and Eadmer (*Historia Nouorum*, Rolls Series, pp. 5 and 107), and to the minor chronicles preserved in MSS. Cott. Nero A VIII and C VII.[4] Of these, the former has *Ymma* (1036) and the latter *Imme* (gen., 1002), while both have *Emma* (1052). The form with ' i ' is to be regarded in Latin texts as a survival from the vernacular chronicles, and from popular usage during the queen's life. The queen's official name *Ælfgifu* does not survive into the post-conquest period at all except in Florence of Worcester, and in a very few documents, where it is derived from older charters or genealogies, as in the St. Edmund's additions to MS. Bodley 297, and the curious sketch of English history inserted in the so-called *Laws of Eadweard the Confessor*.[5]

Of the Anglo-Norman writers, Gaimar, Wace, Benoît de Sainte-Maure, and the author of the *Estoire de Seint Aedward le Rei* use the form *Emme*, which the first once expands to *Emmeline* for the sake of rhyme (*Lestoire des Engles*, 4530). The only English

---

[1] See below, note 5.
[2] Liebermann, *Ungedruckte anglo-normannische Geschichtsquellen*, p. 274.
[3] Rolls Series ed. of Symeon of Durham, ii. 373.
[4] These minor chronicles are edited by Liebermann, *op. cit.*, pp. 56 ff.
[5] Liebermann, *Gesetze*, i. 663. Most manuscripts of this text have the double form of the queen's name, the English name appearing in forms more or less assimilated to its Norse equivalent *Álfífa* (appearing as *Alueua*, *Alfueua*, *Eluiua*), the foreign one as *Emma*, except in one manuscript, which has *Iunia* (< *Imma*). Cf. also above. Liebermann (*op. cit.*, iii. 342 ; cf. his *Über die Leges Edwardi Confessoris*, pp. 36–7) mentions as one of the sources of this law-book an unknown sketch of English history from 975 to 1042, and it is obviously from this that the double form is derived. This sketch of history, or one very closely related to it, is a source used by the surving form (thirteenth century) of the *Historia Norvegiae* and hence we find Emma there referred to as *Elfigeua* (Storm, p. 123).

document to use the form *Emma* is W. 23, which is a forgery, or at least much modified in its extant form.

Foreign sources do not use the name *Ælfgifu* in referring to Emma.[1] Her Flemish Encomiast, the Norman chroniclers, William of Jumièges, William of Poitiers, Ordericus Vitalis, and Robert of Torigni, and also the Norse saga-writers, all use the name *Emma*. Adam of Bremen, however, has the form *Imma* (ii. 51, 52, 72) and Schol. 38 to ii. 51, shows that he derived it from a Bremen record, which recorded that Knútr and his wife and son had recommended themselves to the prayers of the Bremen community. From Adam, the form *Imma* passes into Saxo and the *Annals of Roskilde*.

From the above paragraphs it is evident that Queen Emma's original name consisted of a single element, which the English heard as ' *imm* ', followed, no doubt, by a declensional ending, which is represented in the English forms by either the -*e* of the O.E. feminine weak declension, or by -*a*, which is a latinised ending. The variation between *y* and *i* found in the first syllable is without phonetic significance in manuscripts of the eleventh century and later. *Imme* was evidently very well known to be the Queen's name, for it is frequently used to gloss her official name, is occasionally found alone (K. 761 ; *Chronicle*, D, 1023, C, 1052), and was the form which came to be used to refer to her in the Norman period in official documents (*Domesday Book*, i. fo. 43v ; writs in *E.H.R.*, xxiv. 423, 425 ; xxxv. 389 ; *Domesday Book*, iv. 535, has, however, *Emme*, gen. sing.). It seems to have been used by the Queen personally on non-official occasions, since she asked the Bremen fraternity to pray for her under it. It is clear that the form with initial E- was never used in writing English : the only English document in which it occurs is W. 23, which, if not an entire forgery, is much modified in its extant form. If the English had heard the name pronounced with initial ' *e* ', they would themselves have spoken and written it accordingly, for ' *e* ' followed by a nasal consonant is a regular sound combination in O.E., and accordingly there can be little doubt that the name was pronounced by the Queen and her compatriots, from whom the English would first hear it, with initial ' *i* '. The Bremen record confirms this, showing that the name was communicated to the German monks with initial ' *i* ', from some source which would undoubtedly be in close contact with the court of Knútr. We cannot determine if this communication was made verbally or in writing. On the other hand, *Emma* evidently early became regarded as the correct Latin form of the name, and is the form invariably found in continental Latin (except in Adam of Bremen and writers who use him), and practically always in Anglo-Latin, though there *Imma* is sometimes found, owing to the use of *Imme* in English texts. If *Imme* were a common O.E. name, it might be argued that the queen and her compatriots used the form *Emma*, and that the English substituted for it a form to them more familiar, but the name is not found in O.E., though the corresponding masculine *Imma* occurs, though it is very rare.[2] It follows from the above remarks that the use of the form *Emma* in the Norse sagas is due to the fact that the nomenclature of those texts represents that of a period in which minor differences of form had been levelled away. The queen's name would undoubtedly reach the North first in the form *Imme*, through English visitors or Scandinavians who had been in England, and this would become in Old Norse *Imma*, with the substitution of the usual weak feminine ending. Historical Old Norse *Emma* undoubtedly represents a coalescence of the forms *Imma* and *Emma*, just as *Eiríkr* represents not only its phonological ancestor, but also the form which appears in O.E. texts as *Yric*.[3] It may be added, that the fact that the

---

[1] Except only the *Historia Norvegiae*, referred to in the preceding note.

[2] See M. Redin, *Studies on uncompounded personal names in Old English* (Uppsala, 1919), p. 67 ; also, on the etymology of the name and the reason for the existence of alternative forms with ' *e* ' and ' *i* ', Th. Forssner, *Continental-Germanic personal names in England* (Uppsala, 1916), p. 69.

[3] See below, p. 66, note 1.

queen is always called *Emma*, and never *Álfífa*, in Norse sources is a further proof of the general popular use of her original name in England.

Queen Emma's official designation in English was always *seo hlæfdige*. It is well known that this was the English term generally used with reference to the queens of the West-Saxon house in the tenth century,[1] but the evidence is not sufficient to decide if it had been used in signatures before Emma's time.[2] Emma signs English documents as *seo hlæfdige* five times : K. 788, R. 81, 86, 98, 101. To these the forgery R. 85 may be added. The only exception is R. 94, where the Latin title used by the queen during the reigns of her sons is translated : *Hearþacnut cyng 7 Ælfgeofu his modor*. The queen is referred to as *seo hlæfdige* in R. 86, 96, Earle, p. 232, as well as in the forged W. 23, R. 114. The only exceptions are the forged R. 118, where Eadweard refers to her as *Elfgyuu Ymme, min moder*, and the documents mentioned above (p. 55), in which he refers to her as his mother, without giving her name. *Cwen* is used only once, in a translation of a Latin document (K. 735). In the *Chronicle*, as we have already seen, her title is always *seo hlæfdige*, except in C, D, 1037, where she is *seo cwen*.[3]

In the time of Æthelred and Knútr, Emma practically always signs Latin documents as *regina*.[4] To this *praescripti regis* is added in K. 734, and *humillima* in a group of six documents of western origin to be considered below (pp. 59–60). There are only two other types of title[5] :

1. Ego Ælfgiua thoro consecrata regio (hanc donationem sublimaui).

This is found in K. 730, from the Shaftesbury Register, MS. Harl. 61, and in K. 709, from MS. Cott. Vit. F. xvi. Although the latter document is a forgery, its list of witnesses does not seem to be influenced by that of K. 730, and, as there does not seem to be any, reason to suspect direct or indirect contact between the two documents, it would appear that we have a type of title and confirmation actually used in recording the queen's witness.

2. Ego Ælfgifu eiusdem (*or* praedicti) regis conlaterana (*or* -ea).

Unlike 1, this form of title is found with a variety of forms of confirmation. It occurs in K. 746, 751, 1303 and 1305, which are all in Abingdon cartularies, and might be assumed to have influenced each other. Yet it is probably a contemporary form of title, for it also occurs in a charter of 1011 in the Burton Register (MS. Hengwrt 150, p. 365), and in one of 1019 preserved in a very early, if not a contemporary, copy at Winchester College,[6] while one of 1002 from an Abingdon cartulary (K. 1296) has the similar *Ego Ælfgifu conlaterana regis*. Knútr refers to the queen as *Algiwa mea collaterana* in K. 1316, but the document is a forgery,[7] and elsewhere he refers to her as *regina* : Stowe Charter 39 ; K. 735 (forgery in various manuscripts) ; cf. the double signature *Ego Cnut rex Anglorum cum regina mea Ælfgyfu*, K. 752 (Winchester Cartulary). The title *collaterana* had previously been used by Ælfthryth : B. 1282 (contemporary

---

[1] The only instance of *cwen* so used seems to be *Chronicle*, D, 946.

[2] In B. 972 and 1174, Ælfgifu, wife of Eadwig, and Ælfthryth, wife of Eadgar, sign as *þæs cyninges wif*, but neither is preserved in a contemporary copy.

[3] In the entry for 1017, E has *to cwene*, while C and D have *to wife*.

[4] On the re-introduction of this title in the time of Ælfthryth, see Stevenson's *Asser*, p. 202. It is not found in the tenth century before her time, although it is used occasionally of Eadgifu in late translations and abstracts of documents : B. 766, 823, 881, 1065, 1133.

[5] The queen receives the title *domina* in the Latin version of R. 85 in Stowe Charter 41, but this is a mere isolated literal translation of *seo hlæfdige*.

[6] Printed in the Ordnance Survey Facsimiles, ii, Winchester College, 4, and in the *Liber . . . de Hyda* (Rolls Series, pp. 324–6).

[7] See above, p. xlvii.

copy) [1]; cf. B. 1143 (from Abingdon Cartulary, MS. Cott. Claud. B. VI), where her husband refers to her as *lateranea*.

In the reigns of her sons Emma signs as *Ego Ælfgifu eiusdem* (once, K. 767, *prædicti*) *regis mater* : K. 762-3, 767, 771, 774-5. Of these 763 is from a contemporary copy, 771 is a forgery in the Record Office, and the others are from the Winchester and Abingdon cartularies. The only exceptions are K. 1330, *Hardecnut rex et Ælfgiua mater eius regina*, where the text is not original in its extant form, but is probably a translation of an O.E. writ, the forgery in Thorpe, p. 353, which has the slight variation *Ego Ælfgyfa mater eiusdem regis*, three documents, K. 761, 779, 962, which vary more or less from the regular formula and have already been mentioned as not using the queen's official name, and K. 1332, which will be discussed below. The title *Ego . . eiusdem* (or *prædicti*) *regis mater* had been previously used by Eadgifu (e.g., B. 748, 763, 810, 818, 820, 824) and the same and other very similar formulae by Ælfthryth (e.g., K. 632, 640, 684, 698, 703, 1282).

There is little uniformity in the expression of Emma's assent, and even the limited uniformity which exists seems to be mainly due to the contamination of one document by another in being copied by monastic scribes. Formulae of assent found more than once are :

1. Ego Ælfgyfu regina humillima adiuui.

This is found in two charters written by the same scribe [2] in a contemporary or nearly contemporary hand, Exeter Cathedral, Charter 11, and K. 744 (MS. Cott. Aug. ii. 69).[3] Although the latter is a grant to a Kentish landowner, and hence came into the possession of Christ Church, Canterbury, and accordingly has a late endorsement of a type often found on charters, which were at one time owned by that foundation, it refers to an estate in Devon,[4] and this explains how the existing copy came to be made in the west, by the same scribe as the Exeter Cathedral document already referred to. The identical formula occurs in four other documents : Exeter Cathedral, Charters 9 (K. 728) and 10, K. 743 (from the Winchester Cartulary) and K. 1332 (from the Sherborne Cartulary). The first two of these are documents concerned entirely with matters of the west country, and are preserved in twelfth-century copies ; the third is a grant to a western bishop [5]; the fourth a grant of a Devonshire estate. All the six documents agree in the title and assent of the king as well as in those of the queen, apart from a deviation in Exeter Cathedral, Charter 9. The formula used is *Ego . . Britanniae totius Anglorum monarchus hoc agiae crucis taumate roboraui.*[6] Exeter Cathedral, Charter 9, omits *Anglorum* and substitutes *meae largitatis donum* for *hoc*, thus producing a formula found in other charters of both Knútr and Æthelred (e.g., K. 736, 1301, 1316). K. 1332 is the only document dated after the death of Knútr, in which Emma uses the title *regina*, except K. 761 and 1330, which have already been noted as suspicious (see above, p. 55), and it is therefore evident that it was drawn up on the model of other charters circulating in the west, without regard to the title and form of assent which the widowed queen had

---

[1] Also in B. 1284, but the signature list of that document seems to be influenced by that of B. 1282.

[2] Mr. N. R. Ker kindly confirmed my opinion that these two documents are in one hand.

[3] Facsimile of the former in Ordnance Survey Facsimiles, ii, Exeter Cathedral, 11 ; of the latter in B.M. Facsimiles, iv, 18.

[4] See Napier and Stevenson, *Crawford Collection*, p. 149.

[5] Lyfing, who accompanied Knútr to Rome, and became Bishop of Crediton in the same year (Florence of Worcester, ed. Thorpe, i. 185) : there can be no doubt that this was in 1027 (see above, p. lxii), and therefore the date of this charter (1026) must be an error.

[6] A very similar formula is used by Knútr in K. 729, which is a very doubtful document, also of western origin.

adopted. It may, therefore, be concluded that all these six documents either originated in one western scriptorium, or were all modelled on some charter issued to the west country by Knútr. They do not provide evidence that the combination of title and assent *regina humillima adiuui* was regularly used by a court scribe, who issued Knútr's charters, for the facts that all the documents are connected with the west country, and that the only two extant in contemporary copies are by the same scribe, practically prove that they follow one model, or have a common source.[1] The assent *adiuui* is, however, also found in Winchester College, Charter 4 (cf. above, p. 58), and may have been a standard form for use to express Emma's assent : it is not frequently used by other witnesses.

2. Ego Ælfgifu regina stabilitatem testimonii confirmaui.

This occurs in K. 736, 1301, 1316. The first is preserved in an early copy (Cott. Aug. ii. 24), and the editors of the B.M. Facsimiles (iv, *Preface*) were unable to decide from what archives it derives, but since it was copied into two Evesham cartularies (MSS. Harl. 3763 and Cott. Vesp. B. xxiv) the matter seems hardly doubtful. K. 1316 is known only from Harl. 3763, and is a mere monastic modification of K. 736. K. 1301 is from the Sherborne Cartulary, and refers to land in Dorset. It agrees with K. 736 (and 1316) exactly in the title and consent of the king (see above, p. 59), as well as in those of the queen, but nevertheless it does not seem likely that there has been contact between the Evesham and the Sherborne documents and, consequently, the formula *stabilitatem testimonii confirmaui* can be regarded as one customarily used for the expression of the queen's assent.

3. Ego Ælfgyfu eiusdem regis mater hanc regalem donationem cum trophaeo agiae cruci ouanter diuulgaui.

This is found in K. 763 and 775 ; with *sigillo* for *trophaeo* in K. 774 ; and in an abbreviated form in K. 753. These four documents are all from the Winchester Cartulary, MS. Add. 15350. K. 763 is also extant on a single sheet, Harl. Charter 43 C. 8, but this is not a contemporary copy, but the work of a post-conquest scribe, who attempts to imitate O.E. writing. The number of occurrences of the formula is therefore to be attributed to the influence of Winchester documents upon each other.

4. Ego Ælfgyfu eiusdem regis mater assensum accomodaui.

This formula occurs in three wild forgeries, K. 771 and 779, and Thorpe, p. 353. These documents have undoubtedly influenced each other, but they do not merit discussion.

---

[1] One or two other points show contact between the documents of this group. In all the six documents, the queen signs after the archbishops, a practice otherwise unknown after 1019, cf. below, p. 65. Of the six documents, four, including the two preserved in contemporary copies, spell the name *Ælfgifu* with final -*o*, a spelling found in none of the other documents which name the queen. K. 744 is dated 1031, and, though it is preserved in a fine contemporary copy, it names Earl Hákon among the witnesses, though he was drowned in 1029 or 1030 (see below, p. 72) : this indicates that the document was concocted in the west, following an older model, and did not issue from the court. Of the six documents under discussion, Hákon also signed K. 743. Lastly, it may be noted that, while of the six documents only two are preserved in contemporary copies, and these two are in the same hand, no other two charters of Knútr are in manuscripts by the same scribe : the only other charters of Knútr preserved in copies, which are contemporary or nearly so with the transactions recorded, are Cott. Aug. ii, 24 (= K. 736), Stowe Charters 39 and 42, Ilchester Charter 2 (= K. 741) and Winchester College, Charter 4, and of these no two are in the same hand, or in that of Exeter Cathedral, Charter 11, and Cott. Aug. ii, 69.

5. Ego Ælfgifu eiusdem regis conlaterana praedictum donum confirmo.

This formula is confirmed to K. 1303 and 1305, which are only known from the Abingdon Cartulary, MS. Cott. Claud. B. vi, so influence of one of them on the other is to be suspected.

6. Ego Ælfgyfa praedicti regis conlaterana istud datum uenerandae crucis uexillo consolidaui.

This formula is again confined to documents known only from Abingdon cartularies, K. 746 and 751.

7. Ego Ælfgiua thoro consecrata regio hanc donationem sublimaui.

On the documents with this formula, see above, p. 58.

8. Ego Ælfgifu regina (or conlaterana regis) consensi.

This occurs in K. 749 (from Reg. Alb. Ebor.) and K. 1296 (Abingdon Cartulary). The word consensi is so frequent an expression of assent that its use in two of Queen Emma's signatures is of no consequence.

It appears from the above that the only formulae used more than once each to express Emma's assent in documents not likely to have influenced each other are : (1) adiuui : this is an uncommon expression of assent, though it is used here and there by ecclesiastics and once by a lay witness (K. 643, 746, 751, 787, from various cartularies) ; (2) stabilitatem testimonii confirmaui : in Emma's period this is only once used by another witness, the Archbishop of Canterbury, in Winchester College, Charter 4 ; (7) hanc donationem sublimaui : this is always combined with the title thoro consecrata regio, and is used by Emma only in her period ; (8) consensi : so frequently used by witnesses of all types that it merits no discussion.

The following formulae occur once each to express Queen Emma's assent ; when the name and title are not given they are Ego Ælfgifu regina, or, after Knútr's death, Ego Ælfgifu eiusdem regis mater. A good many of the documents are of a suspicious nature.

1. Reign of Æthelred : K. 714, sciens testimonium adhibui (Eynsham Cartulary) ; K. 719, domini mei regis dono arrisi (Textus Roffensis) ; K. 1304, deuota mente concessi [1] (Crawford Chart. 11 ; etc.) ; Burton Register, ego Ælfgyuu collaterana eiusdem regis hoc mihi placere professa sum (MS. Hengwrt 150, p. 365).

2. Reign of Knútr : Ord. Survey Facs., iii, 39, beneficium hoc predicto archiepiscopo a domino meo rege impetraui (Stowe Charter 39) ; K. 727, ego Emma regina signo crucis confirmo (Reg. C.C. Cant. A. 1) ; K. 734, praescripti regis cum omni alacritate mentis hoc sanciui ut perpetualiter inconcussum sit (Gale and MS. Cole xviii) ; K. 735, omni alacritate mentis hoc confirmaui (Bury Cartulary, Camb. Univ. Lib., MS. Ff. ii, 33) ; K. 739, hanc regiam dapsilitatem collaudaui (Winchester Cartulary) ; K. 740, hanc regiam donationem augendo confirmaui (MS. Cott. Galb. E, ii) ; K. 742, consensi et subscripsi (Cotton Charter X, 11) ; K. 752, ego Cnut rex Anglorum cum regina mea Ælfgyfu propriam donationem regali stabilimento confirmo (Winchester Cartulary) ; K. 1322, hanc largitionem benigniter subarraui (Sherborne Cartulary).

3. Reign of Hörthaknútr : K. 761, ego Ymma regina mater ipsius Hardcnut gaudenter assensum praebui (Bury Cartulary, Camb. Univ. Lib., MS. Ff. ii, 33 ; etc.) ; K. 762, regium munus trophaeo uenerandae crucis corroboro (Abingdon Cartularies).

4. Reign of Eadweard : K. 767, ego Ælfgyfa praedicti regis mater regium munus corroboraui (Abingdon Cartulary, MS. Cott. Claud. B. vi) ; [2] K. 962, ego Ælfgyfa Imma mater regis Eadwardi concessi (St. Alban's Cartulary, MS. Cott. Nero D. i).

---

[1] Napier and Stevenson read consensi.
[2] Cf. K. 762, also an Abingdon document.

APPENDIX II

THE STATUS OF QUEEN EMMA AND HER PREDECESSORS

Queen Emma signs many documents during the reigns of her husbands and sons, and her name is invariably in a high position. She never signs after the bishops, as her husband's mother and great-grandmother frequently do. Nevertheless, this high position of the queen's signature was not introduced by Emma, for it had already appeared towards the end of the life of Æthelred's mother.

It is open to question how far back in West-Saxon history the custom of placing the signatures of queens in a high position may be considered to go, for there is no reliable evidence for the period before the death of Æthelstan. The signature of Eadgifu, the widow of Eadweard the Elder, is amply evidenced during the reigns of her sons, Eadmund and Eadred, and of her grandsons, Eadwig and Eadgar. She signs next after the king, before all other witnesses including archbishops and princes, in a large number of documents [1], e.g., B. 748, 763, 774, 775, 776, 780 (here she signs before, but Prince Eadred after, the Archbishop of Canterbury), 786, 789, 795, 801, 810, 818, 820, 821, 822, 824, 830, 831, 833, 834, 862, 864, 865, 866, 869, 870, 871, 878, 885, 887, 888, 891, 892. She also signs a number of documents after other members of the royal family, but before archbishops, e.g., B. 766, 779, 791, 792, 794, 798, 807. One curious document, B. 880, preserved in two eleventh-century copies, is signed by Eadgifu and Dunstan after all the other witnesses, but their long forms of assent show that they are the chief witnesses after the king, and are placed at the end in the extant manuscripts in a peculiar attempt to give them prominence. In view of the many documents in which Eadgifu signs before the archbishops, B. 770 (Winchester Cartulary) and 803 (Hyde Cartulary), where she signs after Eadred and the archbishops, must be regarded as fabricated or tampered with. This prominent position of Eadgifu's signature is, however, to be regarded as evidence for her powerful personality, rather than to any exceptional West-Saxon respect for the queen as such. This is shown by B. 779 (*Textus Roffensis*), the only charter signed by a living king's wife in this period,[2] where, although Eadgifu occupies her usual high position, Queen Ælfgifu signs in the twelfth place, after all the bishops, but before the

---

[1] With regard to these lists and to similar ones in the pages which follow, it is, of course, true that the documents are by no means all of equal authority. For the purposes of the present enquiry, however, this is not of prime importance, for forgers and modifiers of charters usually had documents before them, which provided models for lists of signatures, and, although they often produce impossible lists, if chronological details are considered, their products, considered in bulk, are not likely to be misleading on broad questions such as, Did the queen usually sign immediately after the king in a given period ? In deciding such a question, quantity rather than quality of evidence is called for : one document, though extant in a fine contemporary copy, may be abnormal, but the agreement of ten, even if they are known only from cartularies, and include some forgeries, provided they are derived from a variety of sources, will point to a norm. I omit from the enquiry, however, documents which are palpably absurd, usually mentioning the omission in a footnote.

[2] Except B. 972, an O.E. abstract of a document of uncertain value belonging to the politically abnormal period of the ascendency of Eadwig's wife and her mother. In the text of K. 404 printed in *Memorials of St. Edmund's Abbey* (Rolls Series, i. 340–1) the name of Ælfgifu, wife of Eadmund I, is added at the top of the list of signatures with the title *regina* (in itself suspicious at that date). No doubt a scribe has ' improved ' this document.

duces. This curious arrangement of signatures can hardly be due to a late forger, unless he had documents before him, which showed him that it was a West-Saxon custom for the queen to sign low. Also, one cannot but suspect that, when the late forger of B. 571 [1] placed the wife of Ælfred in very low position, he had some early document before him, which suggested so doing.[2] It is, however, evident that, from the death of Æthelstan till well into Eadred's reign, the queen-mother never signed after the archbishops, and frequently signed before the princes. The princes, on the other hand, sometimes signed after the Archbishop of Canterbury (B. 753, 780).

A decided change takes place in Eadred's reign. Eadgifu signs B. 895 (A.D. 952), after the king and the Archbishop of Canterbury, but before the bishops (the Archbishop of York does not sign).[3] In 955 she signs B. 905 (Winchester Cartulary) and 906 (Abingdon Cartulary) after all the bishops. In Eadwig's reign, she signs B. 1046 after the Archbishop of Canterbury, but before the bishops, in Eadgar's, B. 1047 after all the bishops. Of these documents, B. 905 is the only one signed by princes, and they sign after Eadgifu. In B. 1190 and 1191 (A.D. 966), the royal family sign between the archbishops, first the princes, then.the queen, and lastly Eadgifu. It should, however, be observed that in the period 952 to 966, although Eadgifu never signs before the Archbishop of Canterbury, and sometimes signs after all the bishops, other royal persons frequently sign in her absence immediately after the king, before the archbishops (e.g., B. 924-7, 930, 932-5), or after the Archbishop of Canterbury only (e.g., B. 931, 938, 941, 949, 968-71), but practically never sign after the bishops (B. 956, where Prince Eadgar signs after the bishops is an exception). In B. 905, therefore, the low position of the princes is perhaps due to a desire to keep the royal signatures together : Eadgifu received a low place, and the princes went into the same position automatically. In any event, it is evident that Eadgifu's status declined in the period from 952 till her death. It is striking that in B. 1190 and 1191, she signs after Queen Ælfthryth : this shows that a change in the relative status of Eadgifu and the reigning king's wife had taken place since B. 779, or the document which suggested its arrangement of signatures, was drawn up.

The signatures of Ælfthryth, Eadgar's wife, present an entirely different picture. The standard place for her signature is amply evidenced as being immediately after those of the bishops, but before all the other witnesses : e.g., B. 1216, 1220, 1230, 1266, 1282, 1284, 1286, 1296, 1302, 1305, 1309. In B. 1303 she signs after the abbots, before the lay witnesses.[4] She rarely signs before any bishops : exceptions are B. 1135, her first recorded signature, where she signs first after the king, before the archbishops, B. 1190 and 1191, which are discussed above, and B. 1175, where she signs[after the archbishops and one prince, but before the bishops. In B. 1295 she signs between the archbishops, but the document is not original in its present form, for Ælfthryth is called mother, instead of wife of the king, the date is wrong,[5] and it should be noticed that the quotation of its list of signatures in B. 1296 is derived from a version in which the queen signed as usual after the bishops. In Eadgar's reign, when the queen and Eadgifu are absent, princes sign immediately after the king, before Dunstan himself (B. 1264, 1310, not good documents, but from different sources), but, when the queen and Eadgifu, or one of them, are present, princes sign with them, after or between the archbishops (B. 1175, 1190, 1191, all mentioned above).

---

[1] See Stevenson's *Asser*, p. 201.
[2] B. 589 is signed by Eadweard the Elder's wife and mother after the king, but there are no other witnesses above the rank of *minister*.
[3] I disregard B. 883, 909, 911, as their lists of signatures have been hopelessly garbled.
[4] Birch has misunderstood the arrangement of the signatures : cf. the reproduction in Ordnance Survey Facsimiles, ii, Charter in Record Office.
[5] See B.M. Facsimiles, iv, *Corrigenda.*

What has been said in the above paragraphs may be summarised as follows. From the death of Æthelstan to 952, the queen-mother signs before the archbishops, in the company of the princes if they are present. In her absence, the princes generally sign before the archbishops (an exception is B. 753, where Eadred signs after the Archbishop of Canterbury). From 952 to the death of Eadgar there is a marked change. The queen and Eadgifu practically never sign before the Archbishop of Canterbury (B. 1135 is the one exception), and are regularly in a low position, after the bishops. On the other hand, in their absence, princes continued to sign as before, first after the king, or after the Archbishop of Canterbury only. (B. 956, where Eadgar signs after all the bishops, is exceptional.) When princes are present with the queens, they sign with them, after the Archbishop of Canterbury (B. 1175, 1190, 1191) or even after the bishops (B. 905). It is evident that the intention before 952 was that the queen-mother should sign next to the king, but, after that time, it was that neither she nor the queen should do so. When other royalties were present, they signed with the queen and Eadgifu, though in their absence they might sign after the king : the desire evidently was to have one place for the royal signatures, and, if one of these were that of the queen or Eadgifu, they all had to be after that of the Archbishop of Canterbury, if not lower. It is unusual in both the periods under discussion to have two groups of royal signatures : the only exceptions are B. 779, discussed above, where the queen and queen-mother sign in different places, and B. 780, where Eadgifu signs before, Eadred after, the Archbishop of Canterbury. In both periods there is inconsistency as to whether the queen and Eadgifu should precede or follow other royalties within the royal group. B. 1190 and the related 1191 have the signature of the queen before that of Eadgifu, but there is no other document of any reliability to enable us to decide if this was the usual practice, for B. 779 is abnormal, being one of the only two charters in the period which split the royal group.

In the first part of the reign of Æthelred, before 1000, Ælfthryth signs after the bishops in K. 633, 640, 696, but in K. 632 and 1282 she signs immediately after the king, before the archbishops. In these five documents no princes sign. In K. 684 and 703, she signs after the bishops, and the princes follow her. In K. 698 she signs after the king, and the princes follow her before the archbishops. In her absence, the princes sign after the bishops in K. 700, between the archbishops and bishops in K. 672 and 705. Doubtful in nature as some of these documents are,[1] the following broad facts may be derived from them. The royal family always sign as a group, and the queen-mother always heads it. There is inconsistency as to whether the royal group shall be the first, second or third after the king. But the royal group never precedes the archbishops in Ælfthryth's absence, but it does so once in her presence. She, on the contrary, precedes the archbishops twice in the absence of princes. It would seem that her status was now definitely higher than that of the princes, whereas in the reign of her husband it had been lower. Also it has improved absolutely, not merely in relation to the princes, for a tendency was arising to put her signature next to that of the king. Just as the status of princes had declined in relation to that of Ælfthryth, so it had declined absolutely, for, in the queen's absence they never sign before the archbishops, as they often did earlier, and sometimes sign after the bishops.

In and after 1000 a decided change takes place. Ælfthryth ceases to sign, and the signatures of Emma soon begin. In the queen's absence, the princes nearly always sign after the king, before the archbishops : K. 707, 710, 711, 1294, 1295, 1307, 1308. They follow the archbishops in K. 1297, 1306, 1310, but never follow the bishops.[2] When the

---

[1] I leave out of consideration the ridiculous forgery, K. 643.

[2] I omit K. 720, where there are no ecclesiastical signatories in the extant text, the wild forgery K. 723, the highly abnormal 1309, where the princes follow the *duces*, and 706, where they are inserted among the bishops.

queen is present, the order varies. In K. 714 and 1301 the royal family precedes the archbishops with the queen last ; in K. 1303 and 1305 it precedes the archbishops with the queen first ; in K. 1296 it comes after the archbishops, with the queen first.[1] In K. 719, in the absence of princes, Emma signs immediately after the king. It can only be concluded that, in this period, it was usual for the royal family to sign immediately after the king, before the archbishops, but that there was some uncertainty as to whether the queen should precede or follow the princes.[2] This implies that the queen's status was rather lower than that of the queen-mother had been in the earlier part of the reign, but that the status of the royal family as a whole had definitely improved.

In the time of Knútr there are no royal signatures except those of the king and queen. Emma can be found signing before, between, and after the archbishops, but never lower. In Stowe Charter 39 (A.D. 1018) and Winchester College, Charter 4 (A.D. 1019), she follows them, in K. 736 (MS. Cott. Aug. ii, 24 ; A.D. 1021-3) she precedes them. In Exeter Cathedral, Charters 9 (= K. 728), 10 and 11, and in MS. Cott. Aug. ii, 69 (= K. 744), she follows the archbishops, and the word *humillima* is added to her title of *regina*, but these documents, which have already been discussed at some length,[3] belong to a group which cannot be regarded as independent of each other, but are all influenced by a model which, since the earliest of them is dated 1018, must have belonged to the beginning of the reign. It would therefore appear that Emma's status was at first lower under Knútr than it had been under Æthelred, but that it improved again about 1020. This is fully borne out by the documents preserved in cartularies : Emma signs between the archbishops in 1018 (K. 727), after the one archbishop present in 1019 (K. 730), but after that always before them : K. 734, 735, 739, 740, 742, 745, 746, 749, 750,[4] 751, 753, 1316, 1322. The only exception is K. 743, which is under the influence of the same model as the Exeter group.[5]

In the reigns of her sons, there is no exception to the rule that Emma signs immediately after the king, except K. 1332, which is again under the same influence as the Exeter group[6] : K. 761, 762, 763, 767, 768, 771, 773, 774, 775, 779, 788, 962, 1330, Thorpe, p. 353, R. 94. The doubtful nature of many of these documents cannot affect the value of their combined evidence, since they are so numerous.

[1] I omit the abnormal K. 709, where the royal family, headed by the queen, come after the archbishops and one bishop, and the rest of the bishops follow them (the document is in any event a forgery), and K. 1304 (= *Crawford Collection*, 11), where the queen comes between, and the princes follow, the archbishops. In the next reign, Emma signs between the archbishops again once (K. 727), but the division of the royal group is confined to K. 1304 in the eleventh century, so the document is to be regarded as abnormal.

[2] This is confirmed by an interesting group of unpublished charters of Æthelred in MS. Hengwrt 150 (Burton Register). In seven documents with dates running from 1007 to 1012 the members of the royal family present sign immediately after the king. Emma signs only one of these seven documents : her signature precedes those of the princes.

[3] See above, pp. 59-60.

[4] This has a joint signature of the king and queen, see above, p. 58.

[5] See above, p. 60.   [6] See above, p. 59.

APPENDIX III

THE SCANDINAVIAN SUPPORTERS OF KNÚTR

A. *Eiríkr Hákonarson jarl*

The Encomiast has a great deal to say about Eiríkr and Thorkell, two Scandinavian supporters of Knútr. A brief account of these two men is called for, as the notes on them in Napier and Stevenson's *Crawford Collection* draw on interpretations of the Scandinavian sources, which date from a period when the interrelationships of these were imperfectly understood.

The statement of the Encomiast (II, 7) that Knútr's great supporter Eiríkr [1] was the ruler of Norway, but was a vassal of the Danish king, puts it beyond doubt that the person referred to is Eiríkr, son of Hákon Sigurtharson Hlathajarl. The power of the earls of Hlathir reached its highest point when Hákon, the father of Eiríkr, became ruler of Norway (as earl, not king) about 970.[2] He owed his success to Danish help. His son Eiríkr's career is dealt with in several poems composed in his honour by contemporary skalds.[3] Norse poets of that period aimed at the artistic decoration of facts known to their hearers rather than at giving information, so it is not surprising that very little is to be learned about Eiríkr from these poems. We have no knowledge of the careers of two of the poets who celebrate Eiríkr, and so we can form no idea as to how good their opportunities were for collecting accurate information about their hero. Of these two, Eyjólfr Dáthaskald appears to have dealt with many early feats of Eiríkr in his *Bandadrápa*.[4] Two verses of this refer to the slaying of one Skopti, another says that its hero had been south over the seas before he began to rule, and five more celebrate feats of viking round the Baltic ; two of these five actually name Eiríkr as their hero. These eight verses are quoted in *Heimskringla*,[5] and *Fagrskinna* quotes the first of them, and summarises most of those on Baltic viking, together, apparently, with a number of lost ones on the same subject.[6] A ninth verse is quoted in Snorri's *Edda*. It names Eiríkr and says that he has taken authority in the land. The second of these skalds is Halldórr Ókristni, who appears to have composed a poem, *Eiríksflokkr*, on Eiríkr's deeds

---

[1] On this name and the various forms in which it occurs, see Napier and Stevenson, *Crawford Collection*, p. 143 ; O. von Feilitzen, *The pre-conquest personal names of Domesday Book*, p. 299 ; D. Whitelock in the Viking Society's *Saga-Book*, xii. 133–4.

[2] By 974 at the latest, see Bjarni Aðalbjarnarson's ed. of *Heimskringla* (i, p. xcii).

[3] It cannot be too clearly emphasised that the verses of the skalds, who composed for the kings of Norway and Denmark in the tenth and eleventh centuries, and occasionally for prominent noblemen, are preserved only in quotations in the Old Norse Sagas, particularly in *Heimskringla* and *Fagrskinna*. Hence, although the basic principle of the study of early Scandinavian history must always be to study the verses separately from the prose in which they are embedded, and to see if they necessarily bear the meaning which the prose alleges them to do, yet, even when this is done, the danger always remains that a verse may not be genuinely early, or may be early but not refer to the events with which the prose connects it. The verses in the Sagas of the kings seem to be given in good faith by the compilers, who appear to avoid the practice, which is not uncommon in other Sagas, of writing verses to fit their narrative, and alleging that characters in their story composed them.

[4] Edited in *Skjaldedigtning*, IA, pp. 200 ff. ; IB, pp. 190 ff.

[5] *Óláfs Saga Tryggvasonar*, chaps. 20, 89–90.   [6] Pp. 105, 136–7.

at Svöld.[1] Eight verses said to be from this poem are quoted in the accounts of the battle of Svöld in the Old Norse translation of Oddr's *Óláfs Saga Tryggvasonar*, in *Heimskringla* and in *Fagrskinna* : only *Heimskringla* has them all. The first verse names Eiríkr, and describes him coming south from Sweden to the battle. The other verses are battle pictures, and, though the sources which quote them are, no doubt, correct in referring them to the deeds of Eiríkr at Svöld, his participation in that battle is so well established a fact, that we are not greatly enlightened as to his career by Halldórr's poem. The passages of *Heimskringla* and *Fagrskinna*, in which the verses so far considered are quoted, define more clearly the circumstances to which the verses allude, and the source upon which they draw in dealing with the earliest part of Eiríkr's career is a lost Saga on the earls of Hlathir (called by modern writers *Hlaðajarla Saga* [2]). They tell us that the Skopti, whom Eiríkr slew, was a friend of Hákon, and that father and son were on bad terms owing to the slaying. Eiríkr withdrew to Denmark, and received from the Danish king a fief in the south of Norway.[3] Whatever may be the truth of this story of Eiríkr's early exile from his father's court, it is clear that the two had composed their differences by the time of the attempted invasion of Norway by forces of unknown composition with Danish backing, which is known to saga as the expedition of the Jómsvíkings.[4] Eiríkr's deeds in the famous battle, in which the Norwegians repulsed their foes, fill a large part in the accounts of it in the Sagas,[5] and verses quoted concerning this battle confirm the presence of Eiríkr. The verses in question are : the tenth of a *drápa* on Hákon by Tindr Hallkelsson,[6] from which we gather that Eiríkr's famous ship, the Barthi, was in the battle ; the first of Thórthr Kolbeinsson's *Belgskaka-drápa*,[7] in which he says that ' Sigurthr's brother ' (Eiríkr had a brother of the name) defeated the Danes ; the first four of the same poet's *Eiríksdrápa*, in which he describes how the hero prepared to defend his father's land on an occasion, which is described in

---

[1] *Skjaldedigtning*, IA, pp. 202 ff. ; I-B, pp. 193 ff.
[2] The best discussion of this lost Saga is that of Bjarni Aðalbjarnarson *Om de norske kongers sagaer*, pp. 199–201, 217–24 ; cf. W. van Eeden, *Neophilologus*, xxxi. 76–8, for a different view.
[3] In the uncertainty, which now prevails, concerning the precise political conditions in Scandinavia in the time of Earl Hákon, it is not possible to estimate the likelihood of this story, that Eiríkr received a grant of Norwegian territory from the Danish king. It is not necessary so to interpret the verse quoted by *Heimskringla* to support the story : see Bjarni Aðalbjarnarson, *Heimskringla*, i. 250–1.
[4] This is to be dated in all probability some time between 980 and 990 : see Bjarni Aðalbjarnarson, *op. cit.*, pp. cix–xii, where the question of the identity of the invaders is also briefly discussed. The latter problem does not concern the present enquiry.
[5] Though he does not appear in Saxo Grammaticus, who also has an account of the battle (ed. Holder, p. 327). The accounts of the battle in *Heimskringla*, *Fagrskinna* and the various extant forms of *Jómsvíkinga Saga* no doubt represent combinations of material from *Hlaðajarla Saga* and the lost original form of *Jómsvíkinga Saga*, but it is now impossible to separate the elements. Eiríkr's presence in the battle is also mentioned in two thirteenth-century Norse poems about it : one is referred to below, p. 73, note 4 ; the other is the *Búadrápa* of Thorkell Gíslason, edited *Skjaldedigtning*, IA, pp. 553 ff. ; I-B, pp. 536 ff.
[6] Tindr was an Icelander, who is stated by *Fagrskinna* and the A.M. 510 version of *Jómsvíkinga Saga* to have been present at the battle. These sources are not independent, however, and the statement may be a mere inference from the fact that Tindr described the battle. His poem is edited *Skjaldedigtning*, IA, pp. 144 ff. ; I-B, pp. 136 ff.
[7] The poems of Thórthr are edited *Skjaldedigtning*, IA, pp. 212 ff. ; I-B, pp. 202 ff. He was an Icelander, who was in Norway on various occasions, but the view that he visited England is pure supposition, based on the fact that he described Eiríkr's English campaign, though it is stated as a fact that he did so by the editors of the *Crawford Collection* (p. 145). He probably based his verses on Eiríkr's voyage to England and his campaign there on travellers' tales, and they are to be used with caution, cf. below, pp. 69–70.

sufficient detail to enable it to be identified with the attempt of the so-called Jómsvíkings against Norway. The second and third verses of *Belgskakadrápa* describe how Eiríkr, despite his triumph over the Danes, withdrew to Sweden when Óláfr Tryggvason returned to Norway (995). We have already seen that Halldórr Ókristni says that Eiríkr came to Svöld from Sweden, so we are no doubt justified in thinking that he withdrew there on his father's fall,[1] and made the country the base for at least some of his viking exploits in the Baltic. To judge by the summary of Eyjólfr's poem in *Fagrskinna* alluded to above, Eiríkr indulged in desultory raiding not only before and after the fight with the Jómsvíkings, but even after the victory of Svöld had made him virtual ruler of Norway.

The part played by Eiríkr in the confederation of Sweden and Denmark, which overthrew Óláfr Tryggvason at Svöld in 1000, and the subsequent division of Norway are known not only from the Saga of Óláfr Tryggvason, in its various forms, but from the Norwegian compendia of history.[2] The problems connected with these events are too exclusively of Norwegian interest to be discussed here. It is, however, clear that Eiríkr and his brother Sveinn became rulers of Norway, but that they recognised some degree of suzerainty on the part of Sveinn of Denmark, and perhaps also on that of Óláfr of Sweden. *Fagrskinna* and *Heimskringla*, no doubt drawing on *Hlaðajarla Saga*, tell us that Eiríkr married Gytha, daughter of the king of Denmark, and Sveinn Hólmfríthr, daughter of the king of Sweden.[3] Not only the poem of Halldórr mentioned above, but also three further verses of Thórthr's *Eiríksdrápa* deal with this period in Eiríkr's career.[4]

The joint rule of Eiríkr and Sveinn in Norway is said to have lasted twelve years by most Scandinavian sources, but Theodricus gives fifteen years, and the *Historia Norvegiae* fourteen. It appears, however, to have been thought both in Iceland and Norway, that

---

[1] In the earliest version of the Saga of Óláfr Tryggvason, written in Latin late in the twelfth century by Oddr Snorrason, an Icelander, and known to us from various recensions of an Old Norse translation (all edited by Finnur Jónsson in *Saga Óláfs Tryggvasonar*, Copenhagen, 1932), Eiríkr and his brother Sveinn chance to be absent from Norway, when Óláfr Tryggvason returns. The versions of the Saga in *Fagrskinna* and *Heimskringla* (both revisions of Oddr's Saga) make Eiríkr withdraw because of Óláfr's arrival, in order to conform with Thórthr's verses, which they quote : *Heimskringla* assumes that Sveinn was with him, but *Fagrskinna* does not mention him. Of the Norwegian compendia of history, *Ágrip* makes the two brothers flee to Sweden on Óláfr's arrival, the *Historia Norvegiae* to Denmark, while Theodricus does not mention the matter. The first of these texts is edited by Finnur Jónsson, Halle, 1929 ; the other two in G. Storm's *Monumenta Historica Norvegiae*, Christiania, 1880. They all belong to the late twelfth century, though *Hist. Nor.* is extant only in a later modified and extended form (thirteenth century). *Ágrip* makes use of both the others, and all three are influenced by Icelandic verse and tradition, so they cannot be regarded with confidence, when they agree with Icelandic sources, as giving confirmation of these from independent Norwegian tradition. The use of literary sources in these works must also be allowed for : e.g., Theodricus has material from William of Jumièges, and *Hist. Nor.* from Adam of Bremen ; cf. also above, p. 56, note 5, and below, p. 78, note 1.

[2] Eiríkr is curiously absent from the accounts of the fall of Óláfr Tryggvason in Adam of Bremen and Saxo Grammaticus, who do not give any information as to what arrangements Sveinn of Denmark made for the government of Norway.

[3] Eiríkr's marriage is mentioned by *Fagrskinna* (p. 136) and Theodricus (Storm, p. 24). *Heimskringla* places it before the conquest of Norway in 1000 (*Óláfs Saga Tryggvasonar*, chap. 90). *Heimskringla* is the only source for Sveinn's marriage, which it places at the time of the conquest (*ibid.*, chap. 113). These marriages were no doubt mentioned in *Hlaðajarla Saga* and hence found their way into *Heimskringla* and *Fagrskinna*. Theodricus may have known of Eiríkr's marriage from independent tradition. When *Ágrip* (ed. Finnur Jónsson, p. 24) and the Legendary Saga of Óláfr Helgi, chap. 10, call Eiríkr a relative of Knútr, they doubtless allude to his Danish marriage.

[4] Also a good many other verses by Hallfrethr and Skúli Thorsteinsson, and the ninth verse of Eyjólfr's poem referred to above.

Sveinn and his nephew, Hákon, Eiríkr's son, ruled for two years after Eiríkr's departure, before the arrival of Óláfr Helgi.[1] It is generally stated that Eiríkr went to England to support Knútr, after the death of Sveinn, and that he died there following an operation.[2] A verse is quoted in *Heimskringla*[3] with reference to Eiríkr's journey, in which it is said that two kings invited Eiríkr to come to meet them.[4] The verse is said by Snorri to be by Thórthr and it is generally assumed to belong to the *Eiríksdrápa*. It is far from clear whether this verse really refers to the occasion when Eiríkr finally left Norway, but, even if it be assumed that it does so, it throws no light on the question of the date of Eiríkr's withdrawal from Norway. By assuming that the kings referred to are Sveinn and Knútr, we can regard Eiríkr as having joined their expedition of 1013, and by assuming them to be Haraldr and Knútr, we can assume that Eiríkr joined the expedition of 1015, which was led by Knútr, but enjoyed Haraldr's support.[5] The latter view is to be preferred, for all the sources, which touch upon the point, are unanimous, that Eiríkr went to England to support Knútr, after the death of Sveinn of Denmark.[6] In *Knytlinga Saga*, chap. 13,[7] two verses are quoted as being from Thórthr's *Eiríksdrápa*, which appear to imply that the fleets of Knútr and Eiríkr joined as they approached the English coast. If this were the case, it would follow that Eiríkr left Norway in 1015 at much the same time as Knútr left Denmark. Now it is highly probable that Óláfr Helgi returned to Norway in 1014,[8] and it is most unlikely that Eiríkr would leave the country, if Óláfr's victorious campaign had begun. If, therefore, seems practically certain that the two kings, Haraldr, king of Denmark, and Knútr, who had been declared king by his crews in 1014,[9] invited Eiríkr to join them, and that he went to Denmark in that year.[10] Thórthr

[1] This was the case in the chronological system of Sæmundr Fróthi, which is known from the late twelfth-century Icelandic poem, *Nóregs konunga-tal* (see *Skjaldedigtning*, IA, pp. 579 ff.; IB, pp. 575 ff.), and used by *Fagrskinna* (p. 144); since *Heimskringla* also allows Eiríkr a rule of twelve years, we may presume that the system of Ari Fróthi here agreed with that of Sæmundr. *Ágrip* has the same system, and Theodricus, while allowing Eiríkr fifteen years, also has the gap of two years thereafter (Storm, p. 25).

[2] So *Nóregs konunga-tal*, Theodricus, *Ágrip*, *Heimskringla*, *Fagrskinna*. Worthless additions to the story in the late expanded version of the Saga of Óláf Tryggvason allege treachery to the part of Knútr or of an old enemy (*Fornmanna Sögur*, iii. 31; *Flateyjarbók*, i. 561). Theodricus differs from the other sources in regarding Eiríkr's departure from Norway as due to uneasy relationships with his brother, and here we may have a separate Norwegian tradition. *Nóregs konunga-tal* does not state why Eiríkr left Norway.

[3] *Óláfs Saga Helga*, chap. 24.

[4] Finnur Jónsson's translation of this verse in *Skjaldedigtning* is an absurdity. The sense is well given by Vígfússon and Powell (*Corpus Poeticum Boreale*, ii. 104).

[5] As the Encomiast tells.

[6] See above, note 2. Theodricus does not make himself clear, whether Knútr or Sveinn was the Danish commander in England when Eiríkr arrived.

[7] Ed. by Af Petersens and Olsen, in *Sögur Danakonunga* (Copenhagen, 1919–25), pp. 44–5.

[8] Óláfr certainly returned in the autumn of 1014 or 1015 (see below, p. 79, note 8) and the evidence points fairly strongly to the former year. If, however, it be assumed that Óláfr returned in 1015, it follows that Eiríkr may have joined Knútr in England, not in Denmark, and that Thórthr's account may be correct. [9] *Old English Chronicle.*

[10] According to the version of the Saga of Óláfr Helgi known as the Legendary Saga, rumours of Óláfr's movements were already current before Eiríkr left Norway. The Legendary Saga, either independently or following the Oldest Saga, here inserts a piece of tradition which clashes with its main narrative, in which Knútr and Eiríkr are already in England before Óláfr leaves that country (see below, p. 80). See the note in Keyser and Unger's edition, p. 104. The Legendary Saga also makes Hákon pay a flying visit to England to ask Knútr's help as Óláfr approaches. On the nature of the Legendary Saga, and the relationships of the various Sagas of Óláfr Helgi, see below, pp. 80–1.

must be assumed to have been ill-informed if he believed that Knútr and Eiríkr joined forces off the English coast. The view, which, as has already been pointed out, appears in many Scandinavian sources, that Eiríkr's rule of Norway lasted only twelve years, cannot be maintained : it presumably takes its origin in the fact that fourteen years intervened between Svöld and the arrival of Óláfr Helgi in Norway, but why that fourteen years should be divided into twelve years of Eiríkr's and Sveinn's rule plus two of Sveinn and Hákon's, instead of into fourteen years of the former plus a few months of the latter, is not clear. The Norwegian Latin compendia are closer to the truth in their estimate of the length of Eiríkr's rule, but Theodricus is in error in that he also allows two years for the rule of Sveinn and Hákon.

On Eiríkr's part in the campaign of 1015–16 we learn nothing from English sources, except that he was appointed earl of Northumbria after the murder of Uhtred in 1016.[1] Uhtred was earl of all Northumbria,[2] so, since Eiríkr was made *eorl eal swa Uhtred wæs*, he must have become ruler, under Knútr, of the entire province, and, when his position was confirmed in 1017, it is evident that his earldom was considered to be a quarter of the kingdom.[3] Nevertheless, Eiríkr is not mentioned in the Northumbrian lists of the earls of that province, for these regard Uhtred's successor as having been his brother Eadulf.[4] It is, of course, possible that Eadulf held part of the province, but acknowledged the superiority of Eiríkr, and succeeded to the whole on Eiríkr's death.[5] Perhaps owing to the remote situation of the earldom held by Eiríkr, it appears that Thorkell took a certain precedence over him early in Knútr's reign (cf. below, p. 75). It may be noticed that Eiríkr never signs documents before Thorkell. Eiríkr's career in England seems to have been short : he signs charters, beginning with the earliest ones issued in Knútr's reign, and ceasing in 1023 (K. 739, Winchester Cartulary), and may be said to disappear from history in that year. He is mentioned in the Thorney *Liber Vitae*.[6] William of Malmesbury says that he was exiled by Knútr and returned to his native land,[7] but nothing is more improbable than that the great Earl of Hlathir returned to Norway without making the slightest impression on the history of that country. The Norse sources say that he died in England owing to loss of blood, following an operation.[8] This story is more probable than Malmesbury's, who probably took a hint from the exile of Thorkell Hávi, the other Scandinavian participant in the fourfold partition of England, in fabricating a story to account for the small part played by Eiríkr in history after 1017.

The activities of Eiríkr during Knútr's conquest of England are the subject of a number of further verses of Thórthr's *Eiríksdrápa*. One of these is quoted by *Heimskringla*,[9] and the substance of it is that the hero fought Úlfkell Snillingr, west of London. (In the *Heimskringla* the verse is taken to imply that Úlfkell was killed, a fault of interpretation which *Knytlinga Saga* corrects in quoting the same verse.) Another of these verses, known only from *Knytlinga Saga*, alleges that Eiríkr (he is actually named) fought victoriously at *Hringmaraheiðr* : this is the Norse name of the spot near Ipswich where Úlfkell fought Thorkell's forces in 1010.[10] If the first of these verses is correctly referred to Thórthr's poem, we must assume that Eiríkr had a brush with Úlfkell near London, and this may have happened at the time of one of the sieges of London in 1016. The Encomiast (II, 7) implies that Eiríkr superintended the siege operations, and his presence

---

[1] *Old English Chronicle.*   [2] See *N.C.*, i. 660.   [3] *Old English Chronicle.*
[4] *N.C., loc. cit.*   [5] So Freeman suggests, *N.C., loc. cit.*
[6] Viking Society's *Saga Book*, xii. 132.
[7] *Gesta Regum*, ii. 181. Henry of Huntingdon follows William.
[8] See references above, p. 69, note 2. Some of these sources say that Eiríkr was then going on a pilgrimage to Rome or had just returned. *Heimskringla* and *Fagrskinna* err in placing his death respectively one and two years after he came to England.
[9] *Óláfs Saga Helga*, chap. 25.   [10] See below, p. 77.

at the taking of London is a Norse tradition, for which the evidence is comparatively early : it appeared already in the oldest version of the Saga of Óláfr Helgi, and finds its way thence into the later versions of the Saga.[1] Accordingly a skirmish with Úlfkell near London may well have taken place. The second of these verses is an obvious forgery. A campaign in the southern part of East Anglia does not fit in well with the lines of the fighting in 1015–16. Accordingly, it seems evident, that the mention of Úlfkell in the first of these verses recalled to some late poet ill-acquainted with English geography the famous verses of Sigvatr and Óttarr, in which the battle of *Hringmaraheiðr* (A.D. 1010) is described,[2] for Sigvatr says that it was *á Úlfkels landi*. This led to the assumption that the brush with Úlfkell took place near *Hringmaraheiðr*, and a verse was produced in which Eiríkr was credited with a battle at the later place.[3] Two further verses are preserved, which are also supposed to belong to Thórthr's poem, but no concrete fact can be derived from them.

Eiríkr was a Christian according to the traditions current in Norway and Iceland in the twelfth century. A picturesque story of his conversion is given by Theodricus, and elaborated by Oddr.[4] The tradition of the church of Bremen was that the faith was well supported in Norway under the rule of Sveinn of Denmark (i.e., in the period when Eiríkr and his brother were viceroys), but Norse tradition is divided on the point.[5]

It is difficult today to decide if the Encomiast's story (II, 15), that Eiríkr acted personally as Knútr's headsman, when the monarch ordered the execution of Eadric Streona, can be true, but he may at least have attended to the matter (cf. however, above, p. lxix).

Eiríkr's son Hákon and brother Sveinn were both defeated by Óláfr Helgi on his return to Norway. The former withdrew to England and the latter soon died. Hákon became Knútr's viceroy in Norway when Óláfr Helgi fled (1028), but perished at sea just afterwards. These events are recorded by Theodricus, *Ágrip*, and the various versions of the Saga of Óláfr Helgi. The *Old English Chronicle*, MS. C, notices that Hákon, *se dohtiga eorl*, died at sea in 1030, before the death of Óláfr Helgi, and obviously Eiríkr's son is referred to. Florence of Worcester repeats this, and adds the interesting remark, that some say Hákon was killed in the Orkneys : Theodricus places Hákon's shipwreck in the Pentland Firth, and so we have here a valuable confirmation of the sound and ancient nature of the notes on Scandinavian matters which Florence so often adds to the material

---

[1] Eiríkr's presence at London during the siege and his being in some way related to Knútr (see above, p. 68, note 3) are the only facts concerning him, which clearly belong to the Saga of Óláfr Helgi in its early form, and are accordingly almost the only ones which appears in the Legendary Saga. (The only exception is the curious tradition recorded by the Legendary Saga which is discussed above, p. 69, note 10.) The additional information concerning his career after 1000, which we find in *Fagrskinna* and *Heimskringla*, comes from *Hlaðajarla Saga*, and Thórthr's verses.

[2] See below, pp. 76–7.

[3] Steenstrup, *Normannerne*, iii. 284, n. 2, hints that he does not consider the verse genuine. The verse is palpably influenced by that of Óttarr, in which the battle of Ringmere of the year 1010 is referred to (see below, p. 77) : both verses have in common the line *rauð Hringmaraheiði*. Nevertheless, Finnur Jónsson (*Knytlingasaga, dens Kilder og historiske Værd*, Copenhagen, 1907, p. 17), prefers to regard the verse as genuine and compares the sporadic raiding attributed by the Encomiast (II, 7) to Eiríkr.

[4] Storm, p. 24 ; *Saga Óláfs Tryggvasonar*, ed. Finnur Jónsson, pp. 220 ff.

[5] See Adam of Bremen, ii. 39. Theodricus states that Eiríkr allowed freedom of religion, but the *Historia Norvegiae* that he and his brother nearly uprooted the faith (Storm, pp. 25 and 119). *Heimskringla* and *Fagrskinna* support Theodricus, and their agreement, as usual in matters concerning Eiríkr, points to *Hlaðajarla Saga* as their source.

in the *Chronicle*. Nevertheless, when Florence states, that Hákon was sent by Knútr on a mission in 1029, later than 11 November, as an honourable exile, and that he was married to a niece of Knútr, his statements are open to grave doubt. The question of Hákon's marriage will be discussed below.[1] With regard to the date and circumstances of Hákon's departure from England, it may at once be said, that it is out of the question that Knútr would have entrusted Norway to a man with whom he was on indifferent terms, after he had at last secured that kingdom after years of intrigue and effort. With regard to the date, the Norse accounts [2] are unanimous that Hákon was made viceroy of Norway by Knútr on his visit to the North in 1028, and this is confirmed by the poem of Thórarinn Loftunga on Knútr's expedition, where it is stated that Knútr made a relative ruler of Norway.[3] (It will be remembered that Eiríkr's wife was a sister of Knútr.) The accounts of the expedition in *Heimskringla* and *Fagrskinna* make Knútr withdraw from Norway, leaving Hákon in charge, before the flight of Óláfr. This, however, is a modification of the version of the Oldest Saga of Óláfr, which, as the Legendary Saga shows, made Óláfr withdraw, while Knútr's bloodless conquest was still in progress.[4] This is supported by the Norwegian compendia,[5] and is obviously much more likely : Knútr would hardly leave Hákon in charge, while Óláfr was still in the field. Accordingly, Hákon's appointment as regent can be placed late in 1028. Using the evidence of three verses of Sigvatr, *Heimskringla* regards Hákon as having been with Knútr on his previous expedition to the North (the year of the battle of Helge-å, on the date see below, p. 82).[6] *Fagrskinna*, however, refers one of these verses to the expedition of 1028,[7] and there seems no reason why this should not be correct, and apply to the others as well : actually, it is not certain that the third one refers to Hákon at all.

Theodricus states that Hákon perished in the Pentland Firth on his way back from England, whither he had gone to fetch his bride, the year after his appointment as viceroy. *Ágrip* is less detailed, but says that Hákon perished in the spring after his appointment. The Sagas of Óláfr Helgi place his death in the autumn, and they give the same object for the journey as Theodricus.[8] It does not seem that there is any means in which one can decide between these Scandinavian sources, which all place Hákon's death in the year after his appointment (1029), and the *Old English Chronicle*, which places it in 1030. Knútr sent his son Sveinn to take Hákon's place. Norwegian tradition seems to have placed Sveinn's arrival in Norway before Óláfr Helgi's return and death in 1030.[9] On the other hand, the oldest version of the Saga of Óláfr Helgi placed the arrival of Sveinn after the death of Óláfr, and this is repeated by *Heimskringla* and *Fagrskinna*, though the Legendary Saga has an unhappy combination of the two accounts,[10] and *Knytlinga Saga*, chap. 17, fails to make itself clear on the point.

Hákon signs Knútr's charters as *dux* from 1019 to 1026.[11] The evidence that, while

---

[1] See p. 85.

[2] Theodricus (Storm, p. 31) ; *Ágrip* (ed. Finnur Jónsson, p. 29) ; and all forms of *Óláfs Saga Helga*.

[3] The poem is known as *Tøgdrápa* : parts of it are quoted with reference to the events of 1028, by all the Sagas of Óláfr Helgi. Edited *Skjaldedigtning*, IA, pp. 322 ff. ; IB, pp. 298–9.

[4] See Legendary Saga, chap. 76.

[5] Theodricus (Storm, p. 31) ; *Ágrip* (ed. Finnur Jónsson, p. 29).

[6] *Óláfs Saga Helga*, chaps. 146, 161.

[7] P. 170.

[8] Legendary Saga, chap. 77 ; *Heimskringla's* version, chap. 184 ; *Fagrskinna*, p. 179.

[9] Theodricus (Storm, p. 34) ; *Ágrip* (ed. Finnur Jónsson, p. 29).

[10] Chaps. 77 and 101 contradict one another. This is merely due to the fact that the Legendary Saga is interpolated from *Ágrip*. See Nordal, *Om Olaf den helliges saga*, pp. 34–5.

[11] On his signature to K. 744, see above, p. 60.

in England, he was earl of Worcester is slight but good (see *N.C.*, ii. 579–80).[1] He is mentioned, like his father, in the Thorney *Liber Vitae*.[2]

B. *Þorkell Strút-Haraldsson inn hávi*

In all versions of *Jómsvíkinga Saga*,[3] and in the *Jómsvíkingadrápa* of Bishop Bjarni of Orkney,[4] two of the leaders of the great assault on Norway, which is the culmination of the story of the Jómsvíkings, are Thorkell Hávi and Sigvaldi, two sons of Strút-Haraldr, Earl of Zealand. They are said to have had a brother, Hemingr, who was very young at the time with which the Saga deals. The presence of Thorkell at the great battle in which the Norwegians repulsed their enemies [5] is not vouched for by any contemporary verse, though that of Sigvaldi is,[6] and, similarly, Saxo Grammaticus, who tells the story of the Jómsvíkings,[7] knows of Sigvaldi, but not of Thorkell. Thorkell also appears in the *Ólafs Saga Tryggvasonar* of Oddr, where he advises Eiríkr to adopt a certain stratagem in order to affect a boarding of Ólafr's ship in the battle of Svöld. This stratagem seems to have been an element in the traditions respecting Ólafr's last fight, for it appears also in the twelfth-century Icelandic poem *Rekstefja*, which deals with Ólafr's career [8] ; but the attribution of it to Thorkell has no authority outside Oddr's work, and the presence of Thorkell at Svöld may be a fiction of Oddr's, occasioned by the undoubted fact that Sigvaldi was at the battle, though it is far from clear whom he was supporting.[9] It will, therefore, be seen that Thorkell's early appearances in history are shadowy and uncertain.

Thorkell Hávi appears again in the Legendary Saga of Ólafr Helgi, a work which is in the main a summary of a Saga, of which only a few fragments are extant, but which was one of the oldest of Icelandic Sagas.[10] The young Ólafr, a rising viking chief, hears that Thorkell is in England and is a mighty and wise man. He joins him, and they win a battle at *Suðrvík* in England. Thorkell's object at this time was to avenge his brother, who had been killed along with all the thingmen, of whom he was the commander. Now this reference to Thorkell's desire to avenge his brother enables us to identify him with the Thorkell whose army appeared in England in 1009, and whose activities are frequently alluded to in both the *Old English Chronicle* and the *Encomium*, for the latter source (I, 2) mentions that Thorkell avenged his brother in England. Florence of Worcester (ed. Thorpe, i. 161) says that Thorkell's fleet, soon after its arrival, was joined by another under Hemingr and Eilífr, and it is tempting to see in this Hemingr the brother whom Thorkell avenged, for he does not appear in history again, and, as is noted above, Icelandic tradition knows of a brother of Thorkell called Hemingr.

[1] *Ágrip* (ed. Finnur Jónsson, p. 26) has an unsupported and obviously impossible story that Ólafr Helgi made Hákon earl of the Sudreys, when he expelled him from Norway.

[2] Reference as above, p. 70, note 6.

[3] That is not only in the five extant recensions, but in the accounts of the attempted invasion in *Heimskringla* and *Fagrskinna* which are derived from the lost early form of the Saga, from which the five extant forms are developed. How far these extant accounts draw also on *Hlaðajarla Saga* is a very obscure problem, see above, p. 67, note 5.

[4] Died 1222. His poem is edited *Skjaldedigtning*, IIA, pp. 1 ff. ; IIB, pp. 1 ff.

[5] Cf. above, p. 67, note 4, on the problem of the composition of the invading forces, a question which again does not effect this enquiry.

[6] In a considerable number of verses : references in *Lexicon poeticum antiquæ linguæ septentrionalis*, Sveinbjörn Egilsson and Finnur Jónsson, s.v. *Sigvaldi*.

[7] Ed. Holder, pp. 325 ff.

[8] Edited *Skjaldedigtning*, IA, pp. 543 ff. ; IB, pp. 525 ff.

[9] See Bjarni Aðalbjarnarson's edition of *Heimskringla*, i. pp. cxxxiii ff., for a brief considera-tion of this vexed question, and further references.

[10] On the relationships of the sagas of Ólafr Helgi, see below, pp. 80–1.

The activities of Thorkell's army in 1009–12 were tremendous, and are fully described in the entries in the *Old English Chronicle* for those years. Of one of the events of this campaign, the murder of Ælfheah, we have another account, given by Thietmar on the authority of one Sewald [1]: it is there stated that Thorkell tried to prevent the murder, but failed to control his men. Thietmar places on Thorkell's lips words which imply that he was a Christian : this may be a mere oversight, but, no doubt, Thorkell went through a form of baptism before he appeared with Knútr at the consecration of the church of Ashingdon in 1020 (see below).

Thorkell's campaign ended with a payment of tribute in 1012, and his army dispersed, except forty-five ships, which entered Æthelred's service. It is clear that Thorkell himself remained with these, for when Sveinn besieged London in 1013, Thorkell and Æthelred were both in the city.[2] Sveinn was repulsed, but later in the year the city submitted to him, being disheartened by his sweeping successes elsewhere. Thorkell and Æthelred were able to withdraw from the city to the ships of the former, which lay at Greenwich. At this point Emma withdrew to Normandy (see above, p. xliv), but Æthelred remained with the fleet till Christmas, when he also made his way to Normandy, by way of the Isle of Wight. That winter, Thorkell's crews, like those of Sveinn, supplemented their allowances by means of plunder.

When Æthelred returned to England after the death of Sveinn in 1014, he paid the forces at Greenwich twenty-one thousand pounds ; in this he displayed a very proper sense of gratitude, for Thorkell's fleet had been his one refuge in extremely dark days. This is the last we hear of Thorkell in the *Chronicle* till the fourfold partition of England in 1017, when it is noted that he received East Anglia.[3]

It is generally assumed that Thorkell changed sides and joined Knútr some time during the campaigns of 1015–16. Two reasons for this have been proposed. The first is Freeman's, who suggested that Thorkell's allegiance was to Æthelred only, and that, on that monarch's death, he felt free to join Knútr.[4] This is not impossible. The second is that defended by Napier and Stevenson, who thought it likely that Thorkell joined the Danes to avenge his brother, who was killed in a massacre of the thingmen.[5] This is out of the question, for, as we have seen, the *Encomium* and the Legendary Saga of Óláfr Helgi, place the death of Thorkell's brother early in Thorkell's career in England, before the death of Sveinn. The only source which places the death of Thorkell's brother after that of Sveinn is late and worthless : it will be discussed below.[6] The Encomiast's account of Thorkell's proceedings during this period have been discussed in the Introduction,[7] but it may be recalled that it is of a very suspicious nature indeed. Firstly, the Encomiast (I, 2) makes Sveinn's warriors expect that Thorkell will join them, if they invade England. He does not actually say that their expectations were fulfilled, but he implies that they were, by suggesting that Thorkell made peace with the English after Sveinn's death (II, 1). Now we know that Thorkell loyally supported Æthelred against

---

[1] This interesting passage is quoted *N.C.*, i. 677–8 ; cf. above, p. lvi. Another sidelight on Thorkell's campaign is provided by Heremannus (*Memorials of St. Edmund's Abbey*, Rolls Series, i. 40).

[2] We can safely reject William of Malmesbury's story (*Gesta Regum*, ii. 176) that Thorkell invited Sveinn to England in 1013, for we know that he loyally supported Æthelred during the invasion of that year. Cf. *N.C.*, i. 668.

[3] It is mentioned in the *Old English Chronicle* that Eadric Streona seduced forty ships to the Danish side late in 1015, and it is usually assumed that these were the remains of the forty-five ships of Thorkell's fleet, which entered English service in 1012. This is highly probable, for it seems unlikely that a native English fleet of such size was then in being. It is open to those who so wish to assume that Thorkell went over to Knútr with these ships.

[4] *N.C.*, i. 356.   [5] *Crawford Collection*, p. 141.
[6] In § D of the present *Appendix*.   [7] Pp. liv ff.

Sveinn. Secondly,.the Encomiast (II, 1) implies as clearly as he can, while avoiding a plain statement, that Thorkell was only able to retain strong forces in England after Knútr withdrew, because the two had a private understanding. In the next chapter, however, he depicts Knútr as expecting opposition from Thorkell, if he returns to England. He then depicts Thorkell hurrying to Denmark after Knútr, to offer apologies for remaining in England against Knútr's wishes, and emphasises that he was doubtful how Knútr would receive him, and that he only made his peace with difficulty (II, 3). Thirdly, he makes the battle of Sherston part of an independent campaign, undertaken by Thorkell before the siege of London. This is mere romancing. He does not mention Thorkell again, except as a vehicle for comments on a supernatural banner at Ashingdon. Obviously, the Encomiast is at pains to make Thorkell behave like a loyal Dane, while knowing perfectly well that he was a thorn in Knútr's side.[1] Accordingly, there is absolutely no evidence that Thorkell was not true to the English cause all through [2] until (like Eadric, who was nominally on the English side at Ashingdon, and instigated the subsequent peace negotiations) he automatically became Knútr's subject, when the latter became king of all England in 1017.

The career of Thorkell is very imperfectly known after he became earl of East Anglia in 1017. He witnesses Knútr's charters from the earliest ones issued till 1019.[3] He invariably signs first of the *duces*, and he is the only magnate actually named by Knútr in the statement of legal policy issued by that monarch on his return from Scandinavia in 1020.[4] It is, accordingly, reasonable to conclude that he was Knútr's first lay subject early in the reign. He is named by Knútr as having been a witness of the ceremony, when the king laid deeds of freedom on the altar at Christ Church, Canterbury.[5] He is mentioned in the Thorney *Liber Vitae*.[6] In the St. Edmund's additions in MS. Bodley 297 alluded to above, Thorkell, the queen, and Ælfwine, bishop of Elmham, are given credit for encouraging Knútr to restore the monastery in 1020.[8] He was present with Knútr at the consecration of the church of Ashingdon in 1020.[8] He was exiled by Knútr at Martinmas in 1021, but in 1023 he and the king were reconciled in Denmark : he was made governor of that country and a guardian of the king's son, while the king brought Thorkell's son back to England.[9] We know that Hörthaknútr was still in England after Knútr returned, for he then made a public appearance with Emma.[10] It would, therefore, seem that Knútr did not entrust Hörthaknútr to Thorkell in 1023, but merely arranged to send him to Denmark in the near future. With Thorkell's appointment in 1023 he

[1] A further motive for the Encomiast's kindness to the memory of Thorkell is suggested below, p. 84, note 8.
[2] On a statement in a worthless source that Thorkell was with Knútr in the invasion of 1015–16, see below, p. 88.
[3] Also K. 742, dated 1026, but this is a ridiculous forgery. It is worth noting that a *Ðurkytel miles* signs a charter of 1012 (K. 719 ; *Codex Roffensis*) ; this was the year in which Thorkell entered Æthelred's service, and it is very likely that this is his signature.
[4] Liebermann, *Gesetze*, i. 273–5.   [5] Thorpe, p. 308.
[6] Reference above, p. 70, note 6.   [7] Reference above, p. 55.
[8] *Old English Chronicle*, MSS. C and D.   [9] *Ibid.*, 1021, and MS. C, 1023.
[10] *Old English Chronicle*, MS. D ; cf. above, p. xlvii. The fact that Hörthaknútr was not physically committed to Thorkell's charge in 1023 has troubled various historians. Some have suggested that Haraldr was the son committed to Thorkell, others that the whole entry of *Chronicle* C for 1023 is a confusion, and that the incident referred to is the appointment of Úlfr as regent of Denmark and Hörthaknútr's guardian some years later (see below, p. 83). There is nothing to be said for either suggestion. It seems evident that there was some crisis in Knútr's dominions just after Thorkell was banished, for Knútr concentrated his fleet in 1022 at Wight, presumably to go in force to Denmark, where we find him in 1023. There is, however, no need to connect these events with Thorkell, or to regard his fall as more than a salutary lesson for a powerful subject, to be followed quickly by a restoration, when its lesson had been learned.

E

disappears from history.[1] He admittedly signs a charter dated 1026, but it is a glaring forgery.[2]

Florence of Worcester [3] adds to the *Old English Chronicle's* notice of Thorkell's banishment, that his wife Eadgyth was banished with him.[4] He had a son, Haraldr, who will be discussed below,[5] and who may or may not have been the one whom Knútr brought to England in 1023.

Finally, it may be recalled that a Norse stanza is extant, which celebrates the fearlessness of Thorkell's army, and which may well be by one of themselves, though the traditional ascription of it to Óláfr Helgi is extremely dubious.[6]

It may at this point be well to discuss the career in England of Thorkell's eminent ally, Óláfr Haraldsson Helgi, for this has given an astonishing amount of trouble to English historians. The future saint was, in the early years of the eleventh century, following a career of desultory violence and robbery round the coasts of the Baltic and the North Sea. In the *Vikingavísur* of Sigvatr Thórtharson, we have an account of his career before he became king of Norway, which is one of the best historical documents transmitted to us by the Scandinavian North.[7] This poem is a series of verses in each of which a battle fought by the young viking is described and, in the case of the first thirteen, carefully numbered. This system of numbering precluded the possibility of additions to the series being forged in later times in the first part of the poem, which includes the battles of Óláfr's English campaign. Fourteen verses are quoted in *Heimskringla* ; some of these are also quoted by the Legendary Saga of Óláfr Helgi, and by *Fagrskinna*, and these sources summarise the verses they do not quote ; all three sources summarise three verses which they do not quote, and in all probability these are all that we have lost of the poem, for Sigvatr, in another poem composed after Óláfr's death, estimates that Óláfr fought twenty battles in all (*Skjaldedigtning*, IA, p. 263 ; IB, p. 244), and he did, in fact, fight in three major actions after he became king of Norway. A verse of Sigvatr's on Óláfr's bloodless victory over Earl Hákon is also quoted in *Heimskringla* and is believed to belong to the same poem, but the incident it records would not count as a battle. Sigvatr was an Icelander, who entered Óláfr's service shortly after his return to Norway. Verses attributed to him are preserved in the Sagas in profusion, and in great measure confirm the statements made about him in those sources. He was always the king's closest confidant and trusted ambassador. His opportunities for learning Óláfr's history must have been unrivalled. The first three verses of the *Vikingavísur* are devoted to battles round the Baltic ; the fourth is at Suðrvík, to the location of which place I will return ; the fifth is off the coast of North Holland. The sixth battle is an attack on London Bridge : the hero offered strife to the English. The seventh was at *Hringmaraheiðr* in Úlfkell's land ; the hero's enemies were English.[8] The eighth was at Canterbury,

---

[1] Cf. below, p. 85. William of Malmesbury's statement (*Gesta Regum*, ii. 181) that Thorkell was murdered when he returned to Denmark, is derived from the worthless account of Thorkell given by Osbern (see *N.C.*, i. 668–9).

[2] See above, p. 75, note 3.   [3] Ed. Thorpe, i. 183.
[4] Her identity is discussed below, p. 89.   [5] Pp. 84 ff.
[6] *Skjaldedigtning*, IA, p. 220 ; IB, p. 210. Some of these curious snatches of verse, apparently by Norse soldiers who fought in England, are edited and discussed by Miss M. Ashdown, *English and Norse Documents* (Cambridge, 1930), pp. 140–3 and 205–8, though she does not include the one mentioning Thorkell. The general sense of it is given in Collingwood's translation, *Scandinavian Britain*, p. 157.
[7] This poem and the similar one by Óttarr Svarti to be discussed below are edited *Skjaldedigtning*, IA, pp. 223 ff. and 290 ff. ; IB, pp. 213 ff. and 268 ff. The verses which concern Óláfr's English adventures may be conveniently consulted in Ashdown, *op. cit.*, pp. 156 ff.
[8] *Ellu kind* : see Ashdown, *op. cit.*, p. 221.

which could not be defended against Óláfr : much sorrow befell the English.[1]   The ninth was at *Nýjamóða*, where the young king smote the English, though the Danes also fell. The tenth and fifteenth battles were in France, the intervening four apparently in Spain,[2] and the sixteenth and seventeenth at places in England of which the sites are quite unknown.

There is another poem dealing with Óláfr's youth by Óttarr Svarti.   This poet was for a short time at Óláfr's court, but he is said to have been on uneasy terms with the monarch, and his poem to him was traditionally supposed to be a *Höfuðlausn*, that is a poem designed to avert a king's anger by a skald in fear of execution.[3]   He confirms a good deal of what Sigvatr says.   He deals with the Baltic viking more fully than Sigvatr, but he does not mention the third, fourth, and fifth battles of Sigvatr's series. He has verses on the battles at London Bridge, *Hringmaraheiðr*, and Canterbury.   These verses do not provide a great deal of fresh information : London Bridge, however, is said to have been broken, the defeated enemy at *Hringmaraheiðr* are clearly described as English, and Canterbury is said to have been taken and burned.   The hero is not named, but, in view of the agreement with Sigvatr in the localisation of no less than three battles, it is hardly open to doubt that these three verses are concerned with Óláfr's English campaign.   Óttarr does not mention *Nýjamóða*, but sums up his hero's campaign by saying that men of English race (*Enskrar ættar öld*) could not withstand him.   It is obvious that both Sigvatr and Óttarr were perfectly clear that their hero fought *against* the English.   It is also worthy of note, that in another poem Sigvatr calls Óláfr *Engla striðir*, ' foe of the English ' (*Skjaldedigtning*, IA, p. 262 ; IB, p. 243).   Of the continental battles, Óttarr mentions only one, the fifteenth of Sigvatr's series, and the remaining verses, which are quoted as being from his poem, deal, with one exception to be considered below, with Óláfr's return to Norway and subsequent deeds.

We gather from the two poets, that Óláfr fought against the English at London, *Hringmaraheiðr* in Úlfkell's land, and Canterbury.   We know from the Legendary Saga that a tradition lingered in Iceland, that Óláfr fought in England in alliance with Thorkell Hávi.   It can, therefore, be concluded with a certainty almost as great as is ever possible in the study of Old English history, that Óláfr took part in Thorkell's campaign of 1009–11. Thorkell attacked London unsuccessfully in 1009, and it should be noticed that neither poet claims that the city was taken by Óláfr : Óttarr says the bridge was broken.[4]   In 1010, Thorkell fought Úlfkell in his own East Anglian land (Úlfkell's land), and Florence of Worcester adds to the notice of the battle in the *Chronicle* that the site was *Ringmere*.[5] This is surely *Hringmaraheiðr*.   The siege and fall of Canterbury followed in 1011, and the burning of the city is no doubt included in the comprehensive *asmeade* of the *Old English Chronicle*.   The site of Óláfr's battle of *Nýjamóða* is quite uncertain, but it is clear that he left Thorkell, either when peace was concluded in 1012, or earlier, and embarked on a career of rapine in France and Spain.

Fagrskinna, Heimskringla and *Knytlinga Saga* all quote a further verse, said to be

[1] *Partar* : see *ibid.*, p. 222.

[2] That Óláfr was active in Spain at this time seems fairly certain : see the two works referred to below, p. 79, note 8.

[3] See the fragment of Styrmir's version of the saga of Óláfr Helgi in *Flateyjarbók*, iii. 242.

[4] In Sigvatr's verse on the fighting at London there is an allusion to the defence of a ditch, and many historians have suggested that there is some confusion with the siege of 1016, in which an operation of circumvallation played a great part, as both the *Chronicle* and the *Encomium* (II, 7) emphasise.   This is possible : Sigvatr was not present in England with Óláfr, and he may have worked on confused accounts of the operations at London, which were influenced by the events of 1016.   We know that the siege of 1016 attracted much attention in Europe (see above, p. lx), and it would tend to obliterate or obscure popular memory of the nature of the earlier siege.

[5] Ed. Thorpe, i. 162.

by Óttarr, which is printed by Finnur Jónsson as the eighth of the poem with which we have been dealing. This verse states that the hero restored Æthelred to the land, which he had previously ruled. Now this verse can only mean that Óláfr assisted Æthelred when he returned to England in 1014, and, if the words *harðr vas fundr* are to be taken literally, they must mean that Óláfr took part in the East Anglian campaign, when Knútr fled before Æthelred. Óláfr seems to have carried out two raids on the English coast on his way back to Norway in 1014—the sixteenth and seventeenth battles of Sigvatr's series—but this is no argument against the assumption, that Óláfr and Æthelred were on good terms in 1014. We may compare the way in which Thorkell Hávi's forces plundered England in the winter of 1013–14 (cf. above, p. 74). It is, of course, open to anyone to assume that the sixteenth and seventeenth battles were fought on Æthelred's behalf, and that Óláfr ' mopped up ' pockets of Danes who remained after Knútr's flight in 1014, or assisted in the punishment of Knútr's English adherents in Lindsey.[1]

It is extremely probable that Óttarr's verse reflects what actually happened in 1014. We know from William of Jumièges,[2] that Óláfr was at the court of Richard of Normandy during a war, which may reasonably be dated about the time when Æthelred was an exile

---

[1] Although Óttarr's verse on Æthelred's return does not name Óláfr, there can be no doubt that it refers to him. If it were a genuine verse, but referred to some other person, no one would have thought that it referred to Óláfr, who was universally and truly believed to have fought on the Danish side in England (see below). On the other hand, it cannot be a forgery : no one would have dreamed of fabricating a verse depicting Óláfr as a friend of Æthelred. It must be an early verse, which was well known to refer to Óláfr, and hence caused saga-writers, who knew Óláfr was an enemy of the English, endless difficulty. The *Historia Norvegiae* (Storm, p. 124) says that Óláfr took four bishops with him to Norway when he left England. This, if true, would show that his last visit to England was friendly in the extreme, but the statement is probably no more than an unjustifiable inference from Adam of Bremen's account (ii. 55) of how English bishops worked for Óláfr.

[2] v. 11–12. William makes it abundantly clear that it is Óláfr, the future king and martyr, to whom he refers, and alleges that his baptism took place in Normandy on this occasion. In view of the statement of the Oldest Saga, that Óláfr spent a winter by the Seine in the course of his European wanderings (see below, p. 81, note 9), and of Óttarr's statement that he brought Æthelred, whose place of exile was certainly Normandy, back to England, there is every reason to believe William's statement that Óláfr had been in Normandy. William says that this was at the time of Duke Richard's war with Odo of Chartres, and, although the evidence for the date of this war is not good, there is no objection to placing it 1013–14 (see F. Lot, *Fidèles ou vassaux*, p. 143), so that it would appear that William is also right as to the time of Óláfr's visit to Normandy. His account of the activities of Óláfr in Normandy is, however, strange. Óláfr and a totally unknown Lacman, called king of the Swedes, are invited by Richard to help him in his war. They hasten to his assistance (William clearly thinks of them as coming from their Northern realms), and, on their arrival in France, destroy Dol. The kings are nevertheless received with delight by Richard, who, however, does not require their active assistance, as the king of France intervenes and stops the war, when he hears of the barbarities indulged in by Richard's new allies at Dol. Now this is an absurd story, for the Bretons were fighting for Richard against Odo, yet, when Richard acquires new allies, they immediately destroy a Breton town, and are, nevertheless, joyfully received by Richard. Attempts to explain Óláfr's attack on Dol are made by Freeman, *N.C.*, i. 460–1, De la Borderie, *Histoire de Bretagne*, iii. 3, Steenstrup, *Normandiets Historie*, pp. 163 ff. It would seem likely that the attack on Dol preceded the duke's invitation to the vikings to assist him, and that William's idea that it followed it arose from his belief that the Northern kings were at home in their own kingdoms when Richard's messengers approached them, and that they then set out for France. Actually they were doubtless ravaging up and down the coast : at least Sigvatr's poem shows that Óláfr was so engaged about this time, and evidence for viking activity on the French coast near Brittany shortly before Knútr became king of England is provided by the contemporary chronicler Ademar, *M.G.H.*, *SS.*, iv. 136 and 139–40, passages which are discussed by Steenstrup, *loc. cit.*

at the Norman court. If Óláfr had then met Æthelred, he would have introduced himself as an ally of Thorkell, who was almost the only friend Æthelred then had in the world, and could have returned to England assured of some help in fitting out an expedition against the rulers of Norway, who were equally his enemies and Æthelred's.

It will not now be difficult to explain the confusions in the Norse accounts of Óláfr's English campaign, of which English historians have so long complained. This confusion is due to the nature of the material which was at the disposal of the saga-writers. The writer of the Oldest Saga about Óláfr, the substance of whose work is preserved in a summarised form in the Legendary Saga,[1] knew the verses in which Sigvatr and Óttarr describe Óláfr fighting in England on the Danish side. He also knew a tradition, that Óláfr had been an ally of Thorkell's, when that chief was in England. He also knew Óttarr's verse in which Óláfr figures as a supporter of Æthelred. Lastly, he knew an international tradition, that Óláfr had helped in the conquest of England by the Danish kings. This last tradition, in which Óláfr's participation in the war of 1009–12 was corrupted into participation in the subsequent invasions of Sveinn and Knútr, is to be found in most of the countries of north-west Europe.[2] In Normandy, William of Jumièges has a story that Óláfr, king of the Norwegians, and the unknown Lacman, king of the Swedes, helped Knútr in his invasion of England.[3] In Germany, Adam of Bremen believed that Óláfr accompanied Sveinn and Knútr, when they invaded England together.[4] In Denmárk, Saxo Grammaticus, although he knew Adam's work, tells an independent story, which shows that he knew that the general view was that Óláfr helped in Knútr's independent expedition : he makes Óláfr assist Knútr after he became king of Norway.[5] The *Annals of Roskilde* have a weird variant of Adam's version.[6] In Norway, the *Historia Norvegiae* repeats Adam's story that Óláfr helped Sveinn, but, in accordance with the more usual tradition, makes him subsequently help Knútr.[7] It need hardly be said that it is quite impossible that Óláfr assisted Knútr in the invasion of 1015–16,[8] for he had only secured a shaky control of Norway at the battle of Nesjar

---

[1] See below, p. 81.

[2] Not apparently in England, where there do not seem to have been any traditional memories of Óláfr, for the reference to him in the so-called *Laws of Eadweard the Confessor* (Hoveden, Rolls Series, ii. 240) is obviously derived from William of Jumièges ; also not in the Celtic lands, where the memory of the warrior saint degenerated till it retained no trace of historical place or time (see *Revue Celtique*, xlii. 336 ff.).

[3] v. 8. This incident is placed shortly before Óláfr goes to assist the Normans in the war discussed above.

[4] ii. 49. Adam believed that Óláfr was a son of Óláfr Tryggvason.

[5] Ed. Holder, pp. 343–4.   [6] Gertz, i. 20. The passage is quoted, *N.C.*, i. 704.

[7] Storm, pp. 121 ff. This version is perhaps merely a literary combination of the versions of Adam and William of Jumièges. *Historia Norvegiae* also uses Óttarr's poem. Theodricus knew nothing of Óláfr's part in the fighting in England, except that he knew Óttarr's verse on the restoration of Æthelred. He was quite ignorant of the circumstances under which Æthelred went into exile, and has to fabricate an explanation, saying that Óláfr *reconciliauit Adalredum fratribus suis et ut in regem sublimaretur obtinuit* (Storm, p. 25). *Ágrip* is silent on the whole matter.

[8] It is one of the most fixed elements in the northern chronology that Óláfr reigned fifteen years, but there is some doubt as to the point from which these were reckoned. If they are reckoned from his arrival in Norway, this must be placed in 1015, but if the first winter, before the defeat of Earl Sveinn, or the period after his flight to Russia in 1028, in which he was a king without power, be excluded from his reign, his arrival must be put in 1014. In the present work, I adopt the latter date, as slightly the more difficult for my argument. If the 1015 date be accepted, it becomes entirely out of the question that Óláfr helped Knútr in his invasion. The early career of Óláfr is carefully discussed in B. K. Brynildsen's *Om tidsregningen i Olav den helliges historie*, and in O. A. Johnsen's *Olav Haraldssons ungdom indtil slaget ved Nesjar* (both

in 1015, and could not have thought of a foreign adventure at that time. It is equally impossible that he was with Sveinn and Knútr in England in 1013, for Sigvatr's carefully numbered list of his battles, and William of Jumièges' account of his visit to Duke Richard, shows that he spent the period following the sack of Canterbury late in 1011 ranging far and wide in Europe. Especially if it be assumed that he remained with Thorkell till that chief allowed most of his forces to disperse after the Easter of 1012— and this is the most probable view—there is little enough time for all his continental adventures before he returned to England with Æthelred in the spring of 1014.

The writer of the Oldest Saga of Óláfr Helgi was not selective in his methods. He included so much self-contradictory material that one scholar has attempted to prove his work to be a blend of various lost older ones, though this view has won little support.[1] He set to work to combine the true tradition, that Óláfr helped Thorkell, with a false one, that he helped Knútr, and to fit in not only Óttarr's statement that he restored Æthelred, but also the battles which Óttarr and Sigvatr say he fought against the English. In the summary of the essentials of this Oldest Saga known as the Legendary Saga, we have seen that Óláfr joins Thorkell in England, and that they there win the battle of Suðrvík (the fourth in Sigvatr's list). Óláfr next wins the battle off the coast of North Holland, which is the fifth in Sigvatr's list. Meanwhile Sveinn dies in England, and Óláfr assists Æthelred to recover the country : not merely this latter statement, but the very words in which it is expressed are clearly derived from Óttarr's verse.[2] Three years after Sveinn's death (which is placed in 1006 !), Knútr attacks Eadmund, who was now king of England. Knútr takes the whole land, and only London holds out. Here the saga writer interrupts himself to mention the severe war of Knútr and Eadmund, their treaty and the succession of Knútr to the whole kingdom on Eadmund's death. He then returns to the siege of London. Knútr hears that Óláfr is in England, asks his help, and Óláfr takes London for him, although Eiríkr had failed to do so.[3] It is also remarked that Thorkell Hávi was with Knútr, but could not offer any effective advice, as to how the city might be taken. Óláfr and Knútr soon quarrel, and part company. Óláfr now goes ranging round England, and wins the battles of Hringmaraheiðr, Canterbury and Nýjamóða. His continental adventures follow, interspersed with various visits to England : this section is made up of Sigvatr's battles plus a mass of wild legend. Finally, Óláfr returns to Norway. Thorkell seems to accompany him from first to last.

The precise relationships of the Sagas of Óláfr Helgi do not concern the present enquiry, but it may be pointed out that Professor Sigurður Nordal's views concerning them have never been successfully challenged, though they have been elaborated in detail.[4] In outline, Nordal's theory is that the Oldest Saga, of which we have only fragments, was modified in various respects (including interpolation from Ágrip, which leads to incongruities of which an example is given above, p. 72, note 10) to produce a ver-

---

Christiania, 1916). The former scholar accepts 1014 as the date of Óláfr's arrival in Normandy, the latter 1015, and I do not consider it possible to decide finally between these years. On the other hand, the fifteen years reign of Óláfr is a firm tradition, and is confirmed by a verse of Sigvatr (Skjaldedigtning, IA, p. 262 ; IB, p. 244), so it is manifestly impossible to make the period from the summer of 1030 back to the autumn of his arrival in Norway include *less* than fifteen winters ; also, since he was present at Æthelred's restoration in 1014, it cannot include *more* than sixteen winters.

[1] J. Schreiner : references to his works and criticism of them in Bjarni Aðalbjarnarson's *Om de norske kongers sagaer*, pp. 177 ff.

[2] Óttarr's verse begins : *Komt í land ok lendir . . Aðalráði* ; the Legendary Saga says that men say that Óláfr *hafðe komet Aðalrað kononge aptr í land.*

[3] One of the only two references to Eiríkr in the Legendary Saga : see above, p. 71, note 1.

[4] Nordal's work is referred to in the Preface.

sion now lost, the Middle Saga (M). The Legendary Saga [1] is in essentials a summary of M. The well-known Icelandic writer, Styrmir Fróthi (d. 1245), wrote a revision and expansion of M, which is lost except for a few fragments.[2] The saga of Óláfr in *Fagrskinna* is a summary, and Snorri's separate version [3] a revision, of Styrmir. The *Heimskringla* version does not differ materially from Snorri's separate version. The latter Sagas of Óláfr [4] take Snorri's version for a basis, but fit into it masses of material from Styrmir, which Snorri had rejected : the results are at times incongruous and absurd.

As far as Óláfr's adventures in England are concerned, Snorri's versions and *Fagrskinna* are in very close agreement, and Snorri here may have used *Fagrskinna's* summary of Styrmir as well as Styrmir's own version. Historically worthless as this form of the story is, it is a credit to the insight of its author,[5] for it must be remembered that he could correct the extraordinary version, which we know from the Legendary Saga, only with the aid of his critical sense and such hints as skaldic verse provided. He decided, probably rightly, that the site of Óláfr's fourth battle at *Suðrvík* (= Søndervig in Jutland ?) was not in England, but in Denmark. He learnt from Óttarr that Óláfr was a supporter of Æthelred, and this led him to think that Óláfr had been fighting for the English during his English campaign. He therefore dropped Óláfr's support of Knútr from the story. He made Óláfr join Thorkell in Denmark,[6] where the two fight the battle of *Suðrvík*, and then the battle off North Holland, before arriving in England.[7] In England, the battles of London, *Hringmaraheiðr*, Canterbury and *Nýjamóða* are all fought as part of a campaign in the service of Æthelred, who had just returned to England after the death of Sveinn. It is at this time that Óláfr is regarded as having restored Æthelred,[8] and, since Óttarr rhetorically addresses Óláfr as *láðvörðr*, ' guardian of the land ', *Heimskringla* assumes that he undertook some sort of wardenship of the country in the English interest. Æthelred dies, his sons succeed, and Óláfr goes on his European wanderings. Meanwhile Knútr conquers England, and drives out the sons of Æthelred, who flee to Normandy.[9] Óláfr meets them there and returns to England with them : his

[1] The fragments of the Oldest Saga are edited by Storm, *Otte Brudstykker af den ældste Saga om Olav den Hellige* (Christiania, 1893). The Legendary Saga is edited by Keyser and Unger, *Olafs saga hins helga* (Christiania, 1849), and by O. A. Johnsen (same title and place, 1922). The Oldest Saga is to be dated 1160–85. The Legendary Saga is the result of a curiously complicated evolution from the Oldest Saga (through M), concerning which D. Seip, *Den legendariske Olavssaga og Fagrskinna* (Oslo, 1929), should be consulted, as well as Nordal. It survives in a thirteenth-century manuscript.

[2] They are printed in *Flateyjarbók*, iii. 237–48.

[3] Snorri's separate version is printed by Munch and Unger, *Saga Olafs konungs ens helga* (Christiania, 1853) ; a new edition (same title and place) by O. A. Johnsen and Jón Helgason has appeared (1941).

[4] These compilations are analysed by Nordal. The most elaborate is printed in *Flateyjarbók*, ii, and a simpler one in *Fornmanna Sögur*, iv–v.

[5] To whom it is to be credited is uncertain. Styrmir perhaps followed the Oldest Saga fairly closely on Óláfr in England, and *Fagrskinna* revised him without mercy. The general similarity of Snorri's story to that of *Fagrskinna* would then be due to the fact that Snorri, while basing his work on Styrmir, consulted *Fagrskinna*. (Nordal leaves the question whether Snorri used *Fagrskinna* open, but Bjarni Aðalbjarnarson has proved that he did so, *Om de norske kongers sagaer*, pp. 173 ff.)

[6] Thorkell is not mentioned at all in Snorri's separate version, nor in *Fagrskinna*.

[7] Note the removal of the meeting with Thorkell and the battle of *Suðrvík* from England to Denmark ; cf. above, p. 73.

[8] From this point *Fagrskinna* is a bare summary, adding little to what the verses tell. I follow *Heimskringla*.

[9] In the course of Óláfr's continental wanderings in the Oldest Saga, he spent a winter by the Seine, and the Legendary Saga and *Fagrskinna* repeat this. This is the starting-point of

sixteenth and seventeenth battles are fought in a vain attempt to restore them.   I refrain from comment on the wild chronology into which all this is fitted.   I also refrain from comment on the extraordinary results achieved by the late saga of Óláfr Helgi in *Flateyjarbók* by fitting into the story of Óláfr in England as told by Snorri elements derived from a late and worthless source concerning the Danish conquest of England.[1]   Sufficient has been said to show the lines upon which the revisers of the early form of the saga of Óláfr worked in the section dealing with the hero's English adventures ; anyone who compares the versions will observe how imperfectly the verses of Sigvatr and Óttarr sometimes bear the interpretations put upon them in the various schemes.

C. Úlfr Þorgilsson jarl ; Eilífr Þorgilsson

Under 1025, MS. E of the *Old English Chronicle* has a notice that Knútr went to Denmark and fought Úlfr and Eilífr,[2] who had considerable Swedish forces both military and naval, at Helge-á (*æt ea þære halgan*).   He was defeated, and suffered considerable losses among both his English and his Danish troops.   This entry is repeated by MS. F, and by Henry of Huntingdon (Rolls Series, p. 187), and is used by William of Malmesbury in compiling his account of Knútr's northern expeditions (*Gesta Regum*, ii. 181), which is, however, confused and useless.   There can be no doubt, that the battle referred to is Knútr's famous reverse at the Helge-á at the hands of Óláfr of Norway and Önundr of Sweden.   In the various Sagas of Óláfr Helgi, this battle is very clearly placed one year before the flight of Óláfr, and that event is placed two years before Óláfr's death by both the Northern chronological system and MSS. C, D and E of the *Old English Chronicle*. Óláfr's death is dated 1030 upon evidence of overwhelming weight, so the battle of the Helge-á is clearly placed in 1027 by Scandinavian tradition.   This tradition seems to be sound, for to move the battle back to 1025 would call for a severe revision of the Northern account of Óláfr's last years, and the evidence of the date in MS. E of the *Chronicle* is not sufficient to justify this, for the entry 1025 is the only one between those for 1024 and 1028, and may, therefore, be regarded as displaced.   Furthermore, we are approaching a period in which the dating of E tends to be bad, and in which its errors re-appear in F and Henry of Huntingdon.[3]   Accordingly, there seems no reason to reject the Northern dating of the battle.[4]

We learn from Saxo Grammaticus [5] that the Swedes and Norwegians were supported at the Helge-á by Earl Úlfr, a Danish subject of Knútr, so that the *Old English Chronicle*

Snorri's story, but when he makes Óláfr be well received in Normandy, and meet the sons of Æthelred there, he is neatly combining two facts recorded by William of Jumièges, firstly that Óláfr was at one time an ally of Duke Richard and secondly that the sons of Æthelred fled to Normandy during the Danish invasions (vi. 10).   William's history was known in the North, and there is not the least difficulty in assuming that Snorri knew it directly or indirectly.

[1] See below, p. 91.
[2] On the various forms of the name, see Napier and Stevenson, *Crawford Collection*, pp. 139 and 142.
[3] For example, E, F, and Henry of Huntingdon place Knútr's death in 1036 (C, D, 1035).
[4] Stenton, p. 397, places the battle in 1026, going against both the English and the Scandinavian evidence without giving his reasons.   It is well known that, when he was at Rome early in 1027, Knútr addressed a letter to his people, in which he says that he is about to go to Scandinavia to deal with a movement of certain peoples against him (Florence of Worcester, ed. Thorpe, i. 188 ; cf. above, p. lxii).   This almost certainly refers to the Swedish-Norwegian alliance, which he was facing in the campaign in which the battle of Helge-á occurred.
[5] Ed. Holder, p. 348.

is supported by Danish tradition in introducing Úlfr into the battle. Úlfr succeeded, according to Saxo, in making his peace with Knútr, but the monarch had him executed somewhat later.

The accounts of the battle in the Sagas are rather different from that of Saxo, but this is largely due to later modifications. The Sagas which cover the history of the period corresponding to Knútr's reign in England have not very much information about him. They know that he conquered England, helped by Eiríkr, took London in the course of the war, married Emma, and died in England.[1] Otherwise, they are concerned only with his long struggle with Óláfr Helgi, and his ultimate success in bringing about the fall of that ruler. There existed, however, a separate Saga about Knútr, which is referred to by name in *Heimskringla* where it is stated to have contained an account of the death of Úlfr (*Magnús Saga Góða*, chap. 22). When we compare the extant fragments of the Oldest Saga of Óláfr Helgi with the Legendary Saga and with *Fagrskinna*, it becomes evident that *Fagrskinna* or its source has inserted a long extract from this Saga about Knútr into the Saga of Óláfr Helgi. The precise limits of the insertion are not certain.[2] It is probable that it was made by Styrmir, of whose Saga of Óláfr the version in *Fagrskinna* is almost certainly a summary. This insertion deals mainly with the reign in Norway of Knútr's son Sveinn and his mother Álfífa (Ælfgifu of Northampton), but it has two other episodes. The second of these deals with Knútr's relations with the Emperor Henry III, and the emperor's marriage to Knútr's daughter. It is very incorrect in detail : it makes Henry already emperor at the time of the marriage, and accompany Knútr on his pilgrimage to Rome. The first of the two episodes is an account of the fall of Úlfr. He is viceroy of Denmark and guardian of Hörthaknútr, and makes use of his position to have the young prince declared king, persuading the thing that he is acting on Knútr's wishes. This he was able to do, because Emma had stolen the royal seal, when Úlfr was in England, and had caused letters to be forged for the earl to take to Denmark. Knútr, however, hears what is afoot, appears in Denmark, and has Úlfr executed. This, it is said, was Knútr's last visit to Denmark. Now in *Fagrskinna* it is said that Úlfr was ruler of Denmark already at the time of the Helge-á battle,[3] and that he accompanied Knútr's son Sveinn to Norway in 1030 after the fall of Óláfr Helgi.[4] (The latter statement comes at the beginning of the insertion from the Saga of Knútr.) It is now evident why *Fagrskinna* does not mention Úlfr's part in the Helge-á battle, though it observes that he ruled Denmark already at that time. The compiler knew that the battle took place some years before Óláfr's fall. He therefore had to disconnect Úlfr's fall from the battle when he digested the Saga of Knútr into that of Óláfr, because in the former Saga Úlfr was still alive at the time of Óláfr's fall. He was automatically forced to add a journey to the North after 1030 to Knútr's career, and no such journey is known from any other source. It would seem that the Saga of Knútr made Úlfr go with Sveinn to Norway, but was sufficiently indifferent to chronology to place the battle

---

[1] Individual sources make small independent additions : *Fagrskinna* and *Heimskringla* revising the early Saga of Magnús Góthi, which we know from *Morkinskinna* and *Flateyjarbók*, are able to add his place of burial ; *Heimskringla* also gives the length of his reign in England correctly. Various scraps of information are also found in *Knytlinga Saga*.

[2] It occurs in *Fagrskinna*, pp. 183–91. One passage of it is already present in the Legendary Saga, chap. 100, but it was not in the Oldest Saga, as the Fragments show. Nordal (*op. cit.*, pp. 162–3) is not convinced that a separate Saga of Knútr is the source of this material, but cf. G. Indrebø, *Fagrskinna* (Christiania, 1917), pp. 101–3, where the best discussion of the question will be found. The only point which concerns the present enquiry is that we have here an addition to the Saga of Óláfr upon the affairs of the Danish royal house.

[3] P. 161.

[4] P. 183.

of Helge-á later than this.[1] Its vague idea of the chronology of Henry III make it quite probable that it was equally vague about that of Ólafr Helgi.

That the Saga of Knútr made Úlfr fight at the battle of Helge-á is clear from *Heimskringla*. There the material from Knútr's Saga is digested thoroughly into the narrative, and not merely inserted in one place. Úlfr's fall is placed at the time of the Helge-á.[2] Úlfr attempts to make Hörthaknútr king very much as in *Fagrskinna*, and Knútr hurries to Denmark. He forgives Úlfr, who helps him at the Helge-á, but has him killed shortly afterwards. Snorri probably made Úlfr fight for Knútr rather than against him at the battle of the Helge-á, because it is mentioned in various poems that two kings opposed Knútr, but there is no word of an earl.[3]

Snorri got round the difficulty attached to making Úlfr fight at the Helge-á, which the compiler of *Fagrskinna* found insuperable, by giving up the story that he accompanied Sveinn in 1030. This however created a new difficulty, for a skaldic poet had declared that an earl accompanied Sveinn to Norway.[4] Snorri had to find an earl to take Úlfr's place, and men of that rank were few in the North at that time. Accordingly he makes Knútr create Haraldr, son of Thorkell Hávi, earl after the death of Úlfr, and lets Haraldr later accompany Sveinn to Norway.[5] Now in this Snorri is falling into a practice in which he is very apt to indulge. When he has to find a person for some purpose, he seizes upon one who had some reality, however shadowy, rather than invent one.[6] Now it seems evident that Thorkell Hávi had a son named Haraldr, who had the rank of earl, though there is no evidence that he was ever in Scandinavia, unless he is to be identified with the son of Thorkell, whom Knútr brought back from Denmark to England in 1023.[7] According to Florence of Worcester (ed. Thorpe, i. 199), Knútr's niece, Gunnhildr, was married to an earl named Haraldr, and her children were called Hemingr and Thorkell. It would be a remarkable coincidence if these two names occurred as those of two brothers outside the family of Thorkell Hávi, and it seems reasonably certain that Gunnhildr's husband was Thorkell's son, and that her children were called after their grandfather and great-uncle.[8] Gunnhildr was banished in 1044 (*Chronicle*, MS. D 1045 = 1944) and Florence (*loc. cit.*) adds that her sons accompanied her. This does not imply necessarily

---

[1] Rather similarly Saxo places the battle of Helge-á after Ólafr's flight to, and return from, Russia.

[2] *Óláfs Saga Helga*, chaps. 148–53.

[3] Snorri quotes a good deal of verse about the campaign, especially from two poems (both in praise of Knútr, and both called *Knútsdrápa*) by Sigvatr and Óttarr. He would reasonably think that, if Knútr had had any important adversary besides the kings of Norway and Sweden, one of the poets would have mentioned it. Modification of a narrative in conformity with the silence of skaldic verse is not an unknown process in the development of the Sagas: for an interesting instance, see Storm, *Snorre Sturlassöns historieskrivning*, pp. 143–4.

[4] The verse is the first of the *Glælognskviða* of Thórarinn Loftunga (*Skjaldedigtning*, IA, p. 324; IB, p. 300). It is quoted by *Fagrskinna* (p. 183) to illustrate the statement in the insertion from *Knúts Saga* that Úlfr accompanied Sveinn, and in *Heimskringla* to support the statement that Haraldr did so (see below).

[5] *Óláfs Saga Helga*, chaps. 183 and 239.

[6] I have drawn attention to examples of this in the Viking Society's *Saga Book*, xii. 232–7.

[7] See above, p. 75.

[8] The Encomiast's desire to depict Thorkell as loyal to the Danish interest at all times may well be due to the fact that at the time he was writing Thorkell's son was alive and married to a near relative of the king (cf. above, pp. 74–5). It is interesting that Snorri knew that Thorkell had a son called Haraldr, although he played no noteworthy part in history. The survival of scraps of genealogical information in the North is often surprising: an example is Snorri's knowledge of the existence of Æthelred's two obscure sons Eadwig and Eadgar (*Heimskringla, Óláfs Saga Helga*, chap. 20).

that they were old enough to be politically dangerous [1] : they were perhaps on the contrary so young that they automatically went with their mother. Florence (loc. cit. and cf. p. 184) says that Gunnhildr had previously been the wife of Earl Hákon, who was drowned in 1029 or 1030. Here, however, he has perhaps made a mistake. Theodricus and the various Sagas of Óláfr Helgi state that Hákon perished on his return from a visit to England to fetch his bride, so it is very likely that she was lost with his ship.[2] Gunnhildr's husband is perhaps the Harald dux, who signs K. 764 (dated 1042).[3] He is commonly believed to be the princeps Danorum named Haraldr, who was murdered at the request of Magnús of Norway, 13 November 1042.[4]

It appears from what has now been said that the Old English Chronicle and Saxo agree that Úlfr opposed Knútr at the battle of the Helge-á, and that, while he does not do this in the accounts of his fall in Fagrskinna and Heimskringla, these accounts appear to be independent efforts to modify an early one in which he did. It would therefore seem to be probable that he replaced Thorkell Hávi, a chief who at that time must have been far advanced in years, as viceroy of Denmark at some time between 1023 and 1027.

Úlfr is said in one wild Norse tale to have been in England in the time of Knútr,[5] and he certainly had connections with this country, for Florence of Worcester,[6] Adam of Bremen (ii. 52, where he is called dux Angliae), the Sagas,[7] and Saxo [8] in all probability, agree that Gytha, the wife of Earl Godwine was his sister, and his son Björn is well known to have held an English earldom in the Confessor's time. (The evidence that this Björn was a son of Úlfr is the agreement of Adam of Bremen, Schol. 65, with Florence of Worcester, i. 202. Adam, iii. 13, says Björn's brother Ásbjörn was expelled from England, when Björn was murdered.) Úlfr's sons Sveinn and Ásbjörn are, of course, famous in Danish history. On Úlfr's marriage to Knútr's sister Ástríthr, I would only add to Freeman's excellent discussion (N.C., i. 771 ff.) that Knytlinga Saga [9] says that Úlfr was already married to Ástríthr, when Knútr invaded England, thus supporting Freeman's conclusion that her marriage to Robert of Normandy was her second marriage. Attention may perhaps be drawn to Adam of Bremen, Schol. 40, where Ástríthr is said to have married a Russian prince ; this would presumably be after her divorce from Robert

---

[1] Cf. N.C., ii. 65, n. 3, where it is suggested that these children of Gunnhildr might be children of her first husband : but her first marriage is doubtful (see below), and the names of her children make it certain that they belonged to Thorkell's family.

[2] It may be noted that the passage in Knytlinga Saga, chap. 75, where Hákon Eiríksson is alleged to have had a daughter is historically worthless. The Worcester Cartulary agrees with Florence that his wife was called Gunnhildr (see N.C., ii. 579-80).

[3] This Haraldr's signature also appears in the forgery K. 1327 (= R. 85). K. 749 is signed by a Haraldr, but he is not described as dux, and many unknown persons with Scandinavian names sign this charter.

[4] See Adam of Bremen, ii. 75, and Stenton, pp. 417-18, for the circumstances. The year, however, was 1042, not 1043 (see Steindorff's Jahrbücher des deutschen Reiches unter Heinrich III, i. 275, footnote 1, and further literature there quoted). The day is known from the Necrology of St. Michael's, Lüneburg, which enters under 13 Nov., obiit Haraldus dux et occisus. This is a good authority, for this Necrology incorporates early material, and St. Michael's had close connections with the Danish royal house in the eleventh century (see Aarbøger for nordisk oldkyndighed og historie, 1927, p. 31, footnote).

[5] See Knytlinga Saga, chap. 11.

[6] Ed. Thorpe, i. 201-2 (clear though by implication) ; ibid., p. 275, and ii. 2, calls her a sister of Sveinn Úlfsson of Denmark : she was, of course, his aunt.

[7] Fagrskinna, p. 279 ; Heimskringla, Óláfs Saga Helga, chap. 152 ; Knytlinga Saga, chap. 11.

[8] Ed. Holder, p. 350 ; but cf. N.C., i. 744.

[9] Chap. 11.

of Normandy.[1] Úlfr signs three charters, K. 735, 740, 1327 (= R. 85). Of these the first and last are obvious forgeries, and the second is not preserved in its original form. Nevertheless, the fact that the three documents are from different sources suggests that Úlfr's name was more frequent in Knútr's charters than the extant specimens would lead us to suppose, for the idea of putting him among the signatories would not have struck the fabricators of K. 735 and K. 1327 independently, unless they had models to follow which he signed. Úlfr is mentioned in the Thorney *Liber Vitae*.[2]

The legendary descent of Earl Úlfr will be found in Florence of Worcester (i. 202) and in Saxo (ed. Holder, pp. 345–6), and it is adopted for Siward in his mythical biography.[3] The identification of his semi-human ancestor ' Bear ' with Styrbjörn, prince of Sweden, which is admitted to Searle's genealogy of the Anglo-Danish kings,[4] is a strange piece of rationalisation originally due to Langebek.[5]

As is mentioned above, the *Old English Chronicle* makes Úlfr and Eilífr the opponents of Knútr at the battle of Helge-á. There can hardly be any doubt about the identity of the Úlfr referred to, in view of the facts that Earl Úlfr Thorgilsson is concerned in the battle in Saxo and *Heimskringla*, and that *Fagrskinna's* account of the earl can easily be regarded as modified for obvious reasons. It is very surprising to find that the *Old English Chronicle* recorded the battle of the Helge-á without mentioning Óláfr of Norway, who was the chief figure among the enemies of Knútr on that occasion, and whose personal presence in the battle is confirmed by skaldic verse.[6] I therefore think that Freeman is most probably right when he suggests that the *Eglaf* of MS. E of the *Chronicle* is a mistake for *Olaf*.[7] Such a slip might very easily be made by a copyist owing to the fact that Úlfr was very closely associated with Eilífr in England : in the three charters signed by Úlfr, his signature and that of Eilífr come together, and the Thorney *Liber Vitae* mentions that they were brothers (see below). The theories, that there were two battles of the Helge-á, or, alternatively, that the Úlfr and Eilífr mentioned by the E *Chronicle* were not Knútr's earls, but two sons of Earl Rögnvaldr of Götland, can be dismissed as mere sophistry.[8]

It is quite certain, on the other hand, that one of Knútr's earls in England was called Eilífr. His signatures run from the earliest in the reign to 1024,[9] and he is mentioned in the Thorney *Liber Vitae*.[10] One document (K. 1317) indicates that he was connected with Gloucestershire, so there is little doubt he is to be identified with the leader of the forces which invaded South Wales in 1022.[11] In fact, he seems to have made a consider-

---

[1] A rather fuller discusssion of Ástríthr's marriages than that of Freeman will be found in K. Maurer, *Die Bekehrung des norwegischen Stammes*, i. 472–3, n. 24 ; Steenstrup, *Normandiets Historie*, pp. 226–7, may also be consulted, though his attempt to place Ástríthr's Norman marriage in the time of Sveinn's negotiations with Normandy (see above, p. xlii, note 4) is not to be supported.
[2] Reference as above, p. 70, note 6.
[3] See *N.C.*, i. 791–2 ; and, for an attempt seriously to connect Siward with Úlfr's family, Steenstrup, *Normannerne*, iii. 437 ff.
[4] *Anglo-Saxon Bishops, Kings and Nobles*, p. 355.
[5] *Scriptores*, iii. 281–2.
[6] Saxo does not make it clear whether Óláfr of Norway takes part in the battle in his version of the story. H. Koht., *Inhogg og Utsyn*, pp. 136 ff., attempts to prove on insufficient grounds that he did not ; cf. J. Schreiner, (*Norsk*) *Historisk Tidsskrift*, xxvii (1927), pp. 311 ff.
[7] *N.C.*, i. 765.
[8] See Napier and Stevenson, *Crawford Charters*, p. 142, for references.
[9] Also the notorious forgery K. 1327 (= R. 85).
[10] Reference as above, p. 70, note 6.
[11] This event is noticed by the only two manuscripts of the Welsh Latin annals which have entries in the period, and by the Welsh vernacular chronicles.

able impression on the Welsh imagination, for his invasion is given a legendary background in one later Welsh source.[1] Therefore, in spite of the absence of his signature in the later part of Knútr's reign, it is unwise to reject the statement of the Welsh chronicles that he fled from England after Knútr's death.[2] The Thorney *Liber Vitae* calls him Úlfr's brother, and this is confirmed by a Norse text to be discussed in the following section.

It is well known that Florence of Worcester states, that Thorkell's army was joined in 1009 by forces under Hemingr and Eilífr. The facts, that Thorkell is known to have avenged a brother in England, and to have had a brother called Hemingr, point to the conclusion that the Hemingr mentioned by Florence was Thorkell's brother.[3] There does not seem any objection to the usual assumption that his companion Eilífr was Knútr's earl, and it is also supported by the text to be discussed below, where Hemingr and Eilífr are said to have been brothers-in-arms in England, although at a wrong date.

In conclusion I may say that many statements are made in well-known works concerning Úlfr and Eilífr, which connect them with the vikings of Jóm, and even argue that Úlfr, when he disappears from English history, became ruler of the Wends in Knútr's interest. These assumptions are as totally without grounds as it is possible to be.[4]

D. *The Account of the Conquest of England in the Supplement to Jómsvíkinga Saga*

At the end of the *Flateyjarbók* text of *Jómsvíkinga Saga* are found three chapters, added by some writer who wished to provide a supplement on the subsequent history of the heroes of the attempted invasion of Norway, which is the main subject of the Saga. The after-history of Sigvaldi had been chronicled in the various Sagas of Óláfr Tryggvason, and Sigurthr Vésetason seems to have left no further mark on northern tradition, but the author thought that he had enough information about Thorkell Hávi to justify him in producing an expanded and modified version of the account of his later career given by the early versions of the Saga of Óláfr Helgi.

The three supplementary chapters are not found in any manuscript of *Jómsvíkinga Saga* except *Flateyjarbók*, nor do the various sources which draw on versions of the Saga older than those known to us give any indication that anything like them was known in early times. The first indication of their existence is that they are used as a source by the *Knýtlinga Saga*, a compilation on Danish history, the composition of which can be dated in the second half of the thirteenth century.[5] These chapters have sometimes been referred to in England, and even in Scandinavia, as if they were an integral part of *Jómsvíkinga Saga*: Napier and Stevenson are, in fact, the only English scholars who appear to have been aware that this is not the case.[6] A considerable number of statements have found their way into English historical works on the unsupported authority

[1] W. J. Rees, *Lives of the Cambro British Saints*, p. 77.
[2] The notice does not appear in the Welsh Latin annals, but there is every reason to regard it as an early one for it appears both in Welsh chronicles of the Red Book type, and in MS. Peniarth 20 in identical words: the death of Knútr is recorded, and it is then said that *gwedy y varw ef y foes Eilaf hyt yn Germania*. In the early Welsh annals *Germania* often means Norway: Knútr is described as king of Germany, Denmark and England, and Haraldr Harðráði and Magnús Berfoetr are both called kings of Germany. On the other hand, the word can have its usual meaning also. [3] See above, p. 73.
[4] Suhm, *Historie af Danmark*, iii. 502 (followed by various authorities), sees in Wolf, the mythical ancestor of Wigbert of Thuringia, confused memories of Earl Úlfr (see *M.G.H.*, *SS.*, xvi. 234 ff.). This is mere nonsense, not worth discussion.
[5] See Finnur Jónsson, *Den oldnorske og oldislandske litteraturs historie*, ii (2nd ed.), p. 778.
[6] See *Crawford Collection*, p. 140, note 2.

of these chapters, so I have considered it desirable to offer an analysis of their contents and a consideration of their reliability. I refer to them as the *Supplement*, and, in Appendix IV, I present a text of them for convenience of reference.

The only Saga which dealt with the later career of Thorkell Hávi was that of Óláfr Helgi in its earlier forms. He practically disappears in Snorri's versions, and entirely in that of *Fagrskinna*. It is, therefore, evident that if the writer of the *Supplement* did not use the Legendary Saga, he used its direct source, M, or its ultimate source, the Oldest Saga, or Styrmir's revision of M.[1] There is no reason to suppose that these sources varied much in what they had to tell of Thorkell, for the Legendary Saga can be shown by comparison with the extant fragments of the Oldest Saga to give the substance of that work (through the medium of M) very fully and accurately, and Styrmir's additions and alterations were concerned with hagiography rather than history. Verbal agreements show that the *Supplement* used a source very much like the Legendary Saga. We may compare :

Supplement	*Legendary Saga*
A þriggia vetra fresti for Knutr . . . . . til Æinglandz . . . . . þeir Knutr konungr [ok] Jatmundr attu nokkura bardaga. eptir þat baðu huorirtueggiu Danir ok Æinglismenn at þeir skylldu sættazst. ok þeir geordu sua ok skyllde 'huorr taka land eftir annan er læingr lifðe. Manaðe sidarr var Jatmundr veginn af fostra sinum Alreki strionu. eftir þat öðladizst Knutr allt Æingland ok red þui fiora vetr ok. XX.	þrim vætrum æftir anlat Svæins for Knutr . . . . . til Ænglandz . . . . . En þæir konungarnir Knutr ok Iatmundr atto bardaga .v. a æinum manaðe. en siðan gengo rikismenn amillum þæirra oc sætto þa. en þat var at sætt at hvar þæirra skilldi haua hælming lannz við annan. en sa þæirra er læingr lifði skilldi æignazt allt Ængland. En a manaðe æftir sætt þæirra Knutz ok Iatmundar. þa svæik Æirikr striona er fostre var Iatmundar ok drap hann þa Iatmund fostra sinn . . . . . En siðan tok Knutr ennriki allt Ængland oc red firir fiora vætr oc. XX.

The Saga of Óláfr Helgi provided a considerable amount of the information used by the author of the *Supplement*. He learned from it, firstly, that Thorkell had a brother, who commanded the thingmen, and was killed with them in England. Secondly, it provided an account of the Danish conquest of England from which he took the following items : (1) Sveinn conquered England and expelled Æthelred, but soon died. (2) Knútr came to England three years later with Eiríkr and Thorkell. The latter is not with Knútr in the Legendary Saga, but the *Supplement* assumes he was, because of the Legendary Saga's remark that neither Eiríkr nor Thorkell knew how London might be taken.[2] In the Legendary Saga, Thorkell appears to be with Óláfr, who is called in to help, while Eiríkr is with Knútr. (3) Knútr had five battles with Eadmund, Æthelred's son. These the *Supplement* spreads over Eadmund's reign, the Legendary Saga says they took place in a month. (4) Knútr took London. (5) The supporters of the two kings made them conclude peace : the one who lived longer was to succeed to the whole land. (6) One month after the peace Eadmund was betrayed and killed by his foster-father, Eadric Streona.[3] (7) Knútr succeeded and ruled twenty-four years.

The *Jómsvíkinga Saga* was naturally a source which the writer who composed the *Supplement* to it would consult. From it he learned that Thorkell had a brother called

---

[1] On the relationships of these Sagas, see above, pp. 80-1.

[2] Cf. above, pp. 70-1 and 80.

[3] It is particularly noteworthy that the *Supplement* gives *Eiríkr* as an alternative name for Eadric Streona, while preferring to use the form *Alrekr* : the use of the name *Eiríkr* for this man is peculiar to the Legendary Saga, where it, no doubt, comes from the Oldest Saga.

Hemingr. He concluded that this must have been the brother of Thorkell who was killed in England. In this he was no doubt perfectly right, for we know that one Hemingr joined Thorkell in England in 1009, and then disappeared from history.[1] The *Supplement* purports to give some of the laws of the thingmen, and various writers have indulged in learned comments on the similarity of these to those of the Jómsvíkings. It is, however, obvious that the writer of the *Supplement* took laws for his thingmen from the Saga, which he was supplementing. These laws are (1) a regulation against spreading rumours ; (2) a prohibition against spending the night outside the camp ; (3) it is implied by the story of the *Supplement*, though not stated, that the thingmen might not keep women in camp. All these laws are among those laid down by Pálnatóki for his men in *Jómsvíkinga Saga*, except that he permitted them to be outside their fortress three nights at a time.

The writer of the *Supplement* has a few fragments of knowledge, which did not come to him from these sources, but which we know to be correct, or correct according to Northern tradition. (1) Sveinn's body was taken to Denmark and buried by that of his father at Roskilde. (2) Knútr married Emma, Richard's daughter, Æthelred's widow. (3) The names of Knútr's children, the story of Gunnhildr's marriage, and the popular belief that Haraldr was not a son of Knútr, though he adheres to the usual Norse belief that he was a son of Emma. (4) The story alluded to above, p. 83, that Henry III went with Knútr to Rome. (5) The fact that Hemingr had a companion-in-arms known as Eilífr. (6) He makes this Eilífr a brother of Úlfr : here the Thorney *Liber Vitae* confirms him, at least if we assume that the Eilífr, who came to England with Hemingr in 1009, was identical with Knútr's earl. (7) He gives the length of Eadmund's reign as nine months, which is approximately correct. (8) He knows that Thorkell was at one time viceroy of Denmark, though he places this period at the beginning of Knútr's reign in Denmark, immediately after Sveinn's death, instead of after the completion. of the conquest of England. (9) He apparently knew, directly or indirectly, that Adam of Bremen estimated the size of Knútr's invasion fleet at 1000 ships, for his 800 is the nearest possible figure to 1000 in round long-hundreds.

The *Supplement* offers a number of statements for which there is no other authority. (1) Eadric Streona is absurdly called a brother of Emma. (2) Thorkell is said to have married Úlfhildr, widow of Úlfkell, and daughter of Æthelred. At the time of his banishment from England, Thorkell was married to a lady named Eadgyth (see above, p. 76), and Úlfhildr is unknown from other sources. Freeman ingeniously suggested that Thorkell's wife Eadgyth might be Æthelred's daughter of that name, and widow of Eadric Streona.[2] (3) Thorkell Hávi is said to have fostered Knútr : this is perhaps a confused memory of Thorkell's guardianship of Knútr's son. (4) Eilífr is made to go to the Eastern Empire before Knútr's invasion of England. This we know to be absurd, but it may be a faint memory of the withdrawal of Eilífr to ' Germany ', of which we learn from the Welsh chronicles. (5) Thorkell is said to have killed Úlfkell and so avenged his brother. But Thorkell's vengeance belongs to the period before the death of Sveinn, and Úlfkell was killed in the general action at Ashingdon. It is, of course, not impossible that he fell by Thorkell's hand, but we do not know that Thorkell had abandoned the English cause at that time.[3] It will be seen from these points that the *Supplement* makes no contribution at all to our knowledge of the history of the time.

The author of the *Supplement* works into his own story all the various scraps discussed above. The object of this story is to enlarge upon the account of the death of Thorkell's brother and of Thorkell's vengeance given in the Sagas of Óláfr Helgi, and to add a sketch of Thorkell's subsequent career. It is not possible to decide if the lively story of the

---

[1] See above, p. 73.   [2] *N.C.*, i. 670.   [3] See above, p. 75.

massacre of the thingmen has any foundation in fact. The part played by the church makes it possible that vague memories of the massacre of Danes at Oxford in 1002 [1] may be the foundation of the whole tale. In any event, the death of Thorkell's brother is to be referred with certainty to the period before the death of Sveinn, and the *Encomium* and the Saga of Óláfr Helgi show that Thorkell's revenge belongs to the years 1009–12.[2] Perhaps Úlfkell was regarded as in some way responsible for Hemingr's death, and Thorkell's victory at Ringmere was felt to be a fitting revenge. This might be sufficient to start a legend that Úlfkell had Hemingr and his men murdered and was slain by Thorkell in revenge.

The *Supplement* has two further anecdotes. The first is that Thorkell intercepted Emma, who was escaping in a boat, brought her to Knútr, and made him marry her. This is obviously a preposterous legend, for Knútr, as we know, had Emma fetched, in all probability from Normandy, in 1017. The second is that Knútr had Thorkell murdered because, when he saw Úlfhildr, he thought that Thorkell had cheated him in keeping her for himself, and letting his king marry Emma. Some memory of the coolness between Knútr and Thorkell, which led to the banishment of the latter in 1021, may underlie this story. The tale is of very common type, based on the motif of the enmity of a king and a subject over a woman.[3] The historical worthlessness of these two episodes does much to undermine faith in the more elaborate tale of the massacre of the thingmen.

Of Authun and Thórthr, the two thingmen who figure in the story of the *Supplement*, nothing is known from any other source. It is idle to attempt to see in Thórthr one of the persons of that name, who sign Old English charters, still less to identify him with Thórthr the Viking, a totally fictitious character, who appears in the late Sagas of Óláfr Helgi in *Flateyjarbók* and *Bæjarbók*.[4]

From what has now been said it will appear that the *Supplement* is of historical value only in that it confirms the statement of the Thorney *Liber Vitae* that Úlfr and Eilífr were brothers, and that of Florence of Worcester that Hemingr and Eilífr operated together in England. It is also possible that there was some massacre of Danes in England between the death of Sveinn and Knútr's invasion, and that this underlies the main story in the *Supplement*. It is, however, chronologically impossible that the brother, whom Thorkell avenged in England, was killed in this massacre.

---

[1] See *N.C.*, i. 648 ff. If the massacre described in the *Supplement* is, in fact, founded, upon no more than vague memories of some of the incidents of 1002, the representation of Knútr's invasion as a mission of vengeance may arise from the fact that the invasion of Sveinn, which followed upon the massacre of 1002, was in some quarters believed to have had personal vengeance as its object. (See Stenton, p. 375, where William of Malmesbury's confused statement, *Gesta Regum*, ii. 177, which literally means that Sveinn's mission of vengeance was the 1013 expedition, is no doubt correctly applied to that of 1003. William of Jumièges, v. 6, also attributes Sveinn's expedition of 1003 to a desire to avenge the massacre of 1002, but Adam of Bremen, ii. 49, makes him wish to avenge a brother, presumably the obscure Hiring, on whom see my *Battle of Brunanburh*, pp. 71–2. William and Adam both telescope Sveinn's expeditions of 1003 and 1013).

[2] Langebek, *Scriptores*, ii. 459, sees the chronological impossibility of Thorkell's brother, who was killed before the death of Sveinn, being in charge of the thingmen after that event, and he solves the problem by bringing Thorkell's other brother Sigvaldi to England. Sigvaldi is killed and avenged before Sveinn's death, Hemingr afterwards. This piece of perverted ingenuity is reproduced by various respected authorities on the history of the period. There is, of course, no shadow of evidence that Sigvaldi was ever in England.

[3] Similar stories will be found referred to in the controversy about the story of Sigurthr Slefa between R. C. Boer and Jón Jónsson in *Arkiv för nordisk filologi*, xviii. 97 ; xxvi. 202 and 346 ; xxvii. 192.

[4] See Nordal, *Om Olaf den helliges saga*, p. 118, on the purely literary reasons which led to the fabrication of this character (probably by Styrmir).

Readers of the Sagas will have no difficulty in classing the *Supplement* with works like *Yngvars Saga*, where a solemn historical background is provided for legends of the wildest type. I forebear from comment on the extraordinary twentieth chapter of the *Flatey-jarbók* version of the Saga of Óláfr Helgi, where the *Supplement*, itself so largely derived from the Saga of Óláfr, is digested back into it.[1] Of more interest is the attempt of *Knytlinga Saga* to build up a connected account of the Danish conquest from the *Supplement*, the *Heimskringla*, and various poems, but an analysis of this would not be strictly relevant to the present enquiry.

[1] Those who wish can study this production in Miss Ashdown's *English and Norse Documents*, pp. 176 ff.

APPENDIX IV

TEXT OF THE SUPPLEMENT TO JÓMSVÍKINGA SAGA

The narrative printed below is preserved only in *Flateyjarbók* (cols. 102–3), where it follows *Jómsvíkinga Saga*, to which it forms a supplement. A facsimile of *Flateyjarbók* is now available (Levin and Munksgaard, 1930) and diplomatic texts of its contents are accordingly unnecessary. The *Supplement* is, therefore, presented below in a normalised Old Norse spelling, and is punctuated according to the system now commonly used in Iceland. It has previously been printed in *Fornmanna Sögur*, xi. (1828), pp. 158–62, and in *Flateyjarbók*, i (1860), pp. 203–5.

Lagasetning Sveins konungs

Sveinn konungr Saum-Æsuson sat nú heima í Danmörk. Knútr óx upp, sonr hans, ok var heima upp fœddr; Þorkell inn hávi fóstraði hann. Sveinn konungr herjaði á ríki Aðalráðs konungs ok gerir hann landflótta um haf. Sveinn konungr setti þingamannalið í tveim stöðum, annat í Lundúnaborg; þar réð fyrir Eilífr Þorgilsson, bróðir Úlfs; hann hafði sex tigu skipa í Temps; annat þingamannalið var norðr í Slésvík; þar réð fyrir Hemingr jarl, bróðir Þorkels háva; þar váru enn sex tigir skipa. Þingamenn settu þau lög, at engi skyldi kvittr kveikjask, ok engi vera um nótt á brott. Þeir höfðu kirkjusókn til Burakirkju; þar var ein stór klukka; henni skyldi hringja, þar er þriðjungr lifði nætr hverja nótt; þá skyldu allir til kirkju ganga ok eigi með vápnum. Slík lög höfðu þeir í Slésvík. Þórðr hét maðr ok Auðun í liðinu.

Frá andláti Sveins konungs ok fœrðr í Danmörk

Sá maðr hafði forráð í borginni, et Alrekr strjóna hét, bróðir Emmu, Ríkarðs dóttur jarls, föður Vilhjálms; hana átti Aðalráðr konungr. Norðr réð fyrir Englandi Úlfkell snillingr; hann átti Úlfhildi, dóttur Aðalráðs konungs. Sveinn konungr andaðisk í Englandi, ok fœrðu Danir hann til Danmerkr ok grófu hann í Hróiskeldu hjá föður sínum. Þá var Knútr tíu vetra. Mikit var ríki þingamanna. Markaðr var þar tvá tíma á tolf mánuðum, í annat sinn um miðsumar, en annan tíma um miðsvetrarskeið. Eigi þykkir Enskum mönnum sýnt, at hœgra sé öðru sinni, at ráða af þingamannalið, er Knútr var ungr, en Sveinn andaðr. Hvern vetr í mót jólum fóru vagnar til borgarinnar, ok var þar fjárhlutr sá, er menn váru vanir at hafa til markaðarins; svá var ok þenna vetr, ok tjaldat yfir öllum; þat var af ráðum, svikum ok vilja Úlfkels snillings ok þeirra brœðra, Aðalráðs sona. Sjaunda dag jóla, gekk Þórðr útan borgar til húsa konu þeirra, er honum fylgdi; hon bað hann vera þar um nóttina. 'Hví biðr þú þess, er víti liggr við?' 'Því bið ek þessa', kvað hon, 'at mér þykkir máli skipta.' 'Vit skulum kaupa saman,' kvað hann, 'at ek mun hér vera, en þú seg mér hvat til berr, er þú biðr þessa.' 'Þat sætir,' segir hon, 'um bœn þessa, at ek veit ráðinn bana öllu þingamannaliði.' 'Hví máttu þat vita,' kvað hann, 'er vér vitum eigi?' 'Þat er svá við látit,' segir hon, 'at menn óku hingat vögnum í borgina ok létu sem þeir fœri með fjárhlut, en þar var fjölmenni í hverjum vagni, en engi fjárhlutr, ok svá hafa þeir gert ok norðr í Slésvík. En þá er þriðjungr er af nótt, mun hringt í borginni; skulu þá hermenn búask um miðnætti; skulu menn búask annan veg í borginni. En þá er þriðjungr lifir nætr, mun hringt at Burakirkju; þá munu þér ætla til kirkju slyppir, en þá mun sleginn hringr um kirkju.' 'Búit er við,' kvað Þórðr, 'at vinsældir þínar sé miklar, ok mun ek segja Eilífi, þótt kvittr þykki vera ; en bú þetta skaltu eiga.' Þórðr gekk í borgina. Hann fann Auðun, félaga sinn ; ganga þeir ok segja Eilífi ; hann gerir menn vara við ; sumir trúðu, en sumir kváðu fælingar. Heyra þeir hringingar eptir vana, ok hyggja margir, at prestar muni hringja. Þeir menn allir, er orðum Þórðar trúðu, gengu með vápnum, en hinir slyppir.

Frá Eilífi ok hans mönnum

Þá er þeir koma í kirkjugarð, var þar fjöldi liðs. Þeir máttu þá eigi ná vápnum, því at þeir kómusk eigi til húsa sinna. Eilífr spyrr þá ráða, en þeir látask engi kunna. 'Eigi þykki mér vel ráðit,' kvað Eilífr, 'at hlaupa í kirkju, ef þat verðr at engu skjóli, en sýna sik í hræzlu. Þat kemr mér í hug, at vér munum hlaupa á herðar þeim, er fyrir útan standa garðinn, ok vita, ef vér kvæmimsk með því undan til skipa.' Ok svá gera þeir. Þat varð mannfall mest, er við skip varð ; Eilífr komsk á burt með þrjú skip, en engir ór Slésvík, ok þar fell Hemingr. Eilífr ferr til Danmerkr. Nökkuru eptir þetta var Játmundr til konungs tekinn í Englandi ; hann var konungr níu mánuðu ; á þeim tíma háði hann fimm orrostur við Knút Sveinsson. Alrekr strjóna, er sumir kölluðu Eirík, var fóstri Játmundar, bróðir Emmu, er átt hafði Aðalráðr Engla konungr. Þorkell hávi hafði þá mest forráð fyrir Danmörk. Þeir áttu þing um várit eptir fall þingamanna. Eilífr eggjaði at fara til hefnda, en Þorkell svarar : 'Vér höfum konung ungan, en eigi hœfir at herja svá, at konungs sé eigi við getit, en á þriggja vetra fresti vænti ek, at eigi muni konung skorta harðfengi en lið óvarast.' Eilífr svarar : 'Ósýnt er, at þeim sé minnisamt á þriggja vetra fresti, er nú þykkir enskis um vert.' Eilífr ferr út í Miklagarð ok gerðisk höfðingi fyrir Væringjaliði ok fell þar um síðir. Á þriggja vetra fresti fór Knútr, Þorkell ok Eiríkr með átta hundruð skipa til Englands. Þorkell hafði þrjá tigu skipa ok drap Úlfkel snilling ok hefndi svá Hemings, bróður síns, ok gekk at eiga Úlfhildi, dóttur Aðalráðs konungs, er Úlfkell hafði átta. Þar fell með Úlfkatli hvert manns barn af sex tigum skipa, en Knútr konungr vann Lundúnaborg. Þorkell fór með landi fram ok fann Emmu dróttning á einu skipi ; hann flytr hana heim í land með sér, fýsir Knút konung at biðja hennar, ok gekk Knútr konungr at eiga hana. Hon ól son um vetrinn, er Haraldr hét, kenningarson Knúts. Hörðaknútr var þeirra sonr. Sveinn var enn sonr Knúts ok Álfífu. Gunnhildr hét dóttir Knúts ; hana átti Heinrekr keisari Konráðsson ; með honum fór Knútr til Róms. Þat var miklu síðarr, er Knútr konungr var at boði hjá Þorkatli háva, þá sá konungr Úlfhildi, ok þótti hann hafa svikit sik í kvennaskipti ok réð Þorkatli fyrir þessa sök bana. Þeir Knútr konungr [ok] Játmundr áttu nökkura bardaga. Eptir þat báðu hvárirtveggja Danir ok Englismenn, at þeir skyldu sættask, ok þeir gerðu svá, ok skyldi hvárr taka land eptir annan, er lengr lifði. Mánaði síðarr var Játmundr veginn af fóstra sínum, Alreki strjónu ; eptir þat öðlaðisk Knútr allt England ok réð því fjóra vetr ok tuttugu.

APPENDIX V

ADDITIONAL NOTES

a. The Encomiast's descriptions of Norse ships and his remarks on the composition of the Norse army

There are no descriptions of Scandinavian fleets so detailed and vivid as those given by the Encomiast in I, 4, and II, 4. Here and there he has given play to his imagination, and has perhaps been influenced by classical models (cf. above, p. xxxii), but in most instances his descriptions agree closely with the evidence of Icelandic literature and with the observations of modern archaeologists. It is well known that, ever since prehistoric times, Scandinavians used to adorn the prows and sterns of their ships with the heads and forms of various beasts, both mythical and natural. Representations of ships furnished with animal heads have been noticed among Scandinavian rock-carvings assigned to the bronze age (cf. G. Ekholm in *Nordisk Kultur, Konst* [ed. H. Shetelig, Stockholm, 1931], pp. 81 ff.; and H. Shetelig and H. Falk, *Scandinavian Archaeology* [1937], ch. X), and the practice was also known among Phoenicians and other Mediterranean peoples in ancient times (cf. R. and R. C. Anderson, *The Sailing Ship* [1926], pp. 30 ff.).

The adornment most frequently described in Icelandic literature is the dragon-head (*drekahöfuð*), and this probably gave rise to the term *dreki* (dragon), used in Icelandic for warships of the largest and strongest class, which were distinguished from smaller craft, such as the *skeið*, *snekkja*, etc. Except in rare instances, the *drekar* were the property of kings or of great princes. The first *dreki* mentioned in literature was built for Haraldr Hárfagri towards the end of the ninth century. This ship was described by the contemporary poet, Þorbjörn Hornklofi, as *ræsinaðr* ('the racing serpent'?, see *Heimskringla, Haralds Saga Hárfagra*, ch. 9). Among the most famous of all *drekar* were Ormrinn langi (the long serpent) and Ormrinn skammi (the short serpent), both of which belonged to Óláfr Tryggvason, and were described in the *Heimskringla* (*Óláfs Saga Tryggvasonar*, chs. 80 and 88, etc.) and in other Sagas about this king. Ormrinn langi contained thirty-four rowing benches, and probably carried seven or eight men on each bench besides a considerable number distributed in the bow and stern, giving a total crew of nearly three hundred. According to the *Heimskringla* (*Óláfs Saga Tryggvasonar*, ch. 94), however, the crew of Ormrinn langi would seem to be nearer six hundred than three hundred, though this is scarcely credible (cf. H. Falk, *op. cit. infra*, pp. 97 ff.). The largest *dreki* mentioned in the sources belonged to Knútr the Great, and contained no less than sixty rowing benches (*Heimskringla, Óláfs Saga Helga*, ch. 147).

Not only the *drekar*, but also lesser craft, sometimes carried figure-heads, in peace as well as in war. In a poem about the battle of Hafrsfjörðr, ascribed to Þorbjörn Hornklofi, the *knerrir*, or merchantmen, which came to support Haraldr, are said to have gaping heads (*Heimskringla, Haralds Saga Hárfagra*, ch. 18). The Oseberg ship, probably built early in the ninth century, was not a *dreki*, but it was apparently equipped with a dragon-head (see H. Shetelig, *Osebergfundet*, i [Oslo 1917], pp. 328 ff.).

Ships furnished with figure-heads were called *höfðaskip* or *höfuðskip*. These figure-heads might be attached both to the prow and the stern. Sometimes the prow alone would have more than one head (cf. Falk, *op. cit. infra*, p. 40). Sometimes the stern of

94

the ship would represent the tail of the beast whose head adorned the prow. E.g., Ormrinn skammi of Óláfr Tryggvason carried a dragon head on the prow, and the stern was shaped like the dragon's tail (*sporðr*), and when the sails were aloft they looked like the dragon's wings (*Heimskringla, Óláfs Saga Tryggvasonar*, ch. 80).

Heads of beasts other than dragons were also carried on the prows and sterns of ships according to the Icelandic sources. One of the settlers of Iceland arrived in a ship bearing the head of a bull (*þjórshöfuð*), after which the river Þjórsá was named (*Landnámabók*, ed. Finnur Jónsson [Copenhagen, 1900], pp. 114 and 223). Óláfr Helgi built a ship called 'Visundr' (Bison), and placed the head of a bison on her prow (*Heimskringla, Óláfs Saga Helga*, ch. 144). Human figures adorning ships are also recorded in sources other than the *Encomium*. Óláfr Helgi once built a ship called 'Karlhöfði' (Man-headed), to which the poet Sighvatr alludes in the *Nesjavísur* (*Skjaldedigtning*, IB, 217). Óláfr himself carved a representation of a king's head, most probably his own, to adorn her prow (*Heimskringla, Óláfs Saga Helga*, ch. 47 ; *Fagrskinna*, pp. 149 ff.). The ship of William the Conqueror, as depicted on the Bayeux Tapestry, bore the full image of a man on the stern (see E. Maclagan, *The Bayeux Tapestry*, [London, 1943], plate V). Mention is also made of a figure representing Þórr, which was carried on the prow of a ship, and this was later replaced by a cross (*Fornmanna Sögur*, x. 358).

It is stated in numerous passages in Icelandic literature that the figure-heads and their necks (*svírar*) were elaborately carved and gilded, and the poets describe how they shone like fire (cf. H. Falk, *op. cit. infra*, p. 41). The heads were detachable, and were sometimes removed or placed upon another ship (e.g., *Heimskringla, Óláfs Saga Tryggvasonar*, ch. 101 ; *Óláfs Saga Helga*, ch. 47).

It is suggested by at least one of the passages quoted above that, to begin with, figure-heads had a magical, as well as a decorative purpose. This conjecture is supported by the laws of pagan Iceland, as they are quoted in the *Landnámabók* (*Hauksbók*, p. 95) and other sources. According to these laws none should approach the coasts of Iceland in ships furnished with figure-heads (*höfuðskip*) ; but if they did so, they must remove the heads before they came within sight of land lest the territorial spirits (*landvættir*) should be scared.

Not only the prow and the stern, but also parts of the gunwale adjoining them (O. Icel. *brandar*) were elaborately carved and decorated (cf. Shetelig, *Osebergfundet*, i. 330 ff. ; H. Falk, *op. cit. infra*, pp. 44 ff.). Moreover the sides of valuable ships were painted (*steind*) above sea-level, as the Encomiast states, sometimes in various colours (e.g., *Fornmanna Sögur*, iv. 277). Each board on the ship of William the Conqueror, as it is shown on the Bayeux Tapestry, was painted a different colour.

The Encomiast mentions bird-like weather-vanes (*volucres*) at the mast-heads. Although the Icelandic sources often mention weather-vanes, these were generally carried on the prow or the stern, and were called *veðrvitar* (Old French *wirewite*, M. French *girouette*). The brilliant gilding of the *veðrvitar* is sometimes described (e.g., *Fornmanna Sögur*, vi. 120). In two passages (*Biskupa Sögur*, i. 422, and ii. 50), moreover, mention is made of another weather vane, or suchlike object, carried on the mast-head, and this was called the *flaug* (fem.). On the Bayeux Tapestry and the Stenkyrka stone (illustrated in Shetelig and Falk, *Scandinavian Archaeology*, pl. 58), the *flaug* appears to be a small flag or pennant.

It need hardly be said that the crews of the *drekar*, and of ships belonging to the great chieftains, were carefully selected, and were superior to those of the *leiðangrsskip* (or *landvarnarskip*), which were supplied by the people and manned largely by conscripts (see W. Vogel, *op. cit. infra*, s.v. *Kriegsflotte*, and references given there). The description which the Encomiast gives of the crews of the ships bears some resemblance to the accounts which Oddr Snorrason (*Saga Óláfs Tryggvasonar*, ed. Finnur Jónsson [Copenhagen, 1932],

p. 160) and later biographers of Óláfr Tryggvason give of the manning of Ormrinn langi. According to Oddr, no man who served in Ormrinn might be younger than twenty, and none older than sixty. Nearly all of the crew had won distinction in one way or another, and none of them were cowards or beggars. According to the *Heimskringla* (*Óláfs Saga Tryggvasonar*, chs. 93–4 ; cf. *Flateyjarbók*, i. 452), Ormrinn was manned chiefly by the king's bodyguard (*hirðmenn*), who consisted of natives and foreigners chosen for their strength and prowess. Somewhat similar statements are made about the crew of the *dreki* of Haraldr Hárfagri (*Heimskringla, Haralds Saga Hárfagra*, ch. 9).

Bibliographical Note : There is an extensive bibliography of this subject. Among the most useful works should be mentioned H. Falk, ' Altnordisches Seewesen ' in *Wörter und Sachen*, iv, 1912, pp. 1–122 ; W. Vogel in *Reallexikon der germanischen Altertumskunde*, Strassburg, 1911–19, s.v. *Schiff, Schiffsarten, Schiffsführung, Kriegsflotte*, etc. ; valuable bibliographies are appended to Vogel's articles. Another useful work is Eiríkr Magnússon, ' Notes on Shipbuilding and Nautical Terms ' in *Saga-Book of the Viking Society*, iv (1906), 182 ff. Good general works are A. Breusing, *Die Nautik der Alten*, Bremen, 1886, and G. H. Boehmer, *Prehistoric Naval Architecture of the North of Europe* (Report of the U.S. National Museum, 1891) Washington, 1892, pp. 527–647.

b. *The Encomiast's description of the magic banner of the Danes*

Banners on which the figure of a raven was depicted are several times attributed to Scandinavian chiefs, both in English and Icelandic sources. According to the *Old English Chronicle* (MSS. B, C, D, E), King Ælfred's army captured a banner called ' Hræfn ' or ' Ræfen ' from the Danes in Devonshire in 878. This same story is told in the *Annals of St. Neots*, where the origin and appearance of the Ræfen (Reafan) are described in some detail. It had been woven by three sisters of Ívarr and Ubbi in a single midday hour. This banner had power to predict the outcome of battle. If those before whom it was borne were to be victorious, a raven would appear upon it flapping his wings. But if those who followed the banner were to be defeated, the raven would seem to droop (cf. Stevenson's edition of Asser, pp. 265 ff.). The passage in the *Annals of St. Neots* bears close resemblance to that in the *Encomium*, and the two must be related (cf. above, p. xxxvii).

Yet another raven banner is described in the *Orkneyinga Saga* (ed. Sigurður Nordal, Copenhagen, 1913–16), chs. 11–12, in *Þorsteins Saga Síðu-Hallssonar* (ed. J. Jakobsen, *Austfirðinga Sögur*, Copenhagen, 1902–3, pp. 216 f.) and in *Njáls Saga* (ed. Finnur Jónsson, Halle, 1908), ch. 157. Allusion to it was also made in the lost *Brjáns Saga*.[1] This banner was called ' Hrafnsmerki ', and once, perhaps derisively, ' Krákr '. It was woven for the Orkney Jarl, Sigurðr Hlöðvésson, by his mother Auðna (Eðna), daughter of the Irish king, Kjarvalr. When the wind blew, the raven embroidered on this banner seemed to flap his wings. Though not oracular, Sigurðr's raven banner had magical properties, for it would always bring victory to him before whom it was borne, but death to him who bore it. When Sigurðr fought on Caithness, he lost three standard-bearers, but gained the victory. The Hrafnsmerki was carried before Sigurðr again at Clontarf, but after he had lost three more standard-bearers, he was obliged to carry it himself, and so lost his life.

In an English text of the twelfth-thirteenth century (*Vita et Passio Waldevi Comitis*, printed by C. E. Wright, *The Cultivation of Saga in Anglo-Saxon England*, 1939, pp. 127 ff. and 267 ff.) mention is made of a banner called ' Ravenlandeye ', which was given to

---

[1] On the *Brjáns Saga*, see A. J. Goedheer, *Irish and Norse Traditions about the Battle of Clontarf* (Haarlem, 1938), pp. 87 ff. ; and Einar Ól. Sveinsson, *Um Njálu* (Reykjavík, 1933), pp. 76 ff. Further references will be found in these works.

Siward by a nameless old man. The name is glossed *corvus terrae terror*. It is reminiscent of Haraldr Harðráði's banner ' Landeyða ' (' land-destruction ' or ' land-waster '), which was also said to bring victory to him before whom it was carried (e.g., *Fornmanna Sögur*, vi. 178).

The raven, as an heraldic symbol, may be associated with Óðinn, god both of war and of wisdom. Óðinn was called the raven-god (Hrafnáss), and kept two ravens, Huginn and Muninn, from whom he derived much of his own wisdom. Nevertheless, it should be emphasised that the cult of the raven is both older and more widespread than that of Óðinn, and examples of it are recorded among the ancient Greeks, and among many other European and Asiatic peoples (cf. A. H. Krappe, *Études de mythologie et de folklore germaniques*, Paris, 1928, pp. 29 ff.).

Banners and suchlike emblems adorned with images of sacred beasts are especially common in Germanic and Celtic legend and history. Among the parting gifts given to Beowulf was an *eafor heafodsegn* (line 2152, see Klaeber, note *ad loc.*). For further examples see O. Hartung, *Die deutschen Altertümer des Nibelungenliedes und der Kudrun* (Cöthen, 1894), pp. 450–5 ; L. M. Larson, *The King's Household in England before the Norman Conquest* (Wisconsin, 1904), pp. 179–81 ; P. W. Joyce, *A Social History of Ancient Ireland* (1913), i. 135 ff.

c. *The Encomiast's etymology of the name Hörðaknútr*

The etymology which the Encomiast gives for the name *Hörða-Knútr* (*Hardocnuto*) appears in several sources, including the *Historia Norvegiae* (Storm, p. 123). Storm (note *ad loc.*) compares the Allemanic name *Hartchnuz*. Sven Aggesøn (Langebek, *Scriptores*, i. 55) also alludes to this etymology of the name, but does not accept it. He associates *Hardo-* (*Harda-*) with the Danish province of Hardesyssel, south of Limfjord in Jutland, and suggests that Hörða-Knútr was born there.[1] Sven Aggesøn's view accords more closely with Icelandic tradition than does that of the Encomiast. It may be deduced from the *Flateyjarbók*, the *Dana Konunga tal* (ed. Kr. Kaalund in *Alfræði Íslenzk* iii, Copenhagen 1917–18, pp. 56 ff.), and from other Icelandic sources, that Hörða-Knútr was called after his great-great-great-grandfather, Hörða-Knútr, son of Sigurðr Ormr-í-auga. It was this first Hörða-Knútr whose nickname was derived from the Danish province Hörð (Hardesyssel), and according to the *Flateyjarbók* he was born in that province.[2]

Nicknames were not uncommonly transmitted to posterity as personal names ; thus Grettir Ásmundarson was called by the nickname of his ancestor Ófeigr Grettir (*Grettis Saga*). Examples of the transmission of the nickname together with the personal name are also recorded in the Icelandic sources, and seem to be favoured when several generations have elapsed between the child and the ancestor after whom he is named. Thus Þórðr Illugi, who lived in the latter decades of the tenth century, was called after his great-great-grandfather Þórðr Illugi Eyvindarson (*Landnámabók*, ed. Finnur Jónsson, Copenhagen, 1900, p. 98) ; Þorsteinn Hólmuðr Skaptason (1004–30) was called after his great-great-grandfather Þorsteinn Hólmuðr Sumarliðason (*Landnámabók*, pp. 93, 257, 259, etc.).

The chief principles according to which children were named were alliteration, variation and repetition. According to the principle of variation, a child would inherit a

---

[1] '. . . quem cognomine Durum vulgo nominabant, non quod austerus vel crudelis extiterit : verum inde, quod tale provinciæ nomen extiterit, ex qua natalem duxit originem '.

[2] *Flateyjarbók*, i. 98 : ' . . . Hann var fœddr á Hörð á Jótlandi ok þaðan af kallaðr Hörða-Knútr '.

part of his father's name (e.g., Oddleifr Geirleifsson). In some cases the child might inherit the whole of his father's name with an addition (Ketilbjörn Ketilsson). According to the principle of repetition, the name of a dead ancestor might be repeated in the new-born child, but it would be contrary to usual practice for a child to inherit his father's name unless his father died before his birth. Thus, Knútr could call his son Hörða-Knútr so long as Hörða-Knútr was regarded as a name distinct from Knútr (variation). If, as the Icelandic sources state, Knútr himself had an illustrious ancestor called Hörða-Knútr, this would give him an additional reason to repeat this name in his son.

Among the more useful works on name-giving the following may be mentioned : G. Storm, ' Vore forfædres tro paa sjælevandring og deres opkaldelsessytem ' in *Arkiv för nordisk filologi*, ix. (1893), pp. 199–222 ; H. Nauman, *Altnord. Namenstudien* in *Acta germanica*, Neue Reihe i (Berlin, 1912) ; M. Keil, *Altisländische Namenwahl*, Leipzig, 1931. Detailed biographical notes are included in the last-named work.

POSTSCRIPT

OVE MOBERG'S *OLAV HARALDSSON, KNUT DEN STORE, OCH SVERIGE*

Owing to the war, the present work was sent to the printers before I had an opportunity to see Ove Moberg's *Olav Haraldsson, Knut den Store, och Sverige* (Lund, 1941). This is a work which every student of the Old English period should study as a severe exemplification of the method mentioned above (p. 66, note 3) of using skaldic verse without allowing the mind to be prejudiced by the prose in which the verse is embedded. Of the problems upon which I touch in the present work, Moberg deals with (1) the early career of Óláfr Helgi and (2) the battle of Helge-å.

(1) Moberg, like myself, considers that Óláfr assisted Æthelred in 1014. He decides the vexed problem of the date of Óláfr's return to Norway in favour of 1015, relying upon Thórthr's poem about Eiríkr. While emphasising that this poem does point to 1015 (p. 69, note 8), I considered that it should be used with caution (cf. especially p. 67, note 7). Moberg, furthermore, considers that the tradition that Óláfr helped Knútr in England is based on an actual friendly contact of the two in 1015, before Óláfr left England, and that Earl Hákon received orders to facilitate matters for Óláfr in Norway. The evidence advanced for this is a verse, attributed to Sigvatr, which Snorri applies to the events of 1027 (*Óláfs Saga Helga*, chap. 146), and which I above (p. 72) suggest may apply rather to 1028, but which Moberg applies to the time of Óláfr's return. The verse certainly alleges that Hákon made an attempt on some occasion to reconcile Óláfr to the Norwegian squires. It remains entirely unknown to what events the verse refers, and accordingly Moberg is unwise to build so much upon it. It may be recalled that Sigvatr was supposed at least in later Norse tradition to have been friendly to Hákon, and to have regretted that he was opposed to Óláfr (*Óláfs Saga Helga*, chap. 161). Accordingly, he may have seen signs of goodwill between his friends with little cause. Concerning Sigvatr's verse Bjarni Aðalbjarnarson's edition of *Heimskringla* should also be consulted (ii, Reykjavík, 1945, p. lxxv).

(2) Moberg wishes to regard Knútr as victorious at the battle of Helge-å, because the king's skaldic panegyrists praise his performance there. This means grimly wrenching the *Old English Chronicle* to mean the opposite of what it says. The skaldic poets, however, do not actually say that Knútr was victorious, and since three poets touch upon the matter, this alone shows that his success, if any, was qualified. Moberg regards the evidence of the verse as pointing to the presence of Óláfr at the battle (cf. above, p. 86, note 6). He accepts the *Old English Chronicle's* date for the battle. This is to extend distrust of the Old Norse prose narratives to their chronological framework. This framework is, however, older than the narratives, is based on the sifting of tradition by professional chronologists, and for the period after 1000 is not to be lightly rejected.

In general criticism of Moberg's work, it may be said that while rightly valuing the skaldic verse above the prose sagas, he is too seldom suspicious of the nature of the verses themselves. His discussion of Eiríkr's alleged battle at Ringmere (p. 50) may in this connection be compared with what I have said above (p. 71, note 3).

GENERAL INDEX

Authorities (medieval and modern) are excluded from this Index, which is mainly one of subjects.
The Additional Notes (Appendix V) are not covered by this Index.

INDEX TO THE TEXT OF THE *ENCOMIUM*

Roman numerals refer to books and
Arabic numerals to chapters of the *Encomium*.
Forms not from MS. L are enclosed in square brackets.
A = Argumentum.
P = Prologus.

GLOSSARY

aduesperat : for *aduesperascit*, II, 10. (Late and very rare, see *Thes.*)

aggrego : *collect*, I, 4. (Sense frequent in late Latin ; first in *Itala*, Ioel ii. 16.)

alterutrum : *mutually, on both sides*, II, 17. (Adverbial use frequent in Late Latin, especially in the *Itala* ; see *Thes:*, s.v. *alteruter*, col. 1760.)

apparesco : for *appareo*, II, 3. (Late and rare ; e.g., *Vulg.*, 4 Esdr. vii. 26.)

appropio : *approach*, I, 4, II, 3. (Late : frequent in *Itala* ; more rarely in *Vulg.*, e.g., Luc. x. 34 ; Act. xxiii. 15.)

ascendo : *disembark*, II, 3, II, 6, III, 4. (A very unusual use : cf. the usual sense ' get on board ', I, 4, II, 7; III, 4.)

auspicor : *be auspicious*, II, 16 (but cf. Textual Note).

batulus : *boat*, II, 5. (Recorded by Baxter in tenth century ; variant of Medieval Lat. *batella*, cf. Ducange, s.v. *2 batus.*)

blasphemium : *reproach*, Prol. (For sense cf. *Vulg.*, Isa. li. 7 ; the neuter declension is fairly frequent, being found in *Itala*, though not in *Vulg.*)

camera : *room*, III, 1. (Sense frequent in medieval period, see Ducange, s.v. *2 camera* ; the earliest occurrence seems to be Aug., *Serm.* cccxix. 7.)

circumquaque : *on all sides*, II, 9. (Late : Aur. Vict., *Orig.* xvii. 6, and Christian writers from Ambrosius onwards.)

coangusto : *besiege*, II, 7. (For sense cf. *Itala*, Isa. xxix. 2, quoted by Jerome, *In Isa.* xxix. 1, where this verb is used where *Vulg.* has *circumuallo* ; and *Vulg.*, Luc. xix. 43.)

complex : *accomplice*, III, 5. (As adj. and noun frequent from Arnobius onwards.)

conciliatus : for *reconciliatus*, II, 3.

confinitas : for *confinium*, II, 16. (Baxter records in the eleventh century.)

coniugatio : *marriage*, II, 18. (Patristic usage : e.g., Ambrosiast., *In I Cor.* vii. 26 (*uirginitas*) *necessitates . . nescit quas patitur coniugatio.*)

conuinculo : *bind*, II, 16. (First instance in Ducange is dated 1081.)

deceni : for *deni*, III, 4. (See on this late form Sommer, *Handbuch der lat. Laut- und Formenlehre*, p. 477.)

delectamen : for *delectamentum*, II, 16. (Very rare : Forcellini quotes from an epigram of uncertain authorship *at nobis casso saltem delectamine amare liceat.*)

diatim : *daily, day by day*, II, 14, III, 3. (Very frequent in Medieval Lat.)

dictamen : *form, style*, Prol. (Recorded by Baxter sixth and eleventh centuries ; Thietmar, Prol. 5, *ornatu splendent dictaminis.*)

diffugium : for *refugium* or *effugium*, II, 6. (Similarly used by Robertus Monachus, e.g., *Patrologia*, clv. 685.)

diiudico : *condemn*, III, 6. (Very rare sense, first in Gregory of Tours, *Iul.* 4, *capitali diiudicatus sententia* : instances later than those in *Thes.*, *s.v.*, are the ' Astronomer ', *Vita Hludowici*, 46, *diiudicatis ad mortem*, and Wipo, *Vita Chuonradi*, 25.)

dirimo : ? *sort*, II, 11. (Cf. Lucan, v. 393, *dirimit suffragia plebis*, ' sorts the votes of the people '.)

exspectabilis : *excellent*, II, 5. (Used for *spectabilis*, as frequently in titles, see Ducange, s.v. *exspectabilis.*)

fastuosus : for *fastosus*, II, 5. (First Schol. on Hor., *A.P.*, 97, and Mart. Cap.)

giro : *draw* (of a circle), Arg. (Cf. Plin., *H.N.* v. 62, *gyratus*, ' made in circular shape '.)

gratulabundus : *delightful, causing delight*, II, 17. (The word can be used as practically

106

equivalent to *laetus*, ' delighted ', e.g., Aul. Gell., v. 14, 14 ; here its meaning is extended by the Encomiast, as is that of *laetus*, to include ' delightful '.)

inconsolabiliter : III, 7.
indicibilis : *indescribable*, II, 15. (Frequent Medieval Lat., see Ducange and Baxter.)
indigeo : *be poor*, III, 7. (For this absolute use, cf. *Vulg.*, Prov. xxviii. 27 ; Eccl. xl. 29.
induro : *dress* (in armour), II, 9. (An unusual usage.)
inpetus : *army*, II, 6 (see Linguistic Note).
intronizo : *enthrone*, I, 5. (Very frequent of both kings and bishops from Cassiodorus onwards ; Freeman suggests that the word is vague and that it would not be used of a duly crowned and anointed king, *N.C.* i. 680 ; this is certainly not the case : cf., e.g., *Vita Aeduuardi*, in Luard, *Lives of Edward the Confessor*, p. 395.)

legatarii : for *legati*, III, 4. (Frequent Medieval Lat., see Ducange.)
legatio : *message of a legation*, II, 13, III, 8. (Medieval Lat. ; Dudo, ed. Duchesne, p. 92 ; Thegan, *Vita Hludowici*, 54 ; *Vita Maior Stephani Regis*, 3 ; cf. Adamnan, *Vita Columbae*, i. 31, *legatiuncula*, in same sense.)
liberalis : *? legitimate*, II, 18. (Or possibly it is here a mere vague word of praise.)

marchio : III, 7. (Frequent in Medieval Lat., here correctly used as title of Baldwin V of Flanders ; see L. Vanderkindere, *La formation territoriale des principautés belges au moyen age*, i [Brussels, 1902], pp. 42–3.)
metallinus : for *metallicus*, II, 4.
milicies : for *militia*, II, 5. (Late instances in Baxter.)
morticina : *dead bodies* (human), II, 17. (Late ; *Vulg.*, frequently, e.g., Psa. lxxii. 2, where *Psalterium Romanum* has *mortalia*.)

obsonium : *entertainment, procuration*, III, 7. (In this sense, Ducange records first 1023, Baxter twelfth century.)
occasiones : *business, affairs*, Prol. (See Linguistic Note.)
ornatitius : for *ornatus*, I, 4. (Cf. *adoptatitius, tractitius* for *adoptatus, tractus* ; etc. See O. Gradenwitz, *Laterculi vocum Latinarum*, Leipzig, 1904, pp. 487–8, for further examples of this formation.)

patria : *country*, II, 1, etc. (Late and medieval ; frequent.)
patriensis : *native* ; noun, I, 4, etc. ; adj., II, 14. (Found occasionally in Medieval Lat. : e.g., *Vita S. Eusebiae abbatissae Hammaticensis*, i. 3 [*Acta Sanctorum Martii*, ii. 452] ; Hariulf, *Chronicon Centulense*, iii. 8, 20, 25.)
pergiro : *traverse*, i. 3. (Baxter records about 1150.)
precatorius : *precatory*, II, 16. (Late : Don. on Ter., *Phorm.* 142 ; cf. *precatoria epistola*, see Ducange and Forcellini, s.v. *precatorius*.)
preconarius : *of a herald*, I, 3. (Baxter records about 1200.)
prelibo : *mention*, I, 2. (Late and medieval ; frequent.)
proci : *deputy-wooers*, II, 16.
propria : *own country, home*, II, 1, 13. (Very frequent in the medieval period, e.g., *Vita Aeduuardi* in Luard, *Lives of Edward the Confessor*, p. 410, etc. ; *Vita Oswaldi* in Raine, *Historians of the Church of York*, i. 406, etc. ; also in continental writers, *passim*.)

reductus : for *reductio*, Arg.
refuto : *refuse*, III, 7. (Baxter records this sense in eighth century and about 1125.)
rememoror : for *memoro*, I, 4.
rudis : ? III, 10. (See Linguistic Note.)

salutamen : *salutation*, III, 3.
scelerose : *wickedly*, III, 5. (Baxter records about 1191.)
sepedictus : *frequently mentioned*, I, 5. (Very frequent in Medieval Latin, see Baxter.)

somniator : *dreamer,* III, 10. (Cf. the sense *Vita Oswaldi* in Raine, *Historians of the Church of York,* i. 409 ; *Miracula S. Bertini,* 44 ; in classical and early ecclesiastical Latin, the word means ' one who believes in or interprets dreams '.)

statutum : *decision,* II, 7.

stipendia : *equipment,* II, 7. (Cf. Saxo, ed. Holder, p. 547 : *Quorum urbem rex . . . . militibus ac stipendiis instruit* ; Robertus Monachus, *Patrologia,* clv. 680 : *paratis suis stipendiis tanto itineri congruentibus.*)

subintro : *enter,* II, 2, 3, III, 1. (Late ; Lewis and Short are wrong in suggesting that the verb necessarily implies stealthy or secret entry.)

tanta : for *tot,* II, 4 (*tanta genera*). (Very frequent late and medieval periods, and already in classical texts, see Forcellini, s.v. *tantus 7.*)

tegna : i.e., *tech(i)na,* I, 3.

theorema : *illustration* (from comparison with a similar case), Arg. (An unusual use of the word, arising from its etymology.)

uallatio : *circumvallation,* II, 7. (Late and rare : cf. for the sense, Hilarian, *Chronologia,* 3 [*Patrologia,* xiii. 1099], *maria conclusione riparum ac montium, ne transcendant quasi uallatione quadam obsessa.*)

uersus : *turn, movement,* I, 4. (Unusual, but etymologically reasonable, use. Cf. Plaut., *Stich.* 770, where *uersus* is used for a movement in a dance.)

INDEX
TO THE SUPPLEMENTARY INTRODUCTION

All references are to the roman numerals in square brackets at the foot of each page

INDEX TO THE SUPPLEMENTARY INTRODUCTION

Printed in the United Kingdom
by Lightning Source UK Ltd.
125194UK00002B/10-12/A